PRIVATE ENTREPRENEURS
IN CHINA AND VIETNAM

CHINA STUDIES

Published for the Institute for Chinese Studies
University of Oxford

EDITORS:

GLEN DUDBRIDGE
FRANK PIEKE

VOLUME 4

PRIVATE ENTREPRENEURS IN CHINA AND VIETNAM

Social and Political Functioning of Strategic Groups

BY

THOMAS HEBERER

TRANSLATED BY

TIMOTHY J. GLUCKMAN

BRILL
LEIDEN · BOSTON
2003

This book was first published in German as *Unternehmer als strategische Gruppen: Zur sozialen und politischen Funktion von Unternehmern in China und Vietnam*, Hamburg (Mitteilungen des Instituts für Asienkunde) 2001.

On the cover: Life-style is an important feature of strategic groups. The photograph shows two major entrepreneurs in the Eastern China city of Qingdao on their wedding reception at the end of December 2002. © Copyright by Wang Weimin.

This book is printed on acid-free paper.

Library of Congress Cataloging-in-Publication Data

Heberer, Thomas.
  Private entrepreneurs in China and Vietnam : social and political functioning of strategic groups / by Thomas Heberer ; translated by Timothy J. Gluckman.
    p. cm. — (China studies, ISSN 0928-5520 ; v. 4)
  Text originally written in German, but published first in English.
  Includes bibliographical references and index.
  ISBN 90-04-12857-3 (alk. paper)
    1. Entrepreneurship—China. 2. Entrepreneurship—Vietnam. 3. Privatization—China. 4. Privatization—Vietnam. 5. Businesspeople—China. 6. Businesspeople—Vietnam. I. Title. II. China studies (Leiden, Netherlands) ; v. 4.

HB615.H229 2003
338'.04'0951—dc21
                                                                    2003051911

ISSN   0928–5520
ISBN   90 04 12857 3

PRINTED IN THE NETHERLANDS

CONTENTS

FOREWORD

This book is the outcome of a comparative survey in China and Vietnam. Until now there has been no such study concerning itself with entrepreneurial strata and the private sector in both those countries. What is more, comparisons of the current developments in the two countries are rare. This study is based on the results of a research project that was supported between 1996 and 1998 by the Deutsche Forschungsgemeinschaft (German Research Foundation). The project included two periods of fieldwork in China and Vietnam. The research in the field was for the most part carried out by two research assistants (Ji Xiaoming in China and Arno Kohl in Vietnam). Immediately after the end of the period of financial support, both colleagues found employment in other areas, and unfortunately were no longer available for the processing of the fieldwork in this book. The goals for the field research in both countries were achieved: in each case quantitative und qualitative surveys of entrepreneurs in three locations with differing levels of development. At the same time, supplementary material from both nations was collected which made possible a deeper and better classification of the empirical material.

For their financial support we would like to thank the Deutsche Forschungsgemeinschaft, the Bundesministerium für Wirtschaftliche Zusammenarbeit (Federal Ministry for Economic Cooperation) and the Gesellschaft für Technische Zusammenarbeit (Corporation for Technical Cooperation, GTZ); they made possible the carrying-out of this research. We would like too to thank partner institutes in China and Vietnam principally the *Institute for Management* under the *State's Commission for the Reform of the Economic Structure* in Peking, in Vietnam the *National Political Academy Ho Chi Minh* (Institute for Sociology) and the *Institute for Sociology* in Hanoi. Above all we would like to express our heartfelt appreciation to the directors of the Institutes Prof. Cao Yuanzheng, Prof. Chong A and Prof. Tuong Lai, who with undoubted commitment did their utmost to enable the implementation of this project on the ground. Our sincere gratitude as well to the administrations of the cities and counties where our study was carried out, and without whose support this research project could not have been so successfully managed. Further thanks go to René Trappel and Christian Bollmann who with great enthusiasm contributed to the formal preparation of this manuscript. Finally, we are grateful to *Internationes* for enabling the translation of this book.

Duisburg, April 2003   Thomas Heberer

PART ONE: THE APPROACH

1. *China, Vietnam, Entrepreneurship and Social Change*

1.1. *Emergence of a new, economic elite*

The processes of change in China and Vietnam differ fundamentally from those in Eastern Europe. Political or systemic transformations were not apparent at the beginning of this process but rather relatively successful economic reforms that were followed by a process of gradual social and political change. As a result in both countries, there were no landslide-like collapses of the political system as took place in Eastern Europe. Relatively successful economic reforms quickly brought about brisk change from below which among other things resulted in rapid social change, a trend to privatization from below, in the formation of new elites as well as in the genesis of a new entrepreneurial strata. In both countries it became apparent that the transition from a planned to a state-influenced market economy under the control of a communist party is possible, and without simultaneous economic decline.

The process of transformation in China and Vietnam can at the same time be differentiated from those which took place in the successful emerging economies of East and Southeast Asia (South Korea, Taiwan, Hong Kong, Singapore, Malaysia etc.), because it (a) was carried out in transition from a planned to a market economy, (b) did not take place under the pressure of the Cold War or with the help of American financial power, and (c) domination by the communist parties imposed ideological barriers on the process of change. As a consequence the developments in both states can certainly be considered to be a special case. We argue that the privatization process that is at the center of our interest, came about as a *bottom-up* privatization, and led to the formation of new entrepreneurial strata that began at least partially to replace the state as an agency of development and modernization. With the entrepreneurial strata a new elite came into being whose social and political function in the processes of social change has been up till now insufficiently studied.

If we start off by assuming the criteria for the determination of an "elite", for instance, a result of a selection process or a positively viewed minority, and that they stand out from other social groups through special qualifications, resources, achievements or social functions, then the elite status of the Chinese and Vietnamese entrepreneurs can be determined by the following parameters:

- A major part of the population now attributes to them a leading role in the socio-economic segment (income, status).
- As one of the social role models of professions, they mold the norms and values of the society.

- They influence changes in economic, social and political structures, as well as the composition of stratification.
- They contribute to changes in the basic conditions of the social system.
- They see themselves as an (economic) elite with a function as social role models.

In contrast to Pareto and Mosca, we do not start off from a Machiavellian concept of an elite defined by power but rather from one that is norm-oriented.[1] According to this classification, entrepreneurs already form an elite but an economic one, whereby as we shall see in Section III, their self-assessment as being an economic elite plays an important role. Self-assessments are an important element of the conscious recognition of a role as an elite and role model, and with that the preconditions for the conscious exercising of such a role.

We concentrate our attention here on functional elites in the sense of heterogeneous groups that are able to formulate and achieve social aims, and in this sense have a strategic effect. The leading cadres (administration, party) represent the ruling political elite whereas aspiring and ambitious, private entrepreneurs form a new, economic elite. A limited, personnel exchange takes place between political and economic elites especially where cadres transfer to the private sector. Moreover in the course of the privatization process a partially shared identity between both elites comes about, since cadres are to some extent active at the same time in private industry. In respect of social stratification there are differences between the periods pre-Reform and Reform. Before the beginning of the Reform period social stratification was mostly about formation of social strata that had political criteria as their basis, whereby party membership and the rank of cadres was the precondition for the membership of an elite, and people who could be classified as "class enemies" such as former large land-owners, rich farmers and their relatives were counted amongst the lowest strata. Nowadays one may increasingly observe a stratification that is derived rather from economic premises.

The entrepreneurial strata are not a *power* or *political* elite but instead a nonruling *functional elite* with an important role in the functioning and change of the society and its sub-systems.[2] In functional terms it is at the same time an *achievement elite* not only because it has to legitimate itself through professional and social achievements, but rather because it produces entrepreneurial achievements in the sense of a significant contribution to economic development. It is simultaneously a *potential elite* because it has potential in terms of function, achievement and change that still is at a relatively early stage of fulfillment. Because the entrepreneurial strata do not merely form an economic elite but rather count amongst their number, managers of state and collective companies too, it represents an economic *partial elite*.

---

[1] On that also Dreitzel 1962: 2-4.
[2] Endruweit 1986.

In the definition of this elite, it is our concern at this stage to document the primary status of this group in the course of the economic and social transformation. This does not yet indicate anything about their goal- or collective-orientations as players in the society as do, for example, terms either related to class or the terminology of a *strategic group*.

The research focus of our study concerns primarily the entrepreneurs as social players whereby we are looking for commonalities as the precondition for political action, without assuming that these players possess a priori unified thought and action in the sense of being collective players. We start out from the hypothesis that entrepreneurs in the course of the reform process play an increasingly important role economically. The private sector demonstrates the highest rate of growth and is developing into the most important source of employment. In terms of their income, the entrepreneurs have a leading position in the society. Consequently not only their economic but also their social prestige is increasing.

1.2. *Entrepreneurship and social change*

Through the reforms, the emergence of new players, new social stratification and the re-definition of relations between Party and society, do not only generate social change but also a process of change of social structures, of institutions, and with that radical alterations in the total societal value and norm systems. Here we are interested first of all only in governmental and party institutions insofar as they stand in direct connection with the privatization process. This is most clearly shown in changes in the number of staff, in the guiding principles and the functions of institutions. The existence of the private sector requires institutions that can behave in harmony with the market. Cadres have to possess the appropriate specialized knowledge in order to match up to the new requirements. Parallel to that new institutions and organizations come into being which serve to represent the interests of the private entrepreneurs.

Values on the other hand form a yardstick for orientation concerning actions and ways in which people act and behave. Here privatization has brought about too a transformation insofar as the non-state sector firstly promotes specific values and attitudes, and secondly attitudes change towards values as they were up till now as well as the ranking order of existing values. All in all a type of "economisation" of the value systems has taken place that has already led to a partial de-ideologization of the political ideology. Marxism-Leninism increasingly has lost its dominant position. Parsons writes in this sense of a transformation of the "normative culture" especially as economic development and industrialization change the societies concerned in the first place politically and culturally (in the sense of value and norm systems) in the form of primary "input effects".[3]

---

[3] Parsons 1970: 43.

Social-political or – to use a more common term – social change refers not merely to an alteration within the relevant economic, political or social sub-system, but rather to the social structures of a system likewise the change in that system in total (the latter can be termed "radical transformation").[4] The rapid and total economic transformation that is taking place in both countries has impacted on the social and political domains, and in the long-term brings about such a social transformation.[5] This process of change was neither in-tended by the political elites of both countries nor can it be controlled without difficulty. The areas named here in which the social change takes place interact interdependently with each other.

The group of prospering entrepreneurs represents in the early phase of the privatization process the most important, but in no way the only human repre-sentative of this social-political transformation. In the long-term, the elite con-tributes to an institutional change which last but not least takes its effect on the political system starting from the lowest level of the bureaucracy: because the entrepreneurs push their way into the bureaucracy in order to obtain for them-selves advantages in competition. The more that functionaries switch to private industry for economic reasons, the easier it is for entrepreneurs to penetrate the bureaucracy.[6]

With that the preconditions for the formation of a new, potentially political elite are created, which for its part can induce a push towards modernization – as the experience from the four small tigers in East Asia demonstrates. In those countries the state likewise the bureaucracy was able to realize the prioritized goals of modernization despite considerable social resistance.[7] In contrast to the economic elite, the state has an advantage in that it can canalize particular in-terests (e.g. economic ones) in the direction of a higher goal, and to implement them if necessary with the use of violence. The precondition for that change process is the existence of new economic elites as well as reorganization in the conventional bureaucracy, since an encrusted political system by itself is hardly in a position to undergo restructuring. Some researchers have already suggested the phenomenon is the genesis of a new "hybrid" class consisting of adminis-trative cadres and private entrepreneurs.[8]

---

[4] Cf. Kohn/Slomczynski et al. 1997.

[5] On that in more detail: Heberer 1993; Heberer/Taubmann 1998. This process of transforma-tion possesses along with an internal aspect an external one too, which comes about through foreign contacts (e.g. tourism, visit of scholars or studying abroad, etc.) and commercial activities abroad. The following expositions are limited to the internal aspects, without wishing to deny the signifi-cance of the contacts abroad.

[6] Cf. *Gongren Ribao*, 12 January 1992, about a study in the province of Guangdong, in which the majority of the newly appointed officials came from the private sector; a study about the prov-ince of Hunan suggested that the number of functionaries who have switched to the private sector is large.

[7] Bürklin 1993; Henderson 1993.

[8] Cf. Unger 1994: 52-59.

At the same time, for the state and Party the possibilities of maintaining control are reduced since not in every case are their interests adequately represented at the lowest level. Particularly in China, this process of transformation is in some provinces apparently already so far advanced that especially in the countryside a dualism of political and economic power exists.[9] Such developments are a cause of concern for the political leaderships of both countries. Hence in China a document put out by the "United Front Department" of the Central Committee instructed party committees at different levels to keep the private economy under observation. Private sector entrepreneurs in the non-state sector turn to the method of buying votes in order to be elected to the local Peoples Congresse's, or buy political advocates for their interests in party committees and parliaments.[10] On the other hand party and administrative cadres use their positions to enrich themselves; in exchange for payments they provide advantages for individual companies or enable commercial activity to take place at all. This form of corruption appears in the course of the privatization process to be very widespread; this is confirmed by the permanent discussions on this topic in China and Vietnam.

A side effect of privatization consists of business activity on the part of members of the state administration and simultaneously the continued exercise of their official positions. Permanent bans on the part of the state have not been able to end such commercial conduct. Among the special effects in China, for example, was a brothel in Guangzhou that was run by the Chinese Women's Federation using a hotel as cover.[11] Easier access to the bureaucracy and to state resources enables the practice of having second jobs to prosper. After an analysis of 800 families in the nation's capital, a researcher at the Hanoi Institute of Sociology commented significantly: "Most of the rich work for the government. With power and access to the market, you can change your life. Without them, you can't get rich."[12] The changes in economic structures and the opening of new possibilities for earning – especially in the cities – increase social mobility and migration into the urban centers.

As a result of the economic process of privatization, new interest groups are engendered which have an urge to participate. Accordingly entrepreneurs have begun to organize their interests in associations. Economic interests can thereby have direct, political effects insofar as they, for example, lead to a liberalization of the economic policies (prices etc.). Out of that results a growing interest in political participation, and this interest manifests itself partially in the impulse on the part of private entrepreneurs to obtain access to membership of the party and to the bureaucracy.

---

[9] Cf. the study by Shue 1990 about Guanghan county, Sichuan province as well as the study by Heberer/Taubmann 1998.

[10] *Dangdai* (Hong Kong), 15 June 1994.

[11] *China aktuell*, April 1994: 413f.; ibid., May 1994: 483f.

[12] Far Eastern Economic Review, 13 January 1994: 71.

In both nations one can discern a significant change in values and attitudes. This applies, for example, to the evaluation of wealth or prosperity. In contrast to the pre-reform socialist phase in which wealth was considered to be a sign of exploitative activity, nowadays prosperity is regarded as a worthwhile goal in life. In China, Deng Xiaoping issued the slogan "Let some become rich first!" Chinese mass media are full of jubilant reports about the rapidly growing "prosperity" of individuals. Luxury articles, the newest technical devices, expensive hobbies among other things develop accordingly into new status symbols.[13]

The quest for profit apparently assumes such a centrally important role that other values in contrast decrease in significance. A well-known Vietnamese pun expresses it clearly: through the omission of two letters of the alphabet, the statement of Ho Chi Minh that: "There is nothing more valuable than independence [doc lap] and freedom," into the snide, "There is nothing more valuable than dollars [do la] ...."[14]. As sociologists of both countries confirm, under this transformation of values the family in particular suffers i.e. one of the most important and basic social institutions. As a result many parents devote hardly any time to the education of their children because the former are busy trying to earn more income.[15] At the same time schoolchildren increasingly play truant from schools in the hope of rapidly obtaining money.[16] An increased I-consciousness at the cost of awareness of the community can be seen especially in the generation that was born after 1970. A survey in the first half of the 1990s amongst Chinese high-school pupils showed that approximately 50% put their own interests above those of the community, while 60% said that the shaping of their own future depended on their own efforts. On the basis of their survey, the interviewers discerned a tendency to accord priority to their own well-being.[17] Officials of the Vietnamese Ministry of Labor, according to these reports, possess both a positive evaluation of wealth and an animosity towards the poorer who have not succeeded in profiting from the reforms.[18]

However, social security factors appear to make the state sector more attractive. This appears to be more the case in Vietnam than in China; in the latter country insecurity within the state sector has significantly increased in recent years due to closure of companies. For example, a survey at five universities and colleges in Hanoi found 85% of those studying would still prefer a job in the state sector.[19] The restructuring of the state companies and the consolidation

---

[13] *China aktuell*, January 1994: 46.

[14] Südostasien Informationen, 4/1991: 7.

[15] Far Eastern Economic Review, 13 January 1994: 71.

[16] *China aktuell*, February 1994: 176; Pfeifer 1990; Tran Trung Dung 1991: 144. In Vietnam at the beginning of the 1990s, about 1.2 m school children aged 6 to 10 and about 1 m aged 11 to 14 finished their school careers prematurely, cf. *Südostasien Informationen*, 4/1991: 8.

[17] *China aktuell*, February 1994: 187.

[18] Far Eastern Economic Review, 13 January 1994: 71.

[19] Le Ngoc Hung/Rondinelli 1993: 17.

of the private sector may lead here to a gradual change, above all, when questions of social security (in terms of employment law) are solved in the private sector.

In general such a complete, deep-reaching process of transformation results in the early phase in a loss of order and orientation during which the old order is shaken severely in its foundations and is undermined without it yet being replaced by a new, generally accepted order. Economic developments and the resulting socio-political changes entail first of all destabilization as well, and increase not only stratification within the former socialist societies but also their polarization (social, regional).

1.3. *Research design and structure of this book*

The present work is based on the results of an empirical study and a comparative analysis, with whose help between 1996–1998 findings about the state, function and socio-political consequences of privatization and entrepreneurial strata in both countries were obtained; in addition questions were explored as to how far the special Chinese-Vietnamese path represents a specific, new "model" of development. As a result it was intended that a better estimate of the economic, social and political development in both countries would be achieved. In that we have confronted less the question of the economic significance of the private sector and of entrepreneurial strata, and much rather its impact on the social and political sub-systems in the sense of social transformation.

The short descriptions in sections 1.1 and 1.2 already indicate that and in what ways entrepreneurs contribute to the stratification of the system, and thereby change it. We are interested as to how far entrepreneurs as endogenous, transformation players have an effect, and in what way they contribute in the long-term to altering the power structure in both countries. It needs to be stated that such a shifting of power is an important factor for initiating political processes of change. While the exogenous factor has an effect, above all nowadays in the form of information on the endogenous factor , but the latter is not the subject of this inquiry. What interests us much more is the basic question of how entrepreneurial players behave and how they can be described in terms of social theory of action. In that the following basic questions are central:

1. To what extent are we observing a **collective player** in the sense of a *social group*? What group interests, shared identity and organizational characteristics emerge?

2. What does the **transformational potential** of entrepreneurial strata consist of i.e. the potential for social and political change?

3. To what extent does a **strategic potential** exist in the sense of a formally or informally followed strategy for the realization of interests and preferred goals?

So we take a player-oriented approach which places a new and rising economic elite at the center of the inquiry. The structure of this study orients itself to that. In the first, conceptional section we concern ourselves with privatization processes in China and Vietnam, as well as with the entrepreneurs as new economic and social players. The second part comes to terms with the results of our field research. Taking as its starting-point this profile of an elite, the third part of this work attempts a summarizing determination of the position of the entrepreneurial strata at the interface of society and politics as well as a classification and categorization of the entrepreneurs (keyword: strategic elite) in the interests of an intended analysis of their future location.

1.4. *China and Vietnam: commonalities and differences*

As already mentioned a development has been taking place in China and Vietnam which differs fundamentally from those in other (former) socialist countries. An extensive privatization "from below" has been going on which leads to a fundamental change of the social and political sub-systems in both nations. At first glance the developments in both countries appears to be for the most part identical.[20] Vietnam is frequently perceived as the "small dragon", as a mirror image of the "big dragon" China. In Vietnam it is widely admitted that one could learn much from China.[21] Above all Vietnam can make use of the Chinese experiences and learn from the mistakes made in China so that they may avoid them.

As a matter of fact both countries do have a number of commonalities:

- Both repeatedly confirm their desire to overtake economically the East and Southeast Asian threshold nations whereby not only the Chinese but also the Vietnamese leadership have recognized the necessity of far-reaching reforms. Singapore, in particular, with its prosperity and at the same time an authoritarian political system that is set on maintaining stability, exercises a role model function for both China and Vietnam. The similarity of the development goals contrasts, however, with differences in the preconditions and pre-determinants for development. This results from the historical starting-points of the threshold nations differing from those of China and Vietnam.
- Due to their economic success both countries are regarded as future NIC states of the third generation. Their successes appear to be derived from a special "Asian" path of development in the sense of a privatization from below with wide-ranging maintenance of political stability whereby they differ basically from the former socialist countries of Eastern Europe.

---

[20] So Pei 1994.
[21] Cf. e.g. *Vietnam Courier*, 1-7 March 1998.

- Economic crises at the end of the 1970s provided the impetus for profound economic reforms in both countries. In China as in Vietnam the gradual reform strategy aimed first of all for an experiment in an (apparently) controllable, small area. The reform process started off in the agricultural sector. Its main focus lay in each case on extensive, long-term economic changes while maintaining the power monopoly of the communist parties.
- China and Vietnam term themselves socialist countries which pursue a development path coined by national experiences and aims. In contrast to Eastern Europe, the political system was not imported by means of Soviet troops but rather supported and made possible for the most part by their own populations (peasantry) in the respective seizures of power by the communist movements. The national molding applies not only to the pre-reform era during which China, in contrast to the Soviet Union, explicitly sought a different path of development whereas Vietnam linked together Chinese, Soviet and national elements of development. It also refers to the reform era in which both countries tried to steer a reform path which differed from the "deterrent" Soviet example.
- China and Vietnam are developing countries stamped by the agricultural sector and have similar problems as other developing countries, and in this way can be fundamentally differentiated both from the former Soviet Union and the rest of what were previously socialist states in Eastern Europe.
- Although the economic systems of both countries prior to reform were marked by Soviet-style communism, both were actually societies whose social structure was – just as it had been before – influenced by a specifically Asian tradition. Among such factors can be counted a somewhat paternalistic, family-oriented, and consensual style of political behavior which was also clientelized; politically hierarchical structures with vertical patterns of decision-making; high status attached to personal relationships or the need for harmony and consensus instead of conflict and competition. Both countries demonstrate similarities from the cultural point-of-view which in the literature are often over-simplified as being "Confucianism". Additionally specific culturally determined business ethics and business culture developed.

These formal similarities relate for the most part to statements in the targets set as well as historical and developmental factors. In general one needs to consider, however, that seemingly similar structures in point of fact are not the same since they represent the results of different historical processes. But the differences too in the conditions at the point of departure make clear the dissimilarities which existed at the beginning of the reform as well as of the privatization:

- Differences in size: Vietnam consists of only 4% of the land mass and 7% of the population of its neighbor. The size of China brings with it a greater plurality and diversification, more complex relations between the central

government and provinces but also a stronger international place and negotiating position.[22]

- Historically perceived China regarded itself as the cultural center of the
  world to which the surrounding peoples and nations for many centuries had
  to pay tribute. The Vietnamese on the other hand, above all in the north,
  see themselves as a people who have over and over again had to defend
  themselves against invasions from outside most of all from the Chinese. In
  contrast to Vietnam, China was never a colony of a foreign power.
- In contrast to China was separated from whom alone the small island Taiwan went its own way, a political creation of its own making, Vietnam was
  between 1954–1976 a divided country with differing political and economic systems. This division while it was overcome at the political level,
  carried on in the form of differing ways of thinking and behaving in the
  minds of the people.
- The Chinese development before the commencement of the reforms was
  stamped by politics marked by political campaigns that to some extent,
  had traumatic consequences for the population; in Vietnam, however, it
  was above all the permanent if mostly successful actions in wars which
  molded the population even if at enormous costs.
- While the Chinese party due to the campaigns of the Mao era and his ambivalent role entered the reform process *politically* significantly weakened,
  the Vietnamese party did not have such a massive, *political burden* to
  carry. What is more the leadership remained stable for decades, and Ho
  Chi-Minh the recognized and undisputed leader of the Vietnamese revolution.
- In Vietnam the reform process commenced **before** *the carrying out of
  complete collectivization in the wealthier southern part* of the country. In
  China in contrast, the collectivization had already been carried out some
  time before the beginning of the Reform. The reform process started there
  first of all in rural areas characterized by poverty.
- The state and collective sector in China is, not least for historical reasons,
  more strongly developed than in Vietnam. While in 1988 less than 1% of
  the Vietnamese population worked in public sector enterprises, in China
  the comparative figure was almost 5% of the population. At the same time,
  in percentage terms the bureaucratic apparatus for controlling the state sector companies is stronger in China than in Vietnam. Also the proportion of
  larger, state-owned companies is in the fields of industry, commerce and
  banks higher in China than in Vietnam. As a result in China the change
  from the state to the private sector was for a long time not so simple and attractive as in Vietnam.

---

[22] See for instance McCormick 1998: 122.

- Measured by the percentage proportion of the GDP, industrialization is more advanced in China than in Vietnam where in this respect the agricultural sector dominates much more.
- The international context of both countries is different. In 1989 Vietnam was to a significant extent financially dependent on the Soviet Union and the socialist states of Eastern Europe. The falling away of Soviet help and support through COMECON had major consequences for Vietnam. Moreover help and cooperation with the West until the end of the 1990s could be estimated as being rather low, and foreign investments up till now were comparatively insignificant. China which for a long time had pursued a policy of self-reliance, since the beginning of the reforms has had a magnetic effect on foreign investors. China had far and away in the 1980s and 1990s the highest foreign investment of all developing nations. In that process investments by Chinese residents abroad (including Hong Kong and Taiwan) played a major role. In Vietnam on the other hand, to what extent the Vietnamese living outside the country sent capital home remains fully unexplored; possibly they did so to a not insignificant degree to their relatives or family members especially in South Vietnam.[23]

In view of the dissimilarities of a historical, economic and political nature between China and Vietnam, there are grave doubts about the claim that Vietnam represents merely a smaller copy of China. Only by filtering out these differences, the possible commonalities in the privatization process as well as the course of the social and political transformation "from below", allow one to establish to what extent a new, specific path of development can indeed be spoken of here.

2. Privatization processes in China and Vietnam – precondition for the emerging of new entrepreneurs

2.1. Privatization initiatives on the part of peasants through collective action and limited fence-breaking

In both countries the starting-point for the development of the private sector was poverty in the countryside. Already in the middle of the 1970s i.e. sometime before the beginning of reform policies, a spontaneous shadow economy had developed primarily in the poverty-stricken areas. As a consequence markets came into being which were considered at that time to be illegal. When in

---

[23] Cf. on that the various contributions in the issue focusing on the relationship China-Vietnam of *China Journal*, July 1998.

the course of the economic crisis in the second half of the 1970s, the pressure from the countryside became ever bigger, in China some provinces with a high level of poverty (Anhui, Sichuan) tolerated this development. The success of private industry and commerce led in 1979 to the emergence of a small-scale private sector (individual businesses) being once again permitted.

Diagram 1: Deviation becomes politics – the case of the private sector (China)

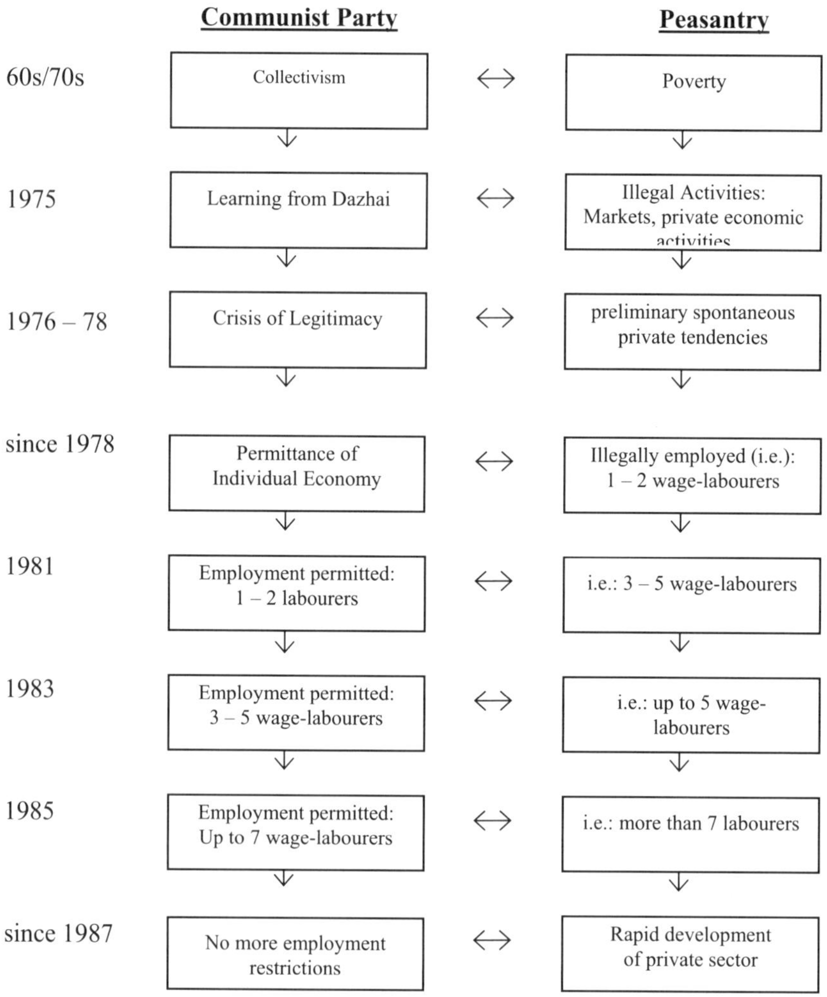

	Communist Party		**Peasantry**
60s/70s	Collectivism	↔	Poverty
1975	Learning from Dazhai	↔	Illegal Activities: Markets, private economic activities
1976 – 78	Crisis of Legitimacy	↔	preliminary spontaneous private tendencies
since 1978	Permittance of Individual Economy	↔	Illegally employed (i.e.): 1 – 2 wage-labourers
1981	Employment permitted: 1 – 2 labourers	↔	i.e.: 3 – 5 wage-labourers
1983	Employment permitted: 3 – 5 wage-labourers	↔	i.e.: up to 5 wage-labourers
1985	Employment permitted: Up to 7 wage-labourers	↔	i.e.: more than 7 labourers
since 1987	No more employment restrictions	↔	Rapid development of private sector

According to Chinese scholars, the return of family management in agriculture finally led to around 150-200 million members of the rural workforce being made redundant who had no access to the urban labor market and to the state sector. The only path to absorbing them was the informal sector i.e. self-employment in commerce and craft-based work. The employment of labor was at first forbidden. Since increasingly the businesses based on individuals employed "family members" or "relatives", paid work became a reality. Hesitantly the state in the first half of the 1980s permitted having two then five then seven members of staff.

The actual developments were always one step ahead of the political decision process. Finally, the development in the private sector was no longer controllable, not least because the advantages for employment, supply of goods and income for the local authorities were very apparent. In June 1988 the State Council issued an edict, 'Provisional regulations of the People's Republic of China for private companies'. Limits on employment were abolished and with that the main block against the development of the private sector.[24]

The political system was not only put under pressure by demands emanating from the rural population but also through political action, whereby at the same time a large section of the political elite grasped the necessity and advantages of those demands and actions, and implemented them in a reform program.

In both countries the beginnings of reform processes were initiated by the spontaneous abandoning by peasants of the collective economy and their return instead to family-style businesses. Since undisguised resistance would have been laden with risk, the peasants shifted their strategy to a permanent but limited process of not heeding regulations (*fence-breaking*). This development was used against the will of the political elite at the local level, and was retrospectively legalized after years of successful practice.

Fforde/ de Vylder ask as a result whether one can talk at all of reforms since in the last analysis what took place was the belated legalization of collective action on the part of the peasantry, and not an active policy shaped by the Party.[25] However, the role which the leadership of the Party played in that should not be overlooked. Although in both countries the first steps originated from the rural areas, without the approval and then the support by the party leadership, the collective action by the peasants could not have coalesced into "reform policies". The stagnation in the 1970s and 1980s, for example, in the Soviet Union by contrast makes all too clear the outcomes of a politics of blockade by a party leadership against collective *bottom-up* actions.

This process of de-collectivization in the primary sector shows a typical prototype of a trend which in similar form was at the basis too of the privatization process in the secondary and tertiary sector, and which is typical for both countries (cf. Diagram 2): at the beginning there are limited transgressions of laws or regulations in order to get around the enormous shortages for the populations which came about due to the socialist systems. The successes of the regulation

---

[24] On this development cf. Heberer 1989. The law in: *Renmin Ribao*, 29 June 1988.

[25] Fforde and de Vylder 1996b: 1.

breaking, possibly accompanied by the toleration by the authorities at the lowest level of administration, induced a copy-cat effect leading in turn to an extensive practice of "fence-breaking". Its success, for example, in solving shortages on the supply side or in the creation of jobs caused political elites subsequently to legalize these activities. The legalization, however, encouraged in
turn new transgressions of laws in other spheres, so that in the end a process
was brought into being which worked in ever greater circles, included ever-
larger areas of the socialist system, and cumulatively entailed a reform from
below.

Diagram 2: Changing Patterns of Reform Processes

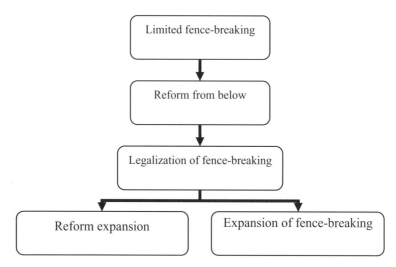

In its starting days, this reform was neither goal-directed nor planned; it arose
spontaneously from the everyday crises of the population and the fundamental
shortcomings of the existing system without any precise design being recognizable for those who were a part of it. The same can be written about the effects
of the reform processes which can neither be confined to a particular area nor
simply – if at all – controllable. In this sense a fundamental difference existed
to the reform processes in what used to be socialist Eastern Europe and the
former Soviet Union.

The Vietnamese development demonstrates parallels but also differences to
the Chinese one. This was determined for instance by the varying processes in
the northern and southern parts of the country. Concerning this geographical
difference, in the North the collectivization of agriculture had commenced in
1958 in a number of stages beginning with the collectivization of the means of

production whereby the land remained in possession of the peasant families. According to official statistics, while at the beginning of the 1960s, 86% of the rural population had been registered as being in 40,000 collectives, in 1980 the number of collectives sank to 12,000 due to their merging. But at this point 95% of the population in the countryside were at least nominally organized in them.[26] At the beginning of their life-spans the collectives may have been greeted with approval, but in the course of time their disadvantages became ever more apparent e.g. the lack of incentive to work, administrative handicaps due to the excessive assemblies and meetings,[27] low productivity etc.

Similarly to China, part of the peasantry took to collective action and limited transgressions of regulations and policies. An example was the breach of the stipulation that 5% of the areas of cultivatable land was to be set aside for private planting by the peasants: however, actually two or three times as much land was privately used. The latter areas were much more intensively cultivated than the collectively used cultivatable land so that the yields per square meter were 100% to 200% above those from the collectively utilized soil. In some places the collective zones even lay fallow. In the 1970s the North Vietnamese peasants obtained 60-75% of their income by means of this privately farmed land, which contrary to official policies had become their primary source of income.[28]

In spite of the widespread collectivization and nationalization of the North Vietnamese economy in the 1950s and 1960s, the peasants had managed to retain a certain economic autonomy (see above) which should also be understood in the context of decentralization resulting from war.[29] Underground, private activities in the economic sphere had continued to exist throughout the period. A study of North Vietnam revealed that already in the 1960s, family businesses in the villages illegally produced everyday needs for the market. In Bat Trang, for example, individual families erected glazing ovens and manufactured ceramic goods. In turn, the raw materials were acquired from other specialized family companies specialized in that domain. As the living conditions deteriorated, correspondingly such functions increased.

Already in the first half of the 1960s, there had been spontaneous privatization tendencies in non-urban areas in North Vietnam. In 1963 in Vinh Bao and Kien Thuy (Province of Kien An), the system of contractual allocation of land for the use of households had been introduced with the approval of local leaderships. In 1963 the Party committee in Haiphong had specifically approved of

---

[26] Kerkvliet 1993: 7.

[27] Ibid.: 10 referred to "45-60 days a year consumed by meetings, seminars, conferences, and other events called by local, district, and provincial leaders." About the reasons for the peasants' rejection of higher levels of development of the collective see ibid.: 7-10.

[28] Cf. Fforde and de Vylder 1996a.

[29] Porter 1993: 44; Werner 1984: 48. The private retail trade had a share of at least 28% of the total turnover of the retail trade in 1974, which shows that even in socialist North Vietnam an officially tolerated private economy still existed.

these illegal measures as a "pilot project". This experiment spread rapidly but
was terminated by the central leadership in 1968.[30]

At the end of the 1960s, state-owned firms allocated contracts for home
work to peasant families, a measure which resulted in an expansion of private
economic activity, and weakened the state and collective sector. Local authorities tolerated such goings-on so long as they were connected by means of contracts with the state sector. Beyond the contractual obligations, households
commenced production for the market. Concurrently independent private work-
shops came into being. Since such activities promised a relatively high income,
more and more workers in the state-owned firms remained absent from work,
and dedicated themselves to their more profitable second jobs. In the course of
the economic crisis of 1978–1980, the government first of all permitted private
work by former state personnel living on pensions; this was done to ensure the
incomes of those concerned. A new branch of independent production centers
was thereby created, and expanded very rapidly. This licensing merely legalized what had already become a widely spread practice which could hardly be
controlled any longer. Collectives metamorphosed into private companies, or
private enterprises operated under the cover of a still nominally existing cooperative.[31] At that time even in Hanoi, the capital city of the North and later of all
of Vietnam, private companies were already in existence albeit to a limited
extent, and primarily in the tertiary sector.[32]

The main causes for the spontaneous widening of private economic activities
were the extent of poverty in the rural areas and Vietnam's economic crisis.
The system of contractual allocation of land to households spontaneously
spread as a result into different regions of the country. In the second half of the
1980s in the North Vietnamese province Tuyen Quang, for example, the state
was no longer in a position to pay the wages of the forestry workers, or to ensure the provision of their basic needs. Consequently the forestry brigade distributed plots of land to the workers for private use on which they planted food,
erected houses with large private gardens and planted fruit trees, or raised livestock. In the end a section of the workforce changed to planting crops for industrial purposes, for the sale of food or rearing livestock. Necessity forced workers to become peasants, artisans and traders. For its part, the forestry company
to some extent released their employees to carry on such activities, gave credits
or acted as mediator for obtaining credits on behalf of the new self-employed.
The new firms gradually started to take on employees themselves. Similar
processes occurred in other regions and sectors.[33]

Latent processes of privatization, however, actually stem from further back.
Already in the middle of the 1960s so-called *sneaky contracts* (*khoan chui*) had

---

[30] Dang and Le 1999: 93f.

[31] Cf. Hy van Luong 1998: 294ff.

[32] A study of 1, 000 small companies suggested that all the same 22.8% had come into being
before 1981. Le Ngoc Hung and Rondinelli 1993: 9.

[33] Liljeström et al. 1998: 59ff.

spread. These were agreements between cooperatives and individual house-holds concerning production; these contracts actually contradicted the statutes of the cooperatives. For example, a household would take over the responsibility for breeding pigs – which would otherwise have been the task of a production brigade – in exchange for a certain payment, or land for growing vegetables would be leased by the cooperative to a household to make use of as the latter saw fit. Often the next step was that private households took charge of rice-growing, a similar development to what happened from the end of the 1970s onwards in China: that is, the "system of responsibility" which was a part of the Chinese agricultural reform. The economic success of such practices which were strictly speaking illegal, lead to their emulation by other cooperatives.[34]

Since the government's reaction which consisted of attempts at stronger controls of the cooperatives did not bring about the hoped-for success, the authorities at the local level made concessions to the peasants. A typical example of these lay in the area of prescribed production quotas and fixed purchasing price for the collectives which together formed the central instrument of state control of the rural markets. When in the 1970s it became ever more difficult for the official departments in question to buy up the quotas at the specified price, the authorities began to negotiate with the cooperatives about both the quotas and the prices instead of setting them bureaucratically without consultation. These concessions on the part of the government were then followed by the step-by-step legalization of practices which had already long been carried out by the members of the cooperatives. So from 1980 onwards, cooperatives were allowed to transfer land lying fallow to individual households for their use. In 1981 the contracts for production made with individuals household units were made legal, and in 1988 the party leadership officially approved the return to family businesses.[35]

2.2. *Development and state of bottom-up privatization*

The privatization processes in China and Vietnam cannot be very precisely assessed at the moment due to the uncertain quality of the statistical data. When working with statistical material, one needs to bear in mind the following problem:

---

[34] On that see also: Tran Thi Que 1998: 30ff.

[35] Ibid.; Großheim 1997: 222-255. This list can be continued; in this spirit in 1993 the Land Law officially permitted what had been standard practice for years i.e. the leasing and inheritance of rights of land use over a longer period of time, whereby depending on the particular region in which it was situated, privately used land could not exceed 3 ha to 5 ha per person. Since then the farmers have gone even beyond this limit: already in 1994 in the Mekong Delta a range of families possessed rice-growing areas of more than 50 ha, and sales of land had long been taking place under the cover of long-term leasing; for instance see Nguyen Tri Khiem 1996.

- Official statistics are to a high degree unreliable and represent instead development *trends* indicatively:
- the secondary literature offers a picture ridden with contradictions;
- a large number of the private companies hide behind false classifications ("collective") so that the private sector actually includes far more companies than are officially registered.

2.2.1. *China*

In the 1950s almost all private companies were transformed into state or collective organizations. In that epoch the privately owned companies were considered to be a capitalist sector with an antagonistic character. Every form of *self-employment* too had been forbidden since the middle of the 1960s. It was not until March 1979 that the political leadership permitted the re-emergence of individual economic structures.[36] In July 1981 a directive of the political leadership characterized individual companies limited as they were to seven employees, as a necessary complement of state-based and collective forms of ownership. Already one year before the creation of this legal basis, 40,000 individual companies had come into existence again in China with the number of those employed in this way given as 806,000.[37]

Although it was to be first in February 1984 that the regulations for individual, rural industrial and trade companies became legally binding, according to official statistics already in 1983 there were around 5.8 m such companies with 7.5 m employees which were then retrospectively legalized.[38] The same phenomenon appeared in 1988 with the regulation for private firms stemming from administrative channels which permitted expansions into various commercial fields excluding the defense and finance sectors. Where there were more than seven employees, such a firm constituted a private company (*siying qiye*). However, already at that point in time (end of 1987), there were de facto 225,000 private companies which had come into being and were registered as individual, collective or cooperative organizations, which employed more than seven members of staff dependent on wages.[39]

The private sector quickly proved itself to be the most dynamic sector and so became a major pillar of economic development. In 1995 as a result, the Party leadership saw it was necessary to make a statement to the effect that all forms of ownership should develop parallel and with equal rights. Above all the prospering provinces in the eastern part of the country soon termed the private sector the "motor" of the "socialist market economy". The 15th Party Congress of

---

[36] I will not describe here the process of development of the private sector after 1949 since I have documented it at length elsewhere; cf. Heberer 1989, but also Jamann and Menkhoff 1988, and Kraus 1989.

[37] Figures based on information from the National Bureau for Administration of Industry and Commerce.

[38] Liu Long 1986: 25; Liu Jianyi 1992: 13.

[39] Liang Chuanyun 1990: 15; Qin/Jia 1993: 32.

the CCP in September 1997 even declared this sector to be a part of the "social-ist" sector. The constitutional change in March 1999 finally established that the individual and private companies were "important constituents of the socialist market economy" which were protected by the state (new Article 16).[40] Tian Jiyun, vice-chairman of the National People's Congress, elaborated then for the first time that some spheres would possibly remain private "forever" (*yongyuan*).[41]

Diagram 3: Classifications of the private sector (China)

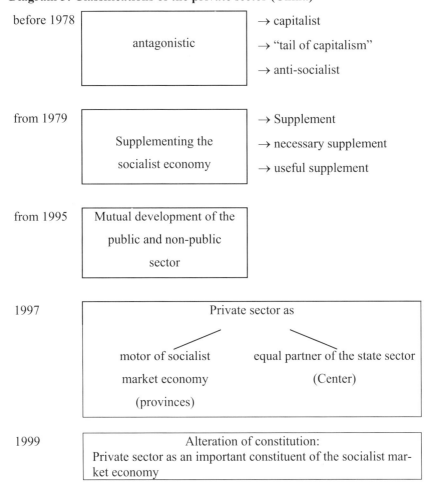

[40] Liang Chuanyun 1990: 15; Qin/Jia 1993: 32.
[41] *Renmin Ribao*, 29 March 1999.

Jiang argued, like workers, peasants, intellectuals, cadres and soldiers private
entrepreneurs were "builders of socialism with Chinese characteristics". The
16th Party Congress in November 2002 agreed to that position so that private
businessmen from now on were permitted to join the Communist Party.[42]

Diagram 4: Number of individual companies (1990–2001, China)

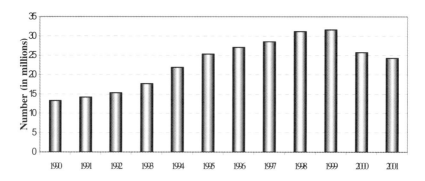

Source: Gongshang xingzheng guanli tongji huibian (1989–2001, different editions).

At the end of 1998 according to official statements, the following kinds of
companies were registered as private industry:

- 31,202,000 individual companies (*getihu* with less than eight employees)
  with 61,144,000 employees involved;
- 1,201,000 private companies (*siren qiye* with more than seven employees)
  with 2,638,000 owners and 17,091,000 employees.[43]

In addition to that the following number of employees were to be found in other
private industrial sectors:

- joint stock companies: 5,460,000;
- limited liability companies: 4,840,000;
- companies with investments from Hong Kong, Macao and Taiwan:
  2,940,000;
- companies with investments from foreign countries: 2,930,000.

This produces for 1997 a figure of around 97 m people engaged in the private
sector.[44] According to figures for 1996 about 25.83 m private companies in

---

[42] Cf. He Yiting 2001. The documents of the 16th Party Congress in Qiushi 22/2002.

[43] On the figures see Gongshang xingzheng guanli tongji huibian 1998.

rural areas with 72.8 m employees, 120,000 private "scientific-technical" firms (mostly in the sphere of consulting) with around 2.1 m employees as well as 220,000 companies with foreign capital employing about 25.1 m people; these likewise have to be classified as private companies.[45] Assuming that these figures remained constant until the end of 1998 (rather one should suppose that they have in fact increased), then at the end of 1998 the private sector might have included more than 200 m people (cf. below).

Diagram 5: Growth rate of the individual companies (1990–2001, China)

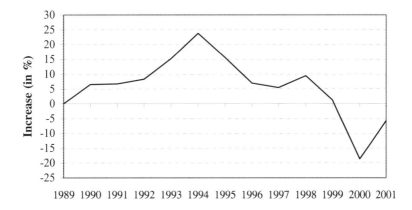

Source: Gongshang xingzheng guanli tongji huibian (1989–2001).

The following diagrams show the development of the private sector economy in recent years:

---

[44] At the end of 2001 there were 24.33 m individual companies with a workforce of 47.6 m and 2.03 m private companies with a workforce of 22.5 m, cf. *Zhongguo Gongshang Bao*, 19 April 2002.

[45] *Zhongguo Gongshang Bao*, 24 April 1997; *Renmin Ribao*, 10 April 1997; Xiangzhen qiye qingkuang (1996).

Diagram 6: Number of private companies (1990–2001, China) (Unit: 1,000)

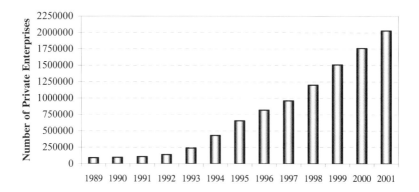

Source: Gongshang xingzheng guanli tongji huibian (1989–2001).

Diagram 7: Growth rate of private companies (1990–2001) (in %)

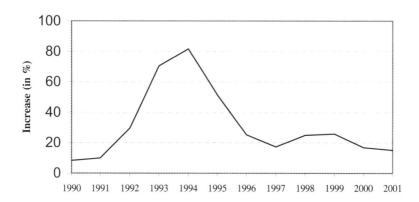

Source: Gongshang xingzheng guanli tongji huibian (1989–2001).

The zone where the private sector had its genesis was the countryside even if the proportion in the urban areas has continually risen as against the rural. But it needs to be noted that there are differences between the private and individual companies: in 1998 more than two-thirds of the private companies but also somewhat more than a third of the individual firms were situated in the rural areas. In terms of staff numbers, the countryside companies are somewhat larger. This may also be discerned in the corresponding percentages for employees in urban or rural areas.

Table 1: Urban–Countryside distribution of private- and individual sector (China, in %)

	1991	1996	1998	2000	2001
Private sector					
Firms: urban	47.3	59.4	62.9	61.3	63.7
Firms: rural	52.7	40.6	37.1	38.7	36.3
Employees: urban	41.8	51.4	56.9	52.7	54.5
Employees: rural	58.2	48.6	43.1	47.3	45.9
Individual sector					
Firms: urban	31.1	34.6	37.7	43.8	46.4
Firms: rural	68.9	65.4	62.3	56.2	53.6
Employees: urban	30.0	34.1	37.0	42.1	44.8
Employees: rural	70.0	65.9	63.0	57.9	55.2

Sources: Gongshang xingzheng guanli tongji huibian (1991-2001).

In 1997 the proportion of urban companies exceeded the 60% barrier for the first time (62.1%), that of the rural under the 40% mark (37.9%).[46] The increase of private economic activity in the urban areas may be the result of the syndrome that more and more rural entrepreneurs base themselves in urban areas with a view to expanding their entrepreneurial activities. They do so for a number of reasons: the proximity of markets to some extent to raw materials is the case rather more than in rural areas; the marketing prospects are better; and bureaucratic controls are not so heavy as in the countryside area.

Chinese development confirms the theory concerning rural entrepreneurs in East Asia which has been for instance propagated by Hayami,[47] according to which a productive upswing in agriculture (as it developed, for example, in the course of the rural reforms and restructurings) has the effect that entrepreneurs are created who make use industrially of a new potential in agriculture (e.g. in the form of firms specializing in processing agricultural produce). In this way the agricultural sector is connected with modern industry and urban markets. The genesis of industrial production potential in the countryside areas is based on traditional bonds there within those communities (clan, village). The latter also contribute to keeping costs at a minimum. Rural industrialization has the

---

[46] Zhongguo Gongshang Bao, 20 March 1998.
[47] Cf. Hayami/Kawagoe 1993.

effect at the same time that increases in income are not only concentrated in the urban areas but rather also include the countryside; consequently the flight from the countryside to urban zones and the urban poverty that results from that process can thereby be restricted to a tenable level.[48] But at the same time, rural entrepreneurs also bring about interconnections of the private sector there with urban areas. What is specific about the developments in China and Vietnam is that the transition from a planned economy to market structures enables new opportunities for entrepreneurs not only in the domain of the market but also in the links between the mixture of elements from both market and planned economies. The latter resulted in the connection between the market and the bureaucracy likewise the private and the state sectors.

Most of the private companies are small firms in such sectors as small industry and crafts, transport, construction, retailing, catering, trade and other service industries. Especially the private rural industries have developed into being a motor of industry whereby, as we shall see below, most of them at the end of the 1990s were still registered as "collective firms" because by doing so they hoped to obtain greater political security, protection by the local authorities and lower tax and payments of social contributions. Larger companies are only gradually emerging even if their number is continually increasing.

Private firms constituting the second economy at first seemed to be standing in the shadow of an over-mighty state sector; they were concentrated in economic niches, and were founded through the initiatives of individuals in contrast to the state sector which is still protected and subsidized. But the private companies by no means exist as an unconnected *second economy* alongside the state and collective sector; instead there are numerous inter-connections. These are evidenced not only in the informal zone (individual relationships or networks between persons in public and private sectors with the goal of reciprocal enrichment),[49] but rather in the form too of delivery firms, relationships linked with supply, and purchaser or providers of capital. At the same time the private sector also appears in the guise of a competitor, and indeed one which in certain spheres of the economy is beginning to oust state and collective companies. There is rivalry too in the labor market between the organizations operating under different forms of ownership, whereby the private companies insofar as they pay higher wages and salaries, attract qualified blue and white collar

---

[48] Although there is a migratory movement made up by rural laborers into the urban areas, (up till now at any rate) they have intended not so much to reside for a long period as to obtain a higher income in the interests of improving the life situation of their families, and acquiring starting capital for self-employment in the region around their native place.

[49] Ever more private firms locate themselves in the proximity of state companies: the former have been dubbed "satellites". In them relatives of some employees in the state sector companies go about associated work. To give an example: according to a Chinese report, customers who showed up at the state Sichuan fridge factory with equipment needing repair were sent by the director of the repair department to a neighboring private repair workshop run by a family member (Yu/Yang 1993: 222/223). Vox populi terms such interconnections as *yi guo liang zhi* (One country, two systems); this is wordplay on the politics of re-unification with Taiwan.

workers from out of the public sector. Due to the possibilities of earning more money and mounting insecurity concerning future developments in the public sector, a continually increasing number of trained employees from the state sector are becoming self-employed. To describe the change to the private sector the familiar word *xiahai* (diving into the sea) enjoys widespread circulation.

Table 2: Private companies in sectors (2000, China, in %)

	Private economy	*Individual economy*
Primary sector	2.3	5.7
Secondary sector	39.5	12.0
Tertiary sector	58.2	82,6
In total	100.0	100.0

Source: *Zhongguo Gongshang Bao*, 23 March 2001.

Turning now to branches of the economy: in 1996 in the private sector, production came first (43.8% of the companies and 53.7% of the personnel) followed by retailing and catering sectors (40.9% of the firms and 30.3% of the employees) of which the industrial sector in rural areas (67.3% of the companies, 71.9% of the employees) was more strongly developed than in the urban areas (27.7% correspondingly 36.5%), where in turn trade and catering dominated (55.1 likewise 45.9%).[50] This rural preponderance may be explained by the fact that the private sector had its origins in the rural areas, and to a major extent it processes agricultural products. However, above all in rural areas there is more space available for industrial production, and reservations on the part of the peasant population are less strongly marked than in the more socialist-oriented, urban centers in which the state sector dominates. In the individual sector, the domains trade and catering with 60% of the firms and 58.3% of the employees are the most important parts of the service industry sector, small industries and public transport/logistics (12.1, 11.7 likewise 11% of the companies). Urban and rural areas are approximately equally balanced.[51]

Seen in terms of space, the private sector concentrated first of all in the more developed areas in East China, where better access to markets and a more developed infrastructure are available. Private companies in East China are qualitatively i.e. in technological and capital terms better equipped and employ on average more personnel. Already in 1996 the initial capital of the companies in East China consisted of 1.24 m, in Central China 1.19 m whereas that in West-

---

[50] Gongshang xingzheng guanli 1997: 64/65.
[51] Ibid.: 74-76.

ern China was 0.91 m Yuan.[52] In the meantime one finds on the quantitative
level, however, a gradual shift.

Table 3: Geographical distribution of private companies (China)

	East China	Central China	West China
1995	69,8	19,0	11,2
1998	64,6	23,0	12,4

Source: According to figures provided by the Administrative Office for Industry and Commerce in
September 1996; Zhang Houyi 1999: 485.

In the 1990s numerous state and collective firms were transformed into forms
of ownership such as shareholding or with limited liabilities (i.e. limited companies), or sold to private firms. In 1995 in the province Zhejiang alone, 758
state and collective companies were sold to private persons and with that were
changed into private companies. In 1995 in Gansu province in total, 2,563 state
companies were transformed into limited companies and 17 into firms with
shareholding arrangements.[53] The emergence of pluralism in company forms
led to a further de-centralization of decision-making in the economy, and to a
change in the structure of company ownership.

The state companies began in this way to lose their dominant position in the
Chinese economy. In 1978 state companies produced 77.6% (collective firms
22.4%) of the gross output. The percentage of private companies at that point
was zero. In 1998 the corresponding amount of state companies had fallen to
only 26.5% (collective firms 36%). The number of private companies (including shareholding companies and firms with foreign capital) was now 37.5% and
already the largest sector. At the same time the private sector has for years been
the one with the highest growth rate.[54] In the total volume of retail trade it had –
as mentioned – in 1998 a share of 62.8%.[55] This share may, however, be underestimated statistically. Chinese studies and our own research show that the
private share in the domains of retailing, catering and service industries in
many provinces comprises more than 90% of the total volume.[56]

However, the statistical data says little about the actual extent of privatization. According to Chinese research for example, the number of non-registered
companies in large and middle-sized cities in the second half of the 1990s was

---

[52] "Zhongguo siying qiye yanjiu" ketizu 1999: 136.

[53] Gansu nianjian 1996: 30.

[54] Cf. Zhongguo tongji nianjian 1999: 421.

[55] Ibid.: 547.

[56] Pan Gang 1997; Heberer/Taubmann 1998: 219ff. A contribution to the theoretical journal of
the CCP attributed to the private sector at the end of 1996 a share of 30.8% of the industrial gross
output, cf. Zhang Sufang 1998: 47.

double or at least as high as those which were registered.[57] In smaller towns this ratio may even be as high as 4:1 and in rural areas the number of non-registered companies is supposed to be even higher.[58] In addition to that there are the private companies which misleadingly let themselves be registered as state or collective companies.

The reasons for that can be divided into (a) *political* such as the need for political correctness and safeguards (in the hierarchy of the companies state and collective firms are still ranked higher than the private ones) or the desire to obtain membership of the CP (officially private companies were refused entry to the party till 2001) as an important entry-point to political networks; (b) *economic*, such as better access to credit, tax advantages, more extensive information about markets or support from the local authorities; and (c) *social* (higher social prestige). The non-registered comprise the following groups for the most part: illegal individual and private companies; family members helping out; persons with a second job; moonlighters who follow a second job in their free time; that section of the rural collective industries which in reality is actually in private hands (approx. 90%); as well as the great number of companies that are nominally state-owned or collective but are actually privately run. If one adds all of those groups together, then one arrives at a figure (end 2001) between 250 and 300 million people who may have been working in the private sector of the Chinese economy, approx. 35–40% of the total workforce.[59]

Meanwhile even the term state ownership has to be put into question. The following phenomena have contributed to it being very difficult to estimate the actual amount of privatization: the multiplicity of forms of ownership (ranging from large, state-sector firms centrally directed and organized according to the planned economy to ones directed by province, city or county, right down to the small ones leased to private persons), the different mixed ownership constructions, misleading classifications and misclassifications.[60]

But there are still a range of problems which stand in the way of a rapid growth of the private sector. Among these are the following:

-   discrimination and handicaps in competition experienced by private companies against state ones (e.g. in the provision of commodities and raw materials, when trying to obtain credit allocation or real estate etc.);

---

[57] According to statements made by the Bureau for the Administration of Industry and Commerce in September 1996; cf. also Li Chengrui 1997: 66; Zhang Houyi 1999b: 51.

[58] Huang Weiding 1997: 90.

[59] On that: Jia/Wang/Tang 1987: 28ff.; *Zhongguo Gongshang Bao*, 25 February 1991; *Renmin Ribao* 9 March 1991. On the statistical problematic cf. Odgaard 1990/91. For the 1990s this was suggested by the sociologist Zhang Houyi, cf. *Gongren Ribao*, 11 August 1997: 2.

[60] Among the forms that constitute private enterprises, may be counted the following: rural industrial companies; joint-stock companies; state and collective firms with internal shares; cooperation between state- and collective firms on the one hand and private companies on the other hand; "firms run by the population" (*minban gongsi*); *Joint-Venture* companies; and/or companies with purely foreign capital (*waizi qiye*).

- absence of legal safeguards;
- interventions by the bureaucracy (for instance in the form of the imposition of higher taxes or contributions) as well as corruption amongst official-dom;
- lack of confidence of the private entrepreneur in the policies of the gov-ernment with the consequence that profits are consumed and not re-invested;
- the existence still of a certain, negative social image of private entrepre-neurial strata.[61]

The problem areas contribute to what has been up till now a grave problem, that is the short lifetimes of companies. In 1999 the average lifetime of private companies was thought to be 2.9 years.[62] As a result an entrepreneur from Shandong demanded in his role as a member of the National People's Congress at the Congress session in early 2000 a "turtle philosophy" for private compa-nies i.e. political measures for guaranteeing longer lifetimes.[63]

Chinese surveys amongst private entrepreneurs at the end of the 1990s sug-gested that confidence in the continuity of policies, social pressure, lack of state support, limitations of the market and distortions of competition in favor of state sector firms were amongst the core problems inducing dissatisfaction.[64] However, the leadership did react to expressions of dissatisfaction. In early 1999 the central newspaper of the Party (*Renmin Ribao*) wrote along these lines: the interests of private entrepreneurs had to be legally safeguarded; the authorities given fixed and unambiguous regulations and guidelines about frameworks; the organizations representing the interests of entrepreneurs strengthened; special banks for private entrepreneurs set up; and they had to have equal status for tax payments and provision of credit.[65]

China's WTO entry will significantly improve the conditions for develop-ment of the private sector because it will provide the private entrepreneurs unlimited access to world markets, access to cheaper, foreign raw materials, better access to credits, a legally more advantageous framework and new chances for growth.

2.2.2. *Vietnam*

In contrast to the northern part of Vietnam, after 1975 a significant section of the southern Vietnamese economy remained outside of state control; already

---

[61] Bai Nanfeng et al. 1993. A survey carried out in 1992 of 2,500 people in Beijing, Shanghai, Guangzhou, Shenyang and Kaifeng about the social consequences of the reforms showed that private entrepreneurs came top concerning assessment of income (out of 11 different professions) but in the assessment of social prestige were in last place but one.

[62] Shi 2000.

[63] Zhongguo Qiyejia, 4/2000: 43.

[64] *Zhongguo Gongshang Bao*, 23 March and 2 April 1999 as well as 28 April 2000.

[65] *Renmin Ribao*, 8 March 1999.

before the separation of the country, there had been considerably more private firms in the South than in the North: "At the end of the 1970s collective and privately-owned industry operating outside the plan still accounted for close to 40% of industrial output." An official guide to investment in Ho Chi Minh City already spoke in 1976 of 731, and in 1980 of 960 private companies. The figure for the industrial sector in the former Saigon already stood at 19,091 and correspondingly 20,581.[66] Especially in the Mekong Delta, the peasants exited relatively rapidly from the newly founded, agricultural production collectives. Of 13,000 founded in the years 1975/76, by 1980 only approx. 3,700 still existed.[67]

Likewise according to official statistics, the private sector nationally is supposed to have produced 38.1% and in 1980 42.8% of the gross national product (GNP); these were at that time incredibly high figures for a socialist economy.[68] In 1985 23% of all employees in the industrial sector were either in an individual or a private economy, whereas one year later already well over 500 private firms were responsible for 15.6% of the entire gross production value.[69] These statistics indicate that a degree of collectivization and nationalization could not be reached in the secondary sector comparable to that in the primary sector, – and definitely not to the same extent as in the socialist economies of Eastern Europe.

So far as the newly founded, collective organizations did not simply come to an end after a short period of time, people under the cover of that form of ownership went about the privately employed business in the sense of "limited fence-breaking" as described above.[70] In the course of a few years, this led to a type of "commercializing" of the planned part of the economy.[71]

The planned and collectivized economy was not accepted by the South Vietnamese population that had been brought up decades long with market economy activities, and been subject to its massive influence from the 1950s to the mid-1970s. Peasants refused to enter into the collective economy, worked hard only on their privately-owned parcels of land but not on the land owned collectively. As a result in reality collectivization existed only for a short period. The literature shows an official toleration of the informal, private sector before 1986 in commerce and small industries, since in this way state-owned companies could be provided with limited *input* goods.[72] The economic crisis between 1978 and 1981 led to a massive rise in additional jobs for which national materials and goods were "diverted" (e.g. building materials and machines from

---

[66] Nguyen/Tran 1992/93: 30.

[67] Quang Truong 1987: 207ff.

[68] Le Ngoc Hung/Rondinelli 1993: 7, Table 3.

[69] Diez/Schätzl 1993: 542; Do Duc Dinh 1993.

[70] Nguyen Xuan Oanh 1991: 3; Sjöberg 1991: 13.

[71] Sjöberg 1991: 13. For more detail on that, see Fforde 1991; Fforde 1993 refers primarily to the north of Vietnam; see too Güldner 1992: 4. Wiegersma 1991 explains this process with the dynamism characterizing the Vietnamese peasant economy, which undermined collectivization.

[72] Andreff 1993: 519; Dinh Qu 1993: 533.

private companies for private jobs in the building sector).[73] Along with this
shadow economy which at least in the South was extensive in size, a gray area
existed in the form of leasing contracts between state/collectivized companies
and private households/persons to whom wide-ranging, economic room for
maneuver was permitted.

In the pre-reform period between 1980 and 1985, Vietnamese policies fluc-
tuated back and forth between a legalization of private business activity and an
extension of the collectivization process without establishing one line in particular.[74] Only after a personnel reshuffle within the CPV, did the reform forces
around Nguyen Van Linh take power at the 6th Party Congress in 1986. With
the heading *doi moi* (renewal), they initiated a extensive program of reform
which put the experiences since 1979 to good account, and on the other hand
attempted to implement the lessons from what had happened in other countries
(China, fast-developing nations, and in a negative sense from the former Soviet
Union and socialist countries of Eastern Europe).

By no stretch of the imagination could the path of reform within the party be
described as regarded with undivided approval. A powerful faction amongst the
members consisting of both the party and state bureaucracies, conservative
ideologists and parts of the military establishment positioned themselves
against those elements linked to Linh who were in favor of a political transformation in favor of the market economy linked to reforms involving a rapid
taking-apart of the planned sections of the economy. Without generally reject-
ing the reforms, this faction urged a slow, cautious, economic transformation
with – if possible for the most part – a retention of the central role of the
Party.[75]

The main goals of the reformers – as in China – lay in the establishing of a
multi-sectoral, commodity economy or *socialist market economy* as the stage
prior to a socialism which was to be established later but which would for the
foreseeable future be postponed indefinitely. The private economy is here explicitly recognized as important and worthy of support. In contrast to the situation earlier, the reforms established the support of agriculture, light industry
and of export.[76] Five sectors of ownership were licensed: that of the state, a
mixture of state-private, collective, private or capitalist, and a family sector.

Among the most important measures for reform which promoted the further
development of parts of the economy not in the public sector should be included a government edict about companies (government, collective, private)

---

[73] Beresford 1989: 183.

[74] On the periodic nature of the Vietnamese reform process cf. Fforde/Vylder 1996b; Kurths
1997: 59-64. The apparent fluctuations could, however, be interpreted as the maneuver of a con-
vinced communist leadership, by which the support of private sector business activities might only
be a tactical decision à la Lenin's NEP which after an economic consolidation could be once again
revised; cf. e.g. Fforde/Vylder 1996b: 13/14.

[75] Cima 1989: 789; *Südostasien aktuell*, 9/1991: 460. Specially about Linh Stern 1989.

[76] Cf. Sixth National Congress 1987.

from 1988. This for the first time created a legal basis for entrepreneurial activities which were de facto already going on in the private sector, as well as three decrees issued by the Council of Ministers concerning the collective, household economy and private economy. Included in the term household economy (also house or home economy), were all private secondary jobs taken on by workers, peasants and civil servants; in contrast, the private economy is understood as meaning all full-time, private business activities.[77]

The 7th Party Congress of the CPV resolved in 1991 that the private economic sector could develop quantitatively and in terms of management without limitations, excluding those areas in which private economic activity was prohibited by law. In that year a law which came into effect about companies legalized the private sector. This law and a further one about companies (limited companies and joint-stock) created for the first time a legal basis for the private sector beyond the sectors limited to individuals or a family. The long-term existence of this sector and equal status with companies governed by other ownership structures was formally recognized and government protection promised. The law allowed at the same time the unrestricted employment of staff dependent on pay.[78] The same points then found their way into the new constitution of 1992 (Articles 15, 16 and 21), through which the private sector was explicitly safeguarded.[79]

Along with the state and the collective sector, Article 16 recognized as further elements in a multi-sectoral economy, private individual businesses as well as the private capitalist and state-capitalist sectors. Within the private sector, the organizational structure of industrial production and commerce can be freely chosen without government specifications (Article 21). The article expressly allowed the building up of private companies to any size without government limitation, a regulation which in the opinion of some successful entrepreneurs in practice was not followed. The same article named the family business sector as especially worthy of support; this sector could be regarded as part of the small company domain. According to Article 22 all sectors have equal rights, and their legal ownership was recognized and protected. The guarantee concerning ownership of the means of production in accordance with the constitution can only be annulled (according to Article 23) when it is required in the national interests. Even then dispossession is not possible without compensation; compensation should be paid which must take into account the current market value of the dispossessed object.[80]

In this way the new constitution is intended to create confidence in the reform policies and the private sector, in the interests of long-term investment and confidence for the purposes of planning. In addition the private economic

---

[77] Economic Sectors 1992: 81; *Südostasien aktuell*, 5/1989: 248.

[78] Law on private enterprises in: *Fundamental Laws and Regulations of Vietnam* 1993: 349-360.

[79] The Constitutions of Vietnam 1995: 160-162.

[80] The Constitution 1993: 18-21.

sector is granted the same status as the state and collective sectors which are still referred to as leading, and so the private sector obtains an unlimited guarantee for its continuing existence. Following the example of China, the term socialism has been expanded to include the private ownership of the means of production.

In 1994 98% of the agricultural companies, 91% of the service industries, 76.5% of the retail trade and 28% of the manufacturing sector are thought to have been privately managed.[81] Parallel to the expansion of the private sector due to the founding of new companies, a restructuring of the state sector took place which led to a decrease in the number of public sector enterprises from approx. 12,000 to 6,310 by the end of 1995, 5,790 by the middle of 1997, and 2,280 in early 2001. Whereas some of the firms above all in rural areas were closed, the majority appear to have been simply merged with larger companies. Over one million jobs were lost as a result, and had to be balanced by the private sector.[82] In spite of what are at first sight impressive, re-structuring measures, to this day the Vietnamese government still does not have at its disposal a clear program for privatization or at the very least for reform for the state sector, a sector which is still not yet effective. The *equitization* of some state companies has been carried out very timidly, and has remained till now (2002) without success.

Although the private sector is considered in Vietnam too as the most dynamic and efficient one,[83] at the same time within the Party leadership differing positions exist concerning the assessment of this sector. The ambivalence manifested itself in the documents emanating from the 8th Party Congress of the CPV. In 'The political report of the Central Committee to the Party Congress', it was stated that in the long-term the sector of smaller individual businesses would play an important role whereby, however, the people concerned, "in their interests and those of the development of production will voluntarily join themselves step by step with collectives or work as satellites for state companies or cooperatives." The larger "private capitalist" sector in contrast, they argued in the paper, could contribute to national reconstruction, and had to be assisted and safeguarded.[84] In the report, 'Guidelines and tasks of the 5-year plan for social and economic development for the years 1996–2000', it is stated on the other hand that they ought to "take suitable political measures," in order that those responsible for the individual firms be "encouraged" to join cooperatives, to found joint ventures with state-owned companies, or take part in business associations with the state sector. The private capitalist entrepreneur in turn should be "encouraged" to sell preferential shares to their employees.[85]

---

[81] Vo Dai Luoc 1996b: 39/40.

[82] General Statistical Office 1996a: 41; Laut Lai Van Cu, Director of the government office, quoted in *Straits Times,* 27 September 1997.

[83] Cf. Le Viet Duc 1999: 133-135.

[84] Communist Party of Vietnam 1996: 54.

[85] Ibid.: 194.

Precisely this latter point contained in a plan for the future for the years up to 2000, can hardly have had an encouraging effect. A direct relapse into collectivist economic structures is indeed hardly likely. But in such views the very strong influence – now as in the past – of conservative circles in the Party becomes transparent. Whereas the 'Orientation and Measures for Vietnam's Industrial Development during 2001-2005' only marginally mentioned the role of the private sector, the 9th Party Congress decided to foster it more strongly.[86]

In the second half of the 1990s, in the discussions which took place inside the Party three basic positions crystallized:[87]

-   One position rejected private entrepreneurial activities in general since they were supposedly based on exploitation of workers, and that contradicted the socialist ideals of the Party. Private entrepreneurial activities on the part of party members and their acceptance by private entrepreneurs in the party altered its character because there was a danger that increasingly entrepreneurial or "bourgeois" interests dominated. Those party members who already possessed private companies were recommended to change their firms into a collective form – amongst which are counted – joint-stock companies.
-   The second position preferred unrestricted entrepreneurial activities by party members. If the party supported the development of the multi-sectoral economy, then party members had to go ahead and set a good example insofar as they themselves founded and led private companies. This created confidence amongst the population in the Party's politics and led to a positive emulation effect. In addition the private sector contributed increasingly to the solution of problems of central socio-economic importance. Very pragmatically this faction pointed to the fact that the existing prohibition had already been circumvented by party members in that they had been increasingly taking part in private economic activity albeit illegally. By doing that they eluded controls. The argument that the supporting of private economic activity entailed a deviation from socialism was not considered valid by supporters of this position. Only if the state were weak and the party members of poor quality would they bring about deviations. The private economy could not be held responsible for that. The opposite was the case, they argued: good party members could act as moral role models, and even orientate this sector to socialism. The pragmatism of this second position, glossed over with ideology, however, leaves open how the private economic sector and socialism could be brought into harmony with each other.
-   A middle position restated in principle the exploitative character of businesses not in the state sector, but raises the question about what could be understood by the term "exploitation". A differentiation between non-

---

[86] Vietnam Economic Review 8/02:7ff.
[87] Le Quang Thuong: 124f.; Vu Hien 1997.

exploitative, small firms and exploitative capitalists made on the basis of the number of employees was rejected as being one-sided and "unscientific". Exploitation could just as well be based on the criterion of financial investment (permitted purchasing of shares versus prohibited investment in manufacturing). Just as in the second position, a special morality was ascribed to party members on the basis of their private economic activity differing fundamentally from that of capitalists.

It is conspicuous that in important reports and reflections about the future development of the economy and economic development policies, the private sector is mentioned either not at all or only at the margins (e.g. in the form of property-overlapping "small and middle-sized companies"),[88] not least in order to cushion ideologically the sensitivity of the terminology. Thus the private sector was not mentioned either by the document '10 development goals in the socio-economic area' issued at the fifth meeting of the National Assembly in May–June 1999, nor by the overall, socio-economic plan of the government for the year 2000.[89]

The "Company Law" which came into effect at the beginning of 2000 upgraded private firms. As a result such firms can be registered without having to obtain official authorization as they did before. Accordingly the registrations doubled between January and April 2000 as opposed to the comparable period of time in the previous year.[90]

The official term for the private sector is "outside of the public sector" (*ngoai quoc doan*), which already indicates at the least a secondary role (alongside the heavyweight "public sector"). Herno argues the language and practice of the division between both sectors creates a normative distance between the "good" socialist or public sector and the private sector a necessary "evil". Not only were two separated sectors of the national economy spoken of but also two different "moral worlds". In this way the private sector was identified with "individualism" which was characterized as being something foreign in Vietnamese culture and as the basic cause of social anomalies. Beyond that this sector represents the negative elements of the market economy. Through the process of privatization as well the "bureaucratic ideal of order" was weakened precisely due to the erosion of control over the economy. Insofar the private economy proves itself to be a "source of disorder".[91] In addition to that comes a further factor in which Vietnam basically differs from China: it recurred in many conversations with functionaries and entrepreneurs above all in the south of the country namely the fear that ethnic Chinese could control important segments of the economy.

---

[88] Cf. for example Vietnam 1997/98 or Le Dang Doanh 1999.
[89] See for instance Weggel 1999: 517/518.
[90] Cohen 2000.
[91] Herno 1998: 6/7.

Finally the dominance of the public sector represents as well the leading role of the Party and with that of the state. As a result of this too, the leading role of the public sector is re-emphasized regularly from time to time. A number of state companies were supposed to be planning to merge (indeed following the South Korean model of the *Chaebol*, the large enterprise conglomerates) in order to shape their work more effectively, and to limit the ruinous competition between state-owned firms which are involved in the same fields of business.

However, there is one thread of the discussion which discusses the private sector without putting it in the middle-point of the debate. Ha and Bui exemplify that: they argue that the transition to an industrial nation presupposed market economic relations even if it was "market mechanisms with a socialist orientation". It needed to be taken into account too that the market economy and communism were not separated spheres but rather were a matching product. They suggest that a Socialist market economy also assumed the existence of a multi-sectoral economy (in terms of forms of ownership) whereby all sectors participated with equal status in industrialization and modernization including the "people's economy" i.e. the non-state sector. These should not be sloppily characterized as the "private capitalist economic sector" given that the criteria for such a terminological classification had to be newly defined (as they see it). It was astounding that the government was cooperating with foreign capitalists but not with private firms in their own country.[92] They point out that others have criticized the term "private capitalist economy" because this terminology already induced in the population a negative connotation and there existed a danger of "left deviations" (i.e. the limitation or the prohibition). It would be better to speak of a "civilian-owned area", a terminology, which made very clear the sensitivity of the question of how to dub the private sector along with its taboo status in political contexts.[93]

This half-latent discussion partially taboo-creating explains the dilemma in which the private sector in Vietnam finds itself: unpopular but indispensable. Diagram 8 shows as of now the officially recognized sectors of the economy and company forms. In contrast to the familial and individual companies, there are for the private companies – similarly to China – no restrictions concerning the number of paid employees; furthermore in the family firms only family members are employed.[94]

---

[92] Ha/Bui 1999.

[93] Market Economy and Socialist Orientation 1999: 82/83.

[94] The classsification follows those which are usual in the statistical yearbook. A diverging classification is to be found in Truong/Gates 1992.

Diagram 8: Enterprise Patterns in Vietnam
(Vietnamese classification)

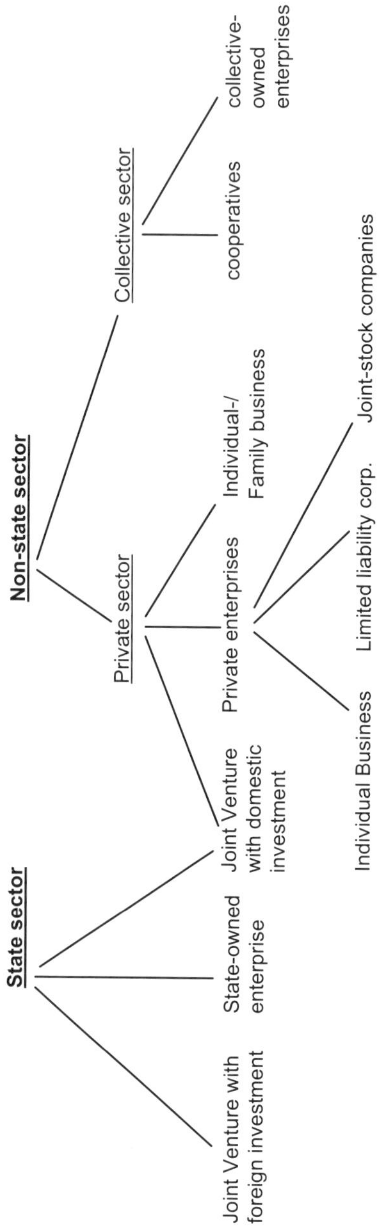

State sector

Non-state sector

Joint Venture with foreign investment

State-owned enterprise

Joint Venture with domestic investment

Private sector

Private enterprises

Individual-/Family business

Individual Business

Limited liability corp.

Joint-stock companies

Collective sector

cooperatives

collective-owned enterprises

Diagram 9: Growth rate of the gross output in Vietnam (in %)

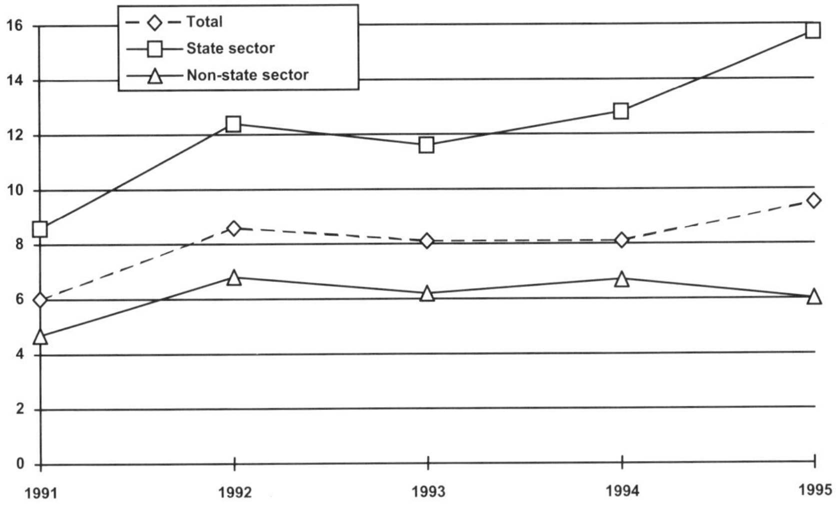

Source: General Statistical Office 1996: 40.

The economic data for the early 1990s show that reform processes which were spontaneously set in motion by the population against the wills of the political leadership brought about extraordinary success with its core area being privatization. So the gross output rose between 1990 and 1995 by 8.1% per year (cf. Diagram 9). The non-state sector grew in the same period by 6.1% but the unhealthy collective and dynamic private sector are both included in this. In 1995 the private sector had apparently already become responsible for 57.8% of the gross output (in 2000 about two-thirds).

The growth rate of the state sector that in contrast with that of China was surprisingly high, is explained by the mixed companies such as joint ventures that are counted as state companies and not private ones. In addition the government supported key industries whereas the private economic growth took place almost entirely out of its own energy and force without any support worthy of note from the government. The crisis-ridden collective sector was included in the category non-public sector, economic activity; as a result the real growth rate of the private sector by itself must have far exceeded the percentages given.

However, in Vietnam too a privatization "from above" had taken place. A large number of state companies were – similarly as in China – allocated to the managers with comparatively few conditions. Those who led their companies taken-over by means of contracts into making a profit could quickly become rich. Beyond that government ownership assets associated with these companies in many cases were re-directed into private firms owned by the manager or members of his family.[95]

So it can be seen that it is precisely these managers who resisted the legal privatization methods proposed by the World Bank. They did so because had they followed those, the managers would have lost their control over the government ownership assets which they had acquired free of charge. This is also why up till 1995 only 19 of 6,000 state companies applied for a privatization and a mere three of these carried it out.[96] At the end of 1997 the Vietnamese leadership declared that there were still 5,790 state-owned companies. At the beginning of 2000 there were thought to be still 5,200. From 1998 until the end of 1999, 403 state companies had been sold; but it was intended that the number of these companies step by step be lowered to 3,200 by means of fusions, sales and being shut down.[97]

But it is not only managers who are opposed to the sale of state-owned companies but also the provinces with a high percentage of state companies; they fear the social unrest which would come with redundancies and closures.[98] The poorer provinces, in contrast, prefer the support of the private sector. Indeed party leaders issue reminders sometimes about the need for speedy privatization of the state sector. For instance, party boss La Kha Phieu in June 1998 demanded such a step not least because only 37% of the state-owned companies work at a profit.[99] Generally nothing much has happened on this issue, an expression of the enormous resistance to such steps.

The distribution of ownership amongst companies (as of the beginning of 1996) is shown in Table 4. It needs to be taken into account that state sector companies are generally larger and have more employees than companies with other forms of ownership.

In 1996 of the total numbers, 74.7% of all privately owned companies in the three big cities (8,815 private firms) as well as in the Mekong Delta (10,287). Central Vietnam (3,153) with 12.0% and the Red River Delta (1,500) with 5.9% are in the middle positions (3,153 private firms). The poorer regions North Vietnam (565), the Central Highlands (524) and Tay Nguyen (734) with in total 7.1% only had a relatively low number of private companies. The latter circumstance is a result of economic under-development and the low density of population in these regions. At the same time the impetus of the individual regions may be discerned from the regional distribution. One can almost formu-

---

[95] Cf. World Bank 1996: 63; Kolko 1997: 56ff.

[96] Kolko 1997: 59ff.

[97] *Saigon Times*, 27 September 1997, followed by *Südostasien*, December 1997: 20. *Bangkok Post*, 9 May 2000. On the development of the state sector companies generally cf. Dodsworth et al. 1996.

[98] Ton Tich Qui 1998. Cf. also Pham Quang Huan 1998, Tran Du Lich and Tran Hong Thai 1998.

[99] Op. cit. in Knappe 1998: 9.

late the following equation: the higher the absolute number of private companies, the lower the number and percentage of state-owned companies.

Table 4: Companies classified by form of ownership (Vietnam, beginning of 1996)

Form of ownership	Number	%
Private companies	25,578	76.6
Of which: private firms	18,101	
Limited companies	7,313	
Joint-stock companies	164	
State-owned firms	6,366	19.1
Others	1,454	4.3
In total	33,398	100.0

Source: Dang Duc Dam 1997: 124/125.

The ownership ratios are shown region by region in Table 5.

Table 5: Companies according to regions and forms of ownership (Vietnam, in %)

Form of ownership	Metropolis[a]	North	Midlands	Red River Delta	Central	Tay Nguyen	Mekong-Delta
Private firm	75.7	48.8	53.0	49.9	78.3	64.4	90.3
State firm	19.0	43.3	41.2	45.0	16.9	31.9	7.1
Others	5.3	7.9	5.8	5.1	4.8	3.7	2.6
Total	100.0	100.0	100.0	100.0	100.0	100.0	100.0

Source: Dang Duc Dam 1997: 124/125.
NB: [a] consists of the cities of Hanoi, Haiphong and Ho Chi Minh City.

Nonetheless, it should not be overlooked that the Vietnamese database is even more complicated in its design than its Chinese counterpart not least due to the depiction of the data which is partly because of rather different classifications. According to the explanations of a Vietnamese social scientist at a conference in Hanoi in 1996, the total number of registered limited companies, private firms and joint-stock companies (on the first of July 1975) was 23, 960, that of

individual/ family firms 1,882,798 and the state-owned companies at 7,179.[100]
For 1996 Ronnas quoted figures as follows: 2.2 m individual companies,
20,000 private companies, 8,300 limited companies, and 190 joint-stock companies. In 1995 about 600,000 small companies were supposed to be in active
existence.[101] The figures in Table 6 taken from Vietnamese sources allow at
least the representation of a trend.

Table 6: Development of private companies (1993-96, Vietnam)

Private companies			Private firms	Limited Liability Comp.	Joint-stock
1991	123	of which:	76	44	3
1992	4,474	of which:	3,115	1,167	65
1993	12,748	of which:	9,344	3,287	117
1994	19,025	of which:	13,772	5,120	133
7/1995	22,438	of which:	16,064	6,226	148
1996	30,090	of which:	ca.21,000	8,900	190

Sources: Nguyen Dinh Phan 1996: 7; Nguyen/Nguyen 1996: 13; Dang Duc Dam 1997: 176;
          Vietnam Economic Times, February 1998: 14; Nguyen Duc Vinh 1999: 16/17.

In the middle of the 1990s, the deputy director general of the Hanoi Chamber of
Industry and Commerce declared that by the year 2000 there would be 200,000
private industrial companies which would employ 60% of the total Vietnamese
workforce and contribute 58% of its industrial output.[102] While this estimation
was all too optimistic, it indicates that the necessity of the development of the
private sector was clearly recognized, but over and over again blocked by sections of the political elite.

What is conspicuous is that the average number of employees per company
between 1991 and 1994 had rapidly fallen namely from 87 to just 10 (cf. Table
8).

---

[100] Official Vietnamese figures admittedly should be treated with some caution. McCartny's
conclusion (1992: 5) that, "official Vietnamese data to 1991 can only be used in an indicative
manner, that is, as little more than signs of possible or probable changes in the economy" is still
valid. The actual share which the private sector has of the GDP may exceed the figures given:
similarly as in China, e.g. many of the collective firms and likewise the state sector companies are
in reality private companies, and private entrepreneurs have their companies registered under other
company forms (e.g. individual firms), cf. the contributions by Do Minh Cuong, Nguyen Minh Tu
and Tran Duc Vinh to the Deutsche Entwicklungsdienst (DED [German Overseas Aid Agency])-
Regional conference Asia (25-28 October 1996) in Hanoi. According to official data, in 2001 there
existed 1.5 m individual enterprises engaged in non-agricultural businesses and 30,000 non-state
enterprises, cf. Vu Dinh Anh 2001: 28. The private sector in 2000 produced one-third of the GDP
and 76.1% of the total revenues of retail trade and services, see *Vietnam Economic Review* 1/01: 43
and 2/01: 44.
[101] Ronnas 1998: 1-2. A detailed study of entrepreneurial strata in Vietnam from an economic
point of view: Ronnas/Ramamurthy 2001.
[102] Murray 1997: 7.

Table 7: Employees in the private sector (1991-94, Vietnam)

	all private companies	of which in private firms	in limited liability companies	in joint-stock
1991	10,683	2,160	6,511	1,967
1992	113,156	29,411	74,753	6,992
1993	228,393	65,687	153,525	9,181
1994	299,540	84,261	202,668	12,611

Source: Dang Duc Dam 1997: 177.

The reason for that is that first of all only the large companies were specially identified (as a private capitalist company), then all firms with more than seven members of staff. Since the absolute majority of them are small firms, the average number of employees per company has lowered. This has at the same time an ideological function because the private companies apparently very small, appear as a result rather marginal and only few very firms are actually to be classified as capitalist. Moreover seasonal workers are not recorded.

Table 8: Companies classified by number of employees (1995, Vietnam)

< 10	Employees	66.3
10-50	Employees	29.3
50-100	Employees	3.0
100-200	Employees	0.7
> 200	Employees	0.7

Source: Dang Duc Dam 1997: 178.

In 1995 companies issuing shares and those with limited liability had on average more members of staff than other private companies. To illustrate this, in simple private companies there were on average 7, in limited companies 53, and in joint-stock firms 106 registered employees per company.[103] Here, above all the quasi-collectivist nature of the latter form plays a role, which politically perceived is supposed to show the correct trend of development for the other private companies, and as a result is considered to be politically more opportune as a form of company ownership. For the limited companies the risk appears to be less, above all after the passing in 1990 of a law about commercial companies.[104] However, the founding of joint-stock companies appeared to move relatively slowly. A Vietnamese study in the middle of the 1990s suggested that the reasons were to be found in the lack of legal security and the absence of a suitable infrastructure (cf. Table 9).

[103] Dang Duc Dam 1997: 178.
[104] The law is to be found in: *Fundamental Laws* 1993: 328-348. This law contains too the regulations about share-holding companies.

Table 9: Reasons for the slow development of joint-stock companies (Vietnam)

Reason	Respondent company agrees with statement (in %)
Lack of unambiguous legal stipulations	64.4
Ownership of shares is not popular	57.8
Absence of a stock exchange	55.6
Complicated company administration	17.8
Lack of confidence in law and politics	15.6

Source: Dang Duc Dam 1997: 214.

Although in Vietnam too, countless laws and decrees were passed which gave the private sector a basic legal framework, in respect of the private sector the Party is primarily concerned with controlling both its power and entrepreneurs, and not in the safeguarding of the rights of individuals.[105]

In March 1998 there were thought to be 34,600 registered private firms, 85 of all companies having 58% of the total investment assets but with only 28.4% of the total turnover. But as was stated in the relevant report, many companies do not possess a license for commercial activity, carry out no book-keeping, and withhold tax payments.[106] Since there is hardly any stimulus for any self-employed activity, the majority of small entrepreneurs are occupied in the informal (i.e. non-registered) sector,[107] which not only includes non-registered business activities but also second jobs held by employees in the state sector. The continuing discrimination and political uncertainty limit both the development of the private sector as well as private investments, and drive many entrepreneurs into the underground economy.

The fluctuation inside the private sector is relatively large. A Swedish-Vietnamese study of 356 private companies in the cities Hanoi, Ho Chi Minh City, Haiphong, Ha Tay and Long An in the years 1991 and 1997 established that 129 (36.2%) no longer existed. In 80 cases the company performance had deteriorated, in 54 they had remained the same or had grown a little, and in 93 cases rapid growth had occurred.[108] Almost 60% had closed or had deteriorated in comparison to 1991. This result which was confirmed by our inquiries at the relevant authorities, showed the phenomenon of fluctuation amongst the entrepreneurial strata. However these results are put into perspective when we take into account that according to the study just quoted almost a third (32.9%) of the entrepreneurs continued to work as self-employed either in a different branch of industry or with a new company in a different field. Almost a third

---

[105] For China: *Zhongguo Gongshang Bao*, 8 December 1998.
[106] Kim Diep 1998.
[107] *Vietnam Economic Times*, February 1998: 14ff.
[108] Ramamurthy 1998: 2.

(32.9%) had retired or died.[109] But at the same time it should be noted that this fluctuation is not the result of an age problem, something which can be established from the fact that 74.1% of the companies which had ceased to exist had been around for more than five years, almost a quarter (22.1%) had existed for more than eleven years, and the transfer of flourishing companies to suitable successors could certainly have been achieved during this time.

Concerning the determination of the quantitative extent of private economic activity, similar problems exist in Vietnam as in China. It is difficult to estimate, for example, the extent of their shadow economies, which feed on the one hand on secondary jobs, and on the other hand on non-registered wheelings and dealings which range from the illegal to the criminal e.g. smuggling. Ronnas estimated the percentage of the registered to the real number of non-registered in the private sector as being merely five per cent.

Le Dang Doanh, the director of the renowned Institute for Business Management (CIEM) in Hanoi confirmed this when he claimed that in 1996 over one million non-registered companies were active in the private economic sector. If we start out by assuming approx 30,000 registered private companies, then merely 3% were registered. As in other countries, work in the informal non-registered sector constitutes an important source of income, and creates in addition jobs in the sphere of simple, labor-intensive work. Even Vietnamese sources nowadays see in the informal sector an important component in terms of the economy and employment policies. At the same time, the sector contributes significantly to the training of a new entrepreneurial strata.[110]

Just as they are in China, false registrations are a central problem which does not only concern the company form of collective firms but also individual firms as well. Although they should have long been counted amongst the private companies according to the amount of capital or the size of the companies (with 20, 30 or 50 workers), many entrepreneurs refrain from re-registering since this would bring with it amongst other things fiscal disadvantages. Many state and collective firms exist furthermore only nominally; in reality they hardly differ from private companies. In some Vietnamese statistics the collective sphere is as a result already classified with the private sector.[111]

Despite the prohibition on their doing so, many cadres work in the private entrepreneurial field in that they founded firms or directed a company via a straw man. Illustrating this, in Danang a third of all registered limited companies are in the hands of party members.[112] Reliable countrywide statistics are not available.

While such companies serve the economic interests of individual cadres, especially since 1994 a hybrid form of company has appeared on the scene,

---

[109] Ibid.: 9.

[110] Cf. on that: Central Institute for Business Management 1997 and Friedrich Ebert Foundation 1998.

[111] Cf. *Vietnam Economic Times*, February 1998: 15.

[112] According to statements by MPI, Danang, January 1997.

which represents the corporate economic interests of organs of the state or the Party. While indeed these are in informal terms private companies, and they generally have a manager who does not hold office either in the government or the Party, the (so-called) manager is nevertheless only nominally responsible. The actual responsibility is borne by committees of the Party, ministries, departments of the administration etc. which have made capital available and then reel in the profits. Such companies appear to be particularly successful if they are concerned with the avoidance of payments of tax. "The overall effect is to ensure that state assets and resources are privatized, in the sense of flowing into peoples' pockets." According to Fforde even approx. 60% of all companies registered as being private firms can be classified as belonging to this hybrid form.[113]

A different form of private, entrepreneurial activity can be observed at many state companies which have de facto been privatized by their managers. The loss of governmental control over the state sector firms in the course of the reform processes combined at the same time with the inability to carry out an official privatization of those companies permitted the managers enough elbow room to use for private ends the government resources placed at their disposal. The managers are not ashamed of admitting in conversation with foreigners the deliberate misuse of state companies. At one of our conversations in Hanoi, a manager declared self-confidently the advantages of "his" company as opposed to other existing state and private firms. He would reach all decisions with two further colleagues he told us, with whom he also divided the profit, had "no problem" with taxes, and any losses they incurred were compensated for by the state. Moreover government resources were at his disposal at very favorable prices – i.e. for free.

Out of this widely-spread, de facto privatization which cannot be seen in the official statistics, an obstacle has come into being to a legal privatization of the state-owned companies, because it would take away from the managers the material basis for their private business activity. Understandably the most resistance to a large-scale privatization of the state sector companies comes from their managers.[114] The privatization program of the government which trades under the unsuspicious name *equitization*, has hardly had very convincing results with seven (!) privatized companies since 1996 out of a total number of over 7,000 state firms. In 2001 there were 2,280 state enterprises left. According to official data, 1,489 from them should be equitized and/or diversified in terms of ownership.

The rapid increase too in the number of registered private and individual companies in the secondary sector makes clear the quick development of the private sector whose share of the industrial production has increased from 15.9% in 1986 to 27.5% in 1994 (cf. Table 10).

---

[113] Fforde 1995: 39f., 68.

[114] Of course there are still other restrictions such as limitations of capital, which alone would be removed by a sale of companies. I do not want to go into this in any more detail here.

Table 10: Number of industrial firms in the private sector (Vietnam)

	Number of private firms	Number of individual firms
1985	920	206,172
1988	318	318,557
1989	1,284	333,337
1990	770	376,930
1991	959	446,771
1992	1,144	368,000
1993	3,322	449,016
1994	4,909	493,046
1995	5,152	517,418

Source: General Statistical Office 1996a: 280; General Statistical Office 1996b: 209.

The exact size of the private sector was not known at the end of the 1990s. The newspaper *Thuong Mai* called it the "dark room" of this sector since the fluctuation (company closures) was said to be large, and de-registrations and registrations often not carried out. The government, they urged, should intervene more strongly, a criticism of the public neglect of the administrative tasks which devolve upon the state. In 2001 there were about 32,000 non-state enterprises, including private enterprises, joint stock companies, cooperations, limited liability companies and enterprises with foreign capital.[115]

3. Entrepreneurs as new economic and social actors

Dietz writes – concerning Eastern Europe – of a "magical triangle" of the process of transformation whereby he means the formation of a market, of "autonomy" (private ownership) as well as "re-structuring". By the latter term he understands economic adaptations to the market as well as the genesis of a strata of entrepreneurs.[116] Such a magical triangle is also in China and Vietnam the starting-point of the process of social transformation with significant consequences for the social structure (changes in elites, institutions and values). With the example of the new entrepreneurial strata, the element of re-structuring and its social and political implications will be examined. Unlike in Eastern Europe

---

[115] Tran Minh Tich 1996. For newer data cf. Nguyen Huy Oanh 2002, Pham Ngoc Kiem 2002, Duong Ngoc 2002.
[116] Dietz 1993: 170ff.

it was in this case not a re-structuring steered from above but rather one that occurred for the most part spontaneously.

Diagram 10: The magical triangle of transformation

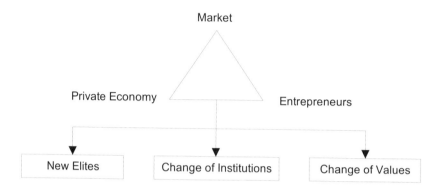

The formation of new entrepreneurial strata will be referred to here as a central factor of radical change. The term entrepreneurial strata is relatively new for both countries. Firstly the authorization once more of private business activities and their ensuing dynamism have led to the creation of new entrepreneurs. But first of all it is necessary to clarify what one can actually classify under this term, and what are the specifics demonstrated by the new entrepreneurs in both countries.

3.1. *Entrepreneur as a category*

In terms of economics the ideal type of an entrepreneur is viewed as a *homo economicus* who as the owner "plans a company, founds it with success and/or independently and responsibly leads with initiative in which [he] takes on the personal risk or the capital risk."[117] Already seen in terms of language, they are regarded as active subjects whereby entrepreneurs with their work first of all set a dynamic, economic process in motion. Joseph A. Schumpeter, the most important theoretician concerning entrepreneurs, in his individualist approach attributed to them creative, innovative behavior as well as leadership qualities. Their function lay in recognizing and carrying out new possibilities in the field of business. Entrepreneurs operate however, more by using their wills than their intellects and, Schumpeter argued, had to defend themselves against accusations of deviant and anti-social behavior.[118]

---

[117] Gabler 1984: 1768f.
[118] Cf. Schumpeter 1928 and 1987b: 149-151.

But the economic side of entrepreneurial strata[119] still tells us nothing about their social and political roles. If we – in the sense of newer system theory – comprehend an enterprise as a "complex, interlocking system of events",[120] whose collective impact brings about processes of transformation, then it becomes clear that the entrepreneur as an actor significantly helps to shape and influence this system. At the same time they do not operate in a vacuum but are rather embedded in social networks, and as a result they have an effect not autonomously but rather in social surroundings. Social relationships make possible first of all successful social effects. So the realization of the economic function requires at the same time social and political commitment since the setting-up and leadership of an organization is not an event but should be understood rather as a process.[121] That process orientation indicates that entrepreneurs have to operate above and beyond a purely economic dimension in order to keep, develop and build up their companies. The Marxist classification of the profit motive as the characteristic of entrepreneurial strata is insufficient. Firstly profit is not only an end in itself but rather appears – as Georg Simmel wrote – at the same time as an "interest center" which "forms its very own norms",[122] and with that takes on a guiding function. Secondly psychic profits[123] certainly also play a significant role for the entrepreneur i.e. non-monetary incentives (such as social recognition). Moreover security and minimization of risks for entrepreneurs require for them a legal framework, the manufacturing of contacts at the individual level to politics, banks and the relevant authorities. In addition the entrepreneurs require being organized (and organizing) in groups which represent their interests, in order to assert advantageous basic economic, legal and political conditions as against the interests of the state (precisely these activities characterize the political). So entrepreneurs possess interests which extend beyond the economic sphere even when these primarily serve the safeguarding of their business activity. As interest actors or players, they are at the same time the promoters of economic and social change. Werner Sombart said of capitalist entrepreneurs (in contrast to those who were lords of the manor), that they were "to a great degree subversive and shakers-up", because they broke with old conventions and directed the existing economic system towards completely new goals.[124] They possessed, he suggested, at the same time a pronounced "will for power" in the form of an entrepreneurial urge which wanted to conquer all domains, not only that of business life, rather that of the state too.[125]

---

[119] A helpful depiction of the economic theory of entrepreneurs: Casson 1982.

[120] On that: Rüegg-Sturm 1998: 3.

[121] Birley 1996: 20.

[122] Simmel 1994: 412.

[123] Lavoie 1991: 39.

[124] Sombart 1987, vol. 1, 2. half-binding: 837.

[125] Sombart 1987, vol. 1, 1. half-binding: 327/328; Schumpeter 1987b: 155.

The element of individualism which Schumpeter and Sombart attributed to the entrepreneur had its effect in the political sphere too, for example, on the values which the entrepreneur not only represents, but rather also popularizes too, about ideas of the role of the government and – in relation to that – their own role, an element which Coleman termed *individualistic industry culture* of the entrepreneur.[126]

The innovative element which Schumpeter attributed rather to the sphere of the economic did not need as a result to be more strongly interpreted in terms of economics because through economic action the social sphere was changed too. By way of economic novelties, entrepreneurs initiated social process of change. Greenfield and Strickon speak of the entrepreneur as "an individual who performs behaviors that are new in his community".[127] The term *creativity* mentioned above also implies permanent change, economically and socially. Concretely applied to China and Vietnam, this implies amongst other things elements such as behavior suitable for the market economy which diverge from the business style and behavior characteristic of the state sector companies. These elements of conduct typical of entrepreneurs in a market economy include: a willingness to take risks; a willingness to achieve; deviant behavior for the assertion of one's own business and social interests; pretial power i.e. the use of assets to assert one's own interests; a higher degree of individualism than in the rest of the society; and last but not least a specific life style and way of consuming (*conspicuous consumption*). As a result larger entrepreneurs can certainly be called "economic leaders":[128] They break through routinized measures and paths, and in this way alter not only values but also institutions.

The question is raised, however, whether the ideal type entrepreneur in the mold which Schumpeter perceived (creative renewer) is also the typical entrepreneur in China and Vietnam too, especially as the "Western" entrepreneur is as a rule viewed as an autonomous individual in the spirit of the Enlightenment.[129] Entrepreneurs are here first of all regarded as being part of that circle of people who have founded and run a company, alternatively somebody who has taken over a government or collective firm, and has run it for the most part by themselves and developed it.[130] The innovative element in this is already there: such people have mostly exited from the more secure state sector, and move in territory divergent in economic, politic and social terms, or at least on

---

[126] Coleman 1988: 5.

[127] Greenfield/ Strickon 1981: 497 following Barth 1967: 664.

[128] Cf. on that Schumpeter 1987a: 128ff.; Kirzner 1989: 62.

[129] See, for instance, Schumann 1992: 13.

[130] Managers of state- and collective companies constitute the sphere of *intrapreneurship* (innovative managers who are employees cf. on that Carsrud, Olm and Eddy 1986: 367f.). This sphere not only in the Chinese but also in the Western literature is to some extent classified under entrepreneurship, and is here not treated as part of the term entrepreneur. Those in question are not self-employed who themselves bear the risk and the final responsibility for the management of the company. This group of people for the most part stems much rather from the strata of officials and are appointed by the administration.

terrain which is full of risks. Kirzner and Codagnone (the latter in relation to the post-socialist society) have pointed out that the element of entrepreneurial *"alertness"* i.e. the recognition of and reaction to faint market signals was of greater importance, they argued, than technical innovation. In difficult and turbulent market conditions as well as economic conditions of shortage, chances and market gaps have to be quickly recognized and made use of.[131] Entirely in this sense a Chinese entrepreneur in Malaysia characterized the (ideal type) *entrepreneur* in the following way:

> A real entrepreneur is someone who looks at the situation...sees a problem in the country...whether it is a bureaucracy or infrastructure or marketing or what. In any problem he sees, the entrepreneur sees opportunity. That is an entrepreneur. But if he is just an ordinary businessman...he just sees a problem.

A corresponding Chinese proverb explicitly makes the point that "in choppy water more fish are to be found than in quiet ones".[132] As a result the element of entrepreneurial alertness can be justified not only systemically but also in the entrepreneurial culture. Alertness and innovative behavior belong together without a doubt whereby the concrete form which these may assume depends on the circumstances in each case.

In this sense particularly under the transitional conditions reigning in China and Vietnam, particularly flexible private entrepreneurs were needed. The relatively new entrepreneurial strata had the task here of contributing to the development of the still incomplete market system. In addition they had to first of all bring with them a large basket of knowledge and connections in the sense of "one makes the market work by working in the market."[133] Abilities and knowledge are not enough for that. Precisely under those conditions where there is little legal security, in which private entrepreneurs as they were before are exposed to partial economic, social and political discrimination, and associations representing particular interests are not allowed to operate openly as *pressure groups*, the significance of informal structures such as social relationships and networks is especially marked. This also applies to the basic goals of entrepreneurs i.e. the wish or urge to attain prosperity and develop one's own firm, and too for a further central element of entrepreneurship, namely the risk factor. Both require not only economic but also social and political safeguards.

Here the point is not only to have personal relationships to people with whom the entrepreneur is in a direct relationship but also more importantly social networks, relationships to local and supra-regional communities, institutions and functionaries with more than a regional base.[134] The formation of networks in China and Vietnam refers to the expansion of the surroundings in

---

[131] Kirzner 1978, 1983, 1985 and 1989: 21f.; Codagnone 1995: 64.

[132] Op. cit. in Stothard 1997.

[133] Reid 1993: 242.

[134] Cf. on that also Hirata/Okumura 1995: 125f.

which people experience trust whereby cultural capital is of significance for entrepreneurs too. Such networks which are termed in the West "Aunt Agatha networks" are as a rule of great significance starting with the founding of companies, access to markets and capital. Who is surprised that entrepreneurs in both countries have to be primarily "social organizers", and that the entrepreneurial aspect lies more strongly in the organization of relationships?

As we shall show in the following sections, this aspect takes up a large part of the entrepreneur's time budget. And here a third characteristic of entrepreneurship is relevant, the "cooperative component" i.e. the manufacture of contacts to the administration and units of supply, and the ability to establish consensus with those above them (bureaucracy) and with those below (employees).[135] But these specific conditions also reveal that the creation of a specific entrepreneur type in Western style is not possible in the conditions which exist in China and Vietnam.[136] Neither in East Asia nor in the Western industrialized countries can companies be understood as purely *relationships of productivity*. But whereas in East Asia companies are more strongly bound in with other companies and the bureaucracy, Western companies are embedded in a network of contracts with their employees, deliverers and customers.[137] In the first case, entrepreneurs are much more woven into non-economic, social and political interaction processes, and in this way they have an effect which is transformative through process.

3.2. *Entrepreneurs – a deviant group?*

In both countries widespread stereotypes of private entrepreneurs positioned them close to speculators or fraudsters as well as people who withhold tax or corrupt officials. While indeed such deviant behavior by entrepreneurs does take place, there has been up till now no study proving that entrepreneurs to any significant degree have committed more crimes than any other social group. Apart from this, payment of bribes or the exertion of influence on the decisions of administrations as well as tax withholding needs to be put into perspective given the high degree of legal uncertainty that exists, and under which the entrepreneurs have to carry on their work.

An important form of legal insecurity manifests itself in the misinterpretation and the interpretative arbitrariness of local functionaries concerning the Party's and state's enactments and decrees. Legal insecurity and randomness of decision-making also make possible and more likely the influencing of decisions, in this case on the part of the entrepreneurs. The partially monopolistic character of state sector businesses e.g. concerning the obtaining of commodities and raw materials, the arbitrary behavior or extortion carried out by many

---

[135] Similarly Hirschman 1967: 16.

[136] Relevant to this Ivory 1994: 55; Brusatti 1979: 7ff. But entrepreneurs are always individualists, even if there may be systemic and cultural differences.

[137] Cf. on that also Albach 1997.

cadres as well as the preferential treatment given to the state companies often make bribery of civil servants, speculative transactions and tax withholding both a precondition and an integral part of the life of successful private-sector economic activity. Consequently private entrepreneurs as such cannot be said to be elements corrupting the society.

The absence of a rational capitalism in the sense which Weber saw it often permits no other choice. Studies from neighboring countries show however, for instance, in South Korea that entrepreneurs obtain their capital out of "non-rational" contexts, that is out of profit from speculation, tax withholding or corruption.[138] And there are certainly parallels to the developments in China and Vietnam.

Advantages in relation to the entrepreneurial strata – which historically seen – is composed of merchants and craftsmen, possesses tradition in both countries.[139] Already in the pre-Christian era, commerce was subject to government interventions, was discriminated against or handicapped through economic-political decisions. In contrast to the agricultural sector which ensured the immediate provision of food, commerce was perceived as unproductive and work as only striving for profit, and doing so only at the cost of others. Confucians, Taoists and Legalists saw in the striving for luxury and money an equal lack of morality and virtue. As a result merchants were regarded as a destructive force and a danger for the social order, precisely because acquiring riches implied repression and exploitation. The drive to obtain money was furthermore viewed as the basis of an alternative prestige ladder and with that as a political risk factor. In the dichotomy public (*gong*) – private (*si*), the first was continually assessed positively in the meaning of jointly or (action) in common, the latter as self-addicted or egoistic. According to this world-view, those who are active for the common good are altruistic, those who are working for themselves are egoistic.[140] This dichotomy between the "public" (*cong*) – "private" (*tu*) existed equally in Vietnam where the striving for private status, riches and power was considered vulgar and egoistic. The public interest had priority over the private, and self-interest (*loi*) on the part of the elites who had lost their honesty (*nghia*) was held to be responsible for the downfall of order or the weakness of the nation (as for instance the colonial subjection to the French).[141]

The parallels between China and Vietnam were in this respect relatively large. The bureaucracy sought to limit the development of commerce and arti-

---

[138] Kim 1976: 469.

[139] This tradition is also to be found in Europe. In the history of European ideas and likewise in the history of the Christian church there was a negative evaluation of entrepreneurial strata, cf. Werhahn 1990: 14ff. Werhahn points out that – very similarly to China – the peasant producing nutrition and raw materials is perceived as the "Idealized figure of successful human existence". His behavior representing continuity was understood as a symbol of peace, whereas the entrepreneur aims at changes and with that was considered to be a social trouble-maker.

[140] Similarly, but somewhat exaggeratedly: Weggel 1999: 926.

[141] Cf. Marr 1981: 116. Vietnamese entrepreneurs argue very similarly in respect of the widespread corruption.

sanship by massive tax deductions and administrative hurdles. The consequence was that the former could hardly develop due to the stigmatization of
business people and entrepreneurial strata. Acquired riches were used to increase social prestige or for the education of the children but only seldom re-
invested. This also had to do with the poor social position of traders and craftspeople who were placed on the lowest steps of the social hierarchy after the
civil service literati and the peasants.[142] In Vietnam, trade was left to the immi-
grant Chinese who had often emigrated out of the over-populated areas of
China, and who were not allowed to work in agriculture. It was the French
colonial power that first supported the development of commerce and the productive trades and with that the formation of strata of business people and entrepreneurs. After WWI which had led to the flowering of a Vietnamese entrepreneurial strata, there was a debate within Vietnamese society about the causes
why so few Vietnamese wanted to become entrepreneurs and thereby grow
rich. Countless Vietnamese went to France so as to train as entrepreneurs.
Amalgamations were agreed between business people that were directed above
all against the Chinese (and not against the French), and which finally tried to
break the French and Chinese monopolies. This development was above all
criticized by traditionalists who perceived the propagation of riches and entrepreneurial strata as a sign of decadence and eroded values.[143]

With the establishing of the socialist system, the traditional stigmatization
synthesized with that of the communists in both countries. Private economic
activities were again limited and forbidden. Standard prejudices – going further
than just business people – characterized the self-employed as greedy, proto-
criminal, immoral and anti-social, were and are widely spread right up to the
present day.

However the low esteem in which traders and business people are held is in
no way only a "Confucian" element. Not only in European history but also in
most developing countries, they were mostly understood as negative fields of
work. As Shils has shown, the political elites do not expect from business people and entrepreneurs any substantial contribution to economic development.
Larger companies, according to Shils, are subject to the "prejudices which
intellectuals and intellectual politicians harbor against private firms."[144]

As I have shown above, it is one-sided to want to insinuate that the entrepreneurs have only one motivation as a driving-force. While it is true that profit is
the necessary result of entrepreneurial activity and mostly the expression of
competence, in turn profit or money also has an effect on its owner. They are
not only an end in themselves but rather, "interest centers …which form their
very own norms, unfold completely autochthonous qualities and generate
someone dependent only on these technologies."[145] Georg Simmel showed that

---

[142] Cf. on that Heberer 1989: 254ff.; Malarney 1998: 269ff.
[143] Marr 1981: 124-126.
[144] Shils 1962: 26.
[145] Simmel 1994: 412.

and how money reduced dependence on others, led to the liberation of the personality, to an "expansion of the ego", and with that to an increase in personal freedom.[146] Money may control ways of behaving and the goal determination of a player, and is the expression of esteem by members of a society.[147] Parsons speaks accordingly of a social mechanism in which money at the same time possesses a symbolic character.[148] Private entrepreneurs in the China or Vietnam of today confirm this in a significant way.

Unlike merchants who buy and sell goods, entrepreneurs organize a production process. They create jobs in a big way, pay taxes and other contributions, contribute to an improvement of the local infrastructure and increase – so far as larger companies are concerned – the prestige of the locality in which they are situated as well as its officials. As a rule public responsibility is also demanded of them i.e. that they let the local community participate in the advantages of their entrepreneurial activity (e.g. through the creation of new jobs, investment in the local infrastructure, and donations to charitable causes). As a result they certainly exercise a public position, they are social bearers of positions at least informally. Informal because the local bureaucracy is often not clear that the larger private entrepreneurs are in reality bearers of functions who beyond their economic tasks at the same time take on important social tasks.

3.3. *The discussion about entrepreneurs in China and Vietnam*

In China and Vietnam the discussion about "entrepreneurs" is comparatively new since (for a period) either there were no longer entrepreneurs or they were not allowed to exist as such. In the 1950s the characterization as "capitalist" or "bourgeois" attributed to them an anti-socialist character, and placed them outside of society. With the economic reforms, individual business and finally private entrepreneurs appeared once again after the period of nationalization of private companies during which only the duo of company director/party secretary had existed. This continues to impact on the contemporary discussion in which often the term for an entrepreneur is only used in reference to the managers or directors of state-owned companies.[149]

3.3.1. *The Chinese discussion*
Self-employed individuals first appeared on the scene again with the onset of the economic reforms at the end of the 1970s, and in the second half of the 1980s larger "private entrepreneurs" emerged. The following diagram repre-

---

[146] Ibid.: 379ff.

[147] Kraemer 1997: 260.

[148] Parsons 1963.

[149] Exemplary for that: Li Junjie 1997; Liu Zhicai 1998: 2ff.; Wu Guangbin 1998: 40ff.; Li Tongwen 1998: 249. Private entrepreneurs are not classified by Li as "Entrepreneurs", rather as "Owners of a business" (*laoban*).

sents the change in the assessment of entrepreneurs up till their re-interpretation as a "traditional" (Chinese) or socialist "entrepreneur".

Only since recently has the rather neutral term "entrepreneur" been discussed again. First of all the "peasant entrepreneurs" (*nongmin qiyejia*) were talked of whereby successful rural managers and entrepreneurs were described as "representatives of advanced productive forces in the countryside" as well as of "the new socialist village", "forerunners of the development of production of goods" and "fighters against poverty in the countryside".[150] Since 1997 contributions in *Jingji Yanjiu* (Economic Studies), the most important Chinese journal of economics have discussed again the Schumpeterian idea of the entrepreneur, and pointed out that an entrepreneurial stratum had once more begun to form itself in China.[151]

Diagram 11: Entrepreneur as a Category in China

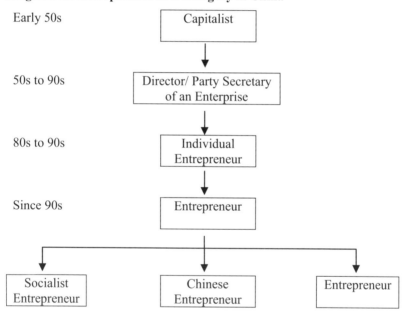

Already in 1994 in a Chinese essay the entrepreneurial stratum were described as the "most valuable" resource of the economy of a country. Such a stratum had to be formed and supported, and the framework conditions needed to be created (such as equal economic, political and legal status) that would favor its development. The article argued that the state sector should no longer be fa-

---

[150] Cf. for instance Wang and Chen 1985.
[151] Xu Zhijian 1997; Zhang and Li 1998.

vored. Intellectuals needed to be encouraged to accept work as entrepreneurs,[152] and there was a need for "scientific entrepreneurs."[153] Accordingly the *Zhongguo Gongshang Bao* (Newspaper for China's Industry and Commerce) wrote that to be an entrepreneur is an "honor" (*rongyaode*), whose direction of the company was a heroic action (*yingxiong zhuyi*), even when it had to be admitted that the path to successful entrepreneurial strata had up till then been an extremely stony one on which many had foundered.[154]

A contribution in the *Shehuixue Yanjiu* (Sociological Studies) noted the existence of a **stratum** of entrepreneurs in China, but this stratum term was not to be understood as ideological (in the sense of a class) or normative (in the sense of an exploitative class). Instead it was said to describe a "living resource" which came into being in the course of social transformation as the product of a market economy, and in turn serves that. One of the books that had a major impact on the discussion on classes was that of the sociologist Lu Xueyi. He argued that in China classes no longer existed, but rather strata and that entrepreneurs were one of them.[155]

At this point it becomes clear how the economization of politics undermines its ideological basis: the category "class" loses its meaning and dissolves itself in an apparently value-free, strata term. Already in 1994 an economist suggested calling all managers of companies irrespective of the form of ownership "entrepreneurs".[156] At the end of 1997, in China the magazine '*The Entrepreneur*' (*Qiyejia*) was established; in the first advert for it in the '*People's Daily*' it was stated that it was "a magazine which will perhaps change your life."[157] Increasingly entrepreneurship is classified as a "profession"; the term no longer possesses political overtones.[158] As far as the apolitical definition of entrepreneur is concerned, Wu Guangbin differentiated 4 different categories: (a) juridical persons with autonomy in management; (b) persons who manage and administer a company well, and who at the same time have to cope with competition and risk; (c) creative manufacturers and innovators; (d) people who with their own capital start a company, lead this creatively, take risks, and manage an enterprise in accordance with the needs of the market. The development of China, so Wu concluded, depends in the final analysis on "Thinkers, politicians, and **entrepreneurs**" (emphasis added). Entrepreneurs must as a result be understood as an "independent, social stratum".[159]

---

[152] Wei and Sun 1994.

[153] Zhao Pozhang 1998: 525ff.

[154] Yu Shaowen 1997.

[155] Mi/Gao 1997: 42ff. This neutrality is demonstrated by a growing number of texts, cf. for instance Wang Xiaodong 1996; Zhou Shulian 1996; Li and Li 1996; Wei and Xu 1996; Wang Qinghai 1997.

[156] Cf. Huang Rutong 1994: 26/27. Compare Lu Xueyi 2002.

[157] *Renmin Ribao*, 27 October 1997.

[158] Zhang and Liu 1996: 6; Li Gang 1999.

[159] Wu Guangbin 1998: 26-31.

Since the socio-political demarcation between Chinese and "Western-capitalist" entrepreneurs has become ever more difficult, the Chinese entrepreneur is also treated as a culturally specific type. The Chinese entrepreneur, according to a book which appeared in 1997, differentiates himself from the Western through his "distinct Chinese qualities" (*Zhongguo tese*): he was, it argued, a "reformer" (*gaigejia*), a "hero" (*yingxiong*) and operates in the interests of social needs as well as increasing the social affluence of China.[160] Another author described the belly-aches which people in China had with the term "entrepreneur" and declared the Chinese entrepreneur to be "socialist" if they indeed helped to build up the "material" and "intellectual culture of Socialism". In contrast to Western entrepreneurs, socialist ones had two central criteria to fulfill: they had to be renewers (*chuangxinzhe*) and at the same time possess political qualities.[161] These were to be found in the special combination of "socialist entrepreneurs Chinese style",[162] whereby such entrepreneurs at the same had revolutionary characteristics; they belonged after all to the "avant-garde of the economic revolution".[163]

An article in the '*People's Daily*' likewise characterized an ideal type of entrepreneur who deviated from that of Western economic theory: "What is required of the political-ideological qualities... he should resolutely put into practice the line, guidelines, the politics of the Party and the governmental legal requirements." It was expected that he would stand on his own two feet professionally, would be hard-working, "honestly and uprightly fulfill his public duties (*lianjie fenggong*), work hard and live simply (*jianku pusu*), voluntarily bring about positive achievements for society (*ganyu fengxian*), and with the leading groups (from Party and state) work together in the public interest." Entrepreneurs were "superior persons" (*gaoshang de ren*), if they engaged themselves in the interests of "strengthening and blossoming of the people and the nation."[164]

In terms of expertise, what was expected from entrepreneurs were qualities of leadership, organization and coordination, market flexibility, specialized further training in modern company and management questions, as well as orientation both to the domestic and the world market. More qualified entrepreneurs were to be trained, the conditions and the environment for the entrepreneurial activity were to be improved, the state had to give them help. The article continued that China needed politicians who were oriented to companies, who could communicate with entrepreneurs, and in particular politics had to serve business interests.[165] On the other hand the entrepreneurs had to be more

---

[160] Liu Yong 1997: 1/2.
[161] Yuan Baohua 1997: 5. However, the "political qualities" are not concretely named.
[162] Zhongguo qiyejia diaocha xitong 1998a: 531.
[163] Zhang/Liu 1996: 41.
[164] Ibid.: 204.
[165] Ibid.: 532.

strongly controlled since they concentrated a relatively large amount of power in their own hands; power corrupted and indeed automatically.[166]

Traditional Confucian ideas about companies which – when they are controlled – act in the interests of the state and society. They are integrated in a corporatist way into the existing structures and correspond to paternalistsocialist ideas. Those traditional themes are linked here to ideas of adaptation to modern world economic structures and qualities; all this, however, without taking into account the element of innovation. The "Chinese" entrepreneur should be a "patriot" i.e. identify with the political system and its values. He should at the same time be "morally superior", possess a good ideology and a good style of working and accordingly they should perfect themselves.[167]

In the socio-economic constellation of both countries, one should note two further, specific characteristics for entrepreneurs. Firstly, there is the combination of the world of officialdom and the world of entrepreneurs i.e. the entry of the cadre into the domain of the company and likewise. This results from a number of factors: the form of ownership of the company; cadres being appointed through higher levels of administration (state or collective companies); the income of the cadres given that incomes from business activities are much higher than those for work in the administration or the party; and the possibilities which officials have due to their connections and their position inside networks.

The second point is that entrepreneurs have to become politically active in order to be able to lead their company successfully on terrain which is legally uncertain. Political means here that they have to strive for membership in the Communist Party or – alternatively – in a body with certain public protective functions (People's Congresses, Political Consultative Conferences, mass organizations). Officials or persons with close contacts to officials possess superior starting conditions without a doubt.[168] The percentage of party members amongst private company owners is relatively high; whereas the percentage of party members out of the total population lay at 4.8% in 1997, out of a 1% sample taken in 1996 15.8% of the entrepreneurs were members of the party.[169] Nevertheless this latter figure lies well below the number of company managers with party membership (96.5%); the same applies to managers of firms with purely foreign capital (41.2%).[170]

Even when the spectrum of opinion swings between the two poles (a) entrepreneurs are primarily capitalists and (b) entrepreneurs and capitalists are dif-

---

[166] Qiu 1997.

[167] Zhongguo qiyejia diaocha xitong 1998a: 545ff.; 567ff.

[168] Cheng and Sun 1996 have discussed that for China.

[169] Zhang, Li and Xie 1996: 179; *Gongren Ribao* 8 July 1997.

[170] *Guanli Shijie* (Management World), op. cit. *Far Eastern Economic Review*, 6 November 1997: 28.

ferent phenomena,[171] the discussion in China is increasingly favorable towards entrepreneurs.

3.3.2. *The Vietnamese discussion*

In Vietnam the debate is much sharper. There the private sector is officially termed the "private-capitalist sector" and private entrepreneurs "private capitalists".[172] Moreover in a text published in 1994, it was stated that due to the development of the private sector and foreign investors, the "bourgeoisie" as well as the percentage of capitalists would increase in numbers. They would bring with them their own ideology and also demand the right for a political voice. Here the state should exercise strict control.[173]

As a result the private entrepreneurs were in effect declared to be anti-socialist elements whose potential should, however, be used for economic development. But the political implications of such a classification appear to be more significant: political controls, surveillance, mistrust and the opportunity for the authorities to proceed arbitrarily against entrepreneurs. This is because according to the statements of the party leadership, those on the sharp end are really capitalists and thus constitute retrogressive elements. The declared goal of the Party is as it was before communism, while the capitalist path is specifically rejected; it argued that the class struggle between the socialist and capitalist paths manifested itself in all social areas.[174] When they examine the entrepreneurial strata, the "dangers" are often foregrounded: the dangers of an all too close interlacing of business and politics, the use of political contacts for personal profit, organized crime, the acquisition of wealth through criminal machinations (quote: "The honest and hard-working are poor, whereas some through corruption and smuggling quickly become rich"), the "foreign-oriented psychology of private capitalists" or other forms of political and social "destabilization".[175]

However, in the meantime a discussion has also begun in Vietnam about the "Vietnamese" or "socialist" entrepreneur. Dao Cong Tien argued on a strongly nationalist basis. He put forward the theory that the socialist market economy differentiates itself from other market economies in that they are "socialist directed" and are subordinate to the "culturally charismatic power of the state". Consequently income earned by employers does not result from exploitation because they serve for the creation of jobs and national development. Therefore the market economy was, he stated, "associated with the culturally charismatic power and the fundamentally socialist direction of the nation, and seen from the cultural viewpoint it is an inextricable part of the development of Vietnam." Derived from this national cultural argumentation, the entrepreneur is defined

---

[171] Cf. Zhang and Li 1998: 31.

[172] Political Report 1996: 115.

[173] Thang 1994: 6/7.

[174] Trong 1996: 5-11; Tien 1996: 33/34.

[175] Exemplary on that: Nguyen Dang Thanh 1997; Le Huu Tang 1997; Tran Ngoc Khue 1997.

as a person who has to take on "the direct tasks of leadership in the economic production process to achieve the goal of being a prosperous people, a strong country, as well as a just and civilized society." The entrepreneur too as a part of the "community of the nation" has to operate in the interests of the nation whereby the state as "state of the people" has to take care of the rule of law, and to endeavor to obtain equal treatment for the entrepreneur too.[176]

The article went on to state that for the shaping of policies, the state should cooperate with private entrepreneurs, listen to their opinions and produce a consensus with them. Entrepreneurs have to be legally safeguarded and protected. Similarly as in the Chinese discussion, it was argued that the entrepreneur has to contribute to making Vietnam strong, the people prosperous and the society egalitarian. All those who follow this path are "socialist oriented".[177] The socialist orientation forces all economic sectors, including the private sector too, to contribute to the "people being prosperous, the country strong and the society equal and civilized".[178]

A stronger Confucianist variant is represented in Nguyen Chuoc's theses in which *business* is seen as a *social concept*. Success in business life is possible only for those who are modest, and who have a good business morality. The ideal is those entrepreneurs who have a "good morality and a strong will" and who enjoy the "respect of the worker and the society". Such entrepreneurs were the "sons of the people".[179] Pham Xuan Nam in turn argued there was a difference to Western conceptions of entrepreneurial strata in which profit-orientation and selfishness were declared to be precisely the basis of successful entrepreneurship; in contrast the Vietnamese entrepreneur was more inclined to take moral factors into account. He followed his "heart" in production, trading and service industry activities. Not only talent is required; much rather this has to be combined with morality.

Morality includes some of the following factors: uprightness (such as the keeping of laws or correct tax payments, good quality of performance); respect for life and the dignity of subordinates, whereby these at the same time had to provided for. A morally good entrepreneur sees his employees as his "brothers". Pham quotes from the Confucian proverb: "Self-perfection has to begin at home, then at the market place, and finally attained in the pagoda." Only such

---

[176] Dao Cong Tien 1999.
[177] Vo Dai Luoc 1996a: 40/41.
[178] Vo Dai Luoc 1996b: 40.
[179] Nguyen Chuoc 1997: 60/61.

behavior ensures success in business, otherwise ruin threatened.[180] Fully in the Confucian sense, entrepreneurial activity is understood as *moral* activity by individuals, less as an economic activity.

4. *Entrepreneurs as a social group: class, middle strata or strategic group?*

One of the central questions which our study is intended to answer is that concerning the political and social location of the entrepreneurial strata and the corresponding theoretical implications which arise out of our study. In the following sections we want to discuss the categories in which the entrepreneurs can be classified as a group. There are basically three categories which present themselves: that of class, that of the "middle strata/middle class", and that of "the strategic group".

4.1. *Entrepreneur as a class*

The term class was dominated for a long time by the Marxist definition according to which classes denote large groups of people who differentiate themselves from others on the basis of their position in a specific system of social production. The decisive criterion of the classification is the class position i.e. the position in the process of production, in the ownership system and the control over or lack of control over the means of production and social wealth. What is important in the Marxist term class is the difference between the classes *in themselves* (objective existence without class consciousness) and the class *for itself* (with class consciousness). The ruling class can be considered as that grouping which possesses not only economic but also political power.

---

[180] Pham Xuan Nam 1997: 35ff.

Max Weber relativized this concept of class in that he understood class not as structures, that is as fixed communities but rather as a process i.e. as potential actors due to a common basis. According to him classes were characterized by shared life chances, determined through economic ownership of goods, and income interests which were pursued in the framework of the commodity market or labor market.[181] We do not want here to describe the total breadth of class theories because the transfer of the term class to the private entrepreneurial strata in China and Vietnam appears to us to be (still) not suitable (cf. our expositions in Part III). Important, however, in this context is that more recent theories of the term class have been uncoupled from the purely economic level. According to these, classes are not only groups which are defined economically and politically but rather groupings with more long-term, broad commonalities in the domains of values and attitudes, of consumer behavior or lifestyle by which one group marks itself from another. In terms of class theory – in the interests of a definition of the term – Bourdieu's concept of class is helpful since he goes beyond the purely economic element and places the classes in a constructed *social* space which includes the different forms of capital which together form the total volume of capital.

A class is for him a "homogenous ensemble of individuals objectively constituting a group differentiated along economic and social lines," in a "space of differences" based on economic and social differentiation.[182] The term capital as a result breaks up into that of *economic, cultural* (education), *social* (resources due to relationships and group membership), and *symbolic capital* (the form of perception of the different types of capital). Persons with similar positions in the total volume of capital in social space – according to Bourdieu – show similar dispositions and ways of behaving. These theoretical classes (classes "in themselves") do not represent, however, real classes in the sense that they (as a class) automatically act together, consciously and goal-directed (classes "for themselves"). Closeness in social space still does not create, according to Bourdieu, an automatic unit so that he would only speak of a tendency to group formation, from a "probable class".[183]

Our hypothesis states accordingly that firstly, the heterogeneity of the entrepreneurial strata and the early stage of development in which entrepreneurs in both countries have found themselves up till now, makes the application of the term class unsuited to the Chinese and Vietnamese entrepreneurial strata. Secondly, the element suggested by Weber of process and potential which forms the basis of the term class, and which Bourdieu then heightens to the term of the probable class, is an indication of the difficulties of classifying groups with class-specific commonalities (class consciousness, class position). These difficulties are particularly relevant for such social processes of upheaval as are

---

[181] Cf. Weber 1964: 678ff.

[182] Bourdieu 1997: 105. Bourdieu 1987 goes into that in more detail.

[183] Bourdieu 1998: 24/25.

currently taking place in China and Vietnam, and in which new strata, new elites, new relations of production and ownership in general first develop and establish themselves anew.

4.2. *Entrepreneur as a "Middle class" likewise "Middle strata"*

Problematic in another way is the terminological field middle class and middle strata. In a system of social stratification "middle class" refers firstly to those professional groups, who carry out *white-collar* work, and have an average or above-average school education. The separation from other classes or strata occurs due to the conditions of the profession and the work, the income, the social prestige, possible values held in common and attitudes as well as of life-style. That the middle class is by no means a homogenous group indicates that it is customary in the literature to speak of an upper, middle and lower middle class, and this indicates that the middle class is not perceived as a homogenous group.

Small traders, peasants and other self-employed professions are typical for the *old middle-class* whereby being self-employed and the small size of the companies are characteristic, as is the use of their own means of production for earning their livings; in contrast the *new middle-class* is composed rather of professionals (self-employed), middle and higher level civil servants and employees as well as smaller and middle level entrepreneurs.[184] The new middle class displays a higher level of education, acts more autonomously, and is based on a world view of professionalism. However, concerning the concept of the middle class, the heterogeneity and fuzziness as regards its content is problematic. Groups which exist in completely different life-, work-, ownership- and income frameworks (entrepreneurs, civil servants, managers, small-sized self-employed, intellectuals and academics) are subsumed under one term, groups too which pursue completely different interests and only show a few commonalities. Consequently our hypothesis runs as follows: the terms middle classes or strata do not represent a suitable analytical instrument, and are not applicable to entrepreneurs because they are a very multi-layered group.

One of the decisive and most discussed questions is the one concerning a (shared) "political mission" of the middle strata, a question which on the one hand is oriented to the role of bourgeoisie and the entrepreneur in modern Europe, whereby the bourgeoisie is often identified with rationality and political liberalism. On the other hand, a whole range of social scientists who have studied this question of the middle stratum and likewise middle strata attribute a decisive role to them in the democratization processes in South Korea and Taiwan even if in cooperation with other social actors.[185] At the same time it is assumed that those who are necessarily most decisively interested in democra-

---

[184] Cf. on that among others Kerbo 1996: 217-245; Glassman 1997.
[185] Exemplary: Koo 1991; Dong 1991; Hsiao 1993 as well as Hsiao and Koo 1997.

tization and democracy, are those who would profit most by such developments.

Protagonists of the viewpoint that the middle class are the forerunners of the democratization process were above all the modernization theoreticians. Along these lines Lipset assumed that the middle class would gradually form the majority in the process of development, and thereby become the driving forces of the modernization process but he failed to recognize their ambivalent role.[186] For Barrington Moore in turn, without an urban bourgeoisie (business people/merchants, entrepreneurs) there could not be any democracy at all.[187]

Sundhausen has demonstrated that the members of the middle strata have not only behaved in varying ways during processes of political transformation, but also that the political framework conditions determine their different ways of acting. Above all in conditions of economic under-development and poverty, business people and entrepreneurs show little interest in a democratization process. He argues that the groups of entrepreneurs who interest us in this context are small in number and prosperous, and therefore from them comes no impetus for democratization. One should rather expect such an impetus from intellectuals, lawyers and journalists.[188] Rüland argues similarly: according to him under the conditions in which there was a dominant state and a middle stratum which was economically dependent on that state and weak, no push for democratization should be expected. The majority of members of the middle strata were interested, he suggests, rather in *good governance* (legal security, battling against corruption, efficiency of the administration and transparency) than in "democracy". The developments in Thailand and South Korea have shown that a large part of the middle strata supported the authoritarian ruler.[189] Above all in times of crisis the middle strata tend towards authoritarian solutions.[190] Hsiao showed using Taiwan and South Korea as examples, that the representatives of the new middle class in the course of the political developments of both states, had behaved in a more liberal and progressive way than the representatives of the old.[191] His analysis makes the heterogeneity of the "middle classes" once again yet clearer. The middle class is thus not per se to be conceived of as the engine of democratic development. This too supports our thesis that the terminology for our context is not a suitable analytic instrument.

In China and Vietnam we find a hybrid middle strata that can be roughly divided into four sub-groups, whereby the edges between them become blurred at points, and at present all four groups are taking root.

---

[186] Cf. Lipset 1962: 63 and 1981: 472 and 131ff.
[187] Cf. Moore 1974: 481ff.
[188] Sundhausen 1991: 110-113.
[189] Rüland 1997: 92-96.
[190] Rüland 1999: 61ff.
[191] Hsiao 1993: 16.

(1) **Systemic middle strata**: Political-ideologically socialized officials below the political decision-making elite, and political-ideologically socialized managers of middle-sized and small state sector enterprises;

(2) **traditional middle strata**: traders and artisans, religious und ethnic personalities;

(3) **professional middle strata**: rather professionally-oriented officials and managers; self-employed in modern sectors (consulting, real estate agencies), scientists, technical and artistic qualified employees, teachers, doctors, lawyers etc.;

(4) **entrepreneurial middle strata**: the new private entrepreneurship.

This differentiation demonstrates that the so-called "middle class" first of all is a highly heterogeneous construction, considering that it is composed of differing groups with different capital, possessions and wealth, interests, values and life-style that basically puts into question the idea of a "class". In addition comes the necessary sub-differentiation. A large part of the entrepreneurial middle class emerged out of the nomenklatura or exists in direct contact with them, others were workers or peasants. The former group is personally and ideologically closely tied to the bureaucracy, the latter as a rule not so.

Giddens has made a meaningful distinction between groups that have formed as a result of different chances in the market and those out of divisions of labor.[192] As far as the entrepreneurs are concerned, they possess more assets, scientists as a rule do not. The self-employed have different interests to those employees dependent on their pay, doctors from those of the petit-bourgeoisie, managers from those of civil servants, etc. On the other hand they are not fixed categories rather fluid ones because under conditions of rapid economic and social change, the stratification structure is certainly not set and constant. As a result the terms middle class likewise middle stratum are controversial in the scientific discussion about them. In our context it is not the middle class as such which is interesting but rather the role of entrepreneurs within this category. Anyway the composition of the middle class in China and Vietnam has changed in the course of the reform policies and the restructuring into market economy formations. Before the era of reform, the term was used rather about that part of the political and economic nomenklatura that took by virtue of income, privileges, social prestige and power something of a "middle" position between the political elite and the "ordinary people" (*administrative middle class*). In addition, it referred as well as persons not in the party who due to their useful function were supported by each regime and provided with material privileges (influential scientists, writers and artists, former "patriotic" entrepreneurs, model workers, war veterans etc.) The reform process has caused this group to expand to include new entrepreneurs, intellectuals who have returned from abroad, artists and writers as well as the self-employed of all kinds. The

---

[192] Giddens 1979: 231.

re-stratification process that is currently taking place with its high degree of fluctuation and processes of polarization renders the use of the term "class(es)" questionable. Moreover the entrepreneurial strata in both countries find itself in both countries still in *status nascendi* (initial state), and do not form a unified, organized class with a class-consciousness. This *status nascendi* situation is indicated by the brevity of entrepreneurial activity.

In China during the period of the survey (1996), merely 14.9% of the firms had been founded before 1990, the rest between 1990 and 1996. For Vietnam the figures were 17.9% (before 1990) and 82.1%. As a result it appears to us to be more useful not to speak of a middle class but rather at the most to talk of the entrepreneurs as a *potential, new middle strata*. Potential because they still find themselves in an upward trend as far as social and political status is concerned. Whereas in terms of income (economic prestige), entrepreneurs fluctuate on a scale between upper-middle and top level incomes, they should be situated, as our study showed, socially in the middle, and politically in the lower-middle part of the scale, not only in terms of their self-estimation but also the estimation of others (assessment by other sections of the population) (cf. Section III, Part 3.1.). But the entrepreneurial strata do find themselves in the process of social ascent.

The discussion about middle strata has also taken place in China. There numerous studies have been carried out on this theme "middle strata" (*zhongchan jieceng*), whereas this theme in Vietnam has up till now been rather a taboo subject. Cheng Guoxia, for example, links the term primarily to income and assets value (cf. Table 11.)

Table 11: Urban population according to standards of living groups (1996, in Yuan)

	Annual income	Average assets /Household	%
Poor (*pinkun*)	< 5,000	3,000	3.8
Persons with basic income (*wenbao*)	5,000-10,000	9,000	36.1
Well-situated (*xiaokang*)	10,000-30,000	28,000	51.5
Well-to-do (*fuyu*)	30,000-100,000	87,000	8.0
Very rich (*fuhao*)	> 100,000	280,000	1.0

Source: Cheng Guoxia 1998: 23.

Cheng counts the well-situated and the well-to-do to the "middle strata". Following that schema, in 1996 almost 60% of the urban population were members of the middle strata, certainly a percentage that is set much too high for the urban areas. In a somewhat undifferentiated way, he attributes the following characteristics to the middle strata: they feared social chaos (*luan*), possessed a great interest in social stability, strove for a higher standard of living as well as a rise in social status. They were socially committed because they wanted to support the poor through donations. They represent an important force for modernization and promoted the democratization process among other things because due to the level of education, they were to a great extent interested in political participation. This makes them protagonists of this process. Cheng hopes in this sense for a political transformation through the middle strata whereby an important part of these strata is made up of the entrepreneurs.[193] Dai and Wan espouse a somewhat modified variant: an annual income of 30,000–100,000 Yuan is the criterion for the membership of the middle stratum.

20-25% of the population according to their opinions are to be counted as belonging to that stratum. But they add yet another category on the basis of areas of business as well as types of property owning. Regionally the middle stratum was concentrated in the larger localities of the coastal provinces.[194] According to Ma Deyong the gap between the rich and the poor was where the middle strata were. So his starting-point is income. Such a differentiation is problematic because it excludes political as well as cultural capital. According to his definition, entrepreneurs would be counted amongst the upper stratum although socially and politically they were to be situated rather in the middle field. Ma attributes to the middle strata an important role in the maintenance of political stability because they weakened the conflict potential between rich and poor, and serve as a buffer between the latter two groupings. Politically moderate they may be, but through their purchasing power they raise the level of consumption and in this way serve general economic development. Above and beyond this, he argued, they were also the most important force for moving forward political democratization.[195] Sun, Li and Shen argue along similar lines: they see in the middle class not only a factor for political stability, rather too a factor for economic and social trend-setting in respect of standards of living and consumer behavior of the society.[196]

Zhang, Hong, Cheng and Wu differentiate between different groups within the middle stratum, and include social indicators in their analysis (level of education, size of family, consumer behavior and social prestige). They reached the conclusion that the middle stratum was composed primarily of people with a university qualification, of *professionals* (also as managers, scientists, technicians and doctors), who for the most part are employed in the state sector. Entrepreneurs are only a relatively small percentage of that.[197]

For Qin Yan who has presented one of the most detailed studies of China's middle class, the new entrepreneurial strata form the core of the new class. He sub-divides the entrepreneurs into four groups depending on assets and income:

---

[193] Cheng 1998.
[194] Dai and Wan 1998.
[195] Ma Deyong 1999.
[196] Sun, Li and Shen 1999: 26ff.
[197] Zhang, Hong, Cheng and Wu 1998.

asset millionaires, household with assets between 500, 000 Yuan and one million; households with assets between 100,000 and 500, 000, and a gross, monthly income of 1,500–5, 000 Yuan; and small entrepreneurs with assets of some tens of thousands of Yuan, and a gross, monthly income of approx. 1,000 Yuan. Viewed politically the new middle classes, he argued, were striving for political participation, up till now primarily still on an individual level. An organizational form to this striving is still in its infancy although the majority of entrepreneurs were said to be interested in such an independent lobby group. Only with the growing significance of representative associations will the potential of the entrepreneurial strata for shaping political events increase.[198]

Zhu Guanglei though does not speak of middle classes but rather hopes that through the new social stratification and the formation of new strata a "civil society" (*shimin shehui*) will come into being. The new strata will not only restrain governmental hegemony but also through new demands promote the creation of democracy and the construction of a legal system. Entrepreneurs as new strata still in *status nascendi* were heading in the future for an important role in that civil society.[199]

For Tian the entrepreneurs still do not form a class. Firstly their economic basis was still unstable, secondly there was still no shared class psychology (*jieji xinli*) and no class-consciousness in common, and thirdly there was no shared association at the national level, not to mention a political organization representing the interests of the entrepreneurs.[200] Although we concur with the argumentation insofar as entrepreneurs do not form a "class", there is meanwhile, however, not only a stable basis for business activity but also a stable social and political basis for entrepreneurship even if this stabilization process still finds itself in a phase of consolidation. That is indicated not only by the increasing acceptance of the entrepreneurs but also their growing "role model function" in surveys and the media, their equal status under the constitution as well as their ideological acceptance in the party. And the work of the relevant representative associations has certainly created overlapping connections, even if here there has been a certain splintering effect brought about by the existence of competing associations.

A discussion about the role of the middle class and entrepreneurial strata had already taken place in China in the first half of the 20th century. To name only a few examples: at the beginning of the 20th century, the entrepreneur Zhang Jian, an important reform politician in the first two decades of this century, proposed specific stimuli for the promotion of the development of an entrepreneurial stratum. In his capacity as Minister for Agriculture and Trade (1913–1915) he tried to implement his proposals. He expected from the entrepreneurial stratum not only economic development but also important inputs for a

---

[198] Qin Yan 1999.
[199] Zhu 1998: 42-44, 381ff. and 641ff.
[200] Tian Weidong 1997.

reform of the political system.[201] In the 1920s in the industrial metropolis Shanghai there was a debate between the orthodox members of the chamber of commerce there and Marxists about the character of the new Chinese entrepreneurial stratum, in which the former argued that Chinese entrepreneurs were not capitalists or members of the bourgeoisie but rather patriotic industrialists who acted in the interest of China and its population, and who had to defend themselves against large foreign capitalists.[202]

In the 1940s in turn it was the renowned journalist Chu Anping, chief editor of the critical liberal magazine *Guancha* (The Observer), which was banned in 1948 by the Guomindang; Chu Anping awaited democratizing effects from the middle classes.

> We should exhaust all the means at our disposal to encourage China's middle classes to take on a firm point of view, and to become the political core of the nation so that we can bring about the goal of the creation of a democratic country.[203]

Insofar the debate about the role of the middle classes is not completely novel in China, but rather connects itself to discussions that were going on the first half of the 20th century. This demonstrates that repressed debates live on in the collective consciousness of societies, discourses that once conceived do not simply disappear, and that later generations may well refer to them again.

However, there is no concurring positive opinion about the role of the middle classes or the private entrepreneur. Wang Xunli represents a rather conservative voice arguing that with the emergence of private entrepreneurs in no way has a new middle class or even a new bourgeoisie come into being. Within socialism the capitalists do not form an independent force, rather the state exerts power over them and their development.[204]

The Chinese terms for middle stratum (*zhongchan jieceng*) or middle class (*zhongchan jieji*) – both are to be found in the discussions of experts – means stratum or class "with average amount of property" which once again makes clear the how problem-ridden the terminology is. The question is raised as to what "average amount of property" means, since the word "entrepreneurs" covers a range which might include very differing amounts of capital, assets, size of company and income, and in this sense they can be clearly differentiated from doctors, teachers, functionaries, technicians or scientists.

It is apparent that the discussion concerning the new social stratification is discussed in ever decreasingly ideological terms, and instead increasingly as a necessary development which leads to a positive i.e. socially constructive po-

---

[201] Cf. on that the essays by Christiansen 1993.

[202] Lee 1991: 90ff.

[203] Chu Anping (1946), "Zhongchanjieji ji ziyoufenzi" (Middle classes and liberals), in: *Keguan*, 12: 1, op. cit. in Barme.

[204] Wang Xunli 1998: 336-340. Starting from the Marxist concept of class, Lu 1999 analyses the middle classes.

larization. In Vietnam in contrast the stratification process is viewed as a purely negative polarization as it was ten years ago in China.[205]

It would be all too reductionist to expect from entrepreneurs alone a change in the political relations in China and Vietnam or even a democratization. Indeed they make a significant contribution to those processes – in the ways described above – but should be viewed as only one of a large number of sets of social actors in the course of transformation especially since they certainly represent particular interests. To achieve the goals of their commercial activity they are, like all other strata concerned to maintain both social and political stability. Legal stability and business activity taking place within a well-grounded and secure economic framework should be counted first of all as their top priorities. When those factors are negatively affected, for instance, through major interference by the bureaucracy, corruption, plundering by tax demands and other such payments, legal uncertainty, or the state refusing or limiting them in their commercial freedom, then they will become more involved in achieving the goals of political change. Economic changes such as safeguarding or expanding the rights of the employees are less likely to gain their support. So it is hardly surprising that an ambiguous role is attributed to the entrepreneurs: on the one hand players for democratization, and on the other supporters of authoritarian rule.[206]

Jones concludes from the ambivalence not of the entrepreneurial strata but rather of the middle strata as a whole, that the idea of a leading political role for these strata in the processes of democratization hardly makes sense due to their ambivalence. The developments in East and Southeast Asia have much rather shown that the new, middle strata to a great extent were dependent on government patronage. He argues that in the last analysis, , they were the product of the state education system, find employment primarily in the state sector, and were as a result dependent on this patronage.[207] Brown et al. argue along similar lines that the middle strata in East Asia were the main beneficiaries and therefore supporters of authoritarian political relations. They suggest that this economic dependence on the state had permitted such a *middle class* to come into being; they experienced angst concerning insecurity and instability, and so clung to the state wanting to live in an "iron security cage".[208] However, both authors under-estimate not only the mobility of *professionals* in times of political upheaval; for example, when the patronage system begins to crumble and loyalty towards the regime evaporates. Their explanations also do not apply to an important segment of the middle strata namely the entrepreneurial strata. They do not apply because as I have shown above, the entrepreneurial strata precisely in these two countries that constitute the subject of this study, are not

---

[205] Cf. e.g. Luu Hong Minh 1999: 25ff.

[206] Similarly: Robison 1989: 52; Jones 1998: 147/148.

[207] Jones 1997 and 1998: 152-155.

[208] Brown and Jones 1995; Jayasuriya 1995.

in any way either dependent on state patronage or the major beneficiaries of an
authoritarian set-up.

4.3. *Entrepreneurs as strategic groups*

Entrepreneurs can be classified in both countries as part of the "new middle
strata" but as I have shown the term as an analytical category is not operation-
alizable. This contrasts with the terminological field occupied by the phrase
strategic group, a term which was introduced by development sociologists at
the University of Bielefeld (Germany). This is an alternative, analytical category for more accurate classification of important new actors for society as a
whole.[209] It refers to a group of persons who are, "connected through a common
interest in the maintenance or expansion of their shared chances of acquisition,"
whereby acquisition refers not only to material goods but rather also to immaterial factors such as power, prestige, knowledge or religious elements. What the
members of the group have in common is a shared, long-term program as well
as an appropriate strategy of action, and an image of themselves as significant
societal players.[210] What also appears consequential in this approach is the
dynamism of this definition: "strategic group" goes further than Dahrendorf's
"quasi-group" because the former term denotes a group which develops strategies for maintaining and pushing through its own interests, and by means of
organizing constitutes itself to an interest group.

So it does not form a fixed class but instead a group that finds itself in the
stages of development that – over and beyond organization in associations –
acts in a potentially strategic manner. The terminology goes beyond that of the
simple interest group because it is not concerned with the short-term implementation of limited interests but rather as a strategic group which perceives itself
to be, "a major force in a power struggle between all strategic groups of the
society in total,"[211] which in cooperation with other groups wants to put through
and achieve long-term economic, social and also political goals.

This strategic groups approach contributes to a clarification of the process of
development of interest groups into classes as well as the coming into being of
classes. In this respect Evers and Schiel distinguish classes from strategic
groups. Classes have a basic program and are organized in political parties.
Their striving is directed to social change ("system change"). Strategic groups,
in contrast do not pursue the goal of changing the system and are not organized
in classes. They are concerned much more with circumscribed goals in the
interest of the maintenance and/or the expansion of their possibilities for acquisition and development.

---

[209] Evers and Schiel 1988; Berner 1991; Korff 1992.

[210] Cf. on that Evers/Schiel 1988: 10ff. and Evers 1997.

[211] Evers 1997: 16.

Nevertheless strategic groups may evolve into classes.[212] In societies in the throes of transformational upheaval (as at present in China and Vietnam), analytical approaches utilizing the terms elite and class are less fruitful because all social groups and strata find themselves in stages of radical change, formation anew and differentiation processes. Peasants turn into workers and (as do many workers) into traders, craftspeople or even entrepreneurs. Likewise cadres and intellectuals to some extent also change into entrepreneurs. Furthermore within the individual groups the degree of differentiation increases significantly. Some examples of this within the work force illustrate the point: workers employed on a regular basis, contract-, migrant- or temporary workers, worker-peasants; or within the peasantry, peasants either large or small scale, agricultural workers, worker-peasants and migrants. Under such conditions of massive and radical social change, the concept of a strategic group as a category of players appears to me to be very helpful.

Such groups emerge primarily under conditions of social change and upheaval i.e. in phases with a high degree of social mobility. New groups and new chances for acquiring assets come about, groups with a strategic orientation try to improve their chances through altering and regenerating the structuring of the framework conditions in their interest. Such a state of becoming active is necessarily a political action so that the strategic group can be assigned the attribute of political activity. In the course of all this such groups strive to build coalitions with other strategic groups.

The term "strategic" refers to the designing and planned implementation of a long-term total plan, whereby in the course of confrontation with others a specific aim should be achieved. This aim is necessarily of more than one dimension since not only economic rather also political and social goals are striven for. This multi-dimensionality is required because optimal chances for asset acquisition and growth cannot be guaranteed only by means of the government's acceptance of economic development processes, but rather also by legal and political safeguarding, social acceptance and political influence.

In the sphere of *strategic management*, strategy is understood at the same time as *organizational strategy* by means of which companies achieve advantages over their competitors. Through their embedding in different networks (competitors, deliverers, customers, the authorities amongst other institutions), they obtain new contacts, information and connections that give them the opportunity to outdo their competitors. Strategy denotes here that firms expand their control over relationships and networks either through cooperation in the form of alliances, coming to arrangements or agreements with their antagonists, or by way of cooperation with suppliers and customers. A strategic variant to those possibilities consists of exerting influence through political activities on the framework conditions in order to alter the market conditions in a direction favorable to the company (e.g. in respect of such factors as *property rights*,

---

[212] Ibid.: 68.

steering or control on the part of the government, or the legal framework). In all cases the strategy of the firm aims to bring about conditions that resemble as closely as possible the maximal goals of the organization.[213]

Transferred to the political dimension, the term strategic group implies that a group with common characteristics, the existence both of shared interests in common and shared goals, will try to achieve those goals whereby these aims emphasize advantages in societal struggles about distribution, as well as the improvement of the framework conditions necessary for that. The goals consist not only of material interests (such as profit or material goods) instead also those of a symbolic nature (prestige) and cognitive (values, self-fulfillment). It is of secondary significance thereby whether the pushing through of these interests and pursuit of goals takes place as a conscious strategy, or in the form of step-by-step collective action by which first of all only the realization of partial goals and partial strategies is intended whereas more far-reaching strategic goals only gradually become apparent.

The latter fluctuate depending on the opportunities which a group objectively and subjectively possess – between the extreme poles of behavior i.e. either cooperative and system immanent or oppositional. Evers emphasizes too embedding in a "paradigm of power". Strategic groups possess the "...power, to effect the societal, economic and political system that thereby the optimal preconditions for the long-term acquisition of assets is brought about."[214] Power here may be understood not only as political power in the form of pushing something through in formal institutions or the potential to threaten or refuse, but rather refers to the following: firstly an informal power i.e. the pushing through of interests outside of formal hierarchies of decision-making; secondly the awareness of power – up till now only economic – for the structuring and assertion of interests.

If goals are reached and plans implemented, then further cognitive elements are required namely information and knowledge, or meta-cognition to use a term from the field of psychology i.e. strategic knowledge. Strategic groups, likewise their representatives, have to be in the position to process information, to formulate group aims, to reach goal-directed decisions, and to put these into practice. The collection of strategic information, strategic analyses, strategic planning and the implementation of this planning are also necessary attributes of strategic goals and their representative interest organizations. The primary goal of strategic planning consists first of all in the choice of steps, which ensure reaching the sought-after goal.[215]

Here the importance of an organization representing interests becomes clear: it makes possible the long-term pursuit of goals, but also the leadership of a strategic group possessing as it does the appropriate meta-cognition. The strate-

---

[213] Galaskiewicz and Zaheer 1999: 238ff.
[214] Evers 1999: 2.
[215] Cf. on that Radford 1988: 127ff.

gic implementation need not always be rational and thought-out but can rather be in the first place thoroughly spontaneous and unstructured. This implies that strategic action is not necessarily an a priori fact but rather represents too a learning process which takes place interactively between organization and group and vice versa.[216]

The term strategy goes far beyond its original military meaning and stands much more for a program strategy. With that the word approaches in its connotations instead the term policy.

Expressed as a summary, the following elements appear to be important for the definition as a strategic group:

- a group possesses an important function for the total societal development as well as the political development, and the radical political change of a society.
- it appears as an organized interest group with power to take part in political negotiations.
- it works "strategically" in the sense described above and possesses the ability to push something through strategically, which might occur either formally or informally.
- the interest organizations have strategic knowledge at their disposal, a strategic plan, and the capacity to implement this plan.
- the disposition and attitudes of the group members have the effect of forming and changing social values.

In all of this, one should not imply that strategic groups were as such protagonists of a democratization process. This depends on the respective, socioeconomic constellations in each case, under which a group operates. Evers and Schiel have differentiated between different forms of appropriation, and on that basis make out varying forms of political behavior. The group being examined here (entrepreneurs) is classified with the attribute "corporative acquisition". They suggest that on the one hand this group guarantees rights of ownership and organizational opportunities, on the other hand they were exposed to the tendency to ameliorate their chances of acquisition through patronage, network connections, and the use of social relationships, and to increase their political influence. They find themselves therefore in an ambivalent "middle position",[217] a classification which appears to me to be applicable to the entrepreneurial strata in China and Vietnam.

The criticism that the strategic groups approach refers to an unclear scale of reference does not apply to the groups of players in question because entrepreneurs despite all divergences increasingly represent a clearly separated-off group with unifying identificatory characteristics. So they can be differentiated from diffuse group terms such as "bureaucracy" or "middle class", and can be

---

[216] On that also: Pettigrew, Ferlie and McKee 1992: 19ff.; Mintzberg 1990.
[217] Evers and Schiel 1988: 46/47.

analytically situated with relative clarity. That does not mean that they as persons think and act unitedly, but rather that they join together in organizations that represent their interests through which they wish to achieve the realization and implementation of common goals. These interest organizations are the expression of the collective desire to act and the needs of the entrepreneurs.[218] The creation of a strategic group follows as a process. That means in this case that the group formation process of the entrepreneur is not completed but rather consists of a trend development precisely because the entrepreneurial strata finds itself in *status nascendi.*

Yet there is a weakness of the strategic groups approach: namely that the term group is in principle too unspecific because it subsumes ruling and aspiring, powerful and less powerful, small and large groups under one term, and with that creates a certain arbitrariness. As a result the inclusion of Bourdieu's concept of the *total volume of capital* (see above) appears to me to be helpful because its components provide information about resources for the introduction, organization and pushing through of interests; this is an area which has been up till now a weak point in the strategic groups approach. It appears helpful to differentiate between *strategic groups* and *strategic elites*, whereby I define elite status as one matching a recognized leadership role in a social partial segment (for entrepreneurs the economic), the societal shaping of norms and values, and the influencing of social change. For classifying an elite one needs to include not only the total capital volume but rather also the different components of influence in reference to social change that stamp the term elite.

As early as 1963, Suzanne Keller had debated the term "strategic elites", and explained that it was necessary to differentiate between different types of elite. All elites are important in one way or another but only a few for the society as a whole. As a result, she argued, those have to be separated off from the others. There existed in fact a hierarchy of elites. Those whose activities, positions and decisions had decisive consequences for the society as a whole represented the *strategic elites.* Whether one needed to speak of a strategic elite, would not depend on activities alone but rather how many members of the society did that directly affect.[219] Although I believe that the activities of the entrepreneurs in China and Vietnam increasingly influence the entire society, I would like to emphasize once more that I am not claiming that the entrepreneurial strata have already become a strategic *elite.* I am writing above much more of a *potential elite* whose potential will be worked out in the following sections. In Part III, I shall return to this formulation of the question.

Finally the term strategy has to be thought through from another vantage point. Strategic methods as part of a total strategy are without a doubt dependent on culture and regime. More so than in Europe the ideas of Taoism have shaped strategic behavior in China and Vietnam. Sunzi's strategic thinking

---

[218] Cf. on criticism of this approach Neelsen 1988 and 1989; Berner 1991 or Schubert, Tetzlaff and Vennewald 1994: 64ff.

[219] Keller 1963: 19/20.

("The true victor is he who does not fight") which was also to be found in Mao's military, strategic reflections stamped the everyday thinking and activities of the Chinese. In conditions of legal and political uncertainty, tactical skill and cunning stratagems were important means in political life for expanding power, social ascent and political survival.[220] Against the background of politically and culturally different developments, the content and meaning of strategy necessarily took different forms in China and Vietnam than they did in Europe. Nothing makes this clearer than Sunzi as quoted above whose words stand diametrically opposed to those of Clausewitz ("The best strategy is to be as strong as possible"). This specific factor needs to be considered too when transferring the term strategy to diverging societies.

---

[220] Cf. on that Sun Tsu 1990 and von Senger 1994.

PART TWO: THE EMPIRICAL WORK: THE PROFILE OF THE
STRATEGIC GROUP ENTREPRENEURS

In this part of the work we are concerned with a profile of the character of the entrepreneurial strata. This requires that at some points we have to go into some detail in order to elucidate this profile, and work through spatial and structural differences. Only in this way can we obtain a differentiated picture of the entrepreneurial strata.

1. *Choice of the research localities, methodological procedures and frameworks in the regions studied*

1.1. *Choice of areas to be surveyed and methodological procedures*

The set of questions described in the introductory chapter cannot be answered for the whole of either China or Vietnam. Apart from the size of China, in the case of both countries an analysis of the entire country would be made more difficult by a significant regional diversification and unequal development. The choice of an area that is representative for the entire country appears to us to be almost impossible. The rapidly developing Southeast and East of China exist in sharp contrast to less developed Central China and the still less developed North-West, whereas in Vietnam the urban centers Ho Chi Minh City and Hanoi constitute the main centers of development. There are at times considerable contrasts between on the one hand the level of appearances or official statements as criteria for selection, and on the other hand the true state of affairs or reality, and these would have made the search for a representative region more questionable in addition. As a result we chose for the survey regions, in each case one which had played a role as forerunner, since in those areas the progress of privatization and the formation of an entrepreneurial strata was at the most advanced stage, and that region may at the same time have played the role of a trendsetter. In order to make a comparison more feasible, our study was also carried out in a rather backwards region as well as one with a "middling" level of development. However one area should not be all too backwards since in such regions only very few private companies exist. It is precisely in poorer areas that entrepreneurial potential, capital and markets are in short supply.

In order to reduce the number of private companies that are the subject of study to a realistic number, we limited them in each case to an urban segment and a township in a rural area. Beyond that the large number of companies as well as forms of companies compelled a limitation to a partial area. As bearers of privatization, private entrepreneurs stood in the middle of our field work. Since within the private sector the percentage share of industrial companies is the highest, we concentrated on this partial segment (industrial entrepreneurs).

Measured by the stated goals of the reforms, the industrial sector has anyway increased in importance. The industrial entrepreneurs can be divided into large and small entrepreneurs. In China we took over the criteria used by the Commission for the Reform of the Structure of the Economy, which in 1996 classified companies with an annual turnover of over five million Yuan (about $500,000) as "large companies". 50 out of 178 companies examined fulfilled these criteria. In Vietnam in contrast there were only a few large companies in this sense, namely only 21 (10.4%). Due to this low proportion, I refrained in the latter case from this differentiation.

Data was collected and ascertained at the macro-, meso- and micro-levels during which the main focus was on the micro-level. At the macro- (central) and the meso-level (provinces), the data that we ourselves ascertained, served the primary function of assisting us in embedding the information gathered in at the micro-level into a larger, superordinated context. At the macro- and meso-levels we obtained new data in each case in a similar way. Through the evaluation of statistics and documents as well by means of interviews, data was gathered in about the state of the privatization process in both national and regional contexts, about the role of the private sector of the national/regional section of the economy, and about local development strategies. Considering the statistical inexactitude, this data collection reflected mostly the state of knowledge of the institution that was in each case asked. As well as what has just been mentioned, legal stipulations and administrative regulations for the private sector were also collected in order to be able to determine the differing regional and local emphases.

The survey of entrepreneurs was completed by interviews with 203 officials (ranging from the lower right up to the ministerial level) at the Central Party School in Beijing in 1996. Since the data from the survey of the Vietnamese officials was not at this author's disposal, no comparison of the answers was possible between the two countries. Not least because of reasons of balance, as a result only selected results of the survey of officials have been included. Of the 203 officials interviewed who gave their answers to a standardized questionnaire, 86% of them were people who had first joined the Party after 1984. Only 2.5% were members at the beginning (1979) of the process of reform.

Readers might derive the impression that the information about China in our study is more complete than that concerning Vietnam. This may be due to the development of the private sector being further advanced and more accepted there. Regular, random survey surveys have been carried out by social scientists there, and the results of those have gone into this study. In Vietnam in contrast, the private sector represents still a rather sensitive area, and this made it more difficult to research into that sector and collect information about it. Consequently the amount of knowledge about the private sector is significantly larger, and more material and information was at our disposal. Beyond this certain questions could not be asked in Vietnam.

As far as the statistical data is concerned, there was in both countries a variety of data principally because the quality of the statistics has improved significantly in the last 15 years. But reports at the lower levels of administration are not always reliable, and in addition there is a certain lack of clarity in the terminological definition and categories of the non-state sector and of the private sector; as a result unambiguous classifications become difficult. Above all, in Vietnam for political reasons data is distorted or covered up. An example of this is that foreign investment is classified as going into the state sector so as to imply a faster level of growth in it as compared to the private sector. As a result we treated official statistical data as trend indicators, and do not expect that they represent reality in a detailed way.

1.1.1. *The survey in China*
The first phase of fieldwork was concentrated on Beijing (survey of administration at the central level) and in the East Chinese coastal province of Zhejiang. In the middle of the 1990s, the province was in first place concerning the growth rate in the private economy and the value of the GDP of that sector. So Zhejiang represents in our study the more developed region. The high level of development achieved manifested itself too in relatively modern company management as well as in the equipping of the companies. Some firms there already possess total capital of more than 100 m Yuan.

Within the province itself, we chose as our urban region the province capital Hangzhou, since here the largest number of registered private companies are based, and the highest growth rate in the private sector has been recorded. Hangzhou consists of 5 urban districts. In both of the central city districts Shangcheng and Xiacheng, private companies predominate in the areas of service industries and trade. In three others the secondary sector dominates. As a result we concentrated on two of those three districts namely Gongshu and Jianggan. As a rural region we chose Fuyang county some 50 km southwest of Hangzhou; in Fuyang in recent years, the private sector has likewise developed well both quantitatively and qualitatively.

The second phase of fieldwork was carried out in the province of Henan (region of middling development) and Gansu (less developed region). Within Henan we concentrated on the city of Luohe in the southern part of the province. At the time of our survey Luohe consisted of one urban district and three counties. Our survey took place in the inner city and in a county approx. 40 km. away (Yancheng).

Within the north-west region of China, Gansu, our partner institution had chosen the city of Baiyin as the urban zone, and Jingtai County some 60 km away which is administered by Baiyin; this was to be our rural region. Baiyin is a newly created city dating from 1956 some 80 km from Lanzhou, the capital of the province. It consists of two urban districts and three counties, and owes its creation to a large state sector company (called Baiyin) working with non-ferrous metal, of which it is the largest producer in the whole of China. About

90% of the inhabitants came – in the course of the company's development – from outside the province.

The choice of private entrepreneurs was made using our specifications (industrial firms of different sizes) by the local administrative officials for industry and trade. When visiting the companies, an employee of the local administrative office to which the company was subject accompanied us. The task of those officials consisted of making the appointment and a short introduction. In each case we carried out a qualitative interview lasting about two hours using guidelines, then followed questions using a standardized questionnaire. The individual questions had been explained to the respondents beforehand so as to avoid misunderstandings. The quantitative statements about the economic state of the company were generally written into a special form by accountants, then checked by the entrepreneur, and in some cases also corrected. After that followed a tour of the company with a concluding round of questions.

In total, we spoke with 178 entrepreneurs, of whom 169 were men and 9 women; 69 in Zhejiang, 60 in Henan and 49 in Gansu of whom 108 were in urban areas and 70 in rural.

1.1.2. *The survey in Vietnam*

In Vietnam we concentrated in the phase of the field work on the capital Hanoi. As far as the number of registered private companies is concerned, it lied in national terms in second place behind Ho Chi Minh City. A further reason for the choice of Hanoi was of a practical research nature: both our partner institutes were situated in Hanoi, and had not only their best contacts in that area but also the most experience there in empirical research.

Since according to our partner institutions in Hanoi, there were no administrative urban districts that one could term purely industrial areas, we chose Hai Ba Trung a district that possesses a comparatively large number of private companies in the productive domain. From the local administrative office responsible for industry there, we obtained a list of private companies in the secondary sector. In the course of our research, it became clear that the list was unreliable since numerous companies had become insolvent, moved, or despite the details contained in the address could not be located, indications of a high degree of fluctuation in the private sector. The lack of telephone numbers or the existence of wrong phone numbers on the list of companies, forced us to seek out the private entrepreneurs using a map of the city and without having previously made contact. Nevertheless this type of surveying was successful in all cases.

Following that, we continued the study in the neighboring district Dong Da. There we were able to note down from an up-to-date list of about 80 registered firms, some 40 addresses and phone numbers. Our visits were usually announced by phone.

Some 25 km north of Hanoi there is Tien Son county in Ha Bac province.[1] We chose this county as our rural area in a highly developed area. In Tien Son our work was more strongly checked by the local authorities than it had been in Hanoi. An employee of the industry department there, arranged for us in each case one day in advance, 3-4 appointments that were all kept with one exception. When visiting, there was first a short introduction made by the official, we explained the questionnaire, and then followed the questions. The visit was concluded with a tour of the company and a final round of questions.

The questions using the question form lasted some 1.5 – 2.5 hours. This was followed by a qualitative interview that took 1 – 1.5 hours in which particular points raised during the questionnaire section were once again explored, and the respondent asked for clarification. During that digressive answers could well be offered in response to sensitive questions. The written answers understandably were throughout more reserved than the oral ones. Only in one case, did a respondent make a fully-blown airing of his grievances in his written answers insofar as he expressed himself critically about the government and the administration, and then personally signed his statements with large strokes. The quantitative answers about the enterprise were partly made by the entrepreneurs themselves, partly by the accountants. In no case did we obtain a view of the company's balance sheets. Moreover their reliability should not be overestimated. In a short conversation that we had during the temporary absence of the official from the local authorities in Tien Son, the interviewed entrepreneur made it known to us that he had a number of balance sheets: one for internal company uses, and for the local authorities. A young, university graduate did the accounts.

All in all 202 interviews were carried out with entrepreneurs, of whom 164 were men and 38 women. In the course of the first phase of the research in North Vietnam, 51 entrepreneurs were spoken with in Hanoi, and 31 in Tien Son county. During the second phase of fieldwork, we interviewed 51 entrepreneurs in Ho Chi Minh City in South Vietnam, 30 in the village Thu Duc about 25 km away to the east, 22 in the central Vietnamese city Danang and 10 in the village Duy Xuyen administered by Danang. As our main emphasis we carried out interviews in the Ho Chi Minh City districts 1, 3, 5 and 10. Districts 5 and 10 belong to that area of the city, Cholon, which the Chinese community had earlier dominated, and that in the course of an administrative reform was split into three.[2] Carrying out the survey in the four city districts made it possible for us to visit not only Vietnamese but also Chinese companies. The inclusion of Chinese companies turned out to be necessary since the ethnic Chinese have once again attained a dominant role in the economy of the city. These firms have already attracted significant amounts foreign capital (we assume a number of billion US $). But that was often unregistered capital from ethnic Chinese in

---

[1] In 1997 Ha Bac was divided into two new provinces Bac Ninh and Bac Giang.
[2] Interview with the director of the Office for Industry in Ho Chi Minh City 26 November 1996.

other countries, in many cases relatives of *Viet Hoa* (Vietnamese Chinese) in Ho Chi Minh City. Vietnamese studies in 1997 suggest that already 2,000 companies owned by ethnic Chinese had been recipients of such investment, and about 30,000 jobs created thereby. The reason for the non-registration is for one thing the tortuous and long-lasting application procedure, secondly in the politically conditioned fear of ethnic Chinese entrepreneurs of declaring investments made by Chinese living abroad.[3]

We sought the entrepreneurs by making use of a publicly available list of industrial companies in Ho Chi Minh City, and visited without any previous announcement whereas in Thu Duc appointments were made in advance. Chinese entrepreneurs reacted in a considerably more reserved and cautious way than their Vietnamese colleagues. The reserve shown by the ethnic Chinese made clear the complicated relationship – weighed down by the past – between the economically, extraordinarily successful Chinese minority and the Vietnamese majority, in which one could detect amongst other things a certain note of envy. A Vietnamese entrepreneur stated that the Chinese products were of better quality, and complained at the same time that the Chinese only share their company secrets amongst themselves, and keep them hidden from the Vietnamese. Apart from two exceptions, all the entrepreneurs that we encountered were available for interviews and to complete the questionnaire. After that a tour of the factories took place that helped us to a better assessment of the respondents and their abilities.

In Danang there were two organizations cooperating with us, the *DACSME (Advisory Center for Cooperatives, Medium and Small Enterprises of Quang Nam Danang Province)*, and the training center linked to them. They put together a list corresponding to the criteria that we had stipulated containing 36 companies of which we interviewed 22 after previously making contact. Of all the places where we conducted research, the conversational atmosphere in Danang was the most open both on the part of the entrepreneurs and the authorities. At that juncture when we were present, an administrative reorganization of the province's administration in Quang Nam Danang was going on, and there was a major burden to the workload of the local government as a result; however they willingly agreed to an appointment for the conversation with us.

The choice of research location in Vietnam had to take into account that private industry has been concentrated in particular places, and is above all located in urban areas. Comparable rural industries as in China do not exist – apart from the traditional craft villages. The two poles of development, Hanoi and Ho Chi Minh City have significantly shaped the Vietnamese developments, whereby the development conditions in the two cities are not identical. Foreign observers have suggested that the northern and southern parts of the country might develop in different directions. Insofar the choice of these two places

---

[3] Cf. *Vietnam Economic Times*, February 1998: 18/19.

appears to have been justified. In addition to that the number of registered private companies is extremely small in the poorer provinces so that research there would hardly have been worthwhile. Thus according to the 'Statistical Yearbook 1995' in the 12 northern provinces of Bac Bo (with the exception of Ha Bac which was studied), in 1994 there were merely 96 industrial companies i.e. an average of 8 per province! So we chose Hanoi and Ho Chi Minh City as two highly developed regions, and Danang as a region of middling development.

1.1.3. *Practical research problems*

We have already mentioned the general set of problems associated with statistics and official data on which however, native and foreign researchers are dependent, and that should be understood primarily as statements about trends. Whereas in China there were only a few objections made to our questionnaire, in Vietnam a whole range of questions had to be reformulated or deleted. The latter applied particularly to those areas that could be classified as politically sensitive because they referred to the party or political assessments. For particular questions as a result, comparisons in some cases cannot be made. Unlike in China, we were not allowed to take the questionnaires home with us to Germany. They had to remain in the partner institutions in Vietnam, and we were only allowed to make copies.

There were less weighty problems resulting from particular groups of questions whose sensitivity was already known from previous research investigations, and resultantly were no surprise:

- Private entrepreneurs understandably spoke unwillingly about their income, profits and taxes. They were also not very forthcoming about the origins of the starting capital for their companies; this could be explained by some of the starting capital having been obtained illegally from community assets likewise governmental/collective assets. To some extent, false answers were given about the number of employees since these figures might be seized on by the fiscal authorities in order to set the amount of tax due; (the tax authorities justified this method with the alleged inexactitude of the book-keeping by private companies from which they could not derive the real turnover of the company).
- The real state of relations with the local cadres was only spoken about freely and openly to a limited extent. The state of such relationships could be estimated, however, through our own personal observations.
- Political attitudes were not expressed freely and openly especially during those interviews where an employee of the local authorities was present.

But in total, the restrictions were far fewer than had been feared before the start of the research.

1.1.4. Cooperation partners and institutional surveys
The main partnership organization in China was the *Institute for Management* which is an offshoot of the *State Commission for the Reform of Economic Structure*, in Vietnam the *National Political Academy Ho Chi Minh* (Institute of Sociology) and the *Institute of Sociology* in Hanoi. In the provinces, counties and cities of China the local departments of the above mentioned State Commission were responsible, in Vietnam varying additional partners.

In addition we visited the *Central Council of Cooperative Union and Small and Medium Enterprises of Vietnam* (*VICOOPSME*), a non-state organization for the private Sector; the Business Club, in which around 500 state and non-state sector companies were organized, and the *Center of Economic Training, Advice and Information (Cetai)* which was linked to it, as well as the *Hanoi Union Association of Industry and Commerce*; in Ho Chi Minh City the *Union Association of Industry and Commerce UAIC*, which with 1,700 members was the largest and most influential association representing private industry in South Vietnam; the *Management Training Center MTC*; in Danang *VICOOPSME Quang Nam Danang* likewise the *DACSME* (see above.) and the training centers connected with them.

We made contact too with German institutions in Vietnam that in their work over many years have collected important practical experience and built up good contacts with the Vietnamese. Amongst those can be included both the Friedrich-Ebert- and Konrad-Adenauer-Foundation, the Deutsche Entwicklungsdienst (DED) (German Development Service), the office for small and middle-sized companies of the Handwerkskammer (Chamber of Handicrafts) of Koblenz city and last but not least the resident experts of the Gesellschaft für Technische Zusammenarbeit (Association of Technical Cooperation, GTZ) all of whom willingly exchanged experiences with us and provided valuable aid and assistance.

1.2. The framework conditions in the research areas

Generally speaking the economic level of development in a region forms the basis for the development of private companies. The level of income influences the sales possibilities, level and extent of industrial development, determines the technical opportunities, the qualifications of the workforce as well as the circle of customers. The infrastructure (such as transport connections, water and energy supply) provides the basic preconditions for production and transport. For a better understanding of the regional development, a short, comparative profile of each of the regions researched into will now be provided, one tailored to our theme, whereby we refer to data which was available at the time of our research.

1.2.1. *Framework conditions in the research areas of China*
At the time of our research (1996/97), the areas where we carried out study had the following populations:[4]
   A comparison between important development indicators in the researched provinces shows that Zheijiang lay clearly above the national average values for all factors, Henan a little and Gansu clearly under. An exception (in the contrast Henan/Gansu) were the average wages in the public sector because the state and large collective industries were concentrated in a few central places in which higher wages were paid. In Henan on the other hand the companies were considerably more widely scattered with for the most part lower wages outside of the urban centers.

Table 12: Development indicators of the provinces researched into in comparison (China, 1995, in Yuan)

	China	*Zhejiang*	*Henan*	*Gansu*
GDP per capita (1996)	5,634	9,455	4,032	2,901
GO Agri. per capita	1,679	2,065	1,433	1,187
GO Ind. per capita	7,587	18,726	5,181	3,383
Urban income p. capita	3,893	5,718	3,029	2,894
Rural income p. capita	1,578	2,966	1,232	880
Average wage public sector per capita	5,500	6,619	4,344	5,493

Source: *Zhongguo tongji nianjian* 1996 and 1997.
(NB: GO= gross output; GDP=gross domestic product; Agri=agriculture; Ind.=Industry)

In a contrast of the area researched into (cf. also Table 13-15), in developmental terms the superiority of Hangzhou as opposed to Luohe and Baiyin was confirmed. Within Zheijiang province, Hangzhou with a quarter of the non-agricultural population, 13.7% of the population of the province and 22% of the gross output had a leading position. Hangzhou represented without a doubt the most highly developed region of urban areas in China. One could state the same about Fuyang whereby in both cities the non-agrarian sector was already of more importance than the agrarian which is shown too by a comparison with the province an under-average per capita of population share of the agricultural production value. But in 1994 in the area Greater Hangzhou, already 31.6% of the working population (in the urban districts 83.9%) were working in the secondary or tertiary sector, in Fuyang only 15.2%. On the other hand in 1998 already 62.5% of the non-agrarian workforce were in the private sector, whereby these created over 50% of the industrial gross output and more than a quarter of the financial income of Fuyang.

---

[4] The dates refer to the end of 1995.

Luohe is situated on the north-south, traffic axis that connects Henan by means of a railway line and a highway with the north and south of China. The cities on the north-south and east-west traffic axes of the province have experienced rapid development in recent years due to their better infrastructure. At the same time the population of Luohe had an agrarian population of 83%, in Yancheng County over 90%. All the same in 1994 about 40% of the workforce were already employed outside the primary sector. But the total indicators for Luohe were only slightly above the average in the province whereas Yancheng only seldom reached the average value. So Luohe can be classified as a place of middling development in Henan, and lower-middle development in contrast to the national standard.

Table 13: Development indicators in the researched cities and counties: Zhejiang (1994, in Yuan)

	Zhejiang	*Hangzhou*	*Fuyang*
GDP per capita	6,149	9,924	7,003
Gross output Agri. per capita	1,629	841	1,200
Gross output Ind. per capita	13,326	18,270	16,313
Urban income per capita	4,691	5,007	no data
Rural income per capita	2,225	2,785	2,647
Average wage public sector per capita	5,597	6,118	5,277

Sources: *Zhejiang tongji nianjian* 1995 and *Hangzhou tongji nianjian* 1995.
(NB: Agri. = Agricultural; Ind.= Industry; Income)

For a large number of the indicators, Baiyin was above the average in Gansu but under the average for the whole of China as well as for that of Luohe. The pay in the public sector was an exception to that; it was relatively high due to the large subsidies for the heavy industrial sector was distant regions. Jingtai did not reach the average in the province very often so that Baiyin/Jingtai may be classified as under-developed regions even if the city has a special role because of the concentration of the state sector there. The urban sector is to be found in markedly agrarian surroundings (in 1995 about 80% agricultural population, 58.5% of the workforce were working in the agrarian sector). Apart from the two centers of the province, Lanzhou (capital of the province) and Tianshui, Baiyin plays an important role amongst the 14 cities and administrative districts (of which five were urban). Calculated in absolute numbers it had the third largest gross output (industrial place two, agricultural place ten), and the sixth highest per capita GDP. Concerning the per capita income of the peasantry, the city only reached place ten. Re-calculated on a per capita basis the leading positions change somewhat.

Table 14: Development indicators in the researched cities and counties: Henan (1995, in Yuan)

	Henan	Luohe	Yancheng
GDP per capita	3,313	3,646	3,429
Gross output Agri. per capita	1,433	1,927	2,329
Gross output Ind. per capita	5,181	6,617	2,051
Urban income p. cap. (1994)	2,398	2,438	no data
Rural income per capita	1,232	1,530	1,563
Average wage public			
sector per capita	4,344	3,477	3,615

Sources: *Henan tongji nianjian* 1996 and *Luohe tongji nianjian* 1995.

Table 15: Development indicators in the researched cities and counties: Gansu (1995, in Yuan)

	Gansu	Baiyin	Jingtai
GDP per capita	2,288	3,067	2,284
Gross output Agri. per capita	1,187	1,147	1,858
Gross output Ind. per capita	3,383	5,331	1,147
Urban income per capita (1994)	2,894	3,020	no data
Rural income per capita	880	833	<800
Average wage public			
sector per capita	5,493	5,789	3,909

Sources: *Gansu nianjian* 1996 and *Baiyin tongji nianjian* 1995.

1.2.2. Framework conditions in the research areas of Vietnam
The statistical volumes that were made available to us in Vietnam had fewer indicators than the Chinese equivalents. Figures for per capita income divided into urban or rural areas, or GDP per capita were not available. Only the following statistics were available for the purpose of comparisons:

Table 16: Output per capita in the regions surveyed (Vietnam, 1996, in m Dong)[5]

	per capita gross output (industry)	per capita gross output (agriculture)
Vietnam	1.144	1.143
Ha Bac*	0.406	1.018
Hanoi	2.950	0.407
Da Nang	1.923	0.301
Ho Chi Minh City	5.331	2.66

Sources: *Nien Giam Thong Ke* 1998.
[NB.: *Ha Bac in 1997 was divided into the new provinces Bac Giang and Bac Ninh]

Table 17: Per capita income according to regions* (Vietnam, 1996, in m Dong)

Vietnam	2,267
Red River Delta (Hanoi)	2,233
North East (Ha Bac)	1,738
Central coast south (Danang)	1,947
Northern South-East (Ho Chi Minh City)	3,781

Source: *Nien Giam Thong Ke* 1998.
[NB:*refers to the large regions; in brackets the corresponding research location]

The superiority of Ho Chi Minh City is shown by the industrial gross output per capita and the per capita income. Its economic power (one exception is agriculture) leaves all other areas and provinces far behind it even the second metropolis Hanoi. So Ho Chi Minh City represents the most advanced level, Hanoi where our research in urban areas was carried out likewise shows an exalted level, Danang a middling one. Measured by the national average, all three areas had a relatively low amount of agricultural population: Ho Chi Minh City 27.5%; Danang 30.5%; Hanoi 46.2% (Vietnam in total: 79.2%). The levels of agricultural gross output were correspondingly low. Ha Bac in contrast is strongly stamped by agriculture. In 1997 the agricultural population made up 94.7% of the population. Tien Son county was the largest one in the province and counted in economic terms amongst the most developed of the province of Ha Bac. Only 47.5% of the gross output stemmed from agriculture and already 30% from the industrial sector. As a result there was a greater concentration of private firms there. In comparison with the three urban areas examined, Tien Son represented the lower middle.

---

[5] 11, 000 Dong in 1996 equalled about one (US) $.

1.2.3. *Framework conditions for the development of the private sector*
1.2.3.1. *China*
Zheijiang displays a number of unusual features. A low level of cultivable land per capita combined with a high rate of population growth traditionally had the effect that the province inevitably lost migrants in the shape of traders and craftspeople. This restriction of agricultural activity formed an important precondition for the rapid revitalization of the private sector. However, the registration of larger companies which had been permitted once again from 1987 onwards at first proceeded rather slowly. Between 1988 and 1992 merely 9,000 enterprises were registered as "private companies". Uncertainties in the political treatment at the central and provincial levels played a role here. It was only in 1993 that the provincial leadership first formulated a specific policy of aid for this sector which among other things envisaged: (1) Expansion of the population groups (up till then pensioners from state institutions could not be active as entrepreneurs); (2) lifting of restrictions on specific branches; (3) at least nominally equal treatment of private, collective and state institutions in giving credit, the use of real estate, taxation as well as supply with water and energy; (4) non-discriminatory political treatment of private entrepreneurs. In 1998 the provincial leadership confirmed that the quantitative und qualitative development of the private sectors cannot have barriers put in its way. The entrepreneurial strata, they went on, had to be protected, their social status raised and politically they had to be marked out from all others.[6] In principle it was being indicated there that Zheijiang would soon declare private industry to be the most important business sector.

In 1993 in Hangzhou a special business zone for the sector was established where local government set up the required infrastructure (road building, water and electricity supply). Private entrepreneurs could there purchase or lease commercial premises, and they obtained tax benefits (such as a two-year tax exemption, and three further years with tax advantages). City hall declared at the same time the growth rate of the private sector to be an important indicator for the assessment of the achievement of the administrative department responsible (such as the Bureau for Administration of Industry and Commerce) and local governments. These measures encouraged the development of the private sector, and in 1995 there were already 71,000 private enterprises officially registered. In the same year the local governmental administration of Fuyang county introduced similar measures for assisting the growth of the private sectors so that the number of private companies which had earlier gone down from 514 (1988) to 400 (1989) and then stagnated up until 1992, nearly tripled between 1993 and 1995 the number growing from 589 (1993) to 1,519 (1995).

After a catastrophic drop in the number of private companies 1989 and 1990 (due to the suppression of the urban protest movement with the corresponding political consequences), in 1992 the provincial leadership in Henan took meas-

---

[6] *Zhongguo Gongshang Bao*, 17 September 1999.

ures for a fast track development of the private sector.[7] These measures corresponded in their main thrust to those in Zheijiang. The latter in every respect acted as role model for Henan. An example of this is that in the first half of the 1990s, the local government organized numerous visits by delegations of private entrepreneurs to Zhejiang so that these could obtain new ideas and motivational impetus. A significant part of the larger entrepreneurs whom we interviewed had taken part in such excursions, and had participated in the experiences.

In 1994 the leadership of Luohe stated that the private sector should grow at an annual rate of 20%. In a special program each year 100 private companies with a turnover of over 1 m Yuan were to be assisted. Our research revealed how problematic such planned objectives (in the style of a planned economy) can be. This is because the civil servants from the Bureau for Administration of Industry and Commerce who earned bonuses for fulfilling the 20% quota, endeavored to persuade or to pressure those with the status of self-employment in order to convince them to change their classification to a private company so that they, the civil servants, could obtain the premiums. In many cases such new company foundings failed because the founders did not possess the necessary know-how or lacked technology, capital and knowledge of the market. The civil servants had, as explained in Part I, reached their "quota" targets even if companies soon afterwards became bankrupt. In 1995 in Luohe there were 310 private companies with a turnover of at least 1 m Yuan. The registration procedure was simplified so that rural private companies were at first allowed to do business at first without registration, and were only required to register after some try-out months .

As early as 1988 the provincial government in Gansu had already decided on special aid packages for the private economy in regions marked by poverty. In 1991 it was stated that an annual growth in the private sector of 10% or 20% was not sufficient. Here too the political discourse in the province also followed a planned economy agenda. In 1992 the province's rulers passed a resolution promising the accelerated development of that sector. This was in contrast to the resolutions in Zhejiang and Henan where there was more emphasis on the transformation into companies issuing shares or with differing modes of ownership.[8] In 1994 in Gansu a policy correction took place in which an appeal was made explicitly to eliminate "left" thinking in respect of the assessment made of the private sector. Those reservations were alleged to be linked to the slow development of this sector, and the increasing gap in development lagging behind East and Central China.

However, for the 9th Five-Year Plan (planned economy oriented) the annual growth-rate of over 15% envisaged a doubling in the number of employees in the private sector within the five-year plan. Although it propagated more lib-

---

[7] See the corresponding resolution in Zhang, Lin and Xin 1996: 25/26.
[8] Printed in *ibid.*: 34/35.

eral policies, it did not go any further than stating the preferred change of ownership form to be either into a company issuing shares or companies with a mixed structure.[9] The arguments of the Gansu Association of Industry and Commerce, one of the most important representative organizations made clear that attitudes towards the private sector in the mid-1990s were still very conservative and distanced.

At the end of 1996 in a report addressed to the leadership of the Party in the province, the Association argued that in every society there are elementary (*jibende*) and non-elementary (*fei jibende*) means of production, classes and strata. State property, workers and peasants were to be counted amongst the first, private properties and entrepreneurs to the second. It was wrong, the report went on, to regard private sector economic activity as a weakening element in communism; much rather it is a strengthening element, and development in the sector could not lead to capitalism. In the last analysis, the state controlled the sector, and would gradually lead it onto the socialist path.

Furthermore most entrepreneurs, the Association argued, obeyed the laws, took the socialist path and served it. Out of that no new bourgeoisie could develop.[10] The argumentation reminded one of the debates about the private sector in the second half of the 1980s and of the debate in Vietnam. Whereas in East China such positions have already been for the most part overcome, in the Western part of the country they still seem to be widespread. This made clear that there are slightly postponed or distorted developments inside one country.

At the lower levels (cities/counties), such abstract theoretical considerations hardly play a significant role any longer. For purely practical reasons, Document No. 31 (1993) of the Baiyin Party committee called for a rapid liberalization and expansion of the individual and private sectors due to unemployment and securing of livelihoods; Document No. 34 (1994) reinforced that appeal and proposed concrete measures. The ninth five-year plan of the city of Baiyin (1995–1999) foresaw a growth in the private sector of 18%. By 2000 alone it expected the founding of 37,292 (!) individual companies with in total 330 m Yuan as starting capital and 946 (!) private companies with 120 m Yuan start capital. Private entrepreneurs were requested to invest in small collective and state enterprises or to take the latter over.[11] Here too the local government established a special business zone but did not see itself as being in a position to finance the water and energy supply of that zone. As a result many of the newly founded companies had to close down soon after.

In all regions the main reason for the growth of the private sector were cited as being the following: aid to the development of the economy, the creation of

---

[9] *Gansu sheng renmin zhengfu wenjian* No. 104 (1994) (Document of the People's Government of Gansu).

[10] Zhengque yindao fei gongyouzhi jingji fazhan 1996.

[11] *Zhonggong Baiyin shi wenjian* 31 (1993) and 34 (1996) (Documents of the city Party committee of Baiyin).

jobs and an increase in state income. As far as the latter goes, the figures are: in 1998 23.3% of the tax income of Zhejiang, 24.7% of the tax income of Fuyang, 50% of the tax income of Gansu, 33.7% of the tax income of Yancheng, as well as 33.3% of that of Jingyuan county were derived from the private sector. In 1994 alone, in Zhejiang 62% of the new jobs were created in the private sector,[12] and half of those made redundant by state sector companies (*xiagang*) found a new job there.[13] In Gansu it was merely 25.1%,[14] and this can be attributed to the comparatively poor development of the private sector in that region.

In the interests of regional and local development, the local leaderships took measures that clearly diverged from those of central government. An official of the Bureau for Administration of Industry and Commerce in Hangzhou stated for example, that according to the regulations of the central government, prospecting and sale of precious metals was forbidden for private companies. In spite of that, the city administration had granted one-year licenses to such companies. If this procedure were to be noted by higher administrative levels and criticized, then the city administration would once again have to withdraw the licenses; however, if that scenario did not take place then the private entrepreneurs in this sphere would be able to continue their work in this sector. Fuyang County in turn ignored a decree emanating from the Central Bank that statutory credit institutes were not allowed to provide credits of more than 10,000 Yuan to private entrepreneurs. Much rather it was the authorities in a county who in the interests of developing the private sector decided whether or not to provide credits of sufficient size to companies which appeared likely to be successful.

1.2.3.2. *Vietnam*
In Vietnam the policies of subsidy still appeared primarily to originate from the central leadership. In the framework of different programs, above all for reasons of employment policy i.e. in the interests of decreasing unemployment, newly founded companies in the private sector are always supported by the state. A large part of the money foreseen for that purpose, stems from the fund started in 1992 the *National Employment Fund* (NEF). In 1992 about 30% of the NEF finance is thought to have been given out to company founders in the form of state subsidized credits (max. 1.2% interest per month) over short periods being made available (cf. Table 18).

---

[12] Zhejiang tongji nianjian 1995: 63.
[13] *Renmin Ribao*, 4 November 1999.
[14] Gansu nianjian 1996: 352.

Table 18: Money in the National Employment Fund (NEF) 1992 (Vietnam)

Components	Volume (billion VND)	Aim
Reform of state sector companies	350	Compensation payments for those made redundant
Support of company founders	250	100 billion VND for *New Economic Zones* (NEZ), 150 for company founders in general
Vocational and further training	10	Improvement of the vocational training systems
Re-settlement program	180	Preparation of NEZs, building up of the infrastructure
Reserves	40	Not further defined
In total	830	

Source: Kurths 1997: 235, Table 61.

Amongst the receivers of the credit, one should note primarily former workers and white-collar employees in the state sector, demobilized soldiers and the poor. Urban craft and service industry companies should be subsidized first of all as well as rural, non-agrarian, entrepreneurial activity. In practice the provision of credit proves to be unnecessarily complicated, and apparently ineffective all things considered. The process of official approval is time-intensive due to the large number of offices involved at the different levels of administration. So far the majority of credits have been awarded to the rural regions and the traditional agricultural activities there, but not – as originally intended – for the secondary sector. Furthermore according to figures given by the *International Labor Organization* (ILO), the average level of individual credits at around (US) $250 is hardly sufficient to create new jobs whose costs are estimated to be about twice that amount.

In contrast to the views of foreign observers, Vietnamese authorities assess the outcome of the NEF Program positively. The Ministry of Labor, Invalids and Social Affairs MOLISA, which administers the money, claims that up to September 1995 about 900,000 extra jobs had been created whereby with 820,000 the overwhelming majority of those were said to be in the rural areas close to the catchment areas of Hanoi and Ho Chi Minh City.[15] None of the

---

[15] Kurths 1995: 235ff.

private entrepreneurs with whom we spoke appeared, however, to have obtained a credit in the framework of the NEF program.

Targeted support of the private sector takes place also through VICOOPSME, the largest association of small and middle-sized entrepreneurs (SME), and its local offshoots such as DACSME. At the same time a large number of foreign institutions and organizations are active in the sphere of SME assistance. Amongst those are the GTZ which has since 1994 cooperated with VICOOPSME within the framework of the GTZ project "Support of small and middle-sized firms" which is run by the organization *Technonet Asia*, a subsidiary of the *Central Association of German Trade* as well as foundations such as the *Friedrich Ebert Foundation* which in Ha Bac run an advisory center for companies together with local people's committees, or the *Konrad – Adenauer Foundation*.

Mass organizations too such as the Communist Youth League or the Women's Federation have recognized the economic significance of SMEs, and have meantime become active in promoting them. They have founded entrepreneur associations at the local level, and organized discussion circles.

A *Center for Management and Development of Entrepreneurship* at the Central Institute for Economic Management was founded at the beginning of the 1990s with the support of the *International Labor Organization*. The UNDP at the beginning of the 1990s, intended first of all for vocational training and further training of managers of state sector companies, was opened too in the second half of the 1990s for private entrepreneurs.

A general method of promotion by the SME existed in tax relief when companies were founded. Production firms enjoyed the largest tax reliefs whereby all forms of companies including state and collective companies were able to make use of them. In the first year of production the sales tax was halved, the profits tax was not levied at all in the first two years. In the third and fourth years the tax on profits was reduced by 50%. As well as that there was a trial period which is used very flexibly by local administrations by which the company did not have to be registered, and accordingly was exempted from all tax payments. The length of the trial period depended on the appropriate agreement between authorities and entrepreneur (and indeed also from the level of certain "donations" to the bureaucracy). However, in reality private entrepreneurs complained that they had to pay significantly higher taxes e.g. a tax on profits at the level of 30–40% whereas companies with foreign capital merely paid tax at a level of 10–20%.

More than in Hanoi, in Ho Chi Minh City one could speak of an active policy of assistance that went beyond national economic policy and was contributing to rapid development in that metropolis. In this manner, for example, the registration procedure for newly founded companies had been simplified, and access to credits from banks with favorable rates of interest made possible.[16]

Unlike Hanoi, Ho Chi Minh City possessed countless advantages that enabled development of private sector economics. Amongst those was the existence of a large private sector both prior to and partially after 1975 in which a number of today's entrepreneurs gathered their first experiences and could obtain capital. About 200,000 Vietnamese were said to possess foreign contacts and these make it possible bringing in the necessary capital for a company.

In Danang too there existed a well-developed policy of assistance to the private sector that would be comparable to that in Ho Chi Minh City at least in its approaches. For a long time the collective rather than the private sector was favored. Even at the end of the 1990s and the de facto collapse of the former sector, the political leadership flirted with a modified collective model in which collectives of a new type, comparable with a joint-stock company, were to come into being. All the same, here too the advantages of the private economy were recognized in terms of employment policies and economic aspects so that some measures of assistance above all in the tax field were adopted and pushed through in the spirit of the national economic policy. The implementation of national policies in concrete measures is certainly worth mentioning since it appears not to be something that can be taken for granted, due to the unusual degree of local autonomy, and the strong tendency of local administrations to give their own ideas priority.

---

[16] Interviews with the director and other employees of the Industry Office of the City Level Business Department People's Committee Districts 3 and 5 of Ho Chi Minh City 26 November, 18 and 19 December 1996.

1.3. *The Development of the private sectors in the regions surveyed*

1.3.1. *Chinese survey areas*
The development of the private sector has taken place in a relatively unbalanced way.

Diagram 12: Development of private companies in the provinces surveyed (China)

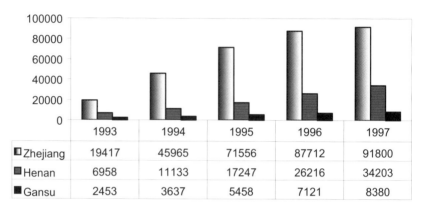

	1993	1994	1995	1996	1997
Zhejiang	19417	45965	71556	87712	91800
Henan	6958	11133	17247	26216	34203
Gansu	2453	3637	5458	7121	8380

Source: *Gongshang xingzheng guanli tongji* 1993-97.

The background of the rapid growth in Zheijiang is more complex than the current, economic-political situation. Non-agrarian, business activities are often associated with migration, and possess a long tradition as already mentioned above. The per capita land available for cultivation is low in relation to the growing size of the population, and this has forced large sections of the population to leave the rural areas and to work as traders or craft persons away from their native places. The example of the city Wenzhou in the south of the province which during the Cultural Revolution was often criticized due to its underground, private, economic activities, and which has been since the early 1980s a model for the development of the private sector (as the dominant one) makes clear the significant role of this sector in the province.

In the 1990s the private sector in the province developed remarkably. The number of registered private companies grew from around 9,000 in 1992 to about 92,000 in 1997 and 100,200 in 1998. Only Guangdong province in 1997 had more private firms (102,320) with the province of Shandong following in third place a long way behind with 76,662. As far as the growth rate of the private sector is concerned, Zhejiang lay in first place.[17] In 1998 42.5% of the industrial gross output and 67.5% of the gross social retail volume were accord-

---

[17] Gongshang xingzheng guanli tongji 1997: 68.

ing to official statements in private hands.[18] Those levels thereby approach again the levels existent at the beginning of the 1950s when 60.3% of the industrial gross output (1949) and 85.1% of the gross, social retail volume were in the possession of individuals or private companies. The same development could be observed in Hangzhou and Fuyang too. At the time of our survey, in the capital of the province 10,002 private firms were registered with a growth of 49.7% compared to the previous year (1994).

While between 1992 and 1997, the number of private firms in Zheijiang and Henan rose by almost 500%, in Gansu it only tripled.

Diagram 13: Development of Employment in Private Companies (China)

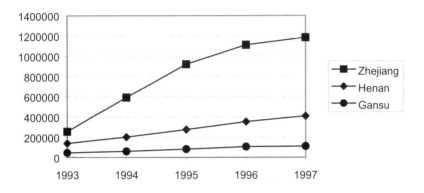

Source: *Gongshang xingzheng guanli tongji* 1993-97.

The positive trend in development was confirmed by figures from Luohe and Baiyin. Between 1986 and 1996, in Luohe the number of private companies rose from 100 to 803, in Baiyin from 49 to 428.

The gap between the three provinces is mirrored not only in the number of registered private companies but also in the fields in which those companies were working. In contrast to Zheijiang where in almost all branches of industry private companies were at work, those in Henan and Gansu were clustered in only a few spheres (such as food, textiles, shoes or the construction industry). Unlike in Zhejiang, those companies in Henan and Gansu were for the most part small and middle-sized firms. These differences were reflected as well in the composition of the firms that we examined:

---

[18] *Zhongguo Gongshang Bao*, 17 September 1999.

Table 19: Distribution of the companies surveyed by branches (China)

	Hangzhou		Luohe		Baiyin	
	Number	%	Number	%	Number	%
1. Machine tools	14	20.3	4	6.7	9	18.4
2. Electronics	12	17.4	0	0.0	0	0.0
3. Building materials	11	15.9	4	6.7	18	36.7
4. Textiles and shoes	9	13.0	11	18.3	3	6.1
5. Food	2	2.9	30	50.0	4	8.2
6. Paper products	7	10.1	1	1.7	1	2.0
7. Ship building	1	1.5	0	0.0	0	0.0
8. Printing	5	7.2	0	0.0	0	0.0
9. Chemistry	2	2.9	5	8.3	5	10.2
10. Furniture	2	2.9	1	1.7	0	0.0
11. Toys	1	1.5	1	1.7	0	0.0
12. Metal goods	1	1.5	3	5.0	4	8.2
13. Mining	0	0.0	0	0.0	4	8.2
14. Others	2	2.9	0	0.0	1	2.0
Total	69	100.0	60	100.0	49	100.0

Source: Own survey.

Table 20: Distribution of companies surveyed by number of staff (permanent workforce, China)

Number of staff	Hangzhou		Luohe		Baiyin	
	Number	%	Number	%	Number	%
8-20	12	17.9	13	21.7	20	41.7
21-50	16	23.9	19	31.7	14	29.2
51-100	16	23.9	16	26.7	4	8.3
101-200	13	19.4	6	10.0	5	10.4
201-500	7	10.4	4	6.7	4	8.3
501-1.000	2	3.0	2	3.3	1	2.1
1.001-2.000	0	0.0	0	0.0	0	0.0
> 2.000	1	1.5	0	0.0	0	0.0
Total	67	100.0	60	100.0	48	100.0

Source: Own survey.

In Hangzhou the companies were superior to those in Luohe and Baiyin in respect of starting capital and technological equipment. In addition, as far as the number of staff goes, the companies in Hangzhou were larger. There only 41.8% employed less than five staff whereas in Henan and Gansu the respective figures were 53.4% and 70.9% respectively. 14.9% of the companies in the capital of Zhejiang had more than 200 staff, contrasted with only about 10% in Henan and Gansu. The reason for the better equipping and quicker development in Zheijiang is related above all to the relatively highly developed state of the province in contrast with the provinces inland, and the more advanced state of affairs in the markets as well as massive support on the part of the local authorities. Better chances in exports, in attracting capital as well as better access to capital, and a qualified workforce also played a role in that.

1.3.2. *Vietnamese survey areas*

At the end of 1994 there were in Hanoi 424 private firms registered as being active in the secondary sector. When one counts the limited companies as well, then the number rises to above 1,000. In the districts of Hanoi (Hai Ba Trung and Dong Da) which we surveyed in 1996 there were 146 and about 80 private firms and limited companies respectively. Especially in the district Hai Ba Trung the private sector had apparently developed well since 1990 when there had been 70 cooperative industrial companies and 30 home firms. Whereas the number of collectives had decreased to 45, the number of home businesses had increased to 980.

These numbers communicate, however, a distorted picture of the existing circumstances. That is because out of the 157 firms in Hai Ba Trung, an estimated 30% had either gone bankrupt or had moved. A further 30% had falsely had themselves registered as industrial companies although they were in business in the tertiary sector. A false registration of this kind is advantageous for the company since the state favors the founding of companies in the field of production. According to the information provided by the director of the Department for Industry in Hai Ba Trung, the number of non-registered firms was "large", although he did not offer an estimate.

Even more unclear was the situation in Tien Son county in Ha Bac province about 25 km northwest of Hanoi. According to information provided by the director of the Industry Department of the People's Committee in Tien Son, in 1996 there were 84 non-state companies registered, consisting of three private firms, seven limited companies, 36 collectives and 38 joint-stock companies. The collectives were in fact disguised private companies. In Bac Ninh (formerly Ha Bac) there was in 1996, however, not a single private company registered![19] The statistics referred merely to 817 individual companies.[20]

Whereas the statistical yearbook communicated the impression that the development of the private sector had stagnated since the mid- 1990s, the authorities painted a rather positive picture of the development of the private sector.

---

[19] Nien giam thong ke tinh Bac Ninh 1997: 88, Table 72.
[20] Ibid.: 89, Table 73.

This image was confirmed by our researches on the ground. Such widely differing estimates and representations are among other things based on the fact that different offices find conflicting data in their researches and – mostly for political reasons – interpret and classify the data differently. In the course of our fieldwork, we did indeed come across a number of companies whose economic figures far exceeded those which were officially recorded. Thus the local authorities had numbered the upper limit of workforce in the large companies at around 300, whereas we encountered at least two companies with over 1,000 staff.

Typical for Tien Son (and Ha Bac in general) was the specialization within villages in particular products. To illustrate this a number of villages were known for their artistic woodcuts which to some extent they sold to Ho Chi Minh City and even exported them abroad. The advantage of such a tradition consists in acquiring specific abilities that in the best case enable the manufacture of products in almost unrivalled quality. An example is the village Dong Ky which is well-known – and not only locally – for the quality of its craft industry. The specialization within a village can, however, be a disadvantage, for instance when its success induces new companies to imitation. Since those mostly lack the requisite experience, their products are often of moderate quality and the profits correspondingly low. We encountered many cases of this kind when we visited villages, and those small entrepreneurs did not conceive of switching to the production of other products with less competitive pressure. More successful entrepreneurs also showed such low levels of flexibility from time to time. A manufacturer of sawing machines who some years ago had supplied the market in the entire province of Ha Bac, complained now about a drop in his customers as a consequence of market saturation. In answer to the question as to why he did not try and sell outside of the province Ha Bac, he replied that he had only ever done business within the province. The economic compulsion to expand was apparently completely foreign to him as an idea.

According to information provided by the department responsible for industry at the city level, in the center of Ho Chi Minh City, there were in 1996 about 600 private companies, 1,500 limited companies and joint-stock companies as well as 25,000 self-employed with in total over 300,000 staff working in the industrial field. They made up about 50% of the industrial production of the city, the other 50% were divided amongst about 700 state sector companies and 100 collective firms (so far as these were still functioning). About 76% of people in employment were in the non-state sector.

Table 21: Distribution of companies surveyed according to branches (Vietnam)

	North Vietnam		Central Vietnam		South Vietnam	
	Number	%	Number	%	Number	%
1. Machine tools	3	2.9		5.7	1	1.2
2. Electronics	4	3.9	0	0.0	0	0.0
3. Building materials	10	9.8	7	20.0	3	3.5
4. Textiles and shoes	19	18.6	4	11.4	13	15.1
5. Food	15	14.7	3	8.6	20	23.3
6. Paper and printing products	12	11.8	6	17.1	2	2.3
7. Chemistry, medicine	3	2.9	0	0.0	1	1.2
8. Furniture	8	7.9	2	5.7	15	17.4
9. Metal goods	8	7.9	1	2.9	7	8.1
10. Plastics, rubber	5	4.9	4	11.4	6	7.0
11. Wood	6	5.9	3	8.6	3	3.5
12. Household goods	3	2.9	1	2.9	5	5.8
13. Craft products	4	3.9	1	2.9	5	5.8
14. Others	2	2.0	1	2.9	5	5.8
Total	102	100.0	35	100.1	86	100.0

Source: Own survey.

Table 22: Distribution of the companies surveyed according to the number of staff (Vietnam, non-casual employees)

Number of staff	North Vietnam		Central Vietnam		South Vietnam	
	Number	%	Number	%	Number	%
< 20	35	39.3	10	31.3	55	67.9
21-50	23	25.8	10	31.3	13	16.1
51-100	16	18.0	6	18.7	7	8.6
101-200	6	6.7	3	9.4	3	3.7
201-500	2	2.3	1	3.1	1	1.2
501-1.000	0	0.0	1	3.1	0	0.0
1.001-2.000	0	0.0	0	0.0	0	0.0
No answer	7	7.9	1	3.1	2	2.5
Total	89	100.0	32	100.0	81	100.0

Source: Own survey.

In the former province Quang Nam-Danang at the end of 1996, there were 58 limited companies and private companies (with 1,520 workers) registered in the industrial sphere.[21] 99 collective firms existed purely nominally which were according to the director of DACSME with one exception either disbanded or functioning as a joint stock or limited company. The joint ventures, specially classified, represented a significant economic factor: of them only 23 were registered but which with 3,246 staff had twice as many employees as the Vietnamese private companies. Alongside those there were 9,000 small firms with over 26,000 employees. Included in these figures is the village Duy Xuyen that we visited as part of our fieldwork; it lies south of Danang. A positive development in Quang Nam-Danang's private sector industry began in particular from 1994 onwards with an annual growth of about 18% between 1994 and 1996. Nevertheless, according to official figures, in 1996 the state sector contributed (1,240 billion VND) more to the GDP of the province than the private sector (831 billion VND).

The following tables make clear the distribution according to branches and size of company the firms that we visited:

In Table 21 the sum of the companies is higher than the total number of companies where the survey was carried out, since some firms were players in a number of different areas. As a result the figures for the total number of stated answers do not match the total number of the surveyed companies.

In comparison to China, in Vietnam branches predominated that are typical for developing countries i.e. textiles/shoes, food processing and paper and print products. In China "modern" sectors such as machine tools, electronics and chemistry count amongst the leading branches with the exception of Luohe where likewise traditional branches dominated. The regional differences were rather low in Vietnam. As far as staff numbers are concerned Chinese companies on average were larger. 12% of the surveyed Chinese but only 2.5% of the Vietnamese companies had more than 200 members of staff. Indeed smaller companies were in the majority in both countries. Whereas in China about half of all companies surveyed had less than 50 staff (53.7%), in Vietnam it was more than two-thirds (71.2%). Even in the region that has the most advanced market economy, Ho Chi Minh City, more than two-thirds (67.9%) were small companies with less than 20 workers in contrast to the most highly developed region surveyed in China in which the proportion of these companies lay under 18%. As a result one can ascertain that all in all the private sector in Vietnam is more traditionally organized and less developed than in China.

---

[21] Interview with the director for the Department for Industry, City of Danang, 21 December 1996.

2. Texture, differentiation and strategic capital

2.1. Composition and starting conditions of the interviewed entrepreneurs

2.1.1. Age structure

The age structure of the interviewed respondents was similar in both countries. More than two-thirds of the Chinese (70.8%) and Vietnamese entrepreneurs (73.0%) were aged between 30 and 50. This result corresponded to the 1995 Chinese 1% sample amongst private entrepreneurs, according to which 74.9% of the entrepreneurs belonged to this age group.[22] But 11.2% (China) and 7.5% (Vietnam) of them were younger than 30. The relatively high total figure for the average of private entrepreneurs in both countries – measured by the average age of the entire population[23] – can be explained very well by the fact that as a rule successful manufacture presupposes specific expertise and material conditions which younger sections of the population possess to a much lesser extent than middle-aged or older ones. Capital and professional experience count amongst the preconditions as well as social contacts and connections which one can only build up over a longer period of time. Younger people are mostly involved in the individual business tertiary sector. The age profile of the tertiary sector diverges therefore from the profile in the secondary sector. Work such as trading often presupposes to a lesser extent expertise in a specific field and the deployment of capital than the production of particular goods. The material preconditions at the starting points are at the same time lower (for example necessary production space or equipping with machines), so that younger people find it easier to make a start in trading, but at the same time can quickly earn a lot of money.

Regional differences depend on specific local factors. The extremely high, youth unemployment rate in centers of heavy industry such as Baiyin may be the reason why the proportion of under 40-year-olds at 53.1% is clearly higher than in Hangzhou (39.1%) and Luohe (48.4%). The higher share of older people in Zheijiang, in turn may be caused by the fact that the more specialized structure of industry there requires a higher level of (age determined) experience.

There were conspicuous regional differences in the age pyramids of the private entrepreneurs on the one hand between South Vietnam and on the other hand in North and Central Vietnam. In the south the proportion of young entrepreneurs aged maximum 29 (16%) was eight times as high as in North Vietnam with 2%; in Central Vietnam there was not one single representative of this age

[22] Zhang, Li and Xie 1996: 157; similarly: Zhang 2000.

[23] According to the Chinese Microcensus in 1995 about 28% belonged to the age-group between 30 and 50, cf.. *Zhongguo renkou tongji nianjian* 1996: 76/77. In the Chinese age pyramid in 1995 53% of the population were younger than 30, 18.9% between 20 and 29 years old. In Vietnam 39% were between 15 and 34, 18,4% between 15 and 24, *Thuc trang Lao Dong - Viec Lam* 1998: 49.

group. If one merged the age group under 40 years with that of the 29s or under, then almost half of the South Vietnamese group of entrepreneurs would be grouped under that heading, whereas in Central Vietnam only one-fifth would belong to it. The high rate of employment amongst young people in the south and the regional strongly marked culture of entrepreneurship may play a role in this trend.

2.1.2. *Familial and social origins*
The majority of the respondents interviewed in China stem from peasant families (44.1%). This can be seen in a different light, however, in the urban-rural comparison. As far as the employment background of the father of the entrepreneurs is concerned, in the urban areas the cadre/manager is the largest group, and in the countryside still the second largest. However, the share of those who had earlier been dubbed "class enemies" (capitalists or large land owners before 1949), as part of their background was relatively low at 3.9%. However, it may very well be that not every respondent was willing to speak openly of that syndrome in his or her family background. A nationwide Chinese survey found a proportion of as much as 7.1% of the respondents interviewed who stemmed from "black families" (former large land-owners, wealthy peasants, capitalists, "reactionary" officers and civil servants).[24]

The proportion of fathers with management experience was at 25% in the urban areas clearly higher than the proportion of administrative cadres (14.8%). The high percentage of peasants indicates on the one hand close relations with the urban area, shows on the other hand, that despite their peasant backgrounds a significant part of the present-day entrepreneurial strata have succeeded in establishing themselves in the non-agrarian sector in the cities. In any case only 4.6% of the entrepreneurs before taking up entrepreneurial activity had themselves been working as peasants. As the qualitative interviews showed, having originated from the peasantry and the lower social prestige associated with it, in the circle of persons concerned, fewer reservations were to be found against becoming an entrepreneur which is for the moment (still) negatively assessed in social terms. On the other hand the low social status of peasants may have strengthened the wish for social ascent, and thirdly the cultural heritage of the peasants provides some motivational impulse. An entrepreneur of peasant origins expressed it thus: "We don't have any anxiety when faced with difficulties and permanently hard work".

---

[24] "Zhongguo siying qiye yanjiu" ketizu (1999): 153.

Table 23: Last profession of the father (China)

Profession	City		Countryside		Total	
	Number	%	Number	%	Number	%
Technician	2	1.9	2	2.9	4	2.3
Cadre/Manager	43	39.8	15	21.7	58	32.8
Blue or white-collar employee	19	17.6	8	11.6	27	15.3
Peasant	38	35.2	40	58.0	78	44.1
Individual laborers	6	5.6	4	5.8	10	5.6
Total	108	100.0	69	100.0	177	100.0

Source: Own survey.

Fathers with a background as cadre or manager are able to pass on their professional and social capital to their children i.e. not only their technical, administration or other professional skills and experiences (this applies too to workers and white-collar employees), but also their professional and social connections (*guanxi*).

This can be well linked with their own experiences and relationships: 10.2% of the urban and 14.5% of the rural entrepreneurs before their self-employment had been cadres working for the civil service or in rural areas, almost half of the urban and more than a third of the rural ones had been working before as a manager in state or collective firms. All in all one can ascertain that a large part of the respondents interviewed had already belonged to elevated social strata before founding their companies. More than half had been working before in state or collective firms as a cadre or manager, 9% as technicians. A Chinese study suggested that at the same time that the former managers amongst the private entrepreneurs possessed lengthy and above-average, professional experience. According to that study 53.5% of the private entrepreneurs had professional experience of longer than ten years, whereas this percentage amongst the total set of respondents (entrepreneurs/managers) lay at only 35.7%. Private entrepreneurs had gathered experiences on average in 7.7 companies, the total set of respondents only in 3.7 firms.[25] Well-founded knowledge of management but also knowledge about administration and useful social contacts may be taken for granted whereby familial capital complements that which is self-acquired. It is precisely cadres and managers with advantageous social relationships who possess better qualifications for the founding of their own companies than other persons.

When we compare the occupational background of the entrepreneurs in the three areas that we surveyed, it can be established that in all three regions a more or less similarly high percentage had been working before as managers in state and collective enterprises. This applies particularly to the developed region Zhejiang. The high proportion of former managers in the urban areas demonstrates that managers from the rural collective sector (township and village firms) apparently used their experiences and contacts in order to make themselves self-employed. Since the development of the rural industrial firms in Zhejiang was thriving, the percentage of that group of people was especially large here.

---

[25] Zhongguo qiyejia diaocha xitong 1998a: 5/6.

Table 24: Occupations of the entrepreneurs interviewed before founding their companies (China)

Occupation	City		Countryside		Total	
	Number	*%*	*Number*	*%*	*Number*	*%*
Technician	13	12.0	3	4.4	16	9.0
Cadres in civil service	7	6.5	3	4.4	10	5.7
Rural cadres	4	3.7	7	10.1	11	6.2
Manager in state or collective firms	48	44.4	26	37.7	74	41.8
Blue or white-collar workers in state or collective firms	20	18.6	7	10.1	27	15.3
Peasants	5	4.6	11	15.9	16	9.0
Individual laborers	11	10.2	12	17.4	23	13.0
Total	*108*	*100.0*	*69*	*100.0*	*177*	*100.0*

Source: Own survey.

In Henan and Gansu, along with former blue-collar workers, a relatively high share of former small entrepreneurs (individual laborers) were involved in that sphere of the private sector defined more loosely. Especially in rural areas, this occupational group lay in second place (Zhejiang) or even in first place (Gansu, Henan). The individual economy is apparently in the countryside an important stage to pass through before moving to larger private sector companies, not only in respect of formation of capital, but also in the sphere of work-related knowledge and experience of the market. For the unemployed and former members of the military, this sector plays a less important role in the first place because it presupposes a significant degree in basic investments and technical qualification.

To some extent, the results of the survey match the 1% Chinese samples from 1995 already mentioned

Table 25: Previous occupation of the entrepreneurs (China, in %)

Profession	Urban	Rural
1. Technically qualified employees	13.0	5.5
2. Cadres	24.2	17.3
3. Blue-collar workers	18.8	16.4
4. White-collar workers	6.5	2.1
5. Former members of the military	0.6	0.7
6. Peasants	11.0	31.7
7. Individual laborers	10.5	10.0
8. No occupation	4.8	1.7
9. Others	10.6	14.5

Source: Zhang, Li and Xie 1996: 158.

Divergences come about through the use of different categories. In the Chinese study the important category "Manager" was missing. It also did not differentiate between different types of cadres (state cadre in civil service and rural cadres). In the Chinese study, managers and rural cadres were in each case classified under the category "cadre" or "peasant" since managers in state and collective enterprises are also considered to be "cadres". And people who live in the countryside without the right to live in the urban areas were lumped together under the label "peasant" whether or not they were active in the primary, secondary or tertiary sectors. In our survey on the other hand, "managers" are considered to be those who had a management function (director, deputy director or head of department) in a company (state, urban or rural enterprise). The second point is that in our questionnaire the question about occupational origins was formulated as an open question. We allowed the entrepreneurs in the course of the interviews to tell how and in which institution they had been employed. Thirdly the occupational background of the entrepreneurs in recent years has rapidly changed. In the course of improved framework conditions as well as due to increasing political and social acceptance, increasing numbers of highly qualified personnel have switched to the private sector.

A further important specific factor for the entrepreneurs we interviewed is that of spatial mobility primarily that of the peasant entrepreneur.

Table 26: Place of birth and current residence of entrepreneurs interviewed as well as headquarters of the company (China, in %)

	Large city	Medium-sized city	Small city
Place of birth	2.3	2.0	10.9
Current place of residence	2.6	0.6	28.4
Headquarters of company	4.0	1.0	26.1
	Township	Village	Total
Place of birth	28.5	56.3	100
Current place of residence	37.4	31.0	100
Headquarters of company	44.4	24.5	100

Source: Own survey.

Many rural entrepreneurs have moved their companies into urban areas in recent years and had them registered there. A civil servant of the Bureau for Administration of Industry and Commerce in Hangzhou termed this phenomenon "Encirclement of the cities by the countryside". Better access to markets as well as more advantageous conditions for marketing and information are decisive for that. An example was an entrepreneur from Hangzhou who stemmed from a peasant family, and had only attended elementary school for three years. At 21 he had already become director of a rural company. In 1979 he had founded in his home county Taishan his first factory, a metal goods firm. This he had registered first of all as a rural company. In 1983 he set up a further factory (to manufacture electric cables), in 1986 a third. In 1991 he moved to Hangzhou. He leased his three factories, and founded in Hangzhou a new private firm in which he invested 2 m Yuan. In 1993 he changed this company into a limited liability company with four subsidiaries. In 1995 he invested 250 m Yuan in building flats and in the development of a tourist park.

The relatively high share of Chinese entrepreneurs who stated that they believe in a religion was conspicuous (in Vietnam unfortunately this question had to be deleted). At any rate 27% professed to one mostly to Buddhism (14.6%).

Surprisingly the proportion in the most developed region was the highest (31.9% Buddhist), in Hangzhou (52.1% professing). Individual statements in the interviews leave one to draw the conclusion that religion is rather perceived as something of a "protective factor" in business life with all its risks, uncertainties and the hard competitive struggle, and less as a directly motivational force for entrepreneurial work in the sense of a business ethic. Studying the interaction between religion and entrepreneurship was not the subject of this research but would have been with certainty a rewarding and interesting target for study.[26]

In Vietnam there were systemically conditioned agreements respecting the composition of the entrepreneurial strata due to historical realities but at the same time also significant differences. Amongst the entrepreneur, the following groups could be identified according to ancestry.

- Former *white-collar employees and managers of state or collective firms* formed in our study the primary group of private entrepreneurs (Managers 12.8%, white-collar staff 38.3%).[27] This corresponds with a study carried out by the National Political Academy Ho Chi Minh (Central Party School) and the Friedrich Ebert Foundation (FES), according to which 42.7% of the entrepreneurs came from the state sector (civil servants, cadres).[28] In 1991 a Swedish-Vietnamese study came to similar conclusions according to which the figure for former civil servants in the urban areas was 48% (in rural areas about 20%).[29] This group of people possesses the best access to government resources and also to premises for production or raw materials, but also have good relationships with state or collective companies as well as to the authorities. With those advantages they have the right prerequisites to found their own firms, into which flow governmental resources as well as relationships with suppliers and customers from their former place of work. Moreover as a result of their earlier work they have at their disposal specific specialized knowledge. A typical example of that was Nguyen Muoi, owner and director of the construction company Kien Tao Mien Trung in Danang. He had trained as a construction engineer and had been former deputy director of the government firm for building, transport and service industries in the same city. He employed not only a section of the employees of his former employer and some of the latter's

---

[26] Cf. on that for example the dissertation by Fiedler (1999).

[27] At least in the metropolis Ho Chi Minh City, the ethnic Chinese Vietnamese are in the majority as far as private entrepreneurs in the secondary sector are concerned. But even the Vietnamese authorities do not know exactly how many of the entrepreneurs are of Chinese descent. Not seldom ethnic Vietnamese are deployed as straw men, behind whom Chinese capital stands In addition the repeated forced Vietnamisation of Chinese names makes it difficult to differentiate clearly between the two population groups Due to the difficulties with the Vietnamese administrations, a not insignificant section of the Chinese entrepreneurs may operate in the shadow economy.

[28] National Political Academy Ho Chi Minh and Friedrich Ebert Foundation 1997: 28.

[29] Ramamurthy 1998:29.

fleet of vehicles, but also looked after the former customer contacts so that his clientele was composed of 50% new customers, and 50% of customers from his former state company.[30]

- Conspicuously low in comparison to China was the percentage of *officials* (3.7%). A significant section of the former cadres preferred out of "reasons of secrecy" to present themselves as "white-collar employees" rather than "cadres" to us especially since at the time of our survey the transition upwards from cadre to manager had just at that point in time been restricted although it was permitted again in 2002. A possible cadre status was indicated by the fact that almost a quarter (22.5%) of the respondents replied that they had been working in a public institution that as a rule is associated with cadre status. According to the 1991 Swedish-Vietnamese study mentioned above, 44% of the interviewed entrepreneurs (in rural areas 16%) were actually former cadres.[31] This number appears to us to be excessively high; but the report does not give any further indication about who was counted as cadre and about how the choice of respondents took place. The study (s. above) of the National Political Academy and the FES suggested likewise that former civil servants and cadres were often classified as a unified category.

- Historically conditioned (the independent republic of South Vietnam till 1975 had a market economy system), *"politically unreliable people"* and former *"class enemies"* were to be found above all in South and Central Vietnam. To some extent they were forced to push into the private economy due to their lack of chances in a socialist country. Since they were trying hard not to be conspicuous in the society, most of this group were small traders. A manufacturer, former officer of the South Vietnamese military forces, reported to us that after the collapse of the Saigon regime and the re-unification he was unemployed while having to support eight children. He could not find work with state companies because of his past. So he had been re-educated as a street trader, after which he opened a small restaurant. This brought him the capital he needed for his food company that he had then founded with members of his family. The quality of his products led to a continual expansion of production and the expansion of his company. He was helped by his knowledge that he had acquired during numerous sojourns abroad in Europe and the USA. With the help of his knowledge of foreign languages he was able to read the corresponding foreign, specialist literature. A French company finally invested in his company so that he was able to expand it. He complained however about the massive difficulties which entrepreneurs face as well as the continuing discrimination.

---

[30] Interview, Danang, 3 January 1997.
[31] Ramamurthy 1998: 29.

- One needs to differentiate them from the "former capitalists" who indeed are counted amongst the "class enemies" but who insofar emphasize that they had acquired through their earlier entrepreneurial activity knowledge and skills which had come of very good use in their renewed entrepreneurial activity. Furthermore a part of this group possessed sufficient capital which they had brought into secure keeping after the communist victory in 1975, and which could now be brought into use as starting capital. Capital and knowledge made possible the development of larger companies. In Ho Chi Minh City the former capitalists count again already amongst the major entrepreneurs that have grouped themselves together in an influential association (UAIC-HCMC). At any rate 23.1% of the fathers of the entrepreneurs interviewed had earlier possessed their own company. Here this could be connected to the collective entrepreneurial family memory.

- The *Vietnamese group of Chinese ethnicity* is not surveyed in more detail in this study. They traditionally form a strong entrepreneurial group that Vietnamese society responded to with extraordinary distrust, prejudice and to some extent also with envy. Due to the strained relations between these two population groups, it is difficult for observers from outside to obtain more exact information. These Vietnamese dominate the urban Vietnamese consumer goods market even in Hanoi.[32] They could draw both on capital from relatives in the Chinese area and on commercial relations abroad that gives them a noticeable advantage against the entrepreneurs who are of purely ethnic Vietnamese origin.

- A section of the private entrepreneurs come from the *individual economy* sector (11.7%). During their self-employed work that often lasted many years, they had accrued the necessary resources (above all good relations with the authorities, steady relationships with suppliers and customers, capital accumulation etc.) and acquired the knowledge to dare the leap into the private sector. This decision does not always take place voluntarily. A successful, individual-run company can reach such a size that the administration cannot tolerate it any longer, and either compels the registration as a private company – which would certainly be disadvantageous in taxation terms for the entrepreneur – or orders its closure. At any rate a quarter (25.1%) had already some experience of their own small, individual company or in another private company.

- The fathers of most of the entrepreneurs interviewed were last of all employed in the public sector (in total 48.6% of whom 25.7% were white-collar employees, 8.7% workers, 6.0% technicians/scientists, 4.4% cadres or 3.8% managers), one-fifth peasants (21.3%), and 19.7% individual self employed entrepreneurs.

---

[32] Most of the inland consumer products which are sold in Hanoi are manufactured by Chinese companies in Ho Chi Minh City; Hoang Kim Giao, interview, Hanoi, 18 January 1997.

In Vietnam one needs to make a differentiation in respect of the wealthy entrepreneurial strata: in the North they were formerly officials or still employed as such from the party and the state, who in their own names or by means of a straw man founded a company, and by using their social capital had achieved riches. In the South on the other hand, they were for the most part members of the former "bourgeoisie" i.e. the well-to-do strata before 1975. According to a Vietnamese sociologist a third of the new rich stem from this group of persons. A further group of the well-to-do stem from the ranks of the ethnic Chinese minority that dominates some sectors in Ho Chi Minh City.[33]

As far as the previous occupation of the entrepreneurs surveyed is concerned, unskilled workers (8.5%), and – differing from China – farmers (1.1%) as well as former members of the armed forces (3.7%) were under-represented. For peasants there are still major restrictions in the way of migratory movements by the peasant population more so than in China, even if they are ever less easy to control. Moreover the peasants tend rather to be working in the smaller sector of individual laborers (craft, trade). A large part of the rural entrepreneurs do not stem from the agricultural sector. The Swedish-Vietnamese study referred to above, on the one hand contains no former peasants for the rural private industry, but on the other hand discerns that for 100% of the companies that had to close between 1991 and 1997, agriculture was the primary source of income for their owners before the founding of the company; this is an apparent contradiction.[34] To a not insignificant extent they may have been working as white-collar employees or rural officials (e.g. in collectives), and so might have been no longer counted as peasants.

In addition there is another explanation: peasants (but also workers and former soldiers) possess in general neither the necessary resources (such as finance capital or special connections) nor specific professional knowledge that would make a start as a private entrepreneur possible, or at least easier. In contrast to China, the agricultural reform in North Vietnam in the late 1980s did not lead to general capital accumulation amongst the rural population that could then have been used for founding a company. Furthermore, rural companies as existent in China appear in Vietnam's secondary sector to be only marginally present, so that here the basis for rapid, private sector development is missing.[35] People who work for state companies are attracted by the social welfare system so that this circle of persons only decide slowly and gradually to switch into the private sector. Rural inhabitants are mostly registered as "indi-

---

[33] Cf. on that Trinh Duy Luan 1995.

[34] Ramamurthy 1998: 34/35.

[35] Vietnamese references to government companies at the local level which have a certain similarity with rural firms in China (township, village, and privately owned enterprises), are not realistic. This is so especially in view of the fact that it is precisely those firms in Vietnam who lost out most of all from the reform of the state enterprises; a large number of them were closed in the course of the reduction of the state companies. they decreased in number from about 12, 000 to about 7,.000 at the beginning of the 1990s.

vidual laborers" even if in terms of occupation, as our survey showed, they actually should be classified in the larger private sector.

Whereas the (familial or occupational) origins from the ranks of cadres were in China fairly openly admitted, in Vietnam the conspiratorial answer prevailed. In the last analysis, one could ascertain that former cadres (or employees in the public services) form an important segment in the question of origins of private entrepreneurs. It was different with the managers. A significant number of Chinese entrepreneurs came out of the rural management area. In Vietnam there is not much of an element of rural and state sector companies, and that is the main reason for the low percentage of managers amongst the Vietnamese entrepreneurs. Instead the proportion stemming from former entrepreneurial families is higher than in China especially in the southern part of the country.

The interviews in both countries made clear the great significance of the entrepreneurship for social ascent in both nations, above all because there are now almost no more legal and system-related limitations for this ascent. Through the business reforms, the social and also the spatial mobility has increased, the old membership of classes as formulated by the party is increasingly dissolving. New social group criteria replace criteria such as familial or class origins, *Danwei* or belonging to urban or rural areas. The transition to market economic relations changes social structures too. The market economy regroups the position of people in this structure, and breaks up "traditional" status symbols and determining criteria such as place of residence.

2.1.3. *Prerequisites for founding an enterprise: material factors*
The preconditions for successfully founding an enterprise and running it can be sub-divided into material factors (capital, land, machines etc.), human capital (specialized knowledge, special skills, training) and social capital (especially connections, networks).

The founding of a company demands first of all access to production factors necessary for that (such as capital, business location, production equipment, machines, raw materials). Since the banks only grant credits to private companies with extreme reluctance, and real estate as locations for manufacturing is difficult to obtain, new entrepreneurs are faced with significant problems. As far as the access to capital for the founding of a company is concerned, the Chinese entrepreneurs we interviewed named the following sources (positions 1-3 characterize the grades of primary importance).

Table 27: Origin of the starting capital (China, in %)

Source	1. Place	2. Place	3. Place
1. Inherited	0.0	0.0	0.0
2. Own finances	60.0	35.3	10.1
3. Borrowed from relatives	14.3	24.2	15.7
4. Bank credits	14.9	23.4	30.4
6. Borrowed from local governments	0.0	0.0	1.1
6. Private credits	1.1	1.3	6.9
7. Financial interest in government firms	0.0	0.7	2.2
8. Financial interest in private companies	6.9	13.1	24.7
9. Foreign investments	1.7	1.3	2.2
10. Others	1.1	0.7	6.7
Total	100.0	100.0	100.0

Source: Own survey.

From Table 27 one can derive the following hypotheses:

- Capital acquisition out of inheritance up till now does not play a significant role in China. Moreover, right up into the 1980s capital accumulation privately was impossible. The first generation of entrepreneurs could not therefore expect any financial contribution from inheritances.
- Having their own capital (60% of the respondents put this in first place) possesses primary importance. Credits too or financial contributions from relatives (at 14.3 in first place) were perceived as part of the self-financing, because this money as a rule was not affected by matters of interest rates, and did not have to be paid out in pecuniary shares. But where do the large sums of money needed for company founding actually come form? Certainly not from regular pay or salaries. In 1996 the official, average, annual per-capita income of urban employees consisted of 4,377 Yuan, the rural equivalent income 1,926 Yuan, the average salary of staff in state enterprises 6,210 Yuan, and the annual salaries of directors of larger state companies (1993) between 10,000 and 12,000 Yuan.[36] Even if a director were to save his or her total salary over 10 years, the accumulated amount would however not exceed 120,000 Yuan, a relatively low sum for the setting-up of an industrial company. This is striking given that the 1% Chinese sample mentioned above (1995), states that the average value of the

---

[36] Zhongguo tongji nianjian 1997: 122, 293.

ple mentioned above (1995), states that the average value of the starting capital was on average 160,000 Yuan at the time of the founding.[37]

- As a result further sources of investment would have been needed. Self-acquired money of their own stemmed either from former work in the individual laborers sectors, out of leasing of state or collective firms or out of provisions, middleman transactions, or profitable side-businesses. In respect of the individual laborers sector, one needs to differentiate. The number of large earners in this sector is thoroughly limited. According to a Chinese study from 1995, the average, annual yearly income for the individual laborers lay at around 14,000 Yuan. 10% earned less than 2, 800 Yuan. The 10% strongest in income had, in contrast, an average yearly income of 84,000 per year.[38] As a result only the successful and better-earning people are in the position to found a larger private enterprise likewise to significantly expand the size of their enterprise. A further examination among 50 private entrepreneurs in Wenzhou demonstrated that people who lease state and collective firms and run them successfully, can earn an annual income of a number of ten thousands of Yuan or even a hundred thousand Yuan. Also those people who have successful work as an intermediary or are working on a performance reward basis (for example buyers and sellers of government companies), can count on an annual income of some hundred thousand Yuan.[39]

- In the course of the interviews, a manufacturer of washing machines in Hangzhou stated that in 1988 he had leased a business. A contract stipulated that he had to pay 15,000 Yuan as leasing. Moreover, he told us, he had been set an annual turnover target of 500,000 Yuan and a profit target of 15,000 Yuan. Leasing and profit were paid to the owner, the government of a municipality. But already in 1988 he had a turnover of 670,000 Yuan. For that he had received 20,000 Yuan. At the same time, he had also taken over the earlier debts of the company that amounted to 170,000, and had in compensation been given semi-finished goods amounting to the same sum. From the profits, he bought second-hand machines, rented a factory building and had it registered as his own company.

- A section of the entrepreneurs acquired their starting capital mostly through bank credits (14.9% of the respondents named this in first place). At any rate a quarter and a third respectively used bank credits as an extra source of income. This was surprising since the entrepreneurs but also the administrative authorities complained about the fact that obtaining bank loans for private entrepreneurs was extremely difficult. At the same time here a certain change had set in. Already in 1995 banks had provided coun-

---

[37] Zhang, Li and Xie 1996: 142.

[38] Geti gongshanghu, siying qiye shouru zhuangkuang diaocha 1996: 27.

[39] Hu Tui et al. 1992: 45.

trywide credits amounting to 10 billion Yuan to private companies.[40] And on the ground governments or financial institutions ignored central regulations that tried to limit the credits for the private sector. In Zhejiang, for example, credit institutions had simply disregarded the official limit of 100,000 Yuan. The thinking of banks is to favor enterprises that promise to be more successful with credits than inefficient state or rural enterprises.[41] The respondents we interviewed told us bank credits were generally acquired in the following ways. Firstly entrepreneurs use loopholes in the bank administration. The owner of the Jinyi firm in Hangzhou told us that first of all he had borrowed 10,000 Yuan from his father and brothers. This contribution he had then deposited in a credit cooperative, and finally borrowed 50, 000 Yuan from this co-op. Finally he deposited a further 50, 000 Yuan into another credit cooperative and thereby obtained another credit. In this way he acquired in total 150, 000 Yuan for the establishing of his company. Secondly entrepreneurs managed by means of social relationships (*guanxi*) to obtain bank credits. A shoe producer in Luohe stated in the course of the interview that he had only owned 4,000 Yuan as starting capital and that was too little to open a company. With the help of his mother who was employed by a credit cooperative, he told us, he had managed it to obtain from this co-op a credit amounting to 80,000 Yuan. The third possibility consists in the support from local authorities. If a local government resolves to support private entrepreneurial projects, whether it due to social relationships or due to economic considerations, then the corresponding company can obtain bank credits. In this way, for example, the owner of Yuwan Ltd. in Luohe planned a project for the manufacture of a patent treatment of bone marrow cancer. For the realization of this project, he needed a credit of about 400,000 Yuan. He managed to acquire 100,000 Yuan in his circle of relatives and friends. The local banks were however, not prepared to grant him a credit. So he created connections with the local mayor who then regarded his project with favor, and had it incorporated into the local development plan. With the approval of the city administration he managed then to obtain a bank credit. For a further large project for the manufacture of artificial manure in cooperation with the Academy of Science in Beijing, he obtained a credit amounting to 15 m Yuan from the Bank of Agriculture. The renown of the Academy, the economic significance of the project for agriculture and the preferential treatment by the city of Luohe, had the cumulative effect that the central government likewise supported the project. As a result, the entrepreneur finally did obtain a credit.

---

[40] Interview with the National Bureau for the Administration of Industry and Commerce, 28 February 1996.

[41] Interview with the Bureau for the Administration of Industry and Commerce in Zhejiang province, 5 March 1996.

The access to real estate for commercial premises is a further problem. According to the national land law only state and collective enterprises have a claim to be granted land. But private companies can lease plots of land. This can take place in two ways: either they find a state or collective institution which in their own name purchases a piece of land, in turn, to be leased to the private companies in question. Or the private entrepreneur undertakes a joint venture with the public sector company. An example of that is the Xiaohesan Ltd. in Hangzhou which set up a large amusement center on land belonging to a municipality. The municipality regarded the granting of the use of the land as a form of capital investment, and received from this "investment" significant royalties. In the three regions examined by us the local governments set up at the same time "business development zones" in which land was also leased to private companies.

In Vietnam the factual circumstances resembled those in China. Bank credits were hardly available, and if they were, then exorbitant rates of interest had to be paid. Often money has to be privatcly loaned for which exorbitant interest rates are charged. The colossal strains created by the interest rates hinder in both countries the qualitative consolidation of the private sector. A specific factor is the capital possessed by Overseas Vietnamese, the Viet Kieu. Officially their willingness to invest in their homeland is welcomed and supported by the Vietnamese government. This is done in the hope of a similar positive impact on the development of the country as has been the case with the Overseas Chinese in China. The two cases are, however, only to a limited extent comparable.

- Overseas Chinese have been able over a longer period of time – to some extent over a number of generations – to accumulate capital abroad successfully. Vietnamese first in the late 1960s and especially in the 1970s went abroad in large numbers. The period of time is comparatively little to accumulate sufficient capital that might be rewarded by investments in Vietnam.
- The geographical closeness of the successful Overseas Chinese in Singapore, Malaysia, Thailand or Indonesia to China made it easier for them to invest in their home country. Many Overseas Vietnamese, in contrast, live far from their native countries in the USA or in Europe.
- At present a significant amount of distrust still exists between Overseas Vietnamese and the Vietnamese state. On top of that there are unrealistic expectations of the financial power of the Overseas Vietnamese.

The official investment activity of the Viet Kieu in Vietnam was as a result up to 1996 relatively modest: merely 34 projects with a volume in total of US-$107 m were officially licensed. At any rate half of that was situated in the secondary sector that implied a more long-term investment activity (in contrast to the tertiary sector which permits short-term investment and promises rapid net profits). That expresses a certain level of confidence in the government's reform policies. But in relation to the total amount of foreign investment, the Viet Kieu investment seems rather modest in comparison. According to official statistics, up till January 1996 merely 1,354 projects with a total volume of (US) $18.59 billion had been officially approved.[42]

The actual impact of Overseas Vietnamese investment is, nevertheless larger than one would expect from these figures. Because on the one hand a section of the (US) $ 600–700 foreign investment which annually flows in to the country and which is transferred to the relatives of the Overseas Vietnamese for the upkeep of the families, is in turn used by the latter to found companies.

On the other hand a significant sum of Overseas Vietnamese capital flows outside of the official bank channels in to the country. Estimates speak of (US) $1-2 billion per year, of which a part runs directly into founding small and micro-companies whereas a further part flows into the illegal finance sector which provide credits to feed those private entrepreneurs who do not get (or want) a bank to provide a credit.[43]

A young female Canadian Vietnamese provides an example. During her period of residence over many years in Canada, she put to one side (US) $50,000 which she invested in a bakery which was registered in the name of her mother who lived in Ho Chi Minh City. Her mother already possessed a house standing empty with floor space of above 200 square meters which could be used as a production and marketing area, so the money could be used to purchase machines and raw materials. The machines were purchased out of the stock left by a Taiwanese bakery firm that went bankrupt. In order to avoid possible complications, the Canadian Vietnamese woman remained in the background as far as the Vietnamese authorities were concerned.[44]

2.1.4. *Prerequisites for founding a company: human capital*
2.1.4.1. *China*

The entrepreneur's skills and qualifications are an important precondition for commercial success. Amongst them count not only education and training but rather economic and social competence too. In our questionnaire we asked about the important factors for social success, 67.4% of the respondents in China named "own skills" and 83.7% "good knowledge of the market" as guarantees for entrepreneurial success.

---

[42] *Vietnam Economic Times*, February 1996: 10, table "Total Foreign Investment by Sector".

[43] On the Viet Kieu see amongst others Cao Ly Dung 1996a and 1996b; Korsmoe 1996.

[44] Interview, Ho-Chi Minh City, 28 November 1996.

Diagram 14: Relevance of different factors of influence for commercial success according to the opinion of the entrepreneurs interviewed (China, in %)

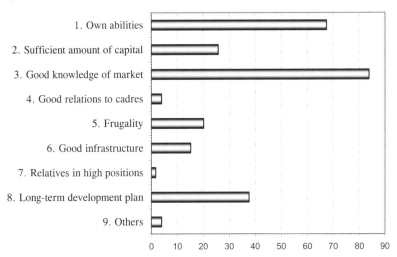

Source: Own survey.

We can hypothesize from Diagram 14 that the three elements thought by Chinese entrepreneurs to be most important (good knowledge of the market, personal abilities and long-term development plan) refer to individual subjective skills. The impersonal objective factors (such as sufficient amounts of capital, good relations to cadres or good infrastructure) were secondary as according to the entrepreneurs. Individual qualifications also influenced the external circumstances of the business activity.

Levels of training and professional experience were considered by the respondents to be indicators of human capital. Table 28 shows the educational level of the respondents. The Chinese entrepreneurs could be termed a well-educated group. 64.4% had reached the upper levels of the junior high, 19.2% were university graduates. With that an above-average share of them possess a qualification from an upper level of the education system – compared with the average level of the working population. In 1993, a study amongst 71,854 managers of state and collective firms found that the length of time spent in educational and training institutions was on average 12.2 years.[45] Amongst the entrepreneurs we interviewed the average length of education and training was 11.3 years.

---

[45] Zhongguo tongji nianjian 1995: 124.

Table 28: Level of education of the entrepreneurs interviewed (China)

Formal education	Urban areas		Rural areas		Total	
	Number	%	Number	%	Number	%
1. Illiterates	0	0.0	0	0.0	0	0.0
2. Primary school	7	6.4	6	8.8	13	7.3
3. Lower levels of junior high	28	25.7	22	32.4	50	28.3
4. Upper levels of junior high school	43	39.5	20	29.4	63	35.6
5. Occupational training institution	11	10.1	6	8.8	17	9.6
6. Polytechnics	14	12.8	12	17.7	26	14.7
7. University	6	5.5	2	2.9	8	4.5
Total	109	100.0	68	100.0	177	100.0

Source: Own survey.

This result approximates to the Chinese 1% sample taken in 1995:

Table 29: Educational level of the private entrepreneurs according to the 1% samples in 1993 and 1995 (China)

	Private entrepreneurs		Total working population
	1993	1995	
Illiterates	1.0	0.3	16.9
Primary school	9.9	8.2	37.8
Lower levels of junior high	36.1	34.9	32.3
Upper levels of junior high school	26.3	28.9	9.0
Occupational training institution	9.6	9.2	2.1
Polytechnics	11.7	13.1	1.2
University	5.5	5.3	0.7

Source: Zhang, Xie and Li 1994: 117; Zhang, Li and Xie 1996: 157.

However, there is a difference here. According to our survey the difference between urban and rural areas was rather low in respect of educational and training qualifications. According to the Chinese 1% sample (1995) on the other hand, the percentage of graduates of higher learning institutes (polytechnics/university) in urban companies was 21%, amongst the rural only 5%.[46] Two reasons for this difference could be responsible: firstly, our survey was only of private entrepreneurs in the industry sector, the Chinese on the other hand surveyed all sectors.

The educational level in the industrial sphere is certainly higher than in the agrarian or tertiary sector. But in the sphere of service industries (catering, repairs, etc.) it is low especially in rural areas. This circle of persons was, however, not the subject of our study. Also to be taken into account is the fact that we chose small and middle-sized cities as the places to survey, whereas the Chinese survey included metropolises such as Beijing and Shanghai in which the educational level of the private entrepreneurs is anyway higher.

According to our study, there appears to be no causal connection between levels of education and training, the size of the company and the private entrepreneurial success. But larger private entrepreneurs possessed on average a higher level of education than the private entrepreneurs in smaller companies. 60% of the smaller ones contrasted with 74% of the larger had a school certifi-

[46] Zhang/Li/Xie 1996: 157.

cate, at least from the upper level of junior high school or higher. Nevertheless education and training is, however, only *one* of the prerequisites for successful entrepreneurial activity. It is self-evident that private entrepreneurs have to read, write and be able to calculate numbers.

But the level of training alone – at least in the current phase of development of the private sector – is not decisive for the quality of the management of the companies, since most of the private companies in contrast to the state companies or to private entrepreneurs in industrial countries are still relatively small and run along traditional-familial lines.

Often they are labor-intensive companies with a low degree of technology. Only from a certain size of firm and with growing pressure from competitors does the use of modern technology become necessary. According to a study carried out by the Bureau for Administration of Industry and Commerce, in the 20 largest Chinese private companies with portfolios of assets of in each case over 100 m Yuan, the level of education of the entrepreneurs interviewed was clearly higher than that of entrepreneurs whom we spoke with. According to the former study 75% of those who completed the upper level of the Junior High School, 45% possessed a university education.[47]

But entrepreneurs have a growing need for new technologies and modern management. For example, prior to 1990 in Fuyang long-term working cooperations already existed between 20 private companies and both scientific research institutes and technical universities. Many private entrepreneurs bring in so-called "Sunday engineers" and "Sunday managers" from state and collective sector, so as to receive advice from consultants in their free time.[48]

According to our study, the educational level of the private entrepreneurs was higher in the rather backward region of Gansu than in highly developed Hangzhou. The Chinese 1% sample of 1993 showed likewise that the percentage of high school graduates in East China was lower than that in Central and West China.[49] Basically the educational level of the population in Zhejiang is of course higher than in Gansu. But in our case one needs to take into account that the City of Baiyin is a rather artificial, industrial settlement with a high percentage of scientific-technical, specialized technicians, so that a higher percentage of private entrepreneurs with university degrees there is not surprising. Secondly a large section of the Baiyin private entrepreneurs have a supply function for the local state sector. Since it is a difficult technical sphere, the work as supplier requires a correspondingly qualified training level. Thirdly, possibly the difficult framework and market conditions in a rather backwards region require as a compensation higher levels of technical qualification than in Hangzhou with its simpler access to markets, raw materials and information; as

---

[47] Geti siying jingji fazhan zhuangkuang 1995.

[48] Interview with the Bureau for the Administration of Industry and Commerce in Fuyang, 1 April 1996.

[49] Zhang, Xie and Li 1994: 118.

a result there people with a lower level of training also find good start-up conditions for private entrepreneurial activity.

Generally seen, occupational experience at the time of the founding of the
company and its development plays a more important role than school education. Amongst the most important experiences, one may count experience in the
specialized technical domain, and experience too in the spheres of business and
management. 42% of those in China we asked before the founding of the company had been working as managers, 9% as technicians, and 12.4% as small,
private entrepreneurs (individual laborers). In those spheres of the economy
those of whom we are writing collect not only experience but also at the same
time social capital (social relationships). The experience-based background
refers as well to knowledge about access to obtaining elements of production
(capital, production location, raw stuffs) or the building up of a circle of customers. More than a few of the private entrepreneurs had worked earlier in the
spheres of purchasing or sales in the state sector.

Our study showed that a close correlation apparently exists between earlier
occupation and size of company:

**Diagram 15: Earlier occupation of entrepreneurs interviewed and size of
their own firm (China, in %)**

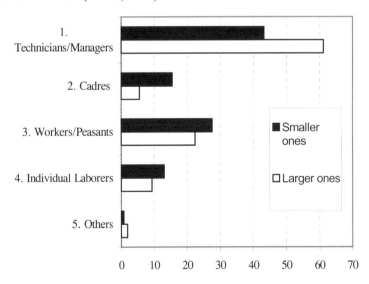

Source: Own survey.

Expertise in professional (technical) work or in business management is of
primary importance for the founding of companies. Peasants play an important
role as private entrepreneurs in the rural areas (processing of agricultural prod-

ucts and locally adapted products); workers in turn use their specialized technical knowledge and experiences for the founding of small companies. Individual
laborers have also collected experiences in enterprises. Cadres rarely become
larger private entrepreneurs; that also applies to rural cadres. Cadres it seems
are not predestined to become private entrepreneurs. Technical-professional
capital is clearly of more importance than social capital, but it is ideal when
both are present in one private entrepreneur.

**Diagram 16: Relationship between earlier occupation and size of output of
private entrepreneurs (China)**

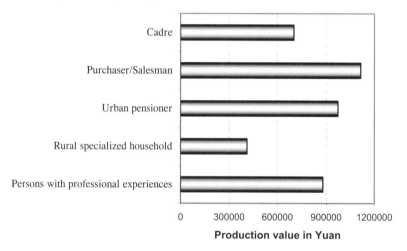

Source: Xiao Liang 1992: 173.

In the Chinese social science literature too there are discussions about the inter-
relation of earlier professional occupation and private entrepreneurial success.
According to Xiao Liang a close correlation exists between them. Diagram 16
makes clear the structure of the relationship between private entrepreneurs and
the level of production output of the private companies that he surveyed. People
with experience in purchasing and sales appear due to that experience at least to
be leaders in terms of level of output produced, whereas cadres themselves lag
behind technically skilled pensioners. But Xiao's structure of categories is too
superficial to be able to make unambiguous statements, especially as the classification "Level of output produced" as a marker of success appears to be thoroughly questionable. The sociologist Li Lulu argues in contrast, on the basis of
a survey, earlier occupations and former social position have no direct influence on private entrepreneurial success.[50]

---

[50] Li Lulu 1996: 103.

Table 30: Relationship between earlier occupation and turnover of private companies (China, in thousands Yuan)

Earlier professional occupation	Average annual turnover (in m Yuan)
Cadre and technician	2.31
Lower level white collar employees in state and collective sector	1.61
Former members of the armed forces	1.28
Urban individual laborers	2.06
Peasants	2.00
Earlier function	
Persons without function	1.89
Director in administrative institutions and enterprises	2.21
Cadres in enterprises	1.95
Rural functionaries	1.86
Persons, who have leased state and collective sector enterprises (*chengbaoren*)	2.27

Source: Li Lulu 1996: 103.

Firstly the table even contradicts Li's statement. The range of the turnovers fluctuates between 1.28 m (members of armed forces) and 2.31 m (cadres/technicians); that is more than one m Yuan in difference. Under the heading "Earlier positions" leading officials and company cadres come before people without a function and ahead of rural officials who often display a lower level of education. As a result Li's results do not differ in principle from ours. At any rate what is problematic is the formation of categories. Cadres and technicians form a common category; managers and workers are completely absent. Li classified all those as "peasants" who live in the countryside. Similarly to the cadres, peasants do not present a unified category. Peasants are on the one hand active in agriculture, others work in rural industrial companies or in the tertiary sector. So Li's classifications do not tell us very much. We hold that the category "turnover" as a defining characteristic for success is questionable.

2.1.4.2. *Vietnam*

In Vietnam too, a large section of the entrepreneurs we interviewed before they founded their company acquired the experiences and skills required either in the state and collective sector (39%) or in private companies (25.1%). In accordance with expectations, the share of private entrepreneurs stemming from the state sector amongst the North and Central Vietnamese with 42 and 54% respectively was clearly higher than amongst the South Vietnamese surveyed (30%).

The high figures for Central Vietnam are based on the collective sector that was massively supported there over a long period of time, whereas in the North state firms dominate. In the south on the other hand more private entrepreneurs come from the private (38%) than from the public sector.

The significance of previous knowledge and skills was emphasized too by a nationwide survey of 1,008 small companies in Vietnam, which was carried out by the Ministry of Labor, Invalids and Social Services, the *Swedish International Development Authority SIDA* and the *International Labor Organization*. According to that survey, about 80% of the managers and the private entrepreneurs of urban private companies or individual laborers had collected experiences in a similar or identical sphere, in which they later became active as private entrepreneurs. In rural areas that applied to almost 70% of the private companies. A relatively high percentage in urban regions acquired specific knowledge through occupations in the informal or illegal sectors (around 30%) whereas the corresponding percentage for the rural regions lay at 13%. The previous occupational experiences according to the private entrepreneurs played a central role in the choice of the sector, and of the product which a private entrepreneur manufactures in his or her company: almost 60% of the urban and 44% of the rural private entrepreneurs named these experiences in the first place as the possible reasons.[51]

Knowledge and skills can be acquired in training whereby it should be noted that it is not only specialist, technical knowledge that is important, but rather too the generally useful skills common in a production firm such as mental flexibility etc. The educational level of private entrepreneurs lies far above the average. According to their own statements, more than the half of the respondents (51.2%) had at least been to university, while a further 30% had passed through junior high school.

But the percentage of university graduates in the countryside (22.5%) was clearly less than in the urban areas (62.5%). The latter corresponded to a Vietnamese survey from the first half of the 1990s, according to which 29.1% of the rural private entrepreneurs had graduated through university.[52]

From the viewpoint of the entrepreneurs, having personal skills (including professional experience) played the main role in commercial success. About

---

[51] Ronnas 1992: 56, table 29, 72; table 42.
[52] Tran Minh Ngoc 1996: 35.

87% of the entrepreneur interviewed by us, a higher percentage than in China (68%) named as one of the three most important success factors having one's own skills, after which came knowing the market (58.9%), long-term orientation (43.6%) and being frugal with resources (39.1%). The factors named in second and third places also refer to particular skills of individuals. Other reasons that are independent of the personality of the entrepreneur such as capital, infrastructure, good relationships with influential people etc. move into the background in contrast.

For one thing a great degree of self-confidence is reflected here without a doubt. Successes were attributed to their own efforts; one accomplished something due to one's own special skills and endeavors, but not primarily on the basis of favorable external circumstances. A Chinese study underscored this high level of self-confidence. According to it, 93.1% of the entrepreneurs believe themselves to be successful, whereas only 83.9% directors of companies with other forms of ownership were of this opinion.[53]

Surprisingly, and in contrast to other answers to our questionnaire as well as to individual statements in the interviews carried out with the entrepreneurs, there was clearly a low degree of significance ascribed to relationships with influential persons (for the explanation see below).

The ranking order of the individual factors did not diverge strongly either between the urban and rural companies or between the regions. But to some extent there were large differences between the percentage share of the individual factors in the total number of answers. What is noticeable in spite of the relatively low total number, is the fact that in North Vietnam "Relationships with state cadres" (15.7%) was named five times more often than in South Vietnam (3.7%).

Many *private entrepreneur*s have acquired occupational knowledge in *state and collective sector*s that can be brought into their own companies with a profit. As an example, a manufacturer of perfume who was registered as an individual laborer, had earlier worked as a chemist in a state firm that amongst other things produced perfume. The chemical analysis of some products carried out secretly by the chemical engineer along with his brother who was employed in the same profession, enabled him first of all to make copies and then to improve on the originals. He was so successful that he could even export (to Russia and the Philippines).[54]

Not only state companies but also private ones were themselves victims of such practices. A worker at the private firm PANA based in Ho Chi Minh City, which produced ventilators for the home market, moved to Hanoi where in his newly founded firm he copied the products, and sold them under his own name. The legal protection against such product piracy is minimal as the owner of PANA, Nguyen Van Tai was to learn. The authorities in Hanoi when he con-

---

[53] Zhongguo qiyejia diaocha xitong 1998a: 18.
[54] Interview, Ho Chi Minh City, 5 December 1996.

fronted them with the matter, demanded 10 m VND in order to start proceedings against his former employee. Since he could not pay the sum, the illegal
production in Hanoi was not forbidden.[55]

In *private companies* whose owner or manager does not possess specialized
knowledge, production difficulties are almost pre-programmed, if the owner(s)
is not in a position in one form or another to draw on expert knowledge. In that
case entrepreneurs are happy to employ the same methods that the Vietnamese-
Canadian woman (mentioned above) did. Neither she nor her mother possessed
knowledge of bakery skills. The decision nevertheless to open a bakery was
among other things borne by a certain opportunistic thinking: many Vietnamese
use their resources (here: access to locations for production, relatively high
degree of personal capital, opportunity to buy machines), in order to make their
entry into the private sector under such apparently favorable circumstances.

Like many of her colleagues, the Vietnamese-Canadian woman tried to lure
qualified workers from her competitors so as to compensate for her own lack of
specialized knowledge. She promised them higher wages as well as free accommodation and catering. Wooing people away has in the meantime become
so common that, for example, large bakeries divide the working process into a
number of steps which are carried out by different employees so that none of
the workers can learn the complete working process. The origins of the raw
material and the composition of the individual recipes are kept secret from the
staff as far as possible.[56]

2.1.5. *Preconditions for founding companies: social und strategic capital in the form of social relationships and networks*
2.1.5.1. *Guanxi as social capital*
Social capital in the form of social relationships (Chin.: *guanxi*) and networks
(*guanxiwang*) are over and over again mentioned as important preconditions for
entrepreneurial success in both countries. The central factor is that they are
woven into the total social structures, and traditionally in both countries by
means of such relationships both individual and group interests were and are
asserted. The outstanding significance of the social phenomenon *guanxi* is not
only for private entrepreneurs but also for the society as a whole is something
that requires a deeper explanation.

Guanxi relationships are based on certain commonalities such as the same native place, shared experiences or other social connections, and are developed
first of all with people to whom a direct connection exists. *Tong*, the commonality, is the most important basis for *guanxi* (see below). But *guanxi* refers also
to personal contacts brought about by a third party or one created by bribery.

---

[55] Interview, Ho Chi Minh City, 6 December 1996.

[56] Interview, Ho Chi Minh City, 28 November 1996. The private entrepreneurs repeatedly complained in the interviews about the often practiced wooing away of staff; e.g. in the interview with
Ms Phuong, owner of the bakery Nhat Phat, Ho Chi Minh City, 18 November 1996.

Relationships can also be built up by means of presents, the granting of advantages, or through a third person acting as intermediary. They contain mutual obligations and expectations. For every action something is expected in exchange. *Guanxi* is less a private relationship than a role-play that induces expectations on the basis of past or present circumstances. Those who grant advantages, as a result gain "face", and are recognized by others as someone who behaves respectfully towards third persons. It is different in the vertical patron–client relationships that represent a vertical relationship of dependence; in contrast *guanxi* refers not only to relationships between unequal players but also to those between equal persons and institutions.

Social relationships have to be polished through favors, gifts or hospitality, whereby according to the deepness of a relationship, the material and social value of the favors and returned favors increases. Friendships and *Tong* relationships bring with them definite obligations such as permanent availability for help and support not only for the people directly involved in the relationships, rather too for members of their family and friends.

The denial of such assistance was and is negatively assessed in social terms as the absence of all form of human feeling, and as proof that someone does not love those with whom he is associated through natural bonding and so is obligated to provide support to. Both are considered to be the highest form of inhumanity and as a breach of moral norms. Making use of *guanxi* requires that both sides are in a position to give something such as the following: influence, protection, access to goods and services that are hard to come by, chances of social ascent or profit. Relationships with influential persons to whom no link exists are "knotted" (*la guanxi*).

That entails one seeks a person from one's own *guanxi* network who may be able to create the sought-after connection by means of different channels. A needs something from D. But between the two no *guanxi* exists. In A's network of relationships there is B, who is in contact with C. C is in a state of *guanxi* with D. A asks B to make contact with C. B helps A and addresses C. C wants to help B and makes contact with D. D wants to do C a favor and as a result helps A. Via such angled relationships new *guanxi* comes into being at the same time also new social obligations. *Guanxi* fulfills too the function of a social investment, and should be understood as relationships between people or institutions that are based on exchange, and are entered into by both parties with a knowledge of the rights and obligations entailed. The concept is as a result embedded in a network of mutual obligations and emotional components.

Guanxi require a high degree of sociability i.e. the ability to make contacts with other people and to maintain them. This requires distinctive informal services in the form of invitations to lavish meals, drinks and other forms of entertainment (invitations to gourmet restaurants, karaoke bars, discos or brothels). As an entrepreneur in Luohe formulated it:

> Eating and drinking together creates an artificial type of community that would otherwise be hard to achieve. We are not related, nor friends or fellow students.

And yet the evening spent together brought us into closer contact. Familiarity grew which is important for the further development of our relationship. *Guanxi* came about this way.[57]

A leading cadre of a local *Bureau for Administration of Industry and Commerce* admitted in a private conversation that familiarity first of all could be created against the will of one of those concerned:

> After a sumptuous meal with a lot of alcohol, the entrepreneur X invited me to a Karaoke Bar in a local hotel. Actually I didn't want to go because it was already very late. "Only just a bit of singing," the entrepreneur said to me, and dragged me to the bar. He invited some women to the bar to sing with us and to dance, and they animated me to consume more alcohol.
>
> Finally they persuaded me to go with one of the women into a separate room in a rear section. The entrepreneur and his friends went likewise into such rooms. At the end we met again. This shared experience was our secret that on the one hand created a certain familiarity, but on the other hand gave me the feeling that I had to show gratitude for the silence of the entrepreneur.[58]

In turn personal familiarity is a basic precondition for trust. Personal trust is insofar an organizational principle because it is based not only on feelings but rather on a specific form of rational calculation. This calculation assumes that participating actors have to follow social norms since confidence and *guanxi* contain mutual obligations. The players are aware of this and so with *guanxi* they enter into a mutual obligation that will be marked by expectations of mutually assisting the other's interests. So this normative contract is based on completely rational calculations. To have confidence in one another, presupposes the belief that the other person is ready to maintain the system of social rules.[59]

While there are clearly similarities between *guanxi* and corruption, the two phenomena are not identical because (at last theoretically) the social and ethical ideas behind them are different. Unlike corruption, *guanxi* is based on actual or imaginary commonalities, and so is associated with personal emotions (*ganqing*, feelings or *renqing*, human emotions). This entails somebody looking after the person concerned and being prepared to help him or her. Such feelings can be polished and expanded by means of favors and presents (*renqingli* i.e. presents in the interests of human feelings). Gift behavior of this kind can be found in the reservoirs of tradition of many peoples, and only becomes a factor in corruption within a more rational state structure.

There are different levels of intensity in *guanxi* that hang together with *ganqing*. The stronger the emotional component, so correspondingly are the relationships closer. And the less these components are present, so the more re-

---

[57] Conversation in Luohe on 7 October 1996.

[58] The informant, who did not want to be named, is known to the writer.

[59] Cf. Kao 1991 and Hamilton 1998: 62/63.

laxed are the relationships. *Guanxi* relationships on the basis of shared experience plus emotional bonding are consequently deeper than those which take place merely through the intermediary work of a third person. And the more profound a relationship is so the larger is its social, political and economic use i.e. its social capital. In China in this context people speak too of "human feelings credit cards" (*renqing xinyongka*).[60]

Under existing conditions, *guanxi* and backdoor practices run right through the total social structure just as they did before: from work (keeping or changing job) via business and finances (granting of commercial licenses, access to credits, size of tax payments) right up to everyday life (obtaining flats, access to good medical treatment) just to name some examples. Almost everyone finds it necessary to resort to *guanxi* in order to ensure living and work processes which are without friction. The era of reform has led first of all to an extension of *guanxi* relationships. Conditions that are strongly stamped by market economic factors with a simultaneous maintenance of the monopoly on power of a party, have brought with them an explosion in gift and hospitality behavior for the upkeep and development of *guanxi*. This has led in turn to significantly rising costs for individuals and institutions.

The basic cause of *guanxi* is the element of social insecurity especially when other structures that induce security such as the clan or the village community are no longer able to provide a socially protective function. Those concerned attempt in this way to achieve personal security and protection above all in conditions of legal and political uncertainty. Distrust and insecurity have the effect that people look for security and trust not in the political but rather in the private sphere and in *guanxi* relationships – an important factor for the formation of factions and cliques. But *guanxi* is not only important at the individual level but rather also for organizations (companies) and institutions (party organizations, associations) in order to achieve particular economic or other goals. So both state and private companies have taken to employing special agents for provision and sales whose task consists in manufacturing and polishing *guanxi*. The development of *guanxi* strategies and tactics has developed into a type of science so that in China people even speak of *guanxixue*, the science of relationships.

It is valid for both countries that *guanxi* represents neither a "typical Confucian" nor a "typical socialist" concept, but rather has to be interpreted as a principle of social organization. It is not only explicable socially or politically, but in the Chinese cultural domain, applies in the People's Republic of China just as it does in Taiwan or amongst the Overseas Chinese. In the modernized conditions prevailing in Taiwan, for example, the phenomenon is visible above all in the *guanxi network* between companies (network or *guanxi* capitalism). Families are considered in business life to be rather hierarchical and "weak

---

[60] Cf. Li and Wang 1993: 49ff.

organizations" (Redding) whereas *guanxi* guarantees family-transcending bonding into a relatively stable network of relationships.[61]

2.1.5.2. *Networks as strategic group capital*

Whereas *guanxi* takes effect more on the individual level and contains individual strategies, networks connect a large number of actors (persons, groups) with one another. So they represent a clustering of *guanxi*, a *guanxi* network that entrepreneurs can use strategically i.e. for the assertion of group and individual interests.

At the same time, networks provide a connection between entrepreneurs and society, given that in China and Vietnam it is less the individual him/herself, and rather the individual embedded in social networks that is understood as the decisive economic actor. The term network refers first of all to a group of persons who stand in social relations to each other. Carl H. Landé summarizes thus:

> all individuals who find themselves in a given field, and who are within direct or indirect reach of each other. That is to say, they include all individuals who are connected directly with at least one other member of the network. Networks thus are not limited to individuals connected directly with the focal member of a given primary star, or those who participate in a specific coordinated action. Rather, networks include all individuals who are not totally isolated from each other, and serve as arenas for all of their interactions.[62]

A network consists of informal relationships between mostly equal social actors (unequal actors would mean patronage). They are based on the elements of cooperation and loyalty. Creation and maintenance of trust form the most important elements of successful networks.[63] The latter connect not only individuals and groups of individuals as well as clusters in which actors belonging to a network are active. As a result a network goes way beyond the individual element, especially as individuals are members of different networks and through individuals, networks are connected with each other. The "ecology of networks" a sociologist dubbed it once.[64]

Landé's definition does not tell us anything about the reason for network formation. As a rule this has the following aims:

- Attaining of economic advantages for organizing the company (easier access to markets, raw materials, public contracts, information, tax waiver or reduction) through social connections to important decision-makers;
- defense against disadvantages (positive use of influence on the local officials, avoidance of excessive restrictions);

---

[61] On *Guanxi* in general compare amongst other: Walder 1986; Oi 1989; Redding 1990; Yang 1994; Yan 1996; Kipnis 1997.

[62] Lánde 1977: xxxi.

[63] Frances, Levacic, Mitchell and Thompson 1991: 14ff.; Reese, Aldrich 1995: 124ff.

[64] Carley 1999: 9ff.

- political advantages (taking on of public offices, party membership, getting round political restrictions); networks provide for cognitive and affective assistance through the members of the network, and so strengthen the identity of the members and ensure their recognition inside and outside the group.[65]

In reference to the entrepreneurs we interviewed, relationships and networks have as their most important functions: (a) on the *political level* the ensuring of influence and the assertion of business-oriented interests; b) on the *economic level* obtaining and exchange of resources, goods and services as well as product cooperation; (c) on the *communicative level* the exchange of information; and (d) on the *normative level* specific expectations due to different commonalities.[66]

Under the conditions of one party rule i.e. prevailing legal uncertainty and strong corporatist and clientelist structures, networks represent on the one hand a strategic infrastructure for entrepreneurial success, and moreover the social capital of the group benefits the individual.

The sociologist Fei Xiaotong has also suggested that according to the Chinese idea of order and society, every person is not only a member of different social networks but rather an involved member inside individual ones too. He or she has to see to the maintenance of this order inside these various networks.[67]

One needs to point out that not all enterprises and enterprise activities are based on network interfaces. There are variations according to the political environment, access to resources and markets, sectors and other factors. There are formal networks, for example, through organized associations e.g. associations of entrepreneurs, through party and other structures as well as informal (clan, family, and *tongxianghui*, native place associations. Intra-familiar networks in turn function differently from inter-familial ones. So one needs to avoid perpetuating over-simplifying stereotypes like, "Chinese entrepreneurs base their business activities on networks."

In our study we referred to the significance of social relationships with two different questions. In Zhejiang we asked whether such relationships are used to obtain raw materials for cheaper prices. 58% of the entrepreneurs answered in the negative, while 42% agreed. The answers make clear that such relationships do not play an important role in all company processes. Especially under conditions of more developed markets such as in Zhejiang, to obtain the goods necessary for production the significance of relationships apparently decreased.

---

[65] On networks in general cf. Thompson, Frances, Levavic. Mitchell and Thompson 1991; Aldrich and Zimmer 1986; Axelsson and Easton 1992; Noriah and Eccles 1992; Nan Lin 1999.

[66] Similarly but without the political aspect: Aldrich and Zimmer 1986: 11ff. as well as Powell and Smith-Doerr 1994: 372ff.

[67] Fei 1992.

Diagram 17: Do social relationships and networks assist the inexpensive acquiring of raw materials? (Province Zhejiang/China, in %)

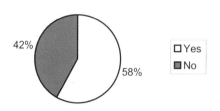

Source: Own survey.

In the interests of precision, we re-formulated the question for the surveys in Henan and Gansu. There we asked whether the membership of a social network had a positive effect on the relevant company. 86.2% of the entrepreneurs agreed, only 13.8% answered in the negative.

Diagram 18: Do social networks assist the development of your company (Henan and Gansu/China, in %)?

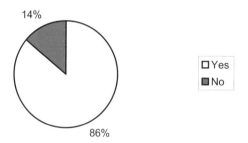

Source: Own survey.

The result made clear the paramount role of social relationships. For that there are different levels of relationships with different functions and varying rules. Four forms can be differentiated which partially overlap each other:

- the level of families and relatives;
- the *tong* level, persons to whom relationships exist due to sharing common geographical origins or common experiences;

- the bureaucratic level, relationships to officials and institutions of party and state;
- The business level (customers, suppliers, banks).

We differentiate in that between the *strong ties* which are based on social commonalities (kinship, *tong* relationships), and the *weak ties* which are not based on such commonalities whereby the degree of strength or weakness depends on the four factors: length of time of a relationship, emotional intensity, familiarity in getting on with another, and reciprocal services that characterize the bond.[68]

Strong-ties relationships refer to rather "broken-in" relationships to persons and groups, with whom an actor is associated through "natural" bonds, *weak ties* refer to looser relationships to persons outside of such natural bonds. As a result *weak ties* bring an actor into new networks of relationships and communicate to him/her new ideas, new information and access to new resources, although *strong ties* go deeper and are easier to mobilize. Above all persons with weakly shaped relationships outside of their immediate life surroundings (family, clan, village) have to rely on a multiplicity of *weak tie* relationships in order to survive as an entrepreneur. Li has pointed out that both types of relationship are important: *strong ties* are more helpful given institutional uncertainty, *weak ties* for market uncertainty.[69]

(1) Strong ties: the levels of family and relatives

The traditional Chinese family differentiates itself from the modern Western ones not because of their patriarchal and hierarchical inner structure, but also above all in the south through the embedding in groups based on descent (clans) whose members are derived from common ancestors, which carry the same family name, and regard themselves as blood related. In the rural areas they mostly live in one place and form stable units with spheres of economic activity, cults and solidarity. Members of a clan are considered to be persons with whom trust exists, and in economic terms, when somebody is given a job a high degree of loyalty is expected from clan members. Many rural enterprises in Central and South China are "clan companies" (*jiazu qiye*), because all the employees or a significant section of them are members of the entrepreneur's clan.

In general, familial relationships in Chinese society play as they did before a paramount role,[70] and are based primarily on trust. But we need to differentiate between urban and rural areas. According to a Chinese study (1993), 64% of the respondents in rural areas named their relatives as the most important group from whom they would expect help; a long way behind followed neighbors (14.3%). Only 33.1% of the respondents in urban areas, named relatives as the

---

[68] Cf.. Granovetter 1973.
[69] Li Fang 1998: 180.
[70] Sun Liping 1996: 20-30.

most important group of helpers, followed by their supervisors (17.7%), work colleagues (14%) and friends (12.%).[71] The urbanization processes apparently leads to a decreasing role for the family. Whereas in traditional societies, economic use was rather of peripheral significance, the economization of society has placed commercial advantages more strongly in the foreground.

Family relationships possess internal and external function areas. Inside a company, this refers to the employment and cooperation of members of the family or relatives (clan members). In almost all of those companies visited by us, members of the family and relatives played an important role, to some extent all leading company positions were in the hands of such persons. This was also confirmed by another Chinese study (1993) according to which 45.1% of leading company personnel in private companies were either directly related with the owner, or at least indirectly connected through being a relative, and this was a factor when being given the job (recommendation by relatives).[72] This applies to a particular extent to wives and children whereby the first in many cases are responsible for the spheres of accounts and finance. According to our study, 45.2% of the wives of the respondents interviewed had taken on such functions. A further Chinese study (1999) confirmed this: according to it over half of the spouses (50.5%) worked in their spouse's company, likewise one-fifth of the grown-up children (20.3%). 37.5% of the respondents interviewed were of the opinion that administration through one's own family members was the basis for their companies to develop in a stable way.[73] In contrast to Western companies, Chinese and Vietnamese family firms are considered to be the property of the family and not of an individual.

Family relationships already play an important role in acquiring capital for founding a company. Since private entrepreneurs as a rule hardly have access to bank credits, members of the family and relatives represent an important source of credit. A company for manufacturing molds in Luohe, for example, was founded for the most part by four brothers sharing in capital provision; they each worked for the company. The oldest possessed as main owner and director 50% of the shares, the other brothers shared the other 50%. The second oldest was responsible for direction of the finance sphere, the third brother for the production, the fourth for distribution.

Amongst the respondents interviewed there were different opinions about the employment and participation of members of the family and relatives in their own companies. As a rule the entrepreneurs welcomed such involvement. The owner of the Juying GmbH in Baiyin thought under the current social conditions that it was problematic, indeed even dangerous to place one's trust in people who were not family members. Despite best pay, he went on, outsiders were seldom truly reliable. The owner of a factory for heat insulation mate-

---

[71] Li and Wang 1993: 47, 48.
[72] Zhang, Xie and Li 1994: 138.
[73] Zhongguo Gongshang Bao, 15 May 1999.

rials in the same city employed both of his children, his daughter-in-law, his brother and sister-in-law, a nephew and another in-law in his company. A further entrepreneur reported that ever since a leading employee had defrauded him, he only gave jobs to members of his family and relatives. He had found employment for all six of his siblings. His older brother was responsible for purchasing, a further brother and a sister directed two branches, and a third brother was responsible for the production at the main factory plant. A sister was in charge of the works canteen, another one the marketing department.

Some entrepreneurs believed that members of the family and relatives should not work in their own companies since this commonly led to conflicts in the course of the company's work and differences of opinion. They argued that one could not measure members of the family and relatives by the performance of a normal employee. One had to behave in the appropriate way; it was difficult to criticize them or to transfer them they thought. So some entrepreneurs had paid off members of the family and relatives network, in that they gave them a sum for the founding of their own company, and in this way were able to complete the separation in a harmonious manner.

Now it is certainly not the case that family companies per se contradict the model of a modern company order as the Bureau for the Administration of Industry and Commerce believed. After all, in the USA 90% and in Western Europe between 75 and 95% of all companies are family companies.

As examples from other countries show, functioning depends primarily on the human factor. The participants must be able to understand each other, and a minimum qualification is necessary to become an actor. That means that the relations of employment have to be based in the first place on qualifications and the interests of the company, and should not be allowed to rest on obligations to relatives.

Secondly it has to be decided from case to case. Under certain circumstances such as a high degree of political, legal or social insecurity, it may be that a family company based on the factor of trust is able to operate more flexibly and securely than others. Employees who exist in a close relationship with the entrepreneur due to the familial obligations are more prepared to continue the work even when a company finds itself in economic difficulties. Lack of confidence in the government, Bowne and Rose argue, contributes to the success of family companies. [74]

Above all with stock corporations the element of family played an important role. In 1995, 36% of all private entrepreneurs in China were registered formally as stock corporations (something equivalent to limited companies), the average number of shareholders or partners consisted of 2.7 persons.[75] Our survey established that 90% of the second shareholders were direct family members (spouse, son, brother). The involvement of people from outside of the

---

[74] Bowen and Rose 1998: 443.
[75] Gongshang xingzheng guanli tongji huibian 1996.

family was rather the exception. As explanation for that, entrepreneurs named as an important reason that when there are business problems, outsiders tended to leave the company, and that when there were company successes conflicts concerning distribution of profits arose. Precisely under conditions in which contracts do not play an important role, family members have to represent the element of trust.

Familial relationships play an important role too in contexts outside the company especially when family members and relatives exercise leading functions in state or party organizations. The reason is that they facilitate the access to resources, capital and markets. According to the 1% sample amongst private entrepreneurs (1995), 58.5% of the relatives to whom the entrepreneurs had closest contacts, were managers and technicians in state companies or officials in public service.[76] Two examples out of our survey underline this point: the owner of the Lanling clothing firm in Hangzhou reported that at the beginning of 1988, he had wanted to have his company re-registered as a "collective company". For that he would have needed a connection with an institution that would approve this (illegal) step. His brother at that time worked at the local university for silk technology, and possessed good relationships to the deputy vice-chancellor of the university. His brother made the contact with the vice-chancellor with the result that the private company could be re-registered as a company belonging to the university, and with this classification it obtained a bank credit amounting to 200,000 Yuan. As a service in return, the entrepreneur was required to divert 50% of the profits to the university. Only in the course of the improvement of the social and political framework conditions, did our private entrepreneur decide, in 1995, to give up the "disguise" as a collective company, and to have his company registered once again as a private firm.

In a further case (the brakes firm Xingfa in Hangzhou), a respondent who wanted to found a private company but who possessed neither the capital nor a location for production, saw himself forced to take over the highly indebted factories of a research institute. The close connections of his brother to the director of the institute enabled him to lease the factory. He took over the debts of the factory, and in return the machine plant was transferred into his possession after some years. He paid the institute both rent and a leasing fee.

In conditions of institutional and legal uncertainty, entrepreneurs acquire capital, and recruit a working force and administrative personnel very often from their own families, or for external processes count on family members with access to the resources needed (capital, raw materials, markets and information). The factors of trust and mutual help are important standpoints. But our conversations suggest that with increasing size and modernization of a company, the family factor is gradually declining in favor of the employment of family members. This is because familial bonding and obligations often impair company processes since criticism or making redundant badly or inefficiently

---

[76] Zhang,Li,Xie 1996: 160.

working relatives may lead to massive, intra-familial confrontations. Family members are often to a lesser degree controllable or guidable, and irrational elements may lead to conflicts.[77]

(2) Strong ties: Tong-relationships

Tong, the commonality, is the most important basis for *guanxi*. The *tongban* (classmate), *tongbao* (regional compatriot), *tonghang* (colleague in a special-ized field), *tongshi* (work colleague), *tongxiang* (compatriot from the same village or township), *tongxue* (school colleague) etc. all exist in special rela-tionships to each other (*tong* relationships). Not all people with whom such relationships exist can be included in the network of a private entrepreneur, rather only those to whom close relationships exist and who hold important positions (such as manager or cadre), and could be of use to the entrepreneur. At the same time *tong* relationships are based not only on the economic advan-tage, but also on friendship and trust too. Assistance that has been completed does not require any direct service in exchange, but is rather to be understood as an investment for the future i.e. the service in return might later become due, but need not necessarily do so at anytime in the future. For state companies, relationships to university and former colleagues play a more significant role than for rural ones, for which familial or village relationships carry more weight.

The owner of the machine tool company Chunfeng in Hangzhou reported, that after a local bank declined his attempts to obtain credit, his deputy director at the company (a female) who was at the same time a shareholder in the com-pany, contacted a former fellow schoolgirl. The latter was working at another bank, he told us, and his deputy director asked her to provide assistance. In this manner it was possible for him to receive a credit amounting to 700,000 Yuan.

The following statement of the entrepreneur of the firm Yangguang in Hangzhou made clear the function of social relationships for the development of the company:

> Because of the conflict with the director of a state company for cameras in Hang-zhou, I switched to the private sector. When founding the company at the beginning of 1986, I put together with seven acquaintances 80,000 Yuan in order to set up this factory for optical equipment as a collective company. My share of the sum (10,000 Yuan) was lent to me by a former fellow-student with an interest rate of 15%. When the company some years later got into difficulties in business, it was above all friends from state companies, former colleagues, but also customers (state compa-nies) who helped us. The relationships to the latter still stemmed for the most part from the days of my work for my former work unit (*danwei*).
>
> When things were going financially better, I invested 300,000 Yuan in a new import and export subsidiary in Ningbo which my younger brother was supposed to take over. The latter was at the same still head of a department in a large, foreign

---

[77] Li Fang made a similar observation: Li Fang 1998: 168ff.

trade company owned by Zhejiang province and wanted himself to become self-employed.

His excellent contacts in this field offered a good basis for a business. In 1990 we transformed our company into a private limited company with two subsidiaries (in Hangzhou and Ningbo). Nowadays there are three shareholders: my younger brother, a former fellow-student of my brother's, who likewise earlier had worked in large state companies, as head of department, and myself. Most of the heads of departments are also former fellow students of my brother's. We possess excellent contacts to the local government that very much supports us. As a result, it is not difficult for our firm to obtain credits. One time we obtained an amount of ten million Yuan as a credit.... Since private companies are not allowed themselves to take part in any import or export work, we were able to complete foreign trade deals only in the name of the foreign trade department of Zhejiang University, of which my brother is a graduate.[78]

(3) Weak ties: the bureaucratic level

Relationships to officials and institutions are an important precondition for successful business activity. From the point of view of entrepreneurs, such social relationships are necessary because the local authorities possess as they did in the past extensive powers concerning important, economic, financial social and political resources.

Wank named three elements with which entrepreneurs are able to influence officials: (a) by financial or substantial contributions (gifts, privileges); (b) through real or fictional employment in companies (as consultant or manager) with correspondingly high salaries; (c) by means of partnerships (patronage). An example of this is through giving a stake in the company, whereby the official in question does not obtain capital shares but rather a share of the power or posts in the advisory board. Since direct contributions are illegal, and could without a doubt be used against an entrepreneur (e.g. in cases such as the uncovering of corruption amongst local cadres protecting an entrepreneur, or in cases of conflict between local cadres), entrepreneurs seek a transition from *clientelistic, one-sided, independent relationships* to *symbiotic clientelism* especially in strongly commercialized regions.[79]

The first contains a significant degree of uncertainty, because every change of cadres makes the building up of new relationships necessary, mostly associated with high costs in terms of time and money. The latter determines *guanxi* to and with authorities that are profitable for both parties. Such institutional relationships are in the rule of longer duration, and are not so strongly based on personal, individual relationships. But in most fields of activity the dependent patron–client relationship predominates. Let us take as an example the access to credits. In the framework of our interviews, private entrepreneurs expressed

---

[78] Conversation on 12 March 1996.
[79] Cf. Wank 1995: 166ff.

themselves relatively openly about credits that they had obtained due to their personal relationships with local officials.

The interest rates for these credits were to some extent far under the official bank interest rates. The owner of the company Yuwang in Luohe e.g. had employed a former leading cadre now in retirement; the latter had formerly worked as a department head in the finance authorities of the province. This person then became head of development planning in Yuwang. Thanks to his connections there to the authorities for whom he had previously worked, he was able to obtain a credit amounting to three million Yuan from his former employer.

A manufacturer of decorating material in Yancheng county was at the same time a member of the People's Congress of the province, the city and of that county, and had at his disposal excellent contacts with the party secretary of the city, Luohe, as well as to the mayor of Yancheng. When in 1987 he wanted to lease a further rural company, around two-thirds of the cadres of the municipality in question were against his proposal. Finally he repeatedly invited the secretaries of the city party and the county, and the mayor of that county to visit his main factory, in order to make clear that the local party leadership supported him. By way of the relationships named, he obtained credits without interest amounting to 100,000 Yuan from the province government, and 100,000 Yuan from the local government. In 1995 he landed in a massive financial crisis due to market fluctuations. He could neither serve the credit repayment installments nor pay his employees. Nevertheless, he was able through his relationships with the government of the province to receive a renewed credit amounting to 500,000 Yuan.

When private entrepreneurs possess good relationships to local cadres, then they are also able to profit from the state and collective companies. In this respect, the XVth Party Congress 1996 passed a resolution to the effect that the majority of the middle- and small-sized state companies should be privatized. After that the local authorities proposed extensive privatizations plans. Private entrepreneurs could buy out state companies at an inexpensive price with the help of their relationships to officials.

In Baiyin during our period of residence there for the research, six state companies and a large number of rural companies were sold. Private entrepreneurs showed themselves at that time to be hardly interested in highly indebted state companies, given that they also still feared conflicts with the blue-collar employees. Instead they were interested rather in rural companies which are easier to deal with.

Furthermore countless company activities require clearance by the local authorities e.g. in the case of larger investment projects or with the purchase of real estate and quality certificates, as well as with environmental or production clearances. Officials often expect for such clearances a service in exchange or the granting of an advantage of some kind. Legal uncertainty and elbow-room for decision-making allow the civil servants responsible either to grant authorization quickly or to put the matter to one side. Two examples of that illustrate the point:

The Hangzhou firm Xiaohesen signed a contract of cooperation with the mayor of a municipality for the construction of an amusement park with an investment sum of 100 m Yuan. The land required for that was quickly made available to the entrepreneur since the mayor could himself grant the clearance without anyone else being involved. At the beginning of the construction, officials of the planning department, the environmental authorities and the city's police all appeared, and demanded the termination of the construction work. They argued that from the viewpoint of the authorities, the plan and its size breached the building regulations. Only after the entrepreneur formed "personal connections" to the party secretary and to the mayor of the city of Hangzhou, did he obtain the authorization for the completion of the project. He did not want to reveal details to us of how he had established contact with them.

A further example comes from the firm Lanyin in Baiyin. The owner narrated his endeavors to broaden his range of products from textile goods to the manufacture of rice wine. For a long period of time, he did not receive an answer to the corresponding application which he had made to the local Bureau for the Administration of Industry and Commerce.

According to a regulation of the local city government, somebody who makes an application can assume that his application has been approved if within 15 days they have not received an answer from the authorities in question. So he started manufacturing rice wine. Three months after commencing production, officials of the local authority appeared to carry out a quality control, and blocked further production; they claimed the quality of the product had not matched up to the standards set by the local authorities. After that the entrepreneur sent a sample of his product to the relevant province authorities, and received a positive answer from them. At the same time the Baiyin authorities continued to forbid further production. The entrepreneur explained: "I know that here only *guanxi* are of any use. But we lack the financial means necessary. In order to build up good relationships to these civil servants, we have to invite them to eat, dance and to karaoke. But a single invitation costs at least 2, 000 Yuan. I can only hope that such civil servants will be fired in the future."

In addition legal insecurity and unpredictable officialdom make *guanxi* something that cannot be done without. Indeed the state has labored for some years to achieve an improvement of the legal framework conditions for companies, but the private sector suffers significantly as it did before from legal insecurity. As a result 64% of respondents interviewed were either not or only partially satisfied with the legal situation.

Although in the meantime there is a broad spectrum of legal constructions (e.g. in the spheres of tax or levies), local authorities try to exploit legal loopholes. As an example the owner of the Hangzhou advertising firm Niaobu reported that he was forced each year to pay levies of different kinds amounting to

10,000 Yuan. Such payments were charged e.g. for the annual inspections by the local Bureau for the Administration of Industry and Commerce and the tax authorities, the environment, police security, for the administration of the rural workforce (migrant workers), or in the form of different street levies.

According to another entrepreneur (the printers Daguan in Hangzhou), the police charged the most different levies for rural laborers such as residence permits (6 Yuan per head), security levies (48 Yuan per head) or levies for physical security (36 Yuan per head). Although the Bureau for the Administration of Industry and Commerce has published a booklet in which all the levy payments were set down, at the same time the entrepreneurs feared any notification of such levies and the accompanying allegation of illegitimate levies or "donations" could lead to revenge-driven actions by the relevant institutions. So from fear of the difficulties as a result they generally refrained from such reports.

Since it was a private company, direct governmental interference in the inner processes of the company is indeed not possible without something further being in question. Indirect interference is, by contrast, relatively common as the following example shows: the owner of the beverages firm Jinyi, a company with a turnover of 200 m Yuan (1995), was in 1997 the Vice-President of the National Youth Association and deputy of the Political Consultative Conference of Zhejiang province. Envious persons in the governments of the province and the city accused the successful and highly-placed entrepreneur of taking too little interest in the province and city, and going over the heads of their leadership to seek the support of central authorities. They criticized his alleged "arrogance", refused to visit his firm, and indicated to the local banks that his company should not be granted any credits. The banks circulated a rumor damaging to his business that the firm Jinyi had financial obligations amounting to 300 m Yuan. The entrepreneur explained:

> Entrepreneurs in China are different from the Western ones in one key point. We have to invest 90% of our energy and time for the manufacturing and upkeep of good relationships to state offices and for social networks.

Without a doubt, cadres possess an especially high degree of social capital especially when they are bonded into cadre networks and the party structures, and are able to make use of their relationships for entrepreneurial activities. According to a Chinese study, private entrepreneurs believed (17.2%) they were better proficient in manufacturing *guanxi* than did the heads of companies with other forms of ownership (10.5%).[80]

Many entrepreneurs declared in the interviews with us the extent of social relationships had played a central role in their consideration of whether or not to make themselves self-sufficient. The head of department for individual firms and private companies under the Bureau for the Administration of Industry and

---

[80] Zhongguo qiyejia diaocha xitong 1998a: 16.

Commerce in Zhejiang explained this with the sentence: "There are not many cadres who without difficulty were able to make the first leap into the sea," (i.e. into self-employed business life, author's comment). "Most of them had earlier worked in the corresponding spheres of state companies."[81]

But the term "cadre" has to be differentiated, given that it includes very different groups (such as leading officials from the party and the state, administrative and rural officials as well as people in official posts at industrial state companies). Unlike administrative cadres, managers in state companies or rural firms, and to some extent village officials are involved to a noteworthy extent in the economy.

Relationships to officials in public office and companies are decisive for the existence and development of the companies. So the entrepreneurs make enormous endeavors for relationships which ensure *guanxi*. Family members, relatives and friends play an important role here. As explained above, to a significant extent the father of entrepreneurs were either former or active cadres. The same applies to their wives: (in China: Urban areas: 23.3%; Rural areas: 13.3%; in Vietnam: 52.5% white-collar employee or cadre), in China but above all for their offspring in employment (Urban areas: 26.0%; Rural areas: 19.2%) as well as for relatives (Urban areas: 39.1%; Rural areas: 26.4%) and close friends:[82]

---

[81] Interview with the Bureau for Administration of Industry and Commerce in Hangzhou, 5 March 1996.

[82] Zhang, Li and Xie 1996: 159,160.

Table 31: Occupations of closest friends from private entrepreneur (China in %)

	Urban Entrepreneurs	Rural Entrepreneurs
Specialists & technicians	16.2	12.3
Administrative cadres	26.6	18.9
Manager	19.6	23.3
Worker	6.2	4.6
Soldiers	0.9	0.5
White-collar employees in service industry sector	8.3	2.6
Peasants	2.9	13.8
Self-employed & craft persons	16.0	20.2
Unemployed	1.0	0.8
Others	2.2	3.1

Source: Zhang, Li and Xie 1996: 160.

The further the distance from relatives, apparently the more the degree of contacts to cadres increases: As a result the entry into networks does not come about by way of family members, relatives and friendship, but rather too by way of the following factor: the choice of leading figures in companies who bring with them into the company the important, social relationships, and thus to some extent only get a job there because of that. More than three-quarters (78.9%) of the deputy heads of the companies in the private company surveyed by us were formerly leading figures in state companies, a further 8.3% were former cadres. Of the heads of departments, 96.3% had been formerly leading, white-collar employees in state companies, 14.7% former administrative officials.

In Vietnam in this field, matters turned out to be very similar. Indeed due to the limited size of companies, the numbers of deputy-directors and heads of department were clearly lower in the Vietnamese areas which we surveyed, but here too 30% of the deputy-directors and 27.9% of the heads of department were formerly leading figures of state companies, and 18.3% and 16.4% respectively were former administrative cadres.

And almost a quarter of the Chinese (24.8%) and over a fifth of the Vietnamese entrepreneurs (20.2%) declared that they had received "consultancy" from party or administrative cadres. Our survey of cadres at the Central Party

School in Beijing determined that almost the half of the officials interviewed stated that they had advised private entrepreneurs with problems.

This is a further indication as to which network relationships are useful for the company leadership. Through the links to cadres, entrepreneurs intend to maximize their room for maneuver, and to minimize the political risk. The relationship between cadres and entrepreneurs is not usually based on friendship, but rather on economically useful considerations.

The relationship between power and money is well explored in the Chinese literature as it is too in the media. Bribery is apparently an effective and widely common means to build up social relationships, although party and government have officially declared war on corruption.[83]

Corruption does not only take place in the form of monetary transactions rather also in the making available of material goods, services and favors (such as presents, costly hospitality, travel both within China and abroad, use of luxury cars provided by entrepreneurs). In Luohe we learned from an employee of the Bureau for the Administration of Industry and Commerce, that e.g. a three-star hotel which stood for sale, through the intermediary services of a deputy mayor was sold to his friend (a private entrepreneur) for an extremely cheap price. The service that the latter had to return, was to make available for the deputy mayor and his guests a suite and costly hospitality free-of-charge on a long-term basis.

A Chinese study of 200 entrepreneurs at the municipality level showed that there are specific relations of exchange between entrepreneurs and local authorities. The latter possess a spectrum of business resources which the entrepreneurs might wish to purchase. So social relationships are necessary, in which the private entrepreneur in turn has to invest. The study came up with the following relation between barters.[84]

What indeed is displayed here is first of all the services and services in interactive exchange to and from a public company, but the services and services in change displayed in Table 32 make clear for the private entrepreneurs what are also important resources which the local authorities have control over, and what these authorities or governments require as a service in exchange for making those resources available.

---

[83] See e.g. a contribution of the Organizational Department of the Central Committee of the CCP, "*Lingdao weihe bang dakuan*" (Why do leading officials help the "Rich"), in: *Jingji Ribao* (Newspaper for Economics and Finance), 6 December 1995; Yin Zhengkun 1996: 11-15; Shi, Pang 1996: 210-236.

[84] Chen Jianpo 1995: 24-32.

Table 32: Barter trade between companies and local authorities (China, in %)

A: Potential offers by the local governments to the entrepreneur:
(1) Local governments controls 37.3% of the available raw materials;
(2) 70.3% of real estate, which belong to counties or municipalities, is placed at the disposal of the entrepreneur free of charge;
(3) The participation in the investment made by local governments in private companies consisted of 28.2% of the starting capital;
(4) 48.5% of the credits are safeguarded by means of a security provided by the administrations of the counties or municipalities;
(5) Local authorities participate with 4.2% in investments made to assist expansion.
B. Service by the companies in exchange for local governments:
(1) 40% of the workforce who were recommended by local governments or by cadres, had to be employed by private entrepreneurs;
(2) 75% of the managing directors were stipulated by the government of the counties or municipalities;
(3) 25% of profits after taxes were paid to the governments of the counties or municipalities;
(4) In 33% of the 13 most important company procedures for making decisions, the local governments had some say in decision making.

Source: Chen Jianpo 1995.

(4) Weak ties: the direct business level

In all societies it is vitally necessary for companies to build up and to maintain relationships and networks (to customers, suppliers, banks and authorities). The difference to Western countries exists in the extent of such networks and their functions. In China they serve principally too for the obtaining of resources necessary for production, and for an expansion of sales.

A concrete example should make this clear. The owner of an aluminum window factory in Fuyang reported that he had earlier worked in a rural aluminum company as director. In 1993 he had decided to found his own private company. In doing that, he told us, he had started out with the following assumptions: first of all, the location was a center of the aluminum industry, secondly there were, he continued, adequate supplies of energy, thirdly the mayor of the municipality in which the headquarters of the company was planned for, was a friend who had already assured him that he could have that piece of real estate, and fourthly the director of the Bureau for Economic Cooperation of Fuyang city was likewise an old friend, who was in a position first of all to offer him five tons of aluminum for 60, 000 Yuan, and for which the payment would be expected only after the attaining of sufficient profit.

The owner of the firm Lubang in the same place (Fuyang) had previously been director of a joint venture company for leather goods. Through this operation he possessed excellent contacts with the province government's foreign trade company. When he founded his own private company for leather products, the former company participated in the firm to the extent of 3 m Yuan. All the products of the company were exported through the governmental company.

The following table underscores our own conclusions that relationships represent a central factor in business life. This is because about a quarter of the methods of obtaining materials and sales are based on personal relationships, in addition to which comes the element of other entrepreneurs which are based less on personal bonds than on the element of mutual advantage (Column 4). The latter likewise is a type of relationship even if this partially may well be based less on affective factors. At any rate, both columns of entrepreneurs when taken together suggest that more than half of all transactions are based on relationships of varying intensity.

Table 33: Methods for obtaining materials and sales of private companies (China, in %)

	East China	Central China	West China
1. Inclusion in government plans	2.3	1.4	2.3
2. Through personal connections	28.1	23.8	24.9
3. Through the market	36.6	47.1	40.4
4. Through different connections on the basis of mutual advantage	33.0	27.7	32.5

Source: Zhang, Li and Xie 1996: 155.

In business relationships *guanxi* and networks only function as a means of help given that the competition on the market continually increases. With good quality and inexpensive prices, relationships and networks can represent an additional means of promoting business: e.g. the owner (mentioned above) of the automobile brakes firm Xingfa in Hangzhou had earlier been a departmental head for marketing in a state company producing cars. Later with an engineer from the same factory, he founded a private company. The two of them developed a new, metal alloy for brakes which originally had to be imported. Due to this development, the Xingfa firm managed to make a supply contract with one of the larger automobile manufacturers in China, the Automobile Factory No 1 in Changchun. In 1995 Xingfa supplied 100,000 semi-finished products for brakes to that automobile factory. Some people believed that the entrepreneur possessed important friends, otherwise he would not have got such an order, they claimed. But this opinion was rejected by the entrepreneur: "The Automobile Factory No 1 twice sent several specialists in our factory, in order to check our manufacturing procedures and the quality of the products, and only then were we able to conclude the contract. Our company possessed advantages over the state companies: we can offer our products more cheaply, and are able to meet the delivery deadlines. So we have no fears about competing with state companies."

In the sphere of credit, relationships and networks play an especially important role because up till now the large government banks have a monopoly of the finance market. If a private entrepreneur has good relationships to banks, this makes it easier as a rule to obtain a credit, in the reverse case, the chances are almost nil. The owner of the Fushun factory for heating pipes in Luohe reported that he possessed personal capital amounting to 300,000 Yuan. After that he did not have enough money to cover the circulating (floating) capital required. A bank credit, he went on, was refused him so that for reasons of survival in business he bred 10, 000 rabbits on the factory lands, and then sold them in order to raise the circulating capital.

Good relationships to banks were achieved by means of different methods. The owner of Water Products Ltd. in Luohe reported that between 1988 and 1990, he had founded first of all a private clothing factory as well as a restaurant. In the interests of expanding his business and creating the necessary framework conditions for that, he had left the private sector for two years, he told us. During that time he took on the post of deputy director in the Agricultural Bank in Luohe, where he earned 800 Yuan a month. He had sold his restaurant, and leased the clothing factory to some relatives. Through the work in the bank, he got to know leading members of the city's government and developed good relationships to the bank director. With his support he founded finally a private company for water products. Due to his good relationships at the bank, it approved a credit to him of 16 m Yuan.

Keeping up social relationships requires – as mentioned – high investment. The entrepreneur has to provide lavish hospitality regularly for those persons important to them, and organize various amusement activities. A Hangzhou entrepreneur reported that he had earlier employed a nephew as a director. After the latter had acquired the necessary know-how, he made himself self-employed, and wooed away with him a number of customers. In order to re-build the good relationships with the old customers (above all a string of large, state sector, steel companies), for the hospitality alone he had to pay out 150,000 Yuan, about 15% of his business turnover.

In Vietnam the situation was reported to be not much different, so that it does not require a separate, detailed description. A high percentage of the entrepreneurs interviewed in Vietnam who were private entrepreneurs thought that specific friendship relationships and those with relatives are of great value for their work in business.

In the interviews this opinion became even more obvious. In a statement typical for many, a producer of packaging materials in the district Hai Ba Trung, Hanoi, named these relationships as "Success factor no. 1". He described his parents-in-law as being in, "Leading positions in the government apparatus".

In contrast to other private entrepreneurs, this entrepreneur had neither experienced problems with the production location (he possessed two of them and intended to acquire a third), nor with the infrastructure (for all his production areas there was unrestricted access to electricity and water).[85]

Table 34: Do relationships with friends and relatives assist obtaining raw or secondary materials? (Hanoi and Tien Son); Do relationships with friends and relatives assist with business processes? (Ho Chi Minh City and Danang; percentage in brackets)

	Yes	*No*
Hanoi	47	11
Tien Son	29	2
Danang	21	
Duy Xuyen	10	
Ho Chi Minh City	50	1
Thu Duc	29	
Total	**186 (93.0)**	**14 (7.0)**
Urban areas	118 (90.8)	12 (9.2)
Rural areas	68 (97.1)	2 (2.9)
North Vietnam	76 (85.4)	13 (14.6)
Central Vietnam	31 (100.0)	0.0
South Vietnam	79 (98.8)	1 (1.2)

Source: Own survey.

Even those entrepreneurs who gave other answers to the written questionnaire, made clear the significance of such relationships. The importance of relationships for Vietnamese entrepreneurs was revealed by the answers to the questions whether they had ever made a donation in the interests of improving rela-

---

[85] Interview Hanoi, 25 May 1996.

tionships to the local authorities, and whether in case they were to come into possession of a large amount of money, they would also use that money for the expansion of their social relationships. In each case 25% said they would. Especially former managers and employees of the state and collective sector possess social capital in the form of good, or not seldom, close personal relationships to local authorities, as well as to government administration. Through their previous work they had already built up contacts with the local authorities before founding a private company, and they were help to further develop them after starting their entrepreneurial work. For one thing dealing with the local authorities whose employees they had to some extent known for years, was familiar to them. Secondly, their private entrepreneurial operation hardly appeared suspicious to the local authorities due to the previous occupational background, whereas the distrust shown by local authorities towards private entrepreneurs with different backgrounds e.g. Overseas Vietnamese was much more marked.

Table 35: Do you talk with other entrepreneurs about your business experiences (%)?

	China	*Vietnam*
Seldom	18.4	28.6
2-3 times/ month	46.9	50.6
1 time/ week	34.7	20.8
Total	100.0	100.0

Source: Own survey.

Table 36: Membership in following organizations (China, in %)

Association for Private Enterprises	75.3
Association of Industry and Commerce	18.3
Association for Individual Laborers	5.1
Communist Party	29.8
Other parties	6.7
Communist Youth League	4.5
Occupational association	19.1

Source: Own survey.

Since the production sector is resource-intensive (not only in relation to the factors named here but also for the processing materials), and key resources are still to some extent under the control of political instead of commercial players, managers or employees from the state and collective sector have in relative terms the best starting chances and conditions for work. The comparatively high rate of this group of persons amongst the total number of industrial private entrepreneurs represents as a result a logical consequence of specific conditions of development not only in China but also in Vietnam.

Network functions are brought into being also through regular meetings, exchanges of information or working dinners.

Table 37: Membership in following organizations (Vietnam, in %)

Association for Small and Medium Enterprises	24.2
Association of Industry and Commerce	7.9
Others	20.5
Without membership	47.4

Source: Own survey.
NB: In contrast to China, there were no overlapping memberships. In Vietnam we were not allowed to ask about membership in political organizations.

More than 80% of the Chinese and over 70% of the Vietnamese entrepreneurs regularly swapped experiences in business, a clear indication that apparently there were network connections through which such an exchange could take place. This occurred via informal meetings, but also in the framework of associations for professionals or entrepreneurs where the degree of organizing was relatively high.

The high degree of organizing in China where the entrepreneur has to be a member of one of the associations for entrepreneurs, but also the membership in professional associations (almost a fifth), in the CCP, in the Communist Youth League or in other parties (41.0%) indicates that entrepreneurs are involved in different network clusters due to their double membership. The degree of organization is much less in Vietnam whereby the voluntary membership in one of the associations for entrepreneurs – as we learned from the interviews _ apparently induces a stronger feeling of identity.

Whereas familial and *tong* relationships are counted amongst *strong ties*, at the levels of bureaucracy and business both *strong* und *weak ties* are to be found. But the rationalization of the business processes and access to markets, market information and resources require the expansion of relationships to new groups, persons and institutions and with that of the *weak ties*. Whether entrepreneurs rely on weak or strong relationships, depends to a significant extent on how far it is possible to create the political, institutional and legal preconditions for equal and fair access to markets. The same applies to ensuring reduction of bureaucratic interference in the market, competition and company, and whether the relationships between firms and local authorities can be designed more rationally through the further promotion of local incentive structures.

2.1.6. *Motivation to found companies*

In both countries it was not material but rather immaterial motives which were of core significance in the decision to work as entrepreneur. Table 38 seems to show that the prospect of higher income to a small extent only was a motivation for founding a company amongst the respondents in China (about 14%). Without a doubt the hope of material reward in the form of higher income formed an important motivating incentive, especially given the economic and social risk associated with self-employment which has to be compensated for by the prospect of higher income.

But this alone appears to be not the main motivation. Similarly to Vietnam, standpoints such as independence (41%) or possibilities of self-development (self-fulfillment) played a major role scoring almost 20%. This was also confirmed by the Chinese 1% sample (1995) according to which 58% and 64% (according to earlier profession) as well as 62% and 80% (according to the forms of ownership of the earlier *Danwei*) had cited self-fulfillment as a major motive for the change into a self-employed occupation.[86]

The occupational factor too played a role in the course of the downturn in the downsizing in the personnel sphere within the state sector above all in regions with significant unemployment. In Baiyin and Luohe, for example, the occupational possibilities in the state sector had significantly lessened in number due to the crisis in that sector, so that the path into self-employment increasingly became one of the most important options. But there were differences between larger and smaller entrepreneurs. For the latter, higher income and the wish for self-sufficiency played a more significant role than with the larger, for whom the development of one's own initiative was a decisive motive for the path into self-employment.

In the interviews, larger entrepreneurs in each case emphasized their own abilities as needed for self-employment, and the motive of professional and social ascent. In this manner an entrepreneur in Luohe pointed out that foreign economists were often of the opinion that China lacked "real" entrepreneurs. In the interests of his country but also himself (social climb), he resolved to become an entrepreneur, and as a result gave up his job at an office of the provincial government.[87]

---

[86] Zhang, Li and Xie 1996: 158f.
[87] Interview, 8 October 1996 in Luohe.

Table 38: Primary motivation for founding a company (China)

Motivation	urban areas		rural areas		Total	
	Number	%	Number	%	Number	%
1. Tense relationships to su-periors	3	2.7	2	2.9	5	2.8
2. No self-fulfillment	25	22.3	11	15.9	36	19.9
3. Higher income	16	14.3	8	11.6	24	13.3
4. Search for steady job	6	5.3	6	8.7	12	6.6
5. Bankruptcy of former com-pany	5	4.5	1	1.5	6	3.3
6. Interest in self-employment	39	34.8	34	49.3	73	40.3
7. Others	18	16.1	7	10.1	25	13.8
Total	112	100.0	69	100.0	181	100.0

Source: Own survey.
NB: Due to some multiple answers the number of answers (181) is higher than that of the respondents (178).

The Chinese 1% sample (1995) came to a similar conclusion although the question about the interest in self-sufficiency was lacking there. But it became clear from the Chinese survey that 57% of the respondents complained about having too few opportunities for self-fulfillment in their earlier *Danwei*. This indicates that founding a company also assisted in the achievement of personal possibilities of self-development.

Diagram 19: Motive for founding a company according to the Chinese 1% sample (1993)

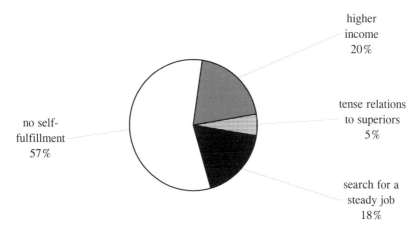

Source: Zhang, Xie and Li 1994: 118.

In the following section I would like to differentiate between four main motivational currents in more detail:

Motivational current 1: improvement of material living conditions

A large number of the entrepreneurs stated that before founding a company they had possessed a (subjectively perceived) low standard of living. An owner of a leather processing factory in Baiyin reported that he had only visited the primary school for two years, since his family was not even in the position to pay his school money. The attainment of a high income and with that the improvement of his living standard was as a result an important factor in his thoughts concerning his occupation. At 15 he had worked as a private slaughterer and meat trader. Through that by the year 1994 he had been able to save 200,000 Yuan whereupon he constructed a factory for leather processing. Likewise the owner of a clothing factory in Luohe in turn had been before the founding of her company a blue-collar worker in a private company. The lower pay had brought the resolve within her to maturity, that she herself should become an entrepreneur. She used her work in a private company in order to acquire the needed know-how as the basis for self-employment, and with the help of savings and credits from her family and circle of friends, in 1995 she bought a small, almost bankrupt clothing industry for a sum amounting to 40, 000 Yuan. Already a year later her company employed 20 people and was once again making a profit.[88] The owner of the shoe-factory Deheng in Luohe declared in contrast, that through contacts to millionaires in the special business zone Shenzen, he had been motivated to found a company. He had himself then in turn become a millionaire.

Retired persons and those on pensions with technical know-how intended through self-employment to reach a higher standard of living in old age, and the creation of an occupational base for their children. The owner of a beverages factory in Luohe reported, for example, that he had begun his retirement in 1987 but had only obtained a small monthly pension. To buy material he then borrowed from members of the family 8,000 Yuan, and invested this in a machine for manufacturing beverages. He said that in this way he had succeeded in increasing his annual net income to around 200,000 Yuan (1996). In 1989 he transferred the company (with 16 employees) to his daughter who had not had a regular occupation before that.

Motivational current 2: The lack of occupational prospects

A further group consisted of former officials who had fallen into political discredit (due to "political mistakes") or had made themselves punishable, and had as a result to look around for a new occupational field. The owner of the Chunfeng Mechanical Engineering Ltd. in Hangzhou, for example, a former member of the party was granted a state company after he had left the army in 1968. During the Cultural Revolution he was sentenced to six years in jail for his criticism of the party's politics at that time. After his release from the prison, he obtained a job as the head of department of the trade union association of Hangzhou city. Due to his alleged misappropriation of 1,000 Yuan he was sentenced once again to a prison sentence, and dismissed from the civil service. After he had discharged his sentence, the only path left open to him was that into self-employment. First of all he leased a small state factory for metal processing. Then he manufactured at first nothing but individual parts of textile machines, later complete machines. Up till 1990 he had earned over one million Yuan, so that in the following year together with seven other shareholders he formed a limited company for machine tools. In 1996 this business had assets worth about 10m. Yuan at its disposal.

---

[88] Interview, 12 October 1996 in Luohe.

Motivational current 3: Professional career and social ascent

Above all it was successful, young entrepreneurs who pointed out in the interviews that at the time, the motivation for founding a company had not been in the first place to have a higher income. Much rather professional careers and social ascent stood in the foreground here. In terms of content the following elements were mentioned: "realization of their own ideas of value and aims", "Possibilities of self-developments", or the wish to become a famous entrepreneur. With that the following motivational current was closely associated with it.

Motivational current 4: Personal responsibility and possibilities of self-

development

Xu Xiaonan, 31 years old, owner of Lubang Leather Products Ltd. in Fuyang had been the director of a rural company before his own entrepreneurial self-employment. The unclear relations of ownership, and conflicts with the administrations of township and village had massively limited the development of his company. Private companies, according to Xu, had the advantage that the relations of ownership would be settled very clearly, and the entrepreneur themselves are responsible for the development of the firm and the company results (inclusive of profit). Private entrepreneurship offers as a result better chances of development also for themselves.

So he resolved to found his own company. "I want to perform on my own stage," he explained; "I am an individualist and I do not want to be restricted by the bureaucracy. I possess the necessary qualifications for an entrepreneur. For my reflections it was not money, but rather the wish for self-fulfillment and entrepreneurial success followed by independence which were decisive."[89]

Sheng Yajun, owner of Yayuan Ltd. in Luohe, was in 1996 37 years old. Before becoming self-employed he had been head of the technical department of a large state cigarette company. Due to his technical experience in the sphere of production processes, he was honored a number of times. In his opinion the prevailing system of administration limited making the state sector more effective. As a result he had not been able to develop his technical skills and ideas. Consequently he resolved to found a company to manufacture aromatic ingredients for cigarettes. High income and professional success were not identical and equal in importance, he argued. Professional success cannot be measured in money. His goal in life consisted of developing the best aromatic materials in the world.[90]

Shi Dongmin (34) is owner of South Ltd. (a food company in Luohe) and had earlier worked in sales for a state sector company. Although it made losses of millions, the company director did not undertake anything to change the

---

[89] Interview, 4 April 1996 in Fuyang.
[90] Interview, 15 October 1996 in Luohe.

running of his company. As a result in 1989 Shi Dongmin left that company with hardly 10,000 Yuan to his name in order to found a company. In 1992 with the profits he had amassed,, he then purchased more modern equipment. In 1996 the company assets amounted to about ten million Yuan and he employed over 1,000 employees. "My goal in life is the creation of a large company. I want to become a second Li Jiacheng"(a well-known Hong-Kong entrepreneur).[91]

There is some controversy amongst Chinese social scientists about the motivation of entrepreneurs. For example, Xiao Liang, is of the opinion that the true motives of the entrepreneur cannot be filtered out of surveys. To underline his point of view he gave two examples: one from 1988 carried out amongst 97 village private companies for the research institute of the Ministry for Agriculture; that survey suggested the following motives for motivation for founding a company:

Table 39: Motives for founding a company [1] (China, in %)

Motivation	%
Self-fulfillment of own abilities with the goal of social ascent	39.2
High income	36.1
Working for the good of the villages and its inhabitants	11.3
Wealth and prestige/ social respect	6.2
Acquiring wealth and property for the family	3.1
Others	4.1

Source: Xiao Liang 1992: 176.

According to a second study amongst 63 private entrepreneurs in Tianjin 1988 the following motivational structure existed.

Table 40: Motivation for founding a company [2] (China, in %)

Motivation	%
Material wealth	8.6
First of all to become rich oneself, in order to assist others to wealth	75.9
Adventure full of risks	12.8
Social recognition through individual skills and values	1.7

Source: Xiao Liang 1992: 176.

---

[91] Interview, 10 October 1996 in Luohe.

Due to the very different results, Xiao comes to the conclusion that entrepreneurs did not want to name their real motives (actually economic in his view). The socialist ideological socialization and egalitarian social pressure have the effect that entrepreneurs disguised their main motivation namely the maximization of income.[92] Xiao sees the desire to make profits and the profit maximization of the entrepreneur as the main economic reasons. But this alone explains little. Entrepreneurdom is not only associated with high profits but rather too with a high degree of risk in personal, economic, political and social spheres.

A study of the biography of Chinese entrepreneurs and interviews they have given show just what stony paths many entrepreneurs have been forced to tread. Entrepreneurdom was often the only alternative in order to survive or for securing their own existence. Certainly for the successful ones, entrepreneurship has a high income associated with it, but the path to that is paved with stones and requires the overcoming of many difficulties. As a result, material profit can hardly be the only reason for the decision to switch to entrepreneurship.

Wang Kezhong, another social scientist, relatively early argued that the motivation for entrepreneurs had to be differentiated into materialistic and non-materialistic reasons. His survey amongst 40 private companies came up with the following results:

Table 41: Motivation for founding a company [3] (China, in %)

	Priority	*%*
Higher income	16	40.0
Career	10	25.0
To promote development of native place area	14	35.0
Total	*40*	*100.0*

Source: Wang Kezhong 1990: 48.

Wang argued on the basis of these results that the material results had been a decisive aim for founding companies. The non-materialistic interests (prestige or political office) could only be achieved on the basis of the materialist interests.[93] Certainly, it cannot be disputed that the basic motivations of the entrepreneurs are those of a material nature, because otherwise investments in the company hardly make sense, given that a firm is supposed to and indeed needs to make a profit in order to be able to survive. But such a definition alone is insufficient.

---

[92] Xiao Liang 1992: 176.
[93] Wang Kezhong 1990: 48.

Most of the entrepreneurs interviewed by us answered that they had made themselves self-employed so as to be able better to develop their own skills. Along with those of an economic nature, entrepreneurs also pursue social and psychological motives.

Social motives and immaterial ones play a role in modern Chinese society. If in earlier times, membership of the party, class origins, "political conscious-ness" or cadre rank were of decisive importance for social status, nowadays there are other factors such as commercial success, assets and income, prestige linked with consumption or demonstrative consumption (*conspicuous consump-tion*).[94] The new prestige factors apply above all to those entrepreneurs who turn economic success into social prestige, and in this way try to raise their social status.

In Vietnam too, the motivation of the wish for independence (30.4%) was named in first place (cf. Table 42). It appears logical to merge the elements of self-sufficiency and independence; these answers then comprise 52.3% of the total. The large majority of the entrepreneurs appear to have chosen the path of the private sector in order to be able to better achieve self-fulfillment, and this thereby becomes a significant element in the entrepreneurial motivation. With the motivation of independence and/or autonomy, a number of elements are now connected such as:

- Emphasis on one's own person and personal skills which are rated more highly than those who are not self-employed;
- Increased willingness to take risks;
- Independence;
- Dissatisfaction with life situation (in material but also in non-material respects);
- Creation of something new which goes beyond what has already been achieved i.e. is active and innovative;
- Indirect criticism of the socialist economic structure which limits people's own economic independence and self-sufficiency.

---

[94] Demonstrative consumption or *conspicuous consumption* characterizes the demonstrative display of consumption of luxury goods externally, with the intention of increasing social prestige.

Table 42: Main motivation for founding a company (Vietnam, percentages in brackets)

	No self-fulfillment possibilities	Higher income	Search for steady job	Former firm went bankrupt	Interest in self-employment	Others
Hanoi	15	3		3	16	15
Tien Son	4	8	2	1	12	9
Danang	4	5	11		4	3
Duy Xuyen		1	1	4	1	2
Ho Chi Minh City		1	21	2	22	5
Thu Duc	1	1	17		10	1
Total	**24 (11.2)**	**19 (8.9)**	**52 (24.3)**	**10 (4.7)**	**65 (30.4)**	**35 (16.4)**
Urban areas	19 (14.6)	9 (6.9)	32 (24.6)	5 (3.8)	42 (32.3)	23 (17.7)
Rural areas	5 (6.7)	10 (13.3)	20 (26.7)	5 (6.7)	23 (30.7)	12 (16.0)
North Vietnam	19 (21.6)	11 (12.5)	2 (2.3)	4 (4.5)	28 (31.8)	24 (27.3)
Central Vietnam	4 (11.1)	6 (16.7)	12 (33.3)	4 (11.1)	5 (13.9)	5 (13.9)
South Vietnam	1 (1.2)	2 (2.5)	38 (46.9)	2 (2.5)	32 (39.5)	6 (7.4)

Source: Own survey.
NB: Due to multiple answers, the number of answers is higher than that of the respondents.

Interestingly it appears not possible to differentiate this motivation (desire for independence and autonomy) from that of the European entrepreneur in early phases of development. Corresponding surveys also see in the process of the formation of an entrepreneurial stratum in Europe, independence as the motivational priority for economic self-sufficiency.[95]

In second place follows the motivation of unemployment (24.3%) whereby the employment problems in Vietnam become apparent. Included in that are clearly widespread if hidden unemployment and under-employment: an illustration of this is the book-keeper and wife of the owner of the firm Pham Thu in Ho Chi Minh City who before founding a company had worked in the foreign trade department of the state sector, import-export firm IMEXCO. After a maximum of two hours work per day there, she had completed her job, and sat around doing nothing.

She was very dissatisfied with her position, and moved to her husband's company.[96] In contrast to the motivations named above for self-employment, this one is more strongly stamped with passivity, since it stresses the rather involuntary loss of the place of work up till then.

In third place the entrepreneurs named other reasons (16.3%) whereby the relatively common motive (the wish to create jobs for other people) also appeared. In that on the one hand there is a reflection of the difficult economic situation of the country with high rates of unemployment, on the other hand there was too within that response a certain feeling of responsibility (or awareness) in relation to society. At the same time this answer legitimated business activity both politically and socially.

In fourth place followed the lack of possibilities for self-fulfillment (11.2%).[97] With that choice, their own personality was stressed more strongly than by the motivation of independence; they experienced a restriction of their personality, and therefore sought a free space for the development of their particular skills, which those concerned subjectively seen had at their disposal. This motivation contained more than the factor of independence – by which for example the hope for financial profit may play a role – a non-materialistic element.

At the same time, of all the answers on the questionnaire this one presupposed the highest degree of ability on the part of the respondents for self-reflection, whereby this entails stressing one's distinctness from other people. As a result, this answer indicates an "active" self-awareness and a significant

---

[95] Cf. e.g. Schumann 1992; Boissevain 1997: 302.

[96] Interview Ho Chi Minh City, 20 November 1996.

[97] Theoretically the lack of possibilities for self-development can also be explained by the restriction of individual skills by a particular employer. In that case one would expect the answer to be the motivation, "Problems with employer". Since this motivation was not mentioned by any of the respondents, it appears that the reason for the lack of self-fulfillment was instead a systemic phenomenon, namely the strong constriction through the socialist system as such.

amount of self-assurance. The answer can also be understood as an expression of especially large limitations in their personal environment.

The desire for more money came only in fifth place (8.9%). That placing, however, does not mean that this motivation is not present in other motives. In the interviews some entrepreneurs stated that along with the motivations named in each case, their hopes of a higher income also played a role.

Independence or unemployment as a motivation might certainly be connected with the hope that through activities in the private sector, they could achieve a materially better position. This interlinkage of motives exists because the idea of attaining material profit belongs to a greater or lesser extent to private entrepreneurial work (which at least needs to suffice in order to ensure earning a living).[98]

The structure of motivation can be differentiated between *pull* and *push* factors. Whereas the motives interests in independence/autonomy imply that occupations were given up, because the "adventure" of independence was exciting and so with that they contain a rather autonomous decision and an active path into *self-employment* (*pull* entrepreneur). Unemployment and conflicts in companies are rather factors, which drive a person into occupational independence (*push* entrepreneur).

As a result, there is a difference in the entrepreneurial impetus between the two groups. On the other hand one can differentiate between materialistic and non-materialistic motives.

Table 43: Compressed answers to entrepreneurs' motives (Vietnam und China)

| | *Vietnam* | | *China* | |
	Pers.	%	Pers.	%
Own initiative	89	52.3	114	73.1
Solving employment problems	62	36.5	18	11.5
Higher income	19	11.2	24	15.4
Total	170	100.0	156	100.0

Source: Own survey.

From Table 43 it becomes obvious that employment problems in Vietnam at least during the period of the survey (1996–1997) were clearly a more important motivation for private entrepreneurship than in China. Actually the issue of unemployment in the 1990s was much more serious in Vietnam as a result of structural problems. In addition the unemployed in China engage themselves much rather in the small individual sector given that involvement in the larger private sector presupposes know-how, capital and a greater willingness to take

---

[98] But it is our considered opinion that it would be an error to reduce private sector business activity entirely to the motivation of earning money.

risks. This (larger) private sector is in Vietnam less developed both quantitatively and qualitatively so that in this sphere a larger proportion of formerly unemployed people is to be found. Furthermore there is in Vietnam a multi-facetted, start-up program run by international organizations for the founding by unemployed of small companies. However, in both countries the predominant motivations for founding a company are opportunities of self-development and/or self-sufficiency.

Similarly too China, in Vietnam the differences in response behavior between urban and rural enterprises are relatively small: for the Vietnamese ratio of urban to rural areas, there is a similarly large percentage that expressed the desire for self-sufficiency in first place (32.3% and 30.7%). Differences exist in the motivation "lack of possibilities of self-development" which amongst urban companies (14.6%) was named twice as often as for the rural areas (6.7%).

One of the reasons for the higher percentage amongst urban entrepreneurs could be in the ability to self-reflect which this answer presupposes. Such an ability to self-reflect demands mental flexibility which can be acquired in the framework of higher education – which is rather the case in urban than in rural areas. In addition the rural, family agricultural companies offer relatively more possibilities of self-development than the urban state sector, so that here a lower amount of restriction of people's personalities is perceived. The responses were of a vice-versa nature in respect of the motivation of higher income: in rural areas it was mentioned almost twice as often (13.3%) as in the urban areas, and amongst other things may be correlated with the disparities in income between urban and rural areas.

The regional differences in Vietnam are noticeably bigger than those between urban areas. As an example, the desire for independence in North Vietnam comes first (31.8%), in South Vietnam second (but with the higher percentage of 39.5%), and in Central Vietnam only in third place (13.9%). This contrasts with the factor "lack of possibilities for self-development" which in North Vietnam comes in second place (21.5%), in Central Vietnam scored 11.1%, and in South Vietnam (only 1.2%) comes merely in fourth place. In North Vietnam, the state sector is much more strongly in evidence than in Central Vietnam or South Vietnam, and as a result the restrictions on individuals at the place of work in North Vietnam are larger. As a result in N. Vietnam it is rather the desire for self-development (and the feeling of being restricted in that) which may occur more often. Furthermore, when people stemmed from an entrepreneurial family, this factor may well have influenced the desire for independence in South Vietnam: twelve of the thirty-two South Vietnamese that we interviewed who stated independence as a motivation, were born into such a family.

It seems rather likely that it is above all, younger people who display a willingness to try self-employment. On the one hand self-employment entails a certain risk, but on the other hand precisely for younger people who are not yet rigidly bound into a specific, occupational context, it represents opportunities of social ascent. A counter-argument to this supposition is that such a relation between age and willingness to take risks cannot be unambiguously ascertained for the group of young entrepreneurs aged 20 to 29. But when one expands the age group to the 20 to 40 year-olds, at any rate 15 of the 22 entrepreneurs in Ho Chi Minh City who gave independence as a motivation can be classified in this group. For the rest of the entrepreneurs interviewed from South Vietnam and Central Vietnam, no such relation can be ascertained.

Unemployment in North Vietnam comes in fifth place (2.3%), since there the state sector absorbs a significant section of the workforce,[99] whereas in South Vietnam (46.9%) and Central Vietnam (33.3%) the unemployment factor plays the main role. In these regions there is no extensive state or collective sector, which could at least superficially absorb the unemployment. By contrast, the number of company bankruptcies in the state sector in total does not play a significant role. Since private company in the 1980s existed only to a limited extent, and bankruptcies in the state sector had been de facto hardly possible (given that the state took over the losses), the motivation of bankruptcy as an answer was only expected to be at a low level. In South Vietnam the range of motivation named was the lowest. The main motivations of unemployment and independence made up 86.4% of the answers given, and the remaining motivations followed in each case with a small percentage. On the other hand, the answers given in Central Vietnam were distributed the most equally amongst the total range of response possibilities (between 11% and 17% with the exception of the most important motivation of unemployment at 33.3%). When one adds together the data divided into material motivation (earning more money, unemployment, company bankruptcy), versus more immaterial motivation (no possibilities of self-development, independence), one finds the following picture:

Table 44: Materialistic and non-materialistic motives (Vietnam)

	Materialistic	*Rather non-materialistic*
North Vietnam	19.3%	53.4%
Central Vietnam	61.1%	25.0%
South Vietnam	51.8%	40.7%
Urban areas	35.4%	46.9%
Rural areas	46.7%	37.3%

Source: Own survey.

Table 44 makes clear yet again the finding already made during the discussion of individual motivation. In North Vietnam there are greater restrictions caused by the state sector, whose comparative absence in South Vietnam and Central Vietnam foregrounds the economic reasons there.

---

[99] Concealed unemployment was not taken into account here.

The immaterial factors were in China (73.1%) significantly higher which in turn may well be related to the structural differences in the private sector named above. In contrast to Vietnam, the percentage of non-materialistic motivations in rural areas of China (75.8%) was slightly above the urban areas percentage for that factor (71.3%).

Materialistic motivations often are to be found in the context of certain material shortages. The loss of somebody's job, or pay which is too low forces people to search for a new occupation. In addition when state or collective companies are no longer able to pay their staff, this is a starting point for the founding of companies for their employees.

An example from Vietnam is the story of Nguyen Van Tai. He had earlier worked in a state sector firm in Ho Chi Minh City which made ventilators. As pay he had often received ventilators instead of money, and he sold the goods privately. In this way it was possible for him gradually to establish relations with customers which he was then able to make use of when he founded his own firm which itself manufactured ventilators.[100]

In some cases a certain naivety or even romantic ideas of private entrepreneurship without a doubt played a role. An example is the female owner of the factory for bakery products, Nhat Phat in Ho Chi Minh City, who started out by assuming that she as a private sector entrepreneur i.e. as the "boss" would not need to work so hard since it was her personnel who would have to do all the donkey work.

She had believed it would be enough for her to draw the profits out of the company. Only when the company landed in a crisis did she grasp how important her entrepreneurial and management functions were for the firm. Nowadays, so she claimed at the time, she worked from six in the early morning until late into the night, not only running her company, but also seeing to the bookkeeping.[101]

In summarizing we ascertain that there is no unified structure of motivation as a reason for entry into entrepreneurial strata. In each case, what we observe are combinations in the considerations of the players, which include the following elements: *improvement of living conditions* (increase of income and standard of living); *improvement of quality of life* (self-fulfillment, independence, increase of social prestige or due to blocked chances of social ascent); *improvement of the chances in the market and access to the market* (capital, chances of investment, expectations of profit); *social and political chances* (social and political capital); as well as *knowledge resources* (occupational and specialized knowledge).

---

[100] Interview Ho Chi Minh City, 6 December 1996.
[101] Interview Ho Chi Minh City, 18 November 1996.

3. *Relations with local government*

The nature of relations between entrepreneurs and the local bureaucracy relate to the following complex of questions:

1. How do entrepreneurs assess the policies of the local government, and how do they react to interventions or interferences on the part of the local bureaucracy?
2. In which way do entrepreneurs influence local politics?
3. What roles do the interest associations play in the structure of relationships which exists between entrepreneurs and local governments?

3.1. *Assessments of local policies by entrepreneurs*

In this respect, the differences between China and Vietnam were relatively large: the dissatisfaction openly expressed by Vietnamese entrepreneurs contrasted with a rather disguised expression of that feeling by their Chinese counterparts. According to our survey, 37.1% of the respondents interviewed in China were of the opinion that their interests were adequately taken into account in the policies of the local governments. 57.3% of the respondents stated that while their interests were taken into account at a basic level it was still inadequate. Only 5.6% of the respondents found that their interests were not at all considered (cf. Table 45).

Table 45: Do you believe that your interests are adequately taken into account in the business policies of the local government? (China)

	Number	*%*
Yes, sufficiently taken into account	66	37.1
To some extent, if they were taken into account more, it would be desirable	102	57.3
Not taken into account	10	5.6
Total	*178*	*100.0*

Source: Own survey.

In the assessment of local government the differences of opinion among Chinese entrepreneurs turned out to be more marked between the three regions surveyed than between the urban and rural areas, likewise large and small companies. An illustration of this is that more respondents in Henan (50.0%) and Gansu (35.4%) thought that their interests were sufficiently taken into account by local administrations than in Zhejiang (26.1%). This result appears to contradict the reality of private sector development, since Zhejiang was generally considered to be exemplary for the private sector. But the reasons may well result from the phenomenon that the degree of differentiation there, and the high level of development of the private sector cause the Zhejiang entrepreneurs to make greater demands on the local government, and these the latter may not be able to fulfill unconditionally.

On the other hand, almost three quarters in Zhejiang (73.7%), almost two thirds in Gansu (64.6%) and half of the respondents we interviewed in Henan (50.0%) perceive their interests as only partially or not at all taken into account; these figures suggest the conclusion that there is a high level of dissatisfaction. Larger entrepreneurs were more dissatisfied than smaller ones, whereas the relation between urban and rural areas was relatively balanced.

Around 60% agreed too, either completely or partially, with the statement: "There are at present still too many restrictions on the private sector and, as a result, it cannot develop well." Merely 40% found that statement to be untrue, whereby in contrast to Zhejiang and Henan (15.9% and 15.0%, respectively), in Gansu it was as many as 22.9%, who completely agreed with this statement. This confirmed our impression, that in rather backward regions, such as Gansu, the policies in respect of privately owned companies are more conservative than in the more highly developed (cf. our statements above to policies concerning assistance for companies).

An illustration is that it was very difficult for private sector construction companies in Baiyin to obtain a permit for construction projects. And unlike other places, in a large number of sectors, no trading licenses were granted e.g. for dispensing chemists. This lead to some extent to entrepreneurs entering into (pseudo-) co-operation with state-owned company firms, or having themselves registered as a collective company for purposes of disguise. Urban area entrepreneurs (65.7%) were more likely to be of the opinion that there were too many restrictions than rural ones (53.6%). This can be explained in the following way: that the local bureaucracies concentrate on the urban areas, and that the net of regulations and byelaws is denser there than in the rural areas. So, it is more difficult for an entrepreneur in an urban area to find a commercial location.

The owner of the clothing factory Lanling in Hangzhou reported for example that establishing a manufacturing company in the city presupposed the inclusion of that company in the city's development plan. At any rate, in the urban areas a large number of authorizations from different departments were required, he went on. The owner of the Xiaohesen company in Hangzhou said that he had been forced to obtain almost 1,000 authorizations from very different departments of government at different levels, before he was able to start on the construction of an amusement park. In rural areas, according to the generally held opinion of the respondents interviewed, the regulations and byelaws were much less bureaucratically dealt with and interpreted; and through relationships too a greater degree of flexibility could be achieved. Almost a quarter of the larger entrepreneurs (24.1%) held the opinion that the private sector could not develop successfully due to excessive limitations. The necessity in the interests of their business activities to create social contacts of the most varying kinds, has the effect that larger entrepreneurs are often able to recognize social problems better than smaller ones.

Table 46: "At present the cadres are not sufficiently prepared for the introduction of a socialist market economy" (China)

	Number	*%*
Completely true	39	21.9
Partially true	79	44.4
False	60	33.7
Total	*178*	*100.0*

Source: Own survey.

At the same time it needs to be pointed out, that larger entrepreneurs require higher standards. They want to be treated no differently than managers of state and collective companies in all economic, social and political matters. Many of the larger entrepreneurs as a result criticized the resolution passed by the party leadership not to permit private sector entrepreneurs to join the party. The owner of Bei'er Ltd. in Fuyang, who was also a deputy of the Political Consultative Conference at the national level, declared that this regulation discriminated against private sector entrepreneurs. They were, he went on, treated like criminals, because only the latter were also denied party membership. Private sector entrepreneurs needed to be given the same status as managers of state and collective companies. Although many of the state and collective companies brought the state little advantage because they ran at a loss, a leading role was attributed to them.

Our survey matches the results established by Chinese studies of entrepreneurs that show that many entrepreneurs would like to have a different structure of relationships between themselves and the authorities. More than half of the respondents interviewed (55.2%), according to a Chinese sample, opted for that, almost half (44.8%) would prefer a reform of the employment system in the civil service. People complained too about the arbitrary levying of special payments and donations by the local authorities: 66.7% stated, that these practices had even increased in comparison with 1996, 33.3% said they had remained the same. They were not satisfied as well by the charging of fees, and only 7.4% of the respondents we interviewed stated, that despite all prohibitions by the central leadership, a decrease of the sums levied had taken place compared to the previous year. Moreover, 37.9% complained about unwarranted bureaucratic interferences in the domain of the market leading to disadvantages for private companies; the same percentage criticized the state monopolization of sectors, 31.0% lamented widely spread corruption in buying and selling.[102]

---

[102] Zhongguo qiyejia diaocha xitong 1997: 13, 17, 34 and 35.

Unlike in Vietnam (see below) in China, at any rate, a third of the respondents we interviewed were of the opinion that the officials were prepared for the market economy. The positive answers were at their highest in Zhejiang (46.1%). Many entrepreneurs regarded the cadres there as more enlightened, and attributed to them a better understanding of relations and conditions in market economies. In Henan, this percentage was only 20.5% and in Gansu 12.5%. The less developed a region is, apparently the less the officials there care to adjust themselves to the market economy. In contrast to rural areas, in the urban areas criticism predominated.

Table 47: Do you believe that your interests are adequately taken into account in the business policies of the local government? (Vietnam, percentages in brackets)

	Yes, sufficiently taken into account	To some extent, if they were taken into account more, it would be desirable
Hanoi	8	32
Tien Son	9	19
Danang	3	15
Duy Xuyen		9
Ho Chi Minh City	12	25
Thu Duc	10	16
Total	**42 (21.2)**	**116 (58.6)**
Rural areas	23 (18.1)	72 (56.7)
Urban areas	19 (26.8)	44 (61.9)
North Vietnam	17 (19.8)	51 (59.3)
Central Vietnam	3 (9.4)	24 (75.0)
South Vietnam	22 (27.5)	41 (51.2)
	Not taken into account	No reply
Hanoi	15	3
Tien Son	3	
Danang	4	
Duy Xuyen	1	
Ho Chi Minh City	13	1
Thu Duc	4	
Total	**40 (20.2)**	**4**
Rural areas	32 (25.2)	
Urban area	8 (11.3)	
North Vietnam	18 (20.9)	
Central Vietnam	5 (15.6)	
South Vietnam	17 (21.3)	

Source: Own survey.

Interestingly, our survey amongst cadres at the Central Party School in Beijing showed, that skepticism about them on the part of officials was significantly greater. Almost a third (32.5%) thought the cadres to be inadequately prepared for a market economy and only 6.2% regarded them as sufficiently so. In this response behavior, skepticism is more strongly expressed than amongst the entrepreneurs as to whether cadres could match up the requirements of a market economy.

In Vietnam, the dissatisfaction showed itself more strongly than in China. 78.8% thought that their interests were either not at all or only partially taken into account. Directly expressed dissatisfaction ("not taken into account") was at more than a fifth of the answers astoundingly large (China 5.6%).

The dissatisfaction was significantly higher in the rural areas than in the urban areas. That is surprising insofar as a policy of promoting the private sector could rather have been expected for the rural areas, since they are considered to be more open, more flexible and receptive to new developments, and the number of private sector companies much higher in the rural areas than in the urban area. Such an assessment may for one thing be a result of the fact that in the Vietnamese rural areas, the preconditions for the private sector are to some extent more difficult than in the urban area (for example, in matters to do with granting production locations or real estate).

Another point is, that the urban anonymity, the size of the administrative and government apparatus as well as the large number of interests competing with each other make it more difficult for individuals to have their specific interests in business policies taken into account by the local authorities. The large number of competing economic and also political interests force people over and over again to compromise. For the individual private sector entrepreneur, it is not simple to find the right contact person in order to assert his or her own interests, due to the size of the administrative machine.

At the village and township level, in contrast, it is easier to have an overview of the local authorities. The right contact person is easier to identify. It is seldom, that there are kinship relationships between the people who work for the local authorities and the entrepreneurs, who, in contrast to the urban areas, are much smaller in number. Many matters can be better and less complicatedly negotiated due to factors such as kinship, belonging to the same village, or other relationship structures.

An absolute majority (58.6%) decided – as in China – to choose the rather "diplomatic" answer that their interests were "partially" considered. Since direct criticism of the authorities was often avoided or diluted, criticism here too, was expressed rather (latently) in more moderate statements ("partially"). Consequently, the high percentage in this category of answers underlined the critical attitudes towards the authorities.

The regional differences are remarkable. In Central Vietnam, only a relatively small percentage of less than 10% believed, that their interests were taken into account, whereas three times as many were of this opinion in Ho Chi

Minh City. That indicates a greater degree of tolerance on the part of the South Vietnamese authorities in respect of the private sector, which is not surprising given the longer period of market economy development in the southern part of the country, above all in order to minimize the conflict potential amongst the population. However, in South Vietnam one cannot deduce from that a general level of satisfaction amongst private sector entrepreneurs with the authorities. On the other hand, dissatisfaction outside of the two metropolises, Hanoi and Ho Chi Minh City, appears to be particularly marked.

The decades-long, centrally administered economy, and the continued presence of elements of the planned economy bring about a tendency to permanent interventions in and control of the private sector. Secondly, in respect of political guidelines issued either by the central or provincial governments, the local authorities often interpret, dilute or boycott these in their own interests due to loopholes whether legal or administratively technical, often with reference to "specific local conditions". As a result, though policies may be decided on centrally, this does not mean that these will actually be put into practice at the local level. This ambivalence finds expression too in the response behavior of the respondents interviewed. The answers to the question "The policy of the government for the private sector is very good, but there are problems in carrying it out," shows, that in China 61% of the respondents agreed with this statement, 37.9% thought it partially correct, and only 1.7% thought it wrong.

Table 48: Evaluate the following statement: "The policy of the government for the private sector is very good, but there are problems in carrying it out." (China in %)

	Zhejiang	Henan	Gansu
Applies	52.2	66.7	64.6
Applies partially	46.4	33.3	31.3
Doesn't apply	1.4	0.0	4.1
Total	100.0	100.0	100.0

Source: Own survey.

In Henan and Gansu, there are actually greater problems in carrying out policies decided on at that level than in Zhejiang. Our survey appears to make clear that the arbitrariness of the local bureaucracies in less developed regions is less marked than in more developed ones. This was emphasized through our own observations. To give one small example: in Hangzhou the official from the Commission for Reform of the Economic Structure, who accompanied us, tried in the course of our interview visits over and over again to acquire donations from the entrepreneurs for the appearance of a year-book about the economic reforms in Zhejiang province. But every entrepreneur answered his request negatively. In Baiyin, on the other hand, corresponding attempts were obligatorily decided positively. In one case, during our visit to a chemical factory half a dozen officials from the local department for environmental protection appeared unannounced and wanted to be invited to lunch. In this case, the entrepreneur asked his deputy director to pay for and accompany the civil servants.

Only a few of the respondents interviewed denied the existence of problems or held them to be insignificant. The absolute majority certainly recognized the discrepancy between policies decided on (centrally or regionally) and the corresponding (local) implementation, which manifested itself in this question. The interviews suggested, that they certainly held the "macro-politics" to be good, whereas the local bureaucracies were predominantly viewed as responsible for problems. In rural areas, the structures of relationships between entrepreneurs and cadres appeared to be less complicated to organize, and entrepreneurs had fewer problems with the local authorities than in urban areas (cf. Table 50).

Table 49: Evaluate the following statements: "The policy of the government for the private sector is very good, but there are problems in carrying it out." (China, in %)

	Entrepreneurs in urban areas	*Entrepreneurs in rural areas*
Applies	67.6	49.3
Applies partially	30.6	49.3
Does not apply	1.8	1.4
Total	*100.0*	*100.0*
	Large entrepreneurs	*Small entrepreneurs*
Applies	51.9	64.2
Applies partially	46.3	34.2
Doesn't apply	1.8	1.6
Total	*100.0*	*100.0*

Source: Own survey.

As an illustration, the owner of a factory producing construction materials, reported that in Fuyang he only had had to come to terms with the Bureau for the Administration of Industry and Commerce and the banks. In the main he had no contact with other official departments,. So far as these were not responsible for private sector entrepreneurs, they did not interfere with company processes. As a result he showed himself to be little interested in personally getting to know the new mayor of Fuyang, since the latter could have only little influence on his work as an entrepreneur. In his opinion, the urban entrepreneurs, in contrast, had to come to terms with many official departments (street committees, police, fire brigade, etc.). Small entrepreneurs agreed more often than did large private sector entrepreneurs, that there are problems with the implementation of policies for the private sector. Large entrepreneurs possess as a rule, good relationships to the local authorities, or themselves have a position in a political organization or institution (e.g. in the Association of Industry and Commerce, the local People's Congresses, or the local Political Consultative Conferences). Local bureaucracies are generally more circumspect with such entrepreneurs because the latter have influence and connections.

In Vietnam, the negative evaluation of implementation of policies at the local level was much more clearly expressed than in China:

Table 50: Evaluate the following statements: "The policy of the government for the private sector is very good, but there are problems in carrying it out." (Vietnam, in %)

	Applies	*Partially applies*	*Does not apply*
Total	78.4	21.6	0.0
Urban areas	77.3	22.7	0.0
Rural areas	80.3	19.7	0.0
North Vietnam	79.5	20.5	0.0
Central Vietnam	75.0	25.0	0.0
South Vietnam	78.5	21.5	0.0

Source: Own survey.

Not a single one of the respondents we interviewed negated the content of the question. Neither the problems nor the positive intentions of the government were, as a result, fundamentally put into question. More than three quarters confirmed the existence of (serious) problems in implementation, more than a fifth admitted problems thereby, or were of the opinion that the policies themselves were problematic.

What is noticeable is that there were hardly noteworthy differences between the individual regions, as well as between urban and rural areas. Consequently, there appear to be no significant differences in the evaluation of the set of problems associated with carrying out policies. That indicates a general dissatisfaction with the local authorities that in the last analysis are required to carry out the government's policies. From an entrepreneurial point of view, the lack of transparency of the administrative apparatus and too few legal safeguards represent core problems; both factors allow the authorities a lot of room to maneuver. Decisions of the authorities are neither unambiguously comprehensible nor is an individual's right to claim – at least on paper – against a government department capable of assertion without complications.

This leads to the grotesque situation that the private sector is supposed in its work processes to stick to the of individual departments' regulations although the latter are largely unknown to the entrepreneurs. Furthermore, the local authorities possess relative autonomy to pass countless local byelaws in addition –

and not seldom in opposition to – the national legislation.[103] For the period between 1989 and 1993 alone, Hoan Kim Giao, an expert on the Vietnamese private sector, stated, the number of laws and regulations passed for the private sector to be 112. And those were only the ones known to him. The total number of regulations passed by the authorities for the private sector is thought to be significantly higher.[104]

Since the private entrepreneurs only know some of the regulations, they often breach them merely out of lack of knowledge, which then in turn can be penalized by the authorities. This makes the levying of fines an additional, administrative source of income, so that, in individual cases, a certain incentive exists to pass regulations that are not publicly made known. Even one of the largest entrepreneurs in Danang, who according to his own statements was protected by the government of the province, complained about this behavior. He saw in that not only a chance for the authorities to enrich themselves, rather he interpreted it also as an expression of the hermaphroditic character of the Vietnamese economic structure: half capitalist, half socialist, without people knowing where they belong and where the train is going to.[105]

To some extent administrations are aware of this problem, and are endeavoring to achieve greater transparency. An illustration of this is that in the third district of Ho Chi Minh City in response to an initiative by the local government in, every three months a meeting took place between administrative officials and entrepreneurs, at which new regulations were made known and general questions of private sector development discussed.

The administration, according to Nguyen Thanh Xe, deputy director of the Department for Commerce in the city district named above, "still doesn't work well". Areas both of competencies and tasks overlapping individual departments combined with the large amount of elbow-room enjoyed by all departments in the interpreting and carrying out national laws limits the efficiency of the administration.[106]

Precisely, in such a sensitive sphere as that of taxation, the private entrepreneurs are sometimes not allowed to have much needed information. The director of the department for structural policies of the fiscal authorities of Quang Nam-Danang, a young cadre, told us that entrepreneurs were not given taxation tables from which they could work out the tax rate applicable to them.[107] In this way, random rates of taxation of companies are made easier to levy, without the entrepreneurs concerned being able to defend against them. Anyway, the offi-

---

[103] Marr 1995: 17f., 26.

[104] Hoang Kim Giao 1993: 183-89.

[105] However, the respondent left no doubt that at least he knew where the road was leading to, namely to capitalism.

[106] Interview, deputy-director of the Industry Department, city administration district 3, Ho Chi Minh City, 18 December 1996.

[107] Interview, tax authorities Quang Nam-Danang, Danang, 4 January 1997. The rates of taxation are published in a book but one which is not obtainable in bookshops.

cial rates of taxation with up to 45% tax on profits are disproportionately high in Vietnamese terms.[108]

Independently of the rate of tax, the actual implementation of the tax levying provides the authorities with considerable scope. In principle, each firm has to pay:

1. an annual business tax;
2. turnover tax or, in the case of luxury goods (e.g. car imports) and semi-luxury foods and tobacco (e.g. alcohol and cigarettes) there is a special turnover tax. The former was paid monthly, the latter annually;
3. a monthly tax on profits;
4. import and/or export tax.

Theoretically, the underlying basis of the payments of the turnover and profit tax was the amount for the previous year. A settlement took place at the end of the year, when all relevant data for the current year was at hand.[109]

Last but not least, for reasons of profit maximization, the entrepreneurs try to wriggle out of the grip of the fiscal authorities. Most common is to keep two sets of accounts, one of which is a false balance sheet for the authorities, and one which is accurate and used for internal company purposes. In the course of the interviews, entrepreneurs and accountants to some extent openly admitted this practice (also known in other countries) and faking the figures.

This falsification does not refer only to the figures directly relevant to tax, such as turnover and profit, rather all the other figures were faked too, from which the real extent of the business operations might be deduced. So, the number of workers was stated to be significantly lower than they actually were. A producer of cosmetics articles in Ho Chi Minh City with 60 regular employees, for example, had only made a notification of 15 of these. The largest, female, private entrepreneur in the district Tien Son officially employed only 600 people, but actually the figure was over 2,000. Many entrepreneurs are falsely registered as state and collective companies or as part of the individual economy, and enjoy because of that certain tax advantages. Companies, which are active in the tertiary sector, one that is particularly highly taxed, are registered as being manufacturing companies, so as to obtain a lower rate of tax. Almost a third of the companies registered in the administrative district Hai Ba Trung in Hanoi, were in this way falsely so. During our fieldwork in Danang, a company for the production of plastic tubes even turned out to be a karaoke bar!

Smaller companies, that do not possess a large amount of machine plant, use the government's policy of assistance in a special way: after four years of production in which they were taxed at a lower level, the production location would be moved and the entrepreneur opened a new one up in order to enjoy

---

[108] Interview, tax authorities Quang Nam-Danang, Danang, 4 January 1997.

[109] Interview, tax authorities Quang Nam-Danang, Danang, 4 January 1997.

tax advantages for a further four years. In some cases, the tax rates were simply negotiated with the local authorities over lunch.

The authorities are aware of countless ruses by inventive entrepreneurs, but constantly lag behind the current developments, since the entrepreneurs regularly come up with new measures. As a result, the authorities have meanwhile resorted to plain-clothes investigators, who work for a period in suspected firms and whose brief is to collect information. In addition, the competitive situation between the companies is used in order to obtain information from firm A about their competitors firm B.

Should it be the case that both firms are withholding taxes, then firm A will escape punishment, if B is convicted on the basis of A's statements. In cases where suspicion exists, the authorities make an unannounced visit to the company in question in order to ascertain the real extent of the company's profits i.e. as a rule to make an estimate.

Since 1993, at lower levels of administration, so-called tax advisory centers have come into being. These consist of representatives of the police, of the Women's Federation, various departments of government, the courts as well as private individuals, who are not employed in the civil service, whose task it is, to report supposed or real tax evaders.[110]

Table 51: At present cadres are not sufficiently prepared for the introduction of a socialist market economy (Vietnam)

	Completely true	*Partially true*	*Untrue*
Hanoi	17	37	2
Tien Son	10	19	
Danang	11	10	
Duy Xuyen	5	5	
Ho Chi Minh City	27	22	1
Thu Duc	16	14	
Total	**86 (43.9)**	**107 (54.6)**	**3 (1.5)**
Rural areas	55 (43.3)	69 (54.3)	3 (2.4)
Urban areas	31 (44.9)	38 (55.1)	
North Vietnam	27 (31.8)	56 (65.9)	2 (2.4)
Central Vietnam	16 (51.6)	15 (48.4)	
South Vietnam	43 (53.8)	36 (45.0)	1 (1.2)

Source: Own survey.

Against this background it is comprehensible, why a very large percentage of the respondents interviewed (cf. Table 51) are of the opinion that there are

---

[110] Interview, tax authorities Quang Nam-Danang, Danang, 4 January 1997.

problems in the implementation of the government's private sector policies, which are in themselves worthy of respect.

Still more negative, and above all significantly worse than in China, was the judgment concerning the preparation of cadres for the introduction of the socialist market economy. Only 1.5% thought it to be adequate and 43.9% classed it as completely insufficient (cf. Table 52). Almost all respondents interviewed expressed themselves critically about the officials. This cannot be interpreted only as a reference to the dissatisfaction concerning the incompetence of the cadres. Since in the last analysis, they are representatives of the party and of the system, dissatisfaction with this system, thereby manifests itself. One can perceive clear, regional differences in the response behavior. In Ho Chi Minh City and Danang, over half of the respondents interviewed attributed insufficient preparation to the cadres, while in North Vietnam "only" somewhat less than a third were of this opinion. This answer reflected too the different historical development of North and South Vietnam: many South Vietnamese have themselves experienced a market economy. Interference by the authorities in business activities and their lack of experience with the market economy system are, as a result, experienced in the South as much more serious than in North Vietnam. This regional difference can be explained as follows: in the North over a long period of time, there had been interventions in the market, the socialist socialization anchored the market as something negative in the minds of the people, and experience with market conditions is relatively new. The response behavior of the Central Vietnamese indicates a similar trend to that in South Vietnam.

3.2. *Negative impacts of the local bureaucracy on private sector companies*

For the most part, there are three problem areas, which impact negatively on the private sector, and which in the following section I would like to go into in some detail: a) slowing down the implementation of legislative specifications for private sector company; b) the pursuit of their own commercial interests by the authorities when administering the private sector; and c) corruption.

(1) Obstruction of the implementation of legislative specifications for private sector company

The difficulties of the entrepreneurs in dealings with the local bureaucracies can be made clear by an example, namely, the odyssey of the entrepreneur Ying Yaoqi. Although the saga took place in the 1980s, the mindset of many authorities, which lies behind it, has changed little. Ying, owner of Aoqi Furnitures Ltd. in Hangzhou, was born into a peasant family in the area. Motivated by the success story of a peasant in Henan province, who had risen to being a transport entrepreneur, Ying sold his house in the countryside and acquired a second-hand car for 8,000 Yuan with three acquaintances.

But the local government in that municipality refused him a trading license with the justification that private individuals were not allowed to run a transport company. After that, he contacted the industry department of Hangzhou. There he was denied any information, since it was a private sector company, which was at issue. Then ensued a heavy confrontation between the entrepreneur and the officials, with the consequence, that the entrepreneur received a rebuke from the party committee responsible. But he did not give up and turned to the local newspaper (*Zhejiang Ribao*). In a conversation with the chief editor he asked, why peasants in Henan were allowed to found a transport company, whereas this had been refused to him in Hangzhou.

In this way he learned, that a document issued by the Central Committee of the CCP, had specifically authorized the founding of such companies by private individuals. He recounted to us that at the Bureau for the Administration of Industry and Commerce, he was able to read this document. However, that institution told him in turn, that this regulation only permitted individuals to use new cars for a private transport company., He gave up discouraged and took the car back to the company that had sold it to him. The director of this company advised him, however, not to sell the car, but instead to rent it out. Since he was now no longer the owner – after all the owner was indeed a state company – he was allowed to pursue without restriction this occupation in the transport field, and in this way he amassed the starting capital for a larger company. A good friend, who worked in a collective company for the manufacturing of (electric) kettles in Hangzhou, told him of the market opportunities for similar companies, and advised him to found a private sector company for the manufacture of kettles. So, in 1983 he founded such a company with five stakeholders, each contributing 20,000 Yuan.

Since at that time larger, private sector companies had not yet been given the status of legality, he had the company registered as a rural collective firm in a nearby township. But this brought with it, some consequences. Hardly had the company begun to make a profit, when the township leadership installed a new company manager and demoted Ying to deputy manager. He did not accept this decision by the township and left the company with his stake of 20,000 Yuan. In 1986, he leased another firm in a rural area. On the basis of a contract certified by a notary, he was supposed to pay 2,700 Yuan for rent per year and 30% of the profits to the township. The contract was valid for five years. After only one year, the township leadership wanted to "correct" the contract, since Mr. Ying had achieved large profits. The township declared to Mr. Ying that such a rapid development of a private company was not allowed. Unnerved, Ying returned to his village. Only in 1987 when private companies were legalized, was it possible for him to found his own company in his home county.

According to the constitution and the law concerning private companies, the property and assets of entrepreneurs are legally safeguarded and arbitrary interventions on the part of the authorities are illegal. In this respect, however, the reality often looks quite different. As an illustration, the owner of the firm Jinyi in Hangzhou reported that when somebody misused the assets of state and collective companies for private purposes, they were almost never punished, although it was indeed against the law. He continued, that if a third party misused money and the assets of an entrepreneur for private purposes, this was not perceived as a breach of the existing law.

Many entrepreneurs complained that fraud and theft on the part of the employees (e.g. the stealing of money or patents) were not prosecuted, rather were treated merely as a civil law "conflict". At the same time they expressed their displeasure that, while they indeed followed labor law and had to sign contracts with employees, many of the latter, in contrast, did not abide by those contracts. Examples of this were the workers often leaving their place of work without prior notification or changing firm without the entrepreneur having any possibilities of invoking sanctions against them.

In terms of the formal laws, private sector companies have the same status as state and collective companies. But in practice they are frequently treated differently. For example, the owner of a company producing decorating material in Luohe told us, that the police there had imprisoned two private entrepreneurs due to delays in repaying to a bank installments for credits received. If they had been managers of state or collective companies, according to the entrepreneur, they would have remained unpunished. When private sector entrepreneurs applied for credit, they were liable not only for the total worth of their company, but also for the total amount of their private assets. Moreover, they had to pay a higher rate of interest than state and collective companies.[111] According to a study in Liaoning province, when private entrepreneurs applied for a credit, banks demanded from them that a large state company be involved as a guarantor, or that thirty percent of the private firm's asset had to be paid as a deposit. According to the law of profit tax, private sector entrepreneurs just like state and collective companies should be taxed at a rate of 33%. But in 1994 in Liaoning, private entrepreneurs were asked to pay a tax rate of 35%. The level of pay in private companies lies between 300 and 500 Yuan. However, outgoing payments for wages are not allowed to exceed 280 Yuan, when factored into the company's costs.[112] According to the regulations of some official departments, payment for interest, depreciation, donations and work-safety in private sector companies cannot be offset as company costs.[113]

Our analysis shows that merely 36.1% of the respondents we interviewed were satisfied with the legal position as it was then, 63.9%, by contrast, were only partially (48.6%), or not at all (15.3%) satisfied. According to a Chinese study in 1997 amongst owners and/or directors of companies with all kinds of ownership structures, 58.6% of the private sector entrepreneurs interviewed (but only 38.2% of all the respondents), stated that the poor state of the legal

---

[111] Interview with the owner of the Hengde Shoe Factory in Luohe and with the Company for Agricultural Machinery Ltd. in Baiyin.

[112] Liaoning sheng siying jingji fazhan de yi er san 1994: 371.

[113] Li Xinxin 1994: 120.

system had been the main reason for the limitations in competition, and 46.4% (contrasted with 36.8% for all respondents) said that unfair competition ought to be legally prosecuted.[114] In this result, the legal uncertainty already described manifests itself. In addition, it becomes clear that and why the private entrepreneurial stratum is so interested in the development of a legal system.

(2) Some departments of local government pursue primarily their own economic agendas when administering private sector companies

In the traditional planned economic system all state and collective companies were subject to a specialized, higher administrative institution. These organs were either assigned to different ministries to do with the economy (ministry for agriculture, textiles, electrical technology, etc.) or the departments of local government (provincial/ urban/county or township administration). They coordinated the companies' affairs with other departments of local government. For private entrepreneurs in contrast no such corresponding institution exists. On the one hand, that is for the entrepreneur an advantage, since the administrative interference is as a result less. On the other hand, this is also a disadvantage, since countless company matters are only realizable with the approval of different departments of local government. For an individual company it is, however, difficult to negotiate with different authorities and administrations (for water and electricity supply alone) and to obtain agreement. If the department responsible for the private entrepreneurs were to coordinate important procedures with other companies, it would be much quicker and simpler to conclude many things.

Up till now there have been no unambiguous central regulations concerning the principal areas of official responsibility for the private sector. Since such responsibilities are usually associated with the payment of administrative levies, some administrative institutions argue amongst themselves (such as the Bureau for the Administration of Industry and Commerce, the Associations for Industry and Commerce, or the authorities responsible for rural enterprises), as to which should be the institution charged with the overseeing and administration for the sector.

Officially, the Bureau for the Administration of Industry and Commerce is the department responsible for the administration of this sector. But it is not only competent for the private sector, rather too for the market regulations (cartel office), for the battle against white-collar crime and for the registration of trademarks. Within this institution a specialized department for the private sector had been set up which has the following tasks:

- registration and approval when companies are founded;
- implementation and checking the implementation of legal regulations for the private sector;

---

[114] Zhongguo qiyejia diaocha xitong 1997: 28 and 34.

- organizing different in-company and further training courses for entrepreneurs (management trainings and different courses about legal regulations etc.);
- legal advice through its own legal department
- controlling the annual accounts.

In 1996 and 1997, the departments of local government demanded from every registered private enterprise an administrative fee amounting to 1–3% of the turnover. The Association of Industry and Commerce in turn objected on the grounds that they were the administrative institution truly responsible for the private sector. In some provinces (Liaoning, Shandong and others), they proposed that first of all, they wanted to check through applications for founding private enterprises, and then put them on the table of the Bureau for the Administration of Industry and Commerce to give the ultimate stamp of approval. At the same time, the Association demanded that the association representing private enterprises (Association for Private Enterprises), which is subordinate to the Bureau for the Administration of Industry and Commerce should in future be subject to it instead, since entrepreneurs were members of both organizations and, therefore, had to pay doubled membership fees. The administrative departments for the rural enterprises also demanded that they be given administrative powers over private companies.

During our conversations with this department in Zhejiang, the official responsible stated, that the Bureau for the Administration of Industry and Commerce merely charged administrative fees, but did not offer in return the proper services appropriate for private enterprises, especially for companies in rural areas e.g. support for the search for real estate, access to credits from banks, and for the provision of water and electricity. He claimed that his department alone was in a position to do that. In some cities of this province (for instance Fuyang and Xiaoshan) the local governments resolved in 1995, that, in future, this department should be responsible for private enterprises. In these places, the administrative fees were charged in a unified manner by the tax authorities, and were then passed on to the authorities responsible.

By a decree of the local government of Fuyang, the administrative fee was fixed at 1% of the turnover (12,000 Yuan as an annual maximum per company). 70% of the fees were to be given to the department for rural enterprises, 15% to the Bureau for the Administration of Industry and Commerce, and 15% to the Association of Industry and Commerce.[115]

Apart from the three institutions named above, there are numerous other departments that have something to do with the private sector companies, and for reasons of their own economic agendas, want to take part in the administration of the private sector. Amongst those one may include, for example, the offices

---

[115] Interview with the Bureau for the Administration of Township and Village Enterprises, 1 April 1996.

responsible in each case for construction, for labor or tax, the departments of local government for environmental protection, land administration and quality control, the police, the street committees responsible as well as the department for supplying water and electricity.

Every department of local government can demand levies from private sector companies for whatever reason they choose. For example, a street committee in Shenyang wanted , from the private sector companies in its administrative area the payment of a monthly fee of 10 to 20 Yuan. If entrepreneurs wanted to employ somebody new, they had to divert 1% of the total wages of the person in question as an administrative fee to the employment office responsible. According to a survey amongst 276 private sector companies in Zhengzhou (Henan province), in 1994 61 types of levies existed, whereas the government of the province officially recognized only 19. The total amount of these fees exceeded the tax paid by entrepreneurs by an average of 50%.[116] Estimates by Jiangxi province indicated, that in the middle of the 1990s the different charges comprised 20% of the turnover of the private sector companies. According to estimates by the National Statistical Bureau in the second half of the 1990s, this overloading through charges threatened the existence of about 20% of the private sector companies.[117]

In the middle of the 1990s, according to the Chinese 1% sample entrepreneurs judged the assistance provided by those departments of local government which were important to them as follows:

Table 52: Assessment of different departments of local governments by private entrepreneurs (China, in %)

	Supports us	*Average support*	*No support*	*No reply*
Local government	71.9	24.4	2.1	1.6
Police	45.2	44,8	4.3	5.7
Department for Environmental Protection	27.4	54.1	6.3	12.2
Office for quality control	40.4	46.6	2.9	10.1
Tax department	63.2	31.6	3.4	1.8
Department for prices	29.4	54.0	3.6	13.0
Health department	27.0	53.5	4.0	15.5
Customs	14.7	30.0	3.8	51.5
Office for the Administration of Industry and Commerce	76.6	20.0	1.6	1.8

Source: Zhang, Li and Xie 1996: 165.

---

[116] Liu Yingjie 1994: 246.
[117] Li Xinxin 1994: 121.

The departments of local government and the Bureaus for the Administration of Industry and Commerce were thought to provide the best assistance. This may have something to do with the fact that both are the most substantial for the development of private sector companies, and that entrepreneurs were dependent on them more than any other: politically (local government) and in terms of administration (Bureau for the Administration of Industry and Commerce).

However, at the same time the development of the private sector is clearly in the interests of both institutions. Through economic development the departments of local government have to legitimate themselves in the eyes of the higher echelons. Since the private sector is nowadays the engine of development, provides a growing share of the tax income, and ever increasingly becomes the sector where the most new jobs are created, it lies in the interests of the local government to develop this sector. There were in Henan (as mentioned above) specific development quotas for the officials responsible for the private sector, for whose fulfillment or over-fulfillment bonuses had been paid. So their incomes had been dependent on that, with the result that the officers tried with the help of all possible measures to increase the number of company start-ups (cf. section 3.3.1). The Bureau for the Administration of Industry and Commerce in turn was interested in growth of the private sector, as more firms also meant increased incomes through administrative fees. Through those fees the wealth and power of that institution grows as do the salaries and bonuses of its employees as well as the extent of their social welfare benefits. Here too, the interest on the part of departments of local government in a rapid development of the private sector assists the economization of politics, and contributes thereby to remodeling of the political and social structures of the society.

Other local government offices glance with envy at the Bureau for the Administration of Industry and Commerce, and try likewise to profit through the private sector. In this way different departments start to compete with each other and there are conflicts of interest. The local government and the Bureau for the Administration of Industry and Commerce present themselves, truly in their own interests, as the protective saints of the entrepreneurial stratum because they attempt to protect the latter from damage. Due to this reason as well, one can explain the high percentage that referred to a large amount of support from the local government and the Bureau for the Administration of Industry and Commerce.

(1) Bribery and corruption

In order to minimize arbitrary behavior on the part of departments of local government or to bring about advantages for themselves from the administration, entrepreneurs in both countries also turn to bribery as a means. Due to their low pay, cadres often tend to "swap" their administrative power for money or other material advantages, or to work for the interests of the entrepreneurs.

Since we have already sufficiently documented this in respect of China in other texts,[118] this theme will be made clear only in respect of Vietnam.

Due to the authoritarian, Leninist, state structures and the lack of legal security, the private sector is dependent on the behavior of the bureaucracy to a great extent. And although China and Vietnam find themselves in a transitional phase from a planned economy to rather market orientated, economic structures, the bureaucracy as it was before is a major economic player, since it has control over key resources (such as energy and land). Furthermore a large number of state companies exist which monopolize key spheres.

The structure of relationships between entrepreneurs, the state and departments of local government possesses as a result core significance for the occupational activities of the former. There are different possibilities to shape this structure of relationships in conditions of legal insecurity, and the monopoly on legal interpretation on the part of the bureaucracy. This can for example take place by means of the expansion of social connections (*guanxi*), or also through bribery, presents or, what is very widespread, regular payments of so-called "donations" to the local administrations (cf. on those practices Part II Section 3). An apparent motive for the demanding by departments of local government or officials of donations consists of making themselves rich, whereby the civil servants due to their positions hardly have to worry about serious legal consequences.

The state, in the form of political leadership, is completely aware of the problem of corruption, but has not been up to now in a position to take effective counter-measures. Even draconian measures such as sentencing people to long periods in prison or indeed the death penalty, could not halt the cancerous growth that is corruption, since people who complain in public, often themselves then become victims of arbitrary measures.

The death penalty is used in cases in which a government employee has accepted more than (US) $27,300.[119] In 1996, according to figures released by the Vietnamese Ministry of the Interior, they exposed only 24 "serious cases of corruption", with a total sum involved of about (US) $30 m, and 50 were put on trial.[120]

Indeed, it does sometimes happen, that even highly ranking cadres are brought before a court. In 1991, for example, six deputy ministers were put on trial, and in 1993 the Minister for Energy lost his position due to allegations of corruption. But before 1996, the penalties set were moderate, and those found guilty could once again take up their earlier posts at the level of province or administrative district after some months.[121]

If at times there have been prosecutions of senior officials, then these were not done due to a principle of equality in the face of the law, but rather against

---

[118] Heberer 1991 and 2001b.
[119] Parry and Tien 1997: 20f.
[120] Ibid.
[121] Hiebert 1993: 160-63; Marr 1995: 16f.

people lacking patronage, or against those politically out of favor. As a result prosecution or penalties for corruption also have to be understood as an instrument of political reprimand.

At the local level, the low salaries of cadres combined with rising costs of living favor the tendency to improve income through "donations". In 1997, administrative employees and policemen earned (US) $ 20–30 each month. A police captain in the Ministry of the Interior earned in comparison as much as US$150.[122] The negative image of the private sector as seen by older administrative cadres, still intensely anchored in socialist thinking, makes corrupt behavior vis-à-vis the new "capitalist exploiters" even easier.

Bribery follows definite rules of play, exact knowledge and maintenance of which are indispensable. Characteristically many Vietnamese do not feel guilty about their own personal attempt at bribery, rather only the *unsuccessful ones*. A talked-about example was related by a Vietnamese official of a foreign company who attempted to bribe a tax official in order to achieve a tax reduction. She described anonymously in the *Vietnam Economic Times,* the course of the bribery attempt:

> I gave [the official] about $40 but I realized afterwards it was too little and that I had approached the wrong person ... I tried to contact other, more senior people, but by the time I found the right person it was too late. She told me if I had come before, the problem could have been avoided. If I'd given her between $1,500 and $2,000, the matter would have been resolved and we wouldn't have had to pay any of the tax bill that my company had been landed with, which was much higher. It was a lot to give but she explained the amount was so high because it was not only her the money had to go to. There were others who knew about the situation, including her boss, and they needed their share.[123]

Out of shame due to her mistake the Vietnamese woman finally gave up her job.

Corruption has in the meantime become an ever-present phenomenon that extends through all areas of life as David Marr the well-seasoned observer of Vietnamese development   confirmed.[124] The insight of an inhabitant of Hanoi that it was now almost impossible, "to find a job, get a license to build a house, receive treatment in a hospital, get a child into a nursery school, obtain a visa to travel abroad, or secure a business or import - export license without paying bribes,"[125] is valid too in this form for the South of Vietnam, merely with the difference that the bribery sums to be paid there, are higher.

The endemic extent of corruption, and above all, the sloppy handling of the problem at the local level, have in village regions repeatedly lead to unrest, and cases of people taking justice into their own hands. An illustration of this is a case in 1992, in which enraged inhabitants of a village, Quang Loc, (district

---

[122] Parry and Tien 1997: 20; Minh Son 1997: 24.
[123] Minh Son 1997: 23.
[124] Marr 1995: 16.
[125] Hiebert 1993: 161.

Quang Xuong, province Thanh Hoa) tried to get hold of the local party secretary, the village chief and his deputy, the chief of police as well as the director of the agricultural administration. Those officials had over a period of years kept a large part of all taxes accrued for themselves, levied additional fees and granted to their relatives the best real estate in the municipality. Two of the accused were able to flee in time whereas the peasants held the rest prisoner over months. A number of attempts to free them by the police failed.[126]

The unrest in Thai Binh proceeded even more spectacularly and among the causes of that was likewise corruption amongst the local authorities. Riots stretching out over months even claimed lives. The Party reacted among other things by sending a commission that was supposed to collect the population's complaints about official corruption throughout Vietnam.[127]

Indeed, the Vietnamese press does report corruption cases extensively, but there are limits to the uncovering of such scandals by the media, as the case of Nguyen Hoang Linh, the editor of the well-known business magazine *Doanh Nghiep*, made clear. In May 1997, Linh had uncovered a corruption case in which Phan Van Dinh, the director of the nationwide customs authority, as well as other party officials had been involved, and which had cost the state many millions of (US) dollars. Some months later Linh was arrested on the grounds of an accusation of betraying state secrets, and in autumn 1998 he was put on trial. Vietnamese journalists interpreted the case as an unmistakable signal to the press not to go too far.[128]

The ever-present corruption is indeed on the one hand a financial load for the entrepreneur, but on the other hand it opens to them the possibility of obtaining and/or "buying" certain advantages. Another motive for the "request for donations" relates to the precarious budget position of departments of local government, which officials try to balance out by acquiring private money for the carrying out of local, infrastructural measures. What is at issue here in the overwhelming majority of cases are measures for the maintenance and/or repair of the existing infrastructure as, for example, in the case of Danang at the end of 1997, where at the time of the survey the main traffic artery was being repaired with the financial involvement of private entrepreneurs.

The need for capital in the infrastructural sphere was extraordinarily high (estimated at [US] $45 billion up to the year 2000), and could not be covered by the government's budget. So in 1996 the finance ministry drew up regulations to place on a legally assured footing the illegal practices covered under the euphemistic slogan, "Government and the people act together" of demanding donations for infrastructural measures. What was intended was

---

[126] Hiebert 1993: 160f.; Stewart 1997.

[127] 'Protest' 1997.

[128] 'Vietnam' 1997. Since Dinh still held his post a half-year after the accusations, Linh's arrest could only have originated from the activities of the former (the accused), without any more far-reaching political signal (from another source).

levying a financial contribution from firms and economic organizations that was to be diverted from profits remaining after payment of all taxes.[129]

The group of problems depicted above show that the activities of departments of local government in a number of ways constitute a significant restriction of the operations of the entrepreneurship. In conditions of legal uncertainty, it is a significant cost factor for companies at the same time, since a certain measure of security for running their businesses has to be purchased. Given that the legal path is still as a rule futile, benevolence on the part of the departments of local government can only be achieved through social relationships or corruption.

3.3. *Associations representing the interests of entrepreneurs*

Guanxi and networks gain in power, if they are formally institutionalized, for example, in associations representing the interests of professions, specialists or entrepreneurs, or in chambers of commerce. This is because in such institutions *horizontal connections* between entrepreneurs merge with *vertical* ones between entrepreneurs and the government bureaucracy (officials, party and state institutions).

Associations (or clubs) entail first of all people joining together for a particular purpose and/or the pursuit of common interests. In China, one can differentiate four groups of associations: those steered by the government (such as the "mass organizations"); government-controlled (such as the associations for occupations or entrepreneurs or clubs for social purposes and hobbies); informal (such as native place associations, clans); and illegal (such as secret societies or groupings which are underground/oppositional/criminal).

Whereas those maneuvered by the government have existed almost throughout the entire history of the People's Republic, the three other types could only be established in the course of the process of reform. The causes for that were, among other things, the coming into being of new social strata and players as well as increasing division of labor and specialization in the course of economic reforms.

Since the 1980s, new groupings with special interests pressed for the formation of functioning professional associations and/or lobby groups representing particular interests. Along with formal groups, informal ones appear too, and alongside traditional forms of organization there are modern ones (such as women's or environmental groups). This development started first of all in rural areas, where the return to familial forms of business activity and the withdraw of the state from villages favored the formation of interest associations representing peasants. Often, these were the revivals of traditional organizations (such as clans, religious and temple associations or secret societies). In the urban areas, peasants then began to group themselves together again in tradi-

---

[129] Kim Oanh 1996: 22.

tional unofficial organizations and associations representing their interests, above all in native place associations and gangs of beggars. Even (illegal) trade unions of migrant workers came into being, and these have organized strikes and demonstrations.

As in other developing countries, the fragmentation of peasants in the urban areas led to a spontaneous creation of associations on the basis of local, ethnic and occupational origins. At the same time, commercial associations were formed in urban areas (for entrepreneurs or particular sectors and occupational groups), hobby and sports associations. Although the non-official associations to some extent were linked to traditional structures, their formation shows that there is a growing need amongst the population for independent organizations.

Social organizations brokering between government and society are not a novelty for the Chinese society. Traditional organizations were based on occupational groups joining together (business people, traders or crafts persons), intellectuals, on kinship (clan) or origins (native place associations). Above all in rural areas, secret societies or communities representing the interests of peasants (irrigation societies, peasant militias) played an important role. In the urban areas towards the end of the Qing era, numerous "modern" organizations were formed for occupational groups or intellectuals, chambers of commerce, trade unions, associations representing students, peasants, women or others. The weakness of the state in the late Qing and early republican era took its effect in the form of a growing amount of autonomy of those associations vis-à-vis the state. In this manner at the end of the Qing era, the chambers of commerce engaged themselves actively for the setting up of parliaments and the working out of a constitution. Associations representing students, workers and occupational groups played an important role in the May 4th movement (1919). With the re-establishing and consolidation of central authority after 1927, the Guomindang pursued a policy of incorporation and limitation against the associations. A law passed in 1941 intended the direct tie to and control by governmental institutions. With the founding of the People's Republic most associations were either dissolved or transformed into organizations controlled by the Party.[130]

Seen in terms of cultural history, independent associations representing particular interests contradict the Confucian command to subordinate all interests vis-à-vis the authorities. This too applied to the guilds that played such a significant role in the European development process. Unlike in Europe, the Chinese craftspeople and businessmen/women never had a determining influence on historical events, and hardly participated in the struggle for political and civil rights.

Guilds, which existed relatively early were mostly organized based on the family structure as a role model, and represented particularistic interests. They conformed to the bureaucracy that dominated the urban areas and markets and

---

[130] Cf. on that the study by Yu Heping 1993.

chose the path of negotiation and petition, seldom that of confrontation. They offered their members material advantages and represented their interests in negotiations with the official departments. Through a rigorous, internal legal code, the guilds encouraged their members to fulfill their obligations to the government, especially given that they were responsible to the authorities for the behavior of their members. The latter were supported in times of crisis, and the guilds took action – when things became intolerable – against the civil servants, who extorted illegal levies from the traders using any pretext whatsoever. The guilds financed themselves mostly through taxes on goods that they themselves imposed. Every guild was headed by a salaried civil servant who thanks to his position negotiated with superior civil servants, and as a representative of the association in question assumed a recognized official position. This corporatist structure which let itself be adapted seamlessly into the monopolistic controlling and manipulative character of the CCP, resembled to a certain extent the current framework existing for associations in the People's Republic of China (for instance the Association for Private Enterprises).

The founding of scientific/occupational/social/artistic/sport or hobby clubs and/or associations has been permitted since the end of the 1980s once again. Hundreds of thousands of clubs and associations sprang up throughout the country, covering a wide range of social interests. Commercial interests make up amongst them an important segment of the associations, and those are expressed in the multiplicity of new occupational and entrepreneurial groupings. With the provisional decree 'Regulations about the registration and administration of social associations', (1989), the rapidly expanding domain of clubs was subjected to stronger governmental regimentation, which moreover was based on the policies towards clubs practiced by the Guomindang.

In 1998, a re-worked version became legally binding.[131] According to these regulations, a formal institution (official departments, state and collective sector companies, party or state institution) had to put forward the formal application for the recognition of the association, and with that took over the supervisory function (guarantor institution). This tie to state or party institutions should not lead one to jump to the conclusion that clubs and associations are governmental hangers-on that only serve the interests of party and state. Much rather, the expansion of the market and the political liberalization associated with that have created a potential social pressure, which has led to an expansion of social autonomy, and through that to a toleration of associations.

This (restricted) autonomy is tolerated, so long as it can be bound in a corporatist manner to the existing structures. Precisely that is the intention behind the linkage to a guarantor institution. But this linkage has allowed the many interconnections between the new associations and the government (likewise the Party) to come into being. As a rule, associations endeavor by means of these

---

[131] An overview about the changes is provided by Woodman 1999. See too Chen Jinluo et al. 1998.

institutions to articulate and assert their interests. This takes place in very different ways e.g. through negotiations or *Guanxi* i.e. the manufacture and utilizations of relationships. It serves the same purpose, namely to win over officials for honorary memberships or as "advisers" in the interests of political protection and social recognition too. In authoritarian societies interests can hardly be asserted in any other way.

The close links with state or party institutions prove at the same time that associations in the shape of autonomous organizations are (still) not possible. As a result in present day China it is not *pressure groups* that are intended, but rather *Guanxi-groups* which solve problems and conflicts according to the principle of patronage. This trend has been continued in the search for protection through powerful guarantor institutions, precisely because the allocation to and/or the linkage to an official department or public institution possess a function that is both protective and enhancing.

In a society in which the independent existence of parallel structures is not permitted, both the representation of interests and participation in processes of negotiation between government and interest groups are not possible without such inter-linkages. The Chinese "bargaining society" in which the interests of social groups are asserted less through formal means and more through indirect negotiation, requires such inter-linkages in the current circumstances, because firstly only in this way is a certain degree of participation on the part of social groupings made possible. Secondly, associations can exert influence on policies through the channels of the government guarantor organization that has been allocated to them. As a result such semi-autonomous organizations should be understood as the forerunners of autonomous economic and political associations. They possess a double character because they not only contain elements of governmental dominance, but also of autonomy. That entails that they are subject to state corporatism whereby the state at the same time allows these associations a certain functional autonomy so long as they do not make any challenge to the government. As a consequence associations have the effect of being organizations that certainly represent particular standpoints vis-à-vis the government either for particular interests, social control, education, and free time activities.

With the development of reform, the element of inclusion has increased i.e. the degree of involvement of a large number of persons, groups and organizations outside of the party in the processes of consultation and decision-making. But the party is trying to bind the newly created associations representing interests into the existing formal structures. All this demonstrates on the one hand that given the increasing economic liberalization, the state is no longer in the position to control all social activities, on the other hand also does not see the necessity to do so long as such structures do not begin to form themselves into parallel political structures. The state tries to bind the new organizations in a corporatist manner into the existing institutional structures. Unlike democratic societies, the corporatist elements in authoritarian ones rely entirely on the state as a decision-making factor. While the state involves existing associations in processes of discussions, it otherwise controls them strictly and prohibits the coming into being of parallel associations which (might) wish to operate independently of the government.

The latter phenomenon is classified too as state or authoritarian corporatism. In East Asia such corporatist structures that are already to be found historically in the political culture, have been created in the course of the individual processes of development in each case, and are strengthened (Japan, South and North Korea, Taiwan, People's Republic of China). In the latter, state corporatism that was authoritarian in style due to historical-cultural factors, synthesized with the Leninist factors.

But the further reduction of the role of the state in economic events and the growing social differentiation may well give the associations an increasingly important function in social and political processes of change.[132] As far as the private entrepreneurs are concerned, there have not been in China up to now any official, *non-state* associations representing their interests. Merely two semi-governmental associations exist which are supposed to formally act on behalf of their interests: the *Association of Industry and Commerce* and the *Association for Private Enterprises*. In the following section the functions and way of operating of both associations will be described in more detail.

(1) *Association of Industry and Commerce (Gongshanglian)*

This is a semi-governmental organization which for the most part accepts larger entrepreneurs, and which is financed partly from the state's budget, and partly from membership dues. It was founded in 1953 as the institution connecting the CCP and representatives of the private entrepreneurial strata. With the beginning of the Cultural Revolution the association had to terminate its activities.

Only in 1979 could they re-start their activities. Up to 1991 only state and collective sector companies could become members, but since 1991 private entrepreneurs as well. By 1995 it had formed 2,676 branches with about 1.02 m members. In 1995, 75% of the new members were private entrepreneurs.[133] The branches which exist up to the county level are not subject to the national association but rather to the United Front Departments of the respective administrative levels. In contrast to the Association for Private Enterprises, membership is voluntary. It is not completely misleading when representatives of the Association of Industry and Commerce declare that the organization pays more attention to the entrepreneurs, the Association for Private Enterprises to the companies.

The current, central official function of the Association of Industry and Commerce consists in promoting the private sector, in supporting measures for

---

[132] In detail on that: Heberer 1996; cf. also White et al. 1996.

[133] Gongshanglian 1996; Interview with the Association of Industry and Commerce, Peking, 27 September 1996.

the state in administrating this sector, and in a bridging function between CCP and private entrepreneurs. The Association itself lists the following set of duties:

- choice and recommendation of representatives of the private entrepreneur as candidates for the Political Consultative Conference through which private entrepreneurs are supposed to participate in political affairs;
- support for the carrying out of government policy for the private sector;
- proposals for the preparation and working out of laws and regulations;
- securing the legitimate rights of their members;
- legal protection for the members through legal services offered;
- making information available about markets and new technologies for members;
- occupational training opportunities for private entrepreneurs (such as management courses);
- arranging contacts to and cooperation with foreign companies;
- administration of the association's own companies.

According to the ideas of the political leadership, the main task of the association consists of influencing private entrepreneurs, and ensuring their inclusion in government policies. In the course of the total social process of economization, the association has come to perceive its main task to be rather in assisting the expansion of economic activities, and in representing the interests of entrepreneurs. In contrast to the Association for Private Enterprises, which is at least to some extent an appendage of the Bureau for the Administration of Industry and Commerce, the Association of Industry and Commerce represents the interests of the large entrepreneurs to a greater extent, given that they are working independently of the state administration. The directing organ is the "United Front Department" of the Central Committee of the CCP, whose task consists of the inclusion of social groups not bound to the party into political discussion processes. In the middle of the 1980s, the Association of Industry and Commerce – similarly to the non-communist parties – obtained a fixed quota of political representatives at the national level of the Political Consultative Conference (1996: 65 representatives). The partial autonomy accepted by the Party permitted the Association of Industry and Commerce to operate within a greater degree of organizational flexibility and interest representation.

The autonomy is strengthened through the formation of chambers of commerce (*shanghui*) at the local level that carry out their duties amongst associations and are not subject to a department of government. In 1993, the Association of Industry and Commerce founded a 'Society for Researching the private sector' that collects materials concerning this sector, edits publications and carries information about entrepreneurs in the media. In a conversation with the President of the Association of Industry and Commerce in Zhejiang province, he declared this prescribed political function to have become meanwhile outdated, much rather the economic activities should be given priority. By the middle of the 1990s, at its first attempt the Association of Industry and Commerce had become the godfather for the founding of about 50 non-state associations representing economic sectors and professions. But due to the political controls as well as interest conflicts with existing *governmental* associations this project collapsed again. Resistance from the Party and associations close to the government or party was simply still too stiff. Already in 1993 the Zhejiang branch association had tried to found a credit fund for private entrepreneurs, in order to make access to credit easier. But this was then once again forbidden by the Central Bank in Beijing.

These examples show that the Association of Industry and Commerce does try to free itself from governmental control and to operate in a more committed way for the interests of their members. The president of the Zhejiang branch association was, however, confident that the potential of the association to assert itself would grow, whereupon much further reaching measures would be capable of implementation.

This was then confirmed insofar as the Hangzhou city government at the end of 1999 approved the setting up of a 'Guarantee Ltd.' (*danbao youxian gongsi*). This company was responsible to the Association of Industry and Commerce, was equipped with 20 m Yuan, and was supposed to take over the guarantee for bank credits granted to private entrepreneurs, in order to resolve the credit problems of the private sector.[134] In 1995, in Henan province alone, 17 branch associations were formed at the level of the city, 157 at the county level and 871 at the township level. In 1996, the Henan Association of Industry and Commerce, (in contrast to the one in Zhejiang), still did not charge membership dues in order to avoid a double charge (entrepreneurs had to pay administration fees to the Association for Private Enterprises). With their support 20 different sector associations were founded (such as the Association of Shoe / Transport / Textile Entrepreneurs or the Restaurateurs). According to the opinion of the Association, the primary functions of these associations should be, to represent the interests of the private entrepreneurs and to limit autocratic behavior on the part of the authorities. But as in the case in Zhejiang, local governments repeatedly opposed such foundings of association branches because they feared losing political, economic and financial control over the private sector.

In order to legitimate everything for the public eye, the association organized amongst private entrepreneurs collections of donations and help for areas stricken by poverty and catastrophes. Between the years 1990 and 1995 alone donations amounting to over 200 m Yuan were collected for the erection of schools and streets in such areas and put into 29 development projects in total.

In poorer regions shortages of means limit the radius of action. As an example, the area of activity of the Association of Industry and Commerce in Gansu province was markedly restricted due to this shortage. The president responsible declared that up to 1996 no membership fees had been charged and the

---

[134] *Renmin Ribao*, 29 December 1999.

provinces themselves could only place small amounts of money at the disposal of the Association. Obtaining computers to establish an information and communication network broke down in the face of shortages of cash. But the national association had made one PC available, and lent the Gansu subsidiary association 200,000 Yuan. The state of affairs in Baiyin looked similar for the Association of Industry and Commerce; there it was at least attempted with the help of donated money from private entrepreneurs to maintain a minimum level of activities. Some of the groups at the county level possessed nothing more than a monthly budget of 500 to 1,000 Yuan and did not even possess their own office. As a result until 1996 in Gansu there were still no branch associations.

The differences in organization, ways of working and influence depend on many different factors: the strength of local or regional entrepreneurs; the financial power and with that the financial independence of a particular branch association; on the local structure of politics (whether a Party committee permitted them more or less autonomy); on the interests of the local authorities concerning the development of the private sector (for instance concerning the amount of taxation); as well as with the prestige of the leadership of the branch association in each place and their relationships to the local political elite. In the 1990s, Presidents of the Association of Industry and Commerce were as a rule vice-presidents of the Political Consultative Conference at the respective level (national / province / city or county level). To some extent the vice-presidents of the Associations for Industry and Commerce were well-known, larger entrepreneurs. In 1993 Rong Yiren, the former chair of the national Association of Industry and Commerce, was deputy president of the nation, a further indication of its high status which in recent years has been continually growing.

In order to gain members, the Association of Industry and Commerce has tried increasingly to represent the interests of the private entrepreneurs in respect of the government and authorities. In the first half of the 1990s, at the national level the Association carried out nationwide surveys amongst private entrepreneurs a number of times, and criticized the negative consequences of the political roller coaster vis-à-vis the private sector. At the same time it circulated to the Central Committee of the CCP and the State Council proposals concerning more assistance to this sector. In this manner in Luohe the president of the Association of Industry and Commerce, a private entrepreneur pointed out in a letter to the association the problem of market organization and administrative discrimination, and complained about the Bureau for the Administration of Industry and Commerce. Following that the Association of Industry and Commerce carried out an investigation and presented the results to the mayor. The latter then personally took on the matter and tried to find a solution of the problems. This makes clear that solutions to the problems as before depend on the attitudes of leading local officials, but on the other hand that due to their position it is possible for the Association of Industry and Commerce to bring problems out into the open and help to solve them.

(2) *The Association for Private Enterprises* (*Siying qiye xiehui*)

At the beginning of the 1980s an association for the small individual entrepreneurs (*getihu xiehui*) had already been set up under the direction of the Bureau for the Administration of Industry and Commerce. After that from 1993 (likewise under the direction of that Bureau) a start was made with the founding of the Association for Private Enterprises. At the province level the Zhejiang branch was the second of its kind (after Guangdong). The Association for Private Enterprises is a semi-official organization that is directly run by the Bureau for the Administration of Industry and Commerce. Compulsory membership (at least until the end of the 1990s) was the order of the day i.e. with the granting of a license for business a private company automatically became a member.

As a result, the Association for Private Enterprises is thoroughly reminiscent of the European guilds, for whom likewise compulsory membership existed, and which were governed first of all by ruling mandarins (only later the elected guild-masters). The regulations of the guild in Germany too had to be approved by the city governments. (Even in today's German Chambers of Industry and Commerce compulsory membership exists.) The chair of the Association for Private Enterprises is generally a deputy director of the Bureau for the Administration of Industry and Commerce at the same level of administration, and larger private entrepreneurs officiate as the deputy chairs. The budget of the Association for Private Enterprises came at the time of our study partly from the administrative fees that private entrepreneurs had to pay to the Bureau for the Administration of Industry and Commerce, partly from membership dues. In 1997 the annual dues usually lay between about 300–500 Yuan (max. 1,000 Yuan). The employees of the Association for Private Enterprises were for the most part employees of the Bureau for the Administration of Industry and Commerce. In Henan the Association for Private Enterprises employed 15 people at the province level, 5–8 at the city level, and 3 at the county level.

In each province the Association for Private Enterprises developed differently. In Zhejiang there were branches in 90% of the urban areas and counties and in 30% of the townships.[135] In Henan and Gansu in contrast at the end of 1996 there were branches only in a few cities. In the cities surveyed by us, Luohe and Baiyin, the Bureaus for the Administration of Industry and Commerce had only begun the preparations for founding branches at the end of 1996.

Officially the Association for Private Enterprises in the 1990s had the following duties:

- "self-education" of the members in the framework of the pursuit of government policies and legal regulations;

---

[135] Interview with the Association for Private Enterprises from Zhejiang, Hangzhou, 7 March 1996.

- self-administration;
- taking care of the needs of their members in respect of legal advice, obtaining information and other services (such as the founding of their own kindergarten, primary school, etc.).

In spite of similar duties, the functions of the Association for Private Enterprises and the Association of Industry and Commerce differed in the following points:

(1) The Association for Private Enterprises is supposed not only to represent the interests of the private entrepreneur but also those of the employees in the private sector. It is not natural persons (entrepreneurs) who are members, but rather juridical ones (firms). In Zhejiang the Association for Private Enterprises also included Party and trade union organizations, which founded corresponding groups in private sector firms and were supposed to direct them. The Association of Industry and Commerce in contrast only accepted entrepreneurs and was supposed to represent their interests.

(2) The Association of Industry and Commerce is meant to exercise primarily political functions. It should among other things contact large and influential private entrepreneurs, in order to win them over to take part in People's Congresses or Political Consultative Conferences. The Association for Private Enterprises, in contrast, is supposed to take care of more internal company processes as well as political socialization and control.

(3) The fact that the Association for Private Enterprises is subordinate to the Bureau for the Administration of Industry and Commerce indeed facilitates contacts and cooperation with other official departments. And on the one hand, the entrepreneurial strata are able through the Bureau for the Administration of Industry and Commerce to place administrative force behind their wishes and interests. On the other hand the 'United Front Departments' of the Party to whom the Associations for Industry and Commerce are subordinate, in hierarchical terms is above the Bureau for the Administration of Industry and Commerce, so that the Associations for Industry and Commerce possess a hierarchical-institutional advantage in negotiations.

The symbiosis between the United Front Department and the Association of Industry and Commerce was apparently intensified further. At the beginning of the year 2000, the vice-president of the Political Consultative Conference and chair of the United Front Department attached to the Central Committee of the CCP appealed at a conference on United Front work in the new century to strengthen cooperation with private companies.[136] He expressly legitimated thereby further support through the Party and inclusion of entrepreneurship in political processes.

---

[136] *Renmin Ribao*, 7 January 2000.

Both organizations find themselves, however, in a permanent conflict of interests. On the one hand they represent the interests of the Party and government, on the other hand those of the entrepreneur. Since the two spheres of interest only seldom overlap, it leads not only to internal confrontations between organizations and members, but rather also to external ones between organizations and the government. In order to ensure political control, as a result Party cells were supposed to be set up in the private sector firms. Already in 1994 the organizational department of the CCP in Zhejiang resolved that such cells should be formed in companies with more than three Party members. It seems that the controls through the Bureau for the Administration of Industry and Commerce alone are not sufficient. Moreover a significant section of the Party membership, namely those who work in the private sector, threaten to elude organizational control by the Party. This means a loss of members and of possible resources for social control.

But only in a relatively small number of the private companies that we surveyed, did organs of the Party, the trade union or the mass organizations exist (cf. Table 53). The absolute majority of the firms were not bound into such organizational structures. As a result private sector firms are important organizations for expanding social liberty. According to a Chinese survey amongst entrepreneurs and directors of companies with all kinds of forms of ownership, 85.7% of the private entrepreneurs interviewed (in contrast 74.9% of all respondents interviewed) expressed the desire for a "simplification" (jianhua), and with that for a reduction of organizational systems controlled by the Party within companies. This was with some distance the largest percentage amongst all interviewed groups.[137]

But the Party leadership tries to build up Party organizations in private sector firms, in order not to lose control over the private sector and with that an important economic and membership segment.[138] At the same time Party organizations in private sector firms represent a different form of organization from those in public sector companies: they are more strongly dependent on the decisions and interests of the entrepreneur, as well as market requirements; furthermore the entrepreneurs are themselves often members of the Party, or at least would like to become one. The conversations with entrepreneurs showed that in spite of all reservations, Party organizations were understood by them to be part of an important network (Party institutions), which can be utilized in the interests of the company, on the other hand they believe that they can shape these organizations according to their own interests.

---

[137] Zhongguo qiyejia diaocha xitong 1998a: 16.
[138] Zhonguo Gongshangbao 19 May, 26 May and 16 June 2000.

Table 53: Which of the following organizations exist in your company? (China, in %)

	Number	% of the total number[1]
1. Party committee	20	11.2
2. Trade union	26	14.6
3. Conferences of workers and staff	30	16.9
4. Communist Youth League	20	11.8
5. Women's Federation	11	6.2
6. None	148	83.1
7. Total	255	

Source: Own survey.
NB: [1] based on persons who answered the question (178).

Neither the Association for Private Enterprises, nor the Association of Industry and Commerce are independent organizations representing interests. In those places where they entirely or almost entirely exist as an appendix of the bureaucracy, they are not perceived by the private entrepreneurs to be organizations representing their interests.

Not only Chinese researches reveal this (a survey amongst entrepreneurs found that over 80% called for the formation of independent associations to represent them),[139] but also our own. So, in this spirit the majority of the entrepreneurs would like to have their own, independent, interests-representing group. Only a low percentage rejected a non-official organization.

Table 54: Is it necessary to set up a non-official association on behalf of private entrepreneurs? (China, in %)

	Number	%
1. necessary	106	59.55
2. not necessary	30	16.85
3. no opinion	42	23.60
4. Total	178	100.00

Source: Own survey.

[139] Qin Nanyang 1999: 109.

Table 55: Is it necessary to set up a non-official association on behalf of private entrepreneurs? (China, in %)

	Zhejiang	Henan	Gansu
1. necessary	53.6	63.3	62.50
2. not necessary	14.5	16.7	18.75
3. no opinion	31.9	20.0	18.75
4. Total	10.0	100.0	100.00
	Larger companies	Smaller companies	
1. necessary	61.1	58,5	
2. not necessary	18.5	16,3	
3. no opinion	20.4	25,2	
4. Total	100.0	100,0	
	urban areas	rural areas	
1. necessary	64.8	50.7	
2. not necessary	18.5	13.0	
3. no opinion	16.7	36.2	
4. Total	100.0	100.0	

Source: Own survey.

Entrepreneurs in Henan and Gansu i.e. in rather less developed regions as well as urban areas entrepreneurs were to a large extent of the opinion that an independent association was required. This was more the case than in the highly developed Zhejiang or in the rural areas. On the one hand this may be associated with the fact that in Henan and Gansu, the paternalism and controls of the associations and entrepreneurs were markedly stronger. In rural areas in turn, officious and arbitrary behavior on the part of the official departments is easier to get around, so that for the peasant entrepreneurs *Guanxi* appears to be more important than an "independent" association, which possibly would also entail a stronger independence from personal relationships, and with that could restrict their personal field of action. In this matter the size of the firms plays a less important role, even if to some extent a higher percentage of larger entrepreneurs expressed a desire for an independent organization. And further factors may be relevant for the differences established between the regions surveyed. In Zhejiang the Association for Private Enterprises was established relatively early, namely in 1993. Almost every company was a member of that association by 1996. In the cities of Luohe and Baiyin, the founding of branches at the end of 1996 was still in the preparatory phase. To some extent entrepreneurs in Zhejiang were of the opinion that the founding of an independent association could not be achieved at that time. Even if an independent organization were to be founded, it would either quickly be placed under state control or it would obtain insufficient competencies to allow it to be able to operate autonomously. Possibly, as some doubters thought, two parallel associations would then exist and the entrepreneurs would have to pay double membership fees.

Due to the current, dominant political culture, the existence of a fully autonomous association is not yet conceivable. In conversations with entrepreneurs it became increasingly obvious, that the majority were not interested in taking part in disputes with the state, that is they did not intend in any way a *pressure group*, but rather set their faith in cooperation with official authorities and *Guanxi* i.e. they sought to assert their interests informally. Associations were perceived rather as organizations for enlarging *Guanxi* not only with other companies, but also to important members of the bureaucracy. A deputy departmental head, who had been nominated to be chairperson of the Association for Private Enterprises in one of the cities surveyed, explained in respect of his tasks:

> I see my tasks in the mediation between the interests of the official departments and those of the entrepreneurs. In addition, I endeavor to bring into being as many and as important relationships as humanly possible.
>
> I did not find this difficult, because due to my administrative occupation, I have access to other directors of department as well as institutions of Party and government. On the other hand, I possess good relationships to the local entrepreneurs based on activities on behalf of the Association for Private Enterprises. I take on their justified desires and demands and I attempt to bring in to the political process the path of negotiations and petition.
>
> For that purpose, I make use of my good relationships to the local Party secretary. For success in negotiations the entrepreneurs for their part have to make concessions to the Party and the authorities [in response to our probe: in the form of donations, support of local guidelines and praise for the work of the authorities].[140]

Interestingly, our interviews with cadres at the Central Party School found that the percentage of cadres who expressed support for the idea of an independent association representing the interests of entrepreneurs, at 68.7% was higher than amongst the entrepreneurs. At the same time a lower percentage of cadres thought (12.9%) that such a network would not be necessary. Apparently, there is amongst officials a relatively high percentage that had nothing against allowing the associations that represent entrepreneurs a greater degree of autonomy. But, this position is at the present moment not capable of becoming reality.

That up till now the entrepreneur prefer a soft negotiating path is confirmed by the answers to the question, "If you favor the setting up of a non-official association, what function should this have?" (cf. Table 56). Cooperation with the government was named here in first place, support for the expansion of social prestige in second, help with the obtaining of information in third, and

---

[140] The informant did not want to be named personally. The name is known to the author.

representing interests in contrast only in fourth place. This ranking order was the same in all three surveyed regions likewise for companies in urban and rural areas.

The difference between entrepreneurs in urban and rural areas lay primarily in that entrepreneurs in rural areas more often than in urban areas emphasized the economic tasks of the association such as obtaining information and assistance with the spadework of business contacts. And those in urban areas underlined more often than entrepreneurs in rural areas the political functions of the association (such as the expansion of social prestige and representing the interests in respect of the authorities). As a result the political consciousness of entrepreneurs in urban areas appeared to be more strongly developed than that of those in rural areas. Representing their interests in respect of the employees did not play an important role, because work conflicts still seldom took place, and the employees in private sector firms are hardly organized (in trade unions for example).

Table 56: What would be the three most important functions of a non-official association? (China)

	Number	%[1]	Ranking order
1. Cooperation with the government	90	84.9	1
2. Support in raising social prestige	53	50.0	2
3. Help in obtaining information	50	47.2	3
4. Representing their interests against the government	39	36.8	4
5. Help with the spadework in making business contacts	36	34.0	5
6. Training	35	33.0	6
7. Representing their interests against employees	17	16.0	7
8. Others	1	0.9	8

Source: Own survey.
NB: [1] Based on persons who answered the question (106).

Although in Vietnam too some official and half-official organizations exist in which the private entrepreneurs can be organized, – just as in China – they felt their interests there to be not adequately represented, and believed that these associations cannot carry out the tasks that they are set. As a result of that, from the point of view of the private entrepreneurs there existed a significant need for the founding of a non-official association representing their interests. The following table shows that three-quarters of the entrepreneurs favored the establishing of such an association:

Table 57: Is it necessary to set up a non-official association for private entrepreneurs or to join it? (Vietnam, percentages in brackets)

	Necessary	*Not necessary*	*No reply*
Hanoi	50	7	1
Tien Son	24	6	1
Danang	17	5	
Duy Xuyen	8	2	
Ho Chi Minh City	32	19	
Thu Duc	18	12	
Total	**149 (74.5)**	**51 (25.5)**	**2**
Urban areas	99 (76.2)	31 (23.8)	
Rural areas	50 (71.4)	20 (28.6)	
North Vietnam	74 (85.1)	13 (14.9)	
Central Vietnam	25 (78.1)	7 (21,9)	
South Vietnam	50 (61.7)	31 (38.3)	

Source: Own survey.

This response behavior shows that the Party and the organizations founded by it apparently do not wish to have the interests of new social groupings represented. But, the large regional differences between North and South Vietnam are conspicuous: in the North 85% agreed with the necessity of setting up an independent association representing private entrepreneurs, in the South in contrast it was only 61.7%. The largest association, the "Central Council for Cooperatives, Small and Middle-Sized Companies" (VICOOPSME), which has its origins in the earlier, official association for cooperatives is mainly active in the North and since the downfall of the collective sector has sought new areas of activity endeavoring to organize private sector firms. Many entrepreneurs still do not perceive it as their own association representing their interests. As a result, there was actually a significant need to establish a new association that is less tied to the state. When one considers the functions such an association would have – according to the responses of the entrepreneurs (cf. Table 58) – it becomes clear that the VICOOPSME is not in a position to carry out those ideas of its role adequately. The situation in Central Vietnam was similar, where half of the companies were members of VICOOPSME and/or its regional offshoot DACSME: here too, over 78% would like to have their own independent association for entrepreneurs.

In South Vietnam in contrast, there existed no offshoot of VICOOPSME, but instead UAIC very much a large association for private entrepreneurs, which personally and organizationally linked up with the era before 1975. At any rate, around 62% of the respondents wished here too to have a non-official association for entrepreneurs. From that one may conclude that the work of the existing associations for entrepreneurs was generally experienced as unsatisfactory, and alternatives were desired.

In 1993, the Vietnamese Chamber for Industry and Commerce accepted private entrepreneurs as members for the first time. Membership still consisted for the most part of the large private entrepreneur. But, in the statutes of the Chamber it is stated that it was the only representative body of the nationwide *business community*. According to its self-description they put forward to the government proposals about political measures and reforms in the sphere of policies concerning companies. They possessed good connections to the political leadership and the president of the Chamber has access to cabinet meetings. A resolution passed by the Prime Minister (1993) re-emphasized the responsibility of all organs of the government to support the Chamber in the following endeavors: advising official departments in all questions relating to the business world; in working out political proposals and ideas, whereby these could be directed straight to the Prime Minister; and assisting in bringing about contacts and dialogues between company representatives and official organs.

Consequently, the space to negotiate appeared to be relatively large. Since this institution felt itself also to be responsible for large, private sector firms, the interests of the entrepreneurs could be directly brought into processes of bargaining with Party and state by means of the Chamber. Since then, political conversations organized by the Chamber between entrepreneurs and prime minister have taken place regularly.[141] As a result, the Chamber appears to be developing into the most important organization representing the interests of entrepreneurs.

The associations for private enterprises were first established in 1996 and operate under the supervision of the People's Committees. So, they are subject to stricter regimentation by the state and, according to interviews, were not regarded by most entrepreneurs as organizations representing the interests of entrepreneurs, but rather as official instruments of control. At the end of 1994 in Ho Chi Minh City, the founding took place of the Association for Young Entrepreneurs who were members of the Youth League. This association understands its role as that of a non-governmental organization (NGO), since it financed itself entirely from membership dues and, according to statements of the deputy president, reached its decisions independently of the Youth Association. The entrepreneurial members were aged 18–40, and for the most part came from the private sector, although it was above all owners of larger companies who were accepted. The largest, private sector firms in the association, the owners of the firms Kinh Do and Hung Duong, in 1996 employed 5,000–6,000 staff in each case, and possessed capital of about 100 billion VND. The concentration on larger companies appeared to have primarily economic rather than political reasons. The functions of the association equal those of

---

[141] Conversation with an advisor to the Prime Minister in Hanoi on 9 March 1998 and Jeong 1998: 189ff.

VICOOPSME (mediating business contacts above all abroad, exchanging experiences, further training, financial support, and representing the interests of the entrepreneurs). Outside of Ho Chi Minh City, the Youth League had up till then merely organized conversation clubs for young entrepreneurs, who due to their more modest set of tasks, size and organizational structure differentiated themselves from the Association for Young Entrepreneurs. In recent years, the latter have worked for non-discriminatory treatment in comparison to the state sector, and have offered legal advice to entrepreneurs.

But over and over again in the second half of the 1990s, entrepreneurs complained that this association only carried out its duties to an unsatisfactory extent, and many young entrepreneurs had therefore not been interested in membership, they stated. The organization had to do more for the support of entrepreneurs, work against discrimination and for equal treatment of private entrepreneurs, they argued.[142] Since 1997 in Ho Chi Minh City there has been a type of counterpart of the Women's Federation to the Young Entrepreneur's Club in the form of a conversation circle on the subject of, "The role of women in the modernization and industrialization of Vietnam". The conversation group in which problems relating to the female employers and employees were supposed to be discussed regularly, was open to all. The Women's Federation themselves had their own department for female entrepreneurs.

In District 5 of Ho Chi Minh City, in November 1996 the first club for female private entrepreneurs was founded, which at the point in time of our survey had only 31 members, financed itself completely from membership dues, and was led by the female director of a limited company making textiles. The setting up of a club at the city level was planned.[143] The specific, hermaphroditic character of the so-called, socialist market economy – on the one hand a state sector which continues to be given preferential treatment, on the other hand a rapid expansion of the private sector – not seldom forces the newly created associations to a tightrope walk: although intended to represent the interests of the private sector, larger state companies were also accepted as members, because they possess good, direct connections to the government, and help to relieve the associations of any suspicion that they are merely organizational centers of exploitative capitalists. In addition they engaged with gusto highly placed officials right up to the level of ministers as "consultants", as for example in the case of the Hanoi Business Club (e.g. 1996: Minister Pham Van Tiem as adviser). The associations can profit through that not only due to the good relationships of the advisers but also from specialized know-how. High-level consultants guarantee in addition not only unrestricted access to the official departments but also to the political elite.

The business club was affiliated to a Center of Economic Training CETAI which among other things organized training courses on subjects in the eco-

---

[142] *Viet Nam News*, 6 August 1996.

[143] Interview with Nguyen The Thanh, Director of the Commission for Communication and Training of the Women's Federation, Ho Chi Minh City, 14 March 1997.

nomic, legal and political spheres (such as market economy, Official Development Assistance [ODA]) in which cadres from all of Vietnam regularly participated. Although the authorities checked through the training materials before being used in the courses, it is noteworthy that the training of cadres at least in the economic sphere no longer lay exclusively in official hands.[144] The privately run, management training center in Ho Chi Minh City founded in 1985, carried out cadre schoolings among other things.[145]

The most important, non-official association for private entrepreneurs in the secondary sector may well be the *Union Association of Industry and Commerce* in Ho Chi Minh City. The association originated out of an entrepreneurial association which had already existed before 1975 in South Vietnam, and was officially founded in its current form in 1989. In 1996, it possessed more than 1,700 members who were organized in twelve industrial sectors and five specialist associations. A section of the members of the committee including the chairperson of the association, who was also a member of the People's Council of Ho Chi Minh City, Ngo Van Phuong, had already been entrepreneurs between 1960 and 1975. After the reunification in 1975, they had lost their firms, and had to begin again from scratch later. In the meantime, according to their own statements, they had once again become dollar-millionaires.[146] After years of cautious tactical maneuvering the private entrepreneurial associations have meanwhile shown a greater degree of self-confidence and with that a sharper and more-defined image. An example of this is that the *Hanoi Union Association of Industry and Commerce* UAIC in April 1996 for the first time called on the government in principle to change the direction of their policies to the private sector. In June of the same year they presented to the Party Congress a report with economic-political proposals. After the Party Congress the chairperson of the UAIC, Vu Duy Thai, expressed criticism of its results arguing that they damaged business interests.[147]

The UAIC see as their most important task advising the government in the formulation and carrying out of economic policies including questions to do with legislation, rather than their usual duties such as advising their members, training, making economic information available, or creating customer contacts. According to the opinion of the President, the UAIC is listened to by the government in Hanoi, and is certainly able to implement its own ideas. Meetings take place annually between representatives of the association and members of the government (right up to the level of prime minister and Party chair),

---

[144] Business Club 1993; conversation with Nguyen Van Bay, Director of CETAI and deputy Director of the Business Club, Hanoi, July 1996.

[145] Conversation with Nghiep, Ho Chi Minh City, 7 November 1997.

[146] Conversations amongst others with Ngo Van Phuong and Vo Van Hien, Ho Chi Minh City, 21 November 1996; Union Association of Industry and Commerce 1996.

[147] Conversation with Vu Duy Thai, Hanoi, 26 June 1996; *Vietnam Investment Review* 10–16 June 1996: 13, 18; Jahn 1996. He based this above all on the announcement of the Party Congress that in all joint ventures they wanted to found Party organizations; this induced amongst the community of foreign investors a significant degree of alarm.

at which current issues are discussed. In 1996 a delegation of ten UAIC members was invited to Hanoi to have conversations with the government and the People's Council. The UAIC also has direct access to the People's Committee of Ho Chi Minh City; at least 4 of the 85 members of the city's People's Council are UAIC members.

Although the possibilities for political action in formal terms are restricted to proposals, they are certainly able to exert influence, for instance in the sphere of legislation. After interventions by the UAIC MPs, for example, the publication date of the trade laws was postponed so as to enable the inclusion of new proposals. Before every decree of new economic laws, which touch on the concerns of the private sector, according to the president the Association was requested to take a clear position on the matter. At the initiative of the Association the government was preparing a law framed to support small and middle-sized companies, as well as new banking legislation.

The UAIC constitutes thereby an organ representing the interests of private entrepreneurs that possesses economic-political influence right up to the national level. On the local stage a whole range of further entrepreneurial associations exist, which in one form or another can exercise influence on local economic policies.[148] Sometimes they are, however, difficult for the non-initiated foreigner to access. Occasionally, disguised behind a harmless "bee-keepers association" lurks a group representing the interests of private entrepreneurs, which first of all serves as a forum for discussion and information for the members. The unsuspicious name hinders unwelcome curiosity on the part of outsiders (e.g. the authorities). According to our survey, unlike in China (84.9%), merely a half of the entrepreneurs (44.2%) see the main task of an association representing the interests to be the promotion of cooperation with official departments. The spread of desired functions was significantly greater here than in China.

Due to the governmental dominance and hegemony mentioned above, it is thoroughly understandable, even when it does not correspond to Western expectations of an association representing the interests as a *pressure group*. Under Leninist authoritarian conditions the existence of independent associations representing interests is hardly conceivable. It is not pressure from the state but rather consensus and consultation, in which concessions from both sides are possible that form the framework inside which such associations are able to maneuver at present. It is necessary for pressure and conflict to be avoided, and consensus behavior is required. At the same time, by means of negotiations and the results there from, they are able to take care of the interests of their members through formal and informal influence on political decision-makers. They influence political output in this manner, a factor to which we have already

---

[148] In Vietnam nobody knows exactly how many such associations exist. A list that is by now outdated, and restricts itself to a few provinces was put together by the association VICOOPSME that perceives itself to be a non-governmental organization. According to it, in the mid-1990s there were in Hanoi alone 32 such registered association.

referred elsewhere. So due to all of this the private entrepreneurs are reliant on good relationships to the authorities, and it was not business-orientated functions such as commercial contacts, advertising or market information, which were named as primary goals of the associations tasks, but rather cooperation with official departments.

In fourth place came the task of representing the interests in respect of the authorities (27.4%) (cf. Table 58). Whereas the duty of cooperation with official departments contains the elements of cooperation, harmony and consensus, contrastingly representing members' interests implies an element of possible confrontation and potential conflict. In those, the private entrepreneurs would confront the authorities as a closed, corporate community of interests, if too such a representation of interests takes on more subtle forms in East Asia. Beyond the relationships to official departments and the representation of interests, business concerns also find expression in the answers: commercial contacts, advertising, information and training for adults. This is especially important for entrepreneurship, because official departments do not place such services at their disposal.

The role of the entrepreneurial association in the sense of a tariff partnership i.e. as an organized interest group against an organized workforce was with 17.9% up till then still assessed at a rather low level. This would first of all require that the government withdraw from this sector and – in the framework of the labor law – allow the wages, salaries, conditions of work, as well as social insurance and welfare matters to be negotiated between tariff partners. Furthermore, independent trade unions could be formed as the corresponding institutions to the association representing private entrepreneurs. Both are in present-day Vietnam inconceivable. At any rate, this answer implies a certain element of independence towards the government, and almost a fifth of the entrepreneurs would see in that an important duty for an independent association. In rural areas and in Central and North Vietnam, there appears to exist here a greater need than in the South, possibly because the relations at the place of work between entrepreneur and employee are more strongly regulated in the North: the Party is more strongly involved. On the other hand, this result may be the expression of regional and structural styles of conflict: where the potential for disturbance or the lack of discipline amongst the staff is greater (as a rule in rural areas), an increased need for the entrepreneurial stratum to have their own organization exists, which could take part as an arbitrating institution in the process of overcoming of and/or regulation of conflicts or differences.

Table 58: What would be the three most important functions of non-official association? (Vietnam, percentages in brackets)

	Cooperation with government	Help with the spadework in making business contacts	Support in raising social prestige	Representing their interest against employees	Help in obtaining information	Training	Representing their interests against the government
Hanoi	30	22	27	9	17	18	26
Tien Son	18	14	10	9	6	2	5
Danang	11	3	5	7	4	4	9
Duy Xuyen	7	1	5	2	3	1	2
Ho Chi Minh City	11	17	5	3	25	9	9
Thu Duc	9	4	2	5	11	8	3
Total	**86 (43.9)**	**61 (31.1)**	**54 (27.6)**	**35 (17.9)**	**66 (33.7)**	**42 (21.4)**	**54 (27.6)**
Urban areas	52 (40.6)	42 (32.8)	37 (28.9)	19 (14.8)	46 (35.9)	31 (24.2)	44 (34.4)
Rural areas	34 (50.0)	19 (27.9)	17 (25)	16 (23.5)	20 (29.4)	11 (16.2)	10 (14.7)
North Vietnam	48 (56.5)	36 (42.4)	37 (43.5)	18 (21.2)	23 (27.1)	20 (23.5)	31 (38.5)
Central Vietnam	18 (56.3)	4 (12.5)	10 (31.3)	9 (28.1)	7 (21.9)	5 (15.6)	11 (34.4)
South Vietnam	20 (25.3)	21 (26.6)	7 (8.7)	8 (10.1)	36 (45.6)	17 (21.5)	12 (15.2)

Source: Own survey.
NB: [1] Based on persons who answered the question (196).

In general, the regional as well as the urban–rural differences in response behavior were at times considerable, and make clear once again the different
historical backgrounds and the varying conditions of development in the different areas. Over half of the respondents in North and Central Vietnam named
cooperation with the government as a desirable function, whereas only 25.3%
in the South wished for that. Due to the strong position of the administration in
the Northern and Central areas (promotion of the cooperatives instead of the
private sector), this response behavior is not surprising. That is indicated too by
the element of representing the interests against the authorities scoring 38.5%
and 34%, respectively, and thereby achieving much higher totals than in the
southern part of the country (only 15.2%). It is noteworthy too, that about one-
third of the private entrepreneurs in North and Central Vietnam started out from
the idea of private entrepreneurial group interests, which should be represented
corporatively in respect of the authorities. The entrepreneurs did not perceive
themselves any longer to be merely the objects of administrative regulations
and benevolence on the part of the authorities, but rather were prepared to articulate their own interests, and where necessary to assert them together.

This desire for the representation of interests may, nevertheless, be less explicable in terms of increased self-confidence on the part of the entrepreneurs,
but instead be the expression of the difficult economic conditions in comparison to the South. More than a quarter of the respondents hoped that an association representing the interests of entrepreneurs would increase the social status
of their group, whereby this task was perceived as much more important for
entrepreneurs in the North (43.5%) and in Central Vietnam (31.3%) than in the
South (8.7%). In the North the image of private entrepreneurs is still significantly more negative due to ideological and socialist ideas, above all amongst
functionaries, than in the South, where the influence of the bureaucracy is less,
and private entrepreneurs possess considerably more prestige. As a result it is
hardly surprising that this function came in last place in the South, whereas in
the North it was second in the list.

Through the formation of new social groups and strata in the process of economic transformation (such as private entrepreneurs), new interests have come
into being which the ruling parties and their "mass organizations" are not able
to represent. The births of new associations representing interests were the
organizational consequence of this process. Without a doubt such functional
organizations are in a position to articulate interests and to participate in society
and politics. They contribute to the pluralization of ideas and assessments and
facilitate in this way the unfolding of pluralistic thinking.[149] Such associations,
whose number continually increases in both countries,[150] are indeed not completely independent of government and Party. At the same time, they are organizations representing interests that are bound into processes of discussion

---

[149] Cf. among others Diamond 1992: 8/9 and 97.
[150] Cf. Heberer 1996; Thayer 1995: 52ff.

and negotiation with institutions of government or Party. Since they are involved in this way at least indirectly in decision-making, their effect is participatory. As a result, the entrepreneurial associations are not simply organs of the official/Party organizational hierarchy as are for example the mass organizations. They are not autonomous associations, but rather semi-official ones and, therefore semi-autonomous in the sense that state and Party are not simply able to steer them in the style of "democratic centralism". This is also no longer intended.

Much rather, government and Party want to organize the members by means of the associations, and create an institution for regulation as well as a structure for communication and information. Through communication and information the behavior of the decision-makers may also be controlled, and demands and wishes of the entrepreneurs flow into the design of policies. These interactive relations permit the associations to formulate interests and provide them with room to negotiate. At the same time, players are brought together through all of these activities, and so networks of entrepreneurs and channels of communication are manufactured at all levels. These networks include not only vertical relationships to officials and institutions but also horizontal ones to other entrepreneurs. At the same time the organizational merging process strengthens group consciousness, and leads to the emergence of a shared identity. Corporate inclusion and expansion of the entrepreneurial space for action connect with each other here. Studies of clubs and associations in the former socialist countries of Eastern Europe emphasize the role of such organizations as *agents of change*.[151]

3.4. *Opportunities which entrepreneurs have to influence local politics*

Our interviews show, that entrepreneurs influence local policies in very different ways. Generally speaking, over 80% of the entrepreneurs interviewed by us in China were of the opinion, that they themselves were in a position to influence politics (cf. Table 59). They expressed this in both of the options, "Find the solution oneself," and, "I try to alter it [decision]". This self-confidence was more strongly characteristic of larger entrepreneurs than smaller ones. The latter were more prepared to accept decisions of the authorities. Due to their economic weight, , as a rule the former possess more influence in local terms, and they also have more pretial capital i.e. assets which they can utilize for the purposes of exerting influence (e.g. in the shape of "donations", material or financial gifts to functionaries, or bribery). In addition, they possess multifaceted social and political capital in the form of positions within organizations (such as the Association for Private Enterprises or the Association of Industry and Commerce) or institutions (People's Congresses, Political Consultative Conferences). These are accompanied by personal relationships to important

---

[151] Cf. e.g. Sadowski 1994.

politicians. Passive acceptance is less marked amongst entrepreneurs in rural areas (15.9%) than amongst urban areas ones (20.4%). The greater self-confidence of the former can be explained by the factor of social relationships and networks being more strongly developed in rural areas, through which individual possibilities of exerting influence are greater. In urban areas, in contrast, a significant degree of anonymity predominates.

Table 59: If you believed the decision of a local department of government were unfavorable for the development of your company, what would you do? (China)

	Number	%
1. I would find the solution myself	88	50.0
2. I would accept the decision	33	18.5
3. I would try to alter it	54	30.3
4. Others	2	1.1
Total	177	100.0

Source: Own survey.

Table 60: If you believed the decision of a local department of government were unfavorable for the development of your company what would you do? (China)

	Larger entrepreneur		Smaller entrepreneur	
	Number	%	Number	%
1. I would find the solution myself	31	57.4	57	46.3
2. I would accept the decision	7	13.0	26	21.1
3. I would try to alter it	15	27.8	39	31.7
4. Others	1	1.9	1	0.8
Total	54	100.0	123	100.0

Source: Own survey.

Policies are not experienced, however, only as a passive factor, but rather as something that they are able actively to shape. So entrepreneurs try to influence local politics in the following ways:

(1) Through membership in interest organizations and political institutions

The entrepreneurs interviewed by us were, according to their own statements, members in the following associations:

Table 61: Of which organizations or associations are you a member? (China)

	Number	*%*[1]
1. Association for Private Enterprises	134	75.3
2. Communist Party	53	29.8
3. Occupational and specialist associations	34	19.1
4. Association of Industry and Commerce	33	18.5
5. Other political parties	12	6.7
6. Association for Individual Laborers	9	5.1
7. Communist Youth League	8	4.5
8. Others	8	4.5

Source: Own survey.
NB: [1] Refers to persons who answered the question (178).

Entrepreneurs perceived not only Party membership but also the Political Consultative Conferences and the local People's Congress as important political instruments for bringing up and asserting their interests. The composition of the People's Congresses constitutes a cross-section of society. Through their roles as representatives, entrepreneurs come into contact with the political elite (of each level respectively), but also with other influential personalities. As a result, 88.2% of the entrepreneurs interviewed by us also expressed an interest in becoming a member of the People's Congresses. Moreover, there have been along with the usual political organizations (parties, mass organizations) once again since the middle of the 1980s occupational and specialist associations.

There was compulsory membership of the Association for Private Enterprises, as already stated. Therefore it is surprising, that only some 75% stated they were members there. But probes led to the answers that the remaining respondents either declared that they did not know anything about this membership, or that they simply ignored it. At any rate, that a quarter did not classify themselves as members indicates that this association is actually not perceived by the majority as an organization representing their interests.

However, this quarter was apparently represented by other organizations: a smaller number in the Association for the Individual Laborers (small entrepreneurs) or in the Association of Industry and Commerce, which endeavors to emerge as the organization which genuinely represents entrepreneurs' interests. The memberships of the entrepreneurs interviewed by us in these three associations grouped together, nevertheless, comprised a degree of membership of about 100%. An above average proportion were members of the Communist Party (29.8%), whereby the proportion arrived at by us was far higher than the percentage of the Chinese 1% sample mentioned above (1993: 13. 1%, 1995: 17. 1%). Membership too in occupational and specialist association plays an important role. All in all, the degree of membership of organizations appeared to be very high and with that too the extent of at least partial exertion of influ-ence. Since the CCP is the ruling party, many entrepreneurs are interested in membership due to possibilities of protection and connections. According to a survey (1995) carried out by the United Front Department of the Party's Cen-tral Committee around 17% of the entrepreneurs were Party members, and 26.6% very much wanted to become members.[152] Yet, according to the Party statute, private entrepreneurs (in contrast to individual laborers) in the 1990s were still denied Party membership.[153]

But this position – also contained in resolutions – had to be reinforced a number of times (1989 and 1995), and this shows that in this respect, there are phenomena which undermine this. In the first half of the 1990s, countless cities and provinces resolved to accept in the Party and Communist Youth League those who were entrepreneurs in the private sector. A book about joining the Party, which appeared in 1993, specifically stated that those self-employed in the small private (individual) sector were allowed to join the Party, since they were "laborers", but not those persons from the larger private sector, who were to be classified as "exploiters". Those who, before taking up private sector self-employment, were already members of the CP could remain in the Party, the book stated, when and depending on to what extent they continued to submit themselves to Party discipline, obtained a legal income, and treated the workers on equal terms.[154]

But our surveys show that at the local level people behaved much more pragmatically. We were introduced in Luohe to a private entrepreneur who had just become a Party member. The person from Beijing who accompanied us asked whether they knew or not that according to the Party statutes, and a recently reinforced resolution of the Party's Organization Department, private entrepreneurs were not allowed to become members of the Party. A local cadre answered him: "We're not aware of this resolution. But even if it does exist, here they are accepted."[155]

Our own researches into private entrepreneurs in various counties within the province of Sichuan in 1999 and 2000, confirmed that the cities and counties apparently for the most part ignored this resolution from the central Party head-quarters. The local Party leaders hoped that membership on the part of private entrepreneurs would bring about better integration and control of that sector. Furthermore, through such an inclusive policy the economic and financial po-tential as well as the capacity of the entrepreneurs could be utilized more effec-tively (for instance with reference to the interests of the Party). Consequently, the clause in question in the Party statutes and its periodic reinforcement by

---

[152] Interview with representatives from the Department Unity Front of the CC of the CCP, Bei-jing, 5 March 1996. My surveys in Sichuan in 1999-2002 revealed that more than 35% of the entrepreneurs were Party members, see Heberer: 2003.

[153] This was changed by the 16th Party Congress of the CCP in November 2002.

[154] Cf. Yan and Cheng 1994: 137 and 140.

[155] Conversation on 11 October 96.

Beijing was over and over again criticized and circumvented by entrepreneurs and local governments. Individual local governments even proposed abolishing this regulation entirely. Resistance to it is especially marked in rural areas, where in 1996 about 40% of the private entrepreneurs were thought to be at the same time director or Party secretary of the villages and townships.[156]

In 1996, 8% of the representatives of the National People's Congress and the national Political Consultative Conference were supposedly private entrepreneurs.[157] In the same year in Henan 149 entrepreneurs were representatives of the People's Congresses and 281 representatives of the Political Consultative Conferences at all levels; in Zhejiang the figures were 431 and 499, respectively. The Association of Industry and Commerce coordinated the choice of candidates, whereby the percentage share as a rule, was stipulated by the Party committee responsible. In 1996 in Fuyang, 24.4% of the private entrepreneurs (584 people) were members of the CP, 83 were Party secretaries or deputy leaders, 79 village heads or their deputies, 158 (6.6%) were representatives of People's Congresses or Political Consultative Conferences ranging from the township up to the province level.[158]

Such memberships and/or positions permit the protection and the assertion of interests, the manufacture of important *guanxi* for political purposes and, through that the exertion of influence on local politics. In this sense, an entrepreneur in Yangcheng county (Luohe) reported that, as a representative of the People's Congress at the province and city level, it had been possible for him to act on behalf of entrepreneurs who had been badly treated or discriminated against by the local authorities. His elevated political position ensured his immunity and with that a certain social protection that he had been able make use of for the assertion of entrepreneurial interests and the influencing of local politics. A further entrepreneur, who was at the same time a member of the Standing Committee of the Political Consultative Conference of the city of Luohe, declared that since that Conference had a stake of 30% in his company, he enjoyed the protection of the local government. His political connections guaranteed not only a frictionless existence for his enterprise, but also were useful in the interests of making business contacts. Moreover, his political position allowed him to take up the interests of entrepreneurs with great force.

The owner of the firm Bei'er in Fuyang, at the same time representative of the Political Consultative Conference at the national level, reported in spring 1996 he had put forward to the national session of the Political Consultative Conference a motion, which would permit private entrepreneurs to join the CP. But it had not been possible, he went on, for him to achieve that, although it would only be a question of time, he stated.

---

[156] Interview with the persons responsible in the organizational department of the Central Committee of the CPCh, Beijing, 5 March 1996.

[157] Interview with the persons responsible in the organizational department of the Central Committee of the CPCh, Beijing, 5 March 1996.

[158] Information from the organizational department of the CCP in Fuyang on 2 April 1996.

The owner of the firm Jingyi, a member of the Political Consultative Conference of Zhejiang province, had with success introduced at the province level session (1996) proposals for the simplification of the authorization proceedings for private sector projects, and the implementation of non-discriminatory treatment in the granting of credit, and the legal safeguarding of assets of private sector firms.

Entrepreneurs also use illegal methods of participation. The social scientific literature records, for example, that private entrepreneurs throughout China often use the tactic of purchasing votes or candidates, in order to influence voting behavior, not only in government but also in the sphere of the Party.[159]

In contrast to China, in Vietnam only a relatively small percentage of entrepreneurs stated that they were members of an organization. Just less than a third were members of entrepreneurial associations (30.2%), almost a half were not organized. The category "others" could refer to the Party, given that we were not allowed to ask about membership of the Party. Unlike in China, there is no compulsory membership in a governmental association. As a result, the entrepreneurs on the one hand are less bonded into government-controlled structures, on the other hand they lack an association through which they could develop a common identity.

Table 62: In which organizations or associations are you a member? (Vietnam)

	Number	%[1]
1. VICOOPSME	46	22.8
2. UAIC (HCM)	15	7.4
3. Others	39	19.3
4. Member nowhere	90	44.6
5. No reply	12	5.9
Total number of respondents	202	100.0

Source: Own survey
NB: [1] There appear to be no double memberships.

In the interviews, it became clear that amongst Vietnamese entrepreneurs there was a strong interest in joining the Party. Here the Party statutes envisage that Party functionaries neither directly, nor indirectly by means of their relatives were allowed to work as private entrepreneurs. This prohibition included the sphere of individual or family companies. In contrast, it was possible for Party members who did not have an official position within the Party to found and direct small companies (family or individual firms).[160]

---

[159] Yi 1996: 11-21.
[160] Le Quang Thuong 1996: 124f.

This regulation was not uncontroversial within the Party. A highly- ranked Party functionary in Hanoi commented on this (in his opinion) mistaken decision with the expressed hope for a biological solution of the problem: those officials, who were against allowing entrepreneurs to join, belonged to the older generation of Party functionaries, whose biological clock would soon wind down. The younger generation were, he went on, in this matter considerably more open. In view of the achievements of the private sector in solving central problems of development, exclusion of the private entrepreneurs by the Party was complete nonsense, he thought.

Whereas ideologically seen, the private sector is disputed at the central level, the Party officials at the local level, exactly as in China, to some extent acted against the ruling emanating from Party headquarters: the secretary of the Party in Tien Son county let it be known openly that he was for the inclusion of private entrepreneurs, since otherwise members would "run away from" the Party. According to his opinion, the private sector was already so widespread and so generally accepted by the population, that the CPV could not afford to stigmatize entrepreneurship by excluding them from the Party.[161]

As a matter of fact, the Party since the beginning of the 1990s had been forced to struggle with a personnel problem, which had induced a deterioration of the Party's work (from the viewpoint of the CPV) and expressed itself in a decrease of members. An example of this is the number of members newly recruited annually: it sank between 1987 and 1991 from 100,000 to 36,000. The number of Party cadres, who resigned from their posts, in contrast, rose from 5% in 1976 to 27% at the end of 1995. Especially amongst the younger population strata, the Party was met with disinterest, which had led to an increase of the average age of Party members of 38.6 years (1976) to 43.6 at the end of 1995.[162]

Even in the districts of Hanoi, the political center of the country, interest in the Party had dropped. An example of that was the lament by the Party committee in Da Ton district in its report (1996) that 42 of the 182 Party members had in the previous year not participated regularly in the Party meetings. Furthermore while one of the twelve Party branches in the district had, they reported, done away with producing minutes of their sessions, the minutes from seven other Party organizations had only been written in a completely superficial way.[163]

The Party is thoroughly aware of the inter-relation between economic reform and the de-ideologization of the population, with which a loss of power by the CP is necessarily connected. Periodically, there are appeals to the mass organizations of the Party that they should produce more and better advertising that, it

---

[161] The CPV leadership decided in 2002 that private entrepreneurs could join the Party, cf. Far Eastern Economic Review 14 March 2002: 12 and 28 March 2002: 8.

[162] Thaaveporn Vasavakul 1997: 125.

[163] Le Van Sinh o.J.: 15.

is hoped, would lead to an increase in membership.[164] Above all, lower levels of the Party include private entrepreneurs who, to some extent are rather more interested in Party membership than other population groups. But one may even note a de-ideologization amongst Party cadres in a process of moving away from the original ideals of the Party. This has a negative effect on the cadres' work in the Party, as the Party views it, and they have complained about it for years: "After we entered the market economy, the seamy side of this economic system had a significant impact on grassroots party organizations, causing not a few cadres and party chapters to become less militant, even paralyzed, thereby unable to fulfill their roles ... Some of [the grassroots party organizations] .. became chronically ineffectual," groused, for instance, the deputy editor of the Party newspaper *Nhan Dan*, Duc Luong. The lack of revolutionary enthusiasm amongst the Party cadres and the members was also one of the themes that were discussed in more detail at the 8th Congress of the CPV in 1996. A four-year reform of the Party, it seems, did not lead to the hoped for resounding success, as Duc Luong admitted: "Generally speaking, the quality and militant strength of grassroots party organizations still do not measure up to the increasingly exacting demands of the revolutionary cause."[165] As a result in future entrepreneurs may well rise to become Party activists.

(2) Exertion of political influence due to personal connections with Party officials

The meaning of *guanxi* at the business level has already been explained (Section 2.1.5.1.). But social relationships and networks are not only important for business contacts, but also contribute to raising social prestige and to the exertion of political influence. Below I shall more strongly foreground the aspect *exertion of political influence*.

In the political sphere, *Guanxi* forms an important instrument of linkage and communication between social groups and communities (villages, clubs, associations, and occupational groups) on the one hand with individuals, and on the other hand with the government and/or Party. Moreover, it makes inter-active processes of negotiation easier and enables decisions to be brought about, which are either impossible or difficult to achieve in other ways. Under the conditions of a lack of formal possibilities for participation and weakly developed institutional mechanisms for implementation, *Guanxi* becomes a means for influencing politics and political decisions, and serves at the same time the linkage between government (Party) and society. But, since individuals and groups by means of *Guanxi* seek to acquire influence, power or advantage and often through it set themselves up above governmental, legal, ethical-moral, social or political standards, and furthermore, with *Guanxi* they consciously

---

[164] Duc Luong 1997.

[165] Cf. also the 'Political Report of the Central Committee (7th Tenure) to the 7th National Congress', Communist Party of Vietnam 1996: 7-109, here: 23.

take breaches of norms for granted, and obtain advantages for those involved, this form of behavior favors corruption and to some extent merges with it.

A Chinese study describes the political influence of private entrepreneurs at the local level as follows: some entrepreneurs used their financial potential too to establish personal relationships with highly placed officials in their own political interests. In this way, the entrepreneurs intended to influence relevant institutions and with that local policies.[166] Since personal connections to cadres, as a rule, are of an informal nature, entrepreneurs did not want to speak about them during the interviews. But, all the entrepreneurs interviewed by us admitted that they endeavor to build up close personal bonds to local functionaries. From the Association of Industry and Commerce in Baiyin we learned e.g. that almost all large private entrepreneurs in the city possessed closer personal contacts to the mayor than did the Association of Industry and Commerce. The owner of the firm Yuwang in Luohe reported in the context of difficulties with an application for credit, that he had turned personally to the mayor. In this way, he said, he had come into contact with the mayor's secretary, with whom he then developed a friendly relationship, and after that with the mayor. With the latter's support not only had the credit been approved, but also he was even able to complete further projects with the help of those two persons.

In Hangzhou, we found out that private individuals were basically forbidden to run karaoke bars and discotheques. As a matter of fact, private entrepreneurs ran nearly all of these establishments, mostly because they possessed very close relationships to the official departments responsible. Social capital of this nature appears to be indispensable to the relationships not only for reason of political security, but rather too in the interests of commercial advantage and favors from the administration.

(2) Donation behavior: strategic philanthropy

Donations are an important element which ensure social capital and possibilities of political influence. They represent as well an important instrument for increasing social prestige. The *strategic management theory* correctly terms this *strategic philanthropy*. According to a Chinese survey, donations count amongst the three most important factors for high social prestige, following the size of the firm and a positive image amongst the public (cf. Table 63).

---

[166] Li and Wang 1993: 49ff.

Table 63: What are the decisive factors in raising the social prestige of the entrepreneurial strata? (China; multiple answers possible, in %)

	%	Ranking order
Expansion of the company	83.3	1
Positive image in the population	60.0	2
Donations in the public interest	55.9	3
Representative of the People's Congress	34.2	4
Good contacts with the local government	27.6	5
Positive and regular proposals to the government	22.2	6
Positive depiction in the media	21.8	7
Joining the CP	18.1	8
Taking on of a position in the local government	11.0	9
Others	1.2	10

Source: Zhang, Li and Xie: 163.

It seems that the size of a company is perceived as the central indicator of the abilities, achievement and the success of an entrepreneur. In principle, the factor of positive image is, not an independent phenomenon, but rather dependent on other variables, amongst other things also on donor behavior. If an entrepreneur regularly donates for social purposes (such as building roads, educational and social institutions for the poor and needy), or for "political" purposes (bonuses or salary for functionaries, donations to the local Party organizations), this contributes to a positive image amongst the local authorities as well as the population (in the case of socially orientated donations), to some extent considerably.

Amongst the institutional factors, joining the Party and taking on a position in the local government is apparently less effective for raising social prestige. Entrepreneurs see in parliamentary membership a higher prestige factor. In contrast to a job in the local bureaucracy, the People's Congresses require less work time, do not entail any entanglement in everyday politics, but nevertheless ensure a high degree of contacts and relationships. Furthermore, to be involved in the People's Congress is to some extent freer because the representatives are not so strictly controlled in their behavior by direct supervisory organs (Party committees, local government in urban areas), as they are in membership of the Party or an activity in local government. So for that reason alone, the post of representative possesses more prestige. At the same time, good contacts to the local bureaucracy, but also taking on participatory tasks (making proposals to the government) appear to be factors that increase prestige.

As far as donor behavior is concerned, in China about 78% of the entrepreneurs interviewed by us stated that they had made donations for social and public interest purposes. In the middle of the 1990s, a Chinese survey in Hebei province, suggested that about 20% of the net profit of private companies was paid out for gifts, donations, and for public welfare.[167] The more developed the private sector in a region, the more the entrepreneurs donated (cf. Table 64). Due to their financial resources larger entrepreneurs donate more often (88.9%) than smaller ones (73.2%). Donations presuppose the financial ability of a company to make them. The owner of the firm Jinyi in Hangzhou declared, that entrepreneurs with company assets of up to 1 m Yuan were for the most parts only occupied with their own firm. Those with assets from 10 m or 100 m Yuan saw it as their duty to concern themselves with societal questions and social duties, he continued. If one compares the percentage of donations with those of the ratios between turnovers (of different firms), this statement appears to be confirmed: the higher the share of larger companies with big turnovers, the larger the percentage of donors.

In rural areas, the percentage of donors was higher (82.6%) than in the urban areas (75%). This is dependent on the stronger social controls existent in the rural areas, where the local communities observe that the well-being of individual families works to the advantage of the larger community (village, clan), and where the moral obligation towards these communities is significantly stronger. Often, entrepreneurs donate to educational institutions and the infrastructure in their native place villages.

One needs to differentiate these donations between voluntary and obligatory ones. Whereas voluntary donations raise the social prestige of the donor or are supposed to improve the *Guanxi* to the local bureaucracy, obligatory donations are paid, so as not to lose *Guanxi* and to circumvent administrative capriciousness. In the villages, the local communities often exert great pressure, given that the wealth of the entrepreneur there is more quickly recognized than in the anonymous urban areas. Pressure, but also envy and resentment have the effect that entrepreneurs remove their firms to urban areas. An entrepreneur from Yancheng County reported that when his factory had stood in his native place village, the village cadres had loaded onto him the electricity bills of the entire village. Inhabitants of the village had demanded products and services without paying for them, he told us. Demands to play host to the cadres of the village and town/township or to cater to them with gifts had assumed massive levels. As a result, he had decided to relocate his firm in the county town.

---

[167] Zhao and Yu 1995: 61.

Table 64: In the last year have you made donations for social and/or public welfare purposes? (China)

	Zhejiang	Henan	Gansu
Yes	60	47	31
as % of answers	87.0	78.3	64.6
	Urban	Rural	
Yes	81	57	
as % of answers	75.0	82.6	
	Larger entrepreneurs	Smaller entrepreneurs	
Yes	48	90	
as % of answers	88.9	73.2	

Source: Own survey.

Social obligation dominated as a motive for making donations. Over 84% held them to be central in the interests of societal development. A long way behind followed obligations to the native place community as well as to the local government ("thankfulness"). Whereas the obligation towards the native place community is based on traditional duties, the donations to the local governments serve a dual function for the manufacture and/or the maintenance of *Guanxi* (concerning voluntary and obligatory donations, see above).

A relatively high percentage complained about the demands ("requests") for donations, although such statements tended not to be made by many entrepreneurs in the presence of representatives from the local authorities. The actual percentage of such donations may, as a result, be much higher than ascertained by us.

Table 65: If you made a donation, what were your main motives? (China, multiple answers possible)

	Number	%[1]
1. Everyone should make a contribution to society	116	84.1
2. Thankfulness to the community in native place	41	29.7
3. Thankfulness to the government	32	23.2
4. Donations were requested	22	15.9
5. Increasing social prestige	13	9.4
6. Improvement of relationships with official departments	13	9.4
7. Other motives	7	5.1

Source: Own survey.
NB: [1] Refers to persons who answered the question (138).

Donor behavior is based not only on calculation, rather – as mentioned – also on internalized social obligation, according to which the public interest has priority over the interests of individuals, and every member of the community is supposed to support them. This applies particularly to persons who have achieved prosperity and wealth. They are then expected to remember that the community, from which they stem had contributed to their success and those, who are successful should now in turn give something back. With their donations, the entrepreneurs demonstrate that they are not only pursuing their own interests, but rather too are fulfilling social norms and obligations. And people who comply with those factors enjoy respect and recognition by society. In the rather traditionally orientated province Henan the element of social obligation and responsibility was more strongly represented amongst the entrepreneurs than amongst those in the two other provinces.

Migratory movements, the amassing of wealth and foreign influence in Zhejiang as well as the artificial structure of Baiyin (only a few decades old) with its many emigrants from other regions may have contributed to a weakening of the traditional obligation. In rural areas, traditional motives play a greater role, firstly because clearly defined communities continue to exist there and the social control over whether someone has met his obligations is stronger. Consequently, entrepreneurs who have close relations with their native place villages are also somewhat obligated to donate, which at the same time explains why only a considerably lower percentage claimed to have had donations demanded from them.

The statements "Thankfulness to the government" (23.2%), "Improvement of relationships with the local authorities" (9.4%), and "Requested donation", (15.9%) imply that the local authorities have created positive political framework conditions for the entrepreneur and/or will create them, whereby the donation is understood as a reward or stimulation. The percentage of donors motivated by thankfulness was higher in Henan (27.7%) and Gansu (25.8%) than in Zhejiang (18.3%), which might well be caused by the fact that the enforcement of the local authorities there might be stronger.

In contrast in Zheijiang, , the entrepreneurs in total were less dependent on local government. But in rural areas the interest in good relationships with the bureaucracy as a motive for making donations was clearly more significant than in the urban areas, given that entrepreneurs in the rural areas are dependent on the local government (which are closer in proximity for control purposes) during many business processes such as the acquiring of credit or real estate or in respect of water and electricity supply.

More markedly than amongst smaller entrepreneurs, the response behavior of the larger ones indicates a higher measure of self-confidence. During the conversations, numerous larger entrepreneurs opined that they themselves did not have to make any more contributions to the society; the fact that they were important employers and tax payers was sufficient proof that they had met their social obligations. Since they themselves took the risk and responsibilities involved in their achievements, they argued, it was not necessary for them to show any special thankfulness to the government. Due to their position they tended to know how to protect themselves from demands for donations. But, almost a third claimed that they regularly met their obligations towards their native place community.

Demands to make donations were more common in averagely/less developed regions than in the developed (Zhejiang). In Zhejiang, the authorities had also taken measures to prohibit the demand for non-approved donations. A lower degree of dependence of the companies on the local bureaucracy made the rejection of donations easier. In less developed regions, entrepreneurs are usually not sufficiently influential to defend themselves against arbitrariness on the part of the local authorities. This applies as well to smaller companies. Whereas larger entrepreneurs usually possess firsthand contacts to more highly placed local officials and so enjoy protection, the smaller ones have to submit to demands for donations so as to avoid immediate impacts on their business life.

In Vietnam almost all entrepreneurs stated that they had made donations in 1995 (see Table 66).

Table 66: Have you in the last year made donations for social and/or public welfare purposes? (Vietnam, Percentages in brackets)

	Yes	*No*	*No answer*
Hanoi	52	3	3
Tien Son	30	1	
Danang	22		
Duy Xuyen	10		
HCM	49	2	
Thu Duc	30		
Total	**193 (97.0)**	**6 (3.0)**	**3**
Urban areas	123 (96.1)	5 (3.9)	
Rural areas	70 (98.6)	1 (1.4)	
North Vietnam	82 (95.3)	4 (4.7)	
Central Vietnam	32 (100.0)	-	
South Vietnam	79 (97.5)	2 (2.5)	

Source: Own survey.

There was no great difference between the various parts of the country or between urban and rural areas. It is not seldom that the initiative comes from the official departments themselves. Above all before national holidays, it is common for them to make groups visits to private entrepreneurs in order to "request" a financial donation for a particular purpose. According to the entrepreneurs, for example, money was collected to support Cuba (!). The authorities tell the entrepreneurs what the lower – and sometimes the upper as well – limit is for the total donation. If the entrepreneurs do not respond to this "request", they will have to expect sanctions, which may range from the non-granting of benefits right up in extreme cases to withdrawal of their business license.

In first place in Vietnam too was the answer, "Everyone should make a contribution to society". As already detailed in the case of China, here too this is in no way merely a question of a legitimating character. Donations for the community, for infrastructural projects, the building of schools and clinics, or the battle against poverty bring with them social and political prestige, and contribute to acceptance of the private sector both in the population and amongst functionaries.

In Vietnam as in China it was shown in the course of the interviews that the prestige of private entrepreneurs is not only dependent on their income, but above all in the achievements which they produce for the community. And prestige, as many entrepreneurs explained, was a basic prerequisite in order to strengthen their own position in negotiations with the authorities about political questions (concerning entrepreneurship), and to ensure greater acceptance amongst the party organizations.

Amongst the motives for a financial donation, there was a range from, "Donations were requested", (from governmental or party institutions [37.3%]), to in third place, "Improvements in relations with the official departments", (25.9%). Here it should be noted that the underlying basis of the first-named answer is also the calculation that there will be an improvement in relationships that of course takes place subsequently to compliance with the donation request. A large sum of money, if it were available to them, would be used by 25.3% of the entrepreneurs interviewed by us to better social relationships, a euphemism, which very clearly refers to the relationships to cadres in the administrations of party and governmental administration.

Table 67: If you made donations, what were your main motives? (Vietnam; multiple answers possible, percentage in brackets[1])

	Everyone should make a contribution to society	Thankfulness to the government	Improvements in relations with the official departments	Increasing social prestige	Donations were requested	Other motives
Hanoi	42	5	20	1	32	12
Tien Son	22	11	14	6	10	2
Danang	18	5	6	2	3	
Duy Xuyen	7	3			4	
HCM	44	3	6		15	
Thu Duc	30	4	4		8	
Total	**163 (84.5)**	**31 (16.1)**	**50 (25.9)**	**9 (4.7)**	**72 (37.3)**	**14 (7.3)**
Urban areas	104 (84.6)	13 (10.6)	32 (26.0)	3 (2.4)	50 (40.7)	12 (9.8)
Rural areas	59 (84.3)	18 (25.7)	18 (25.7)	6 (8.6)	22 (31.4)	2 (2.9)
North Vietnam	64 (78.1)	16 (19.5)	34 (41.5)	7 (8.5)	42 (51.2)	14 (17.1)
Central Vietnam	25 (78.1)	8 (25.0)	6 (18.8)	2 (6.3)	7 (21.9)	
South Vietnam	74 (93.7)	7 (8.9)	10 (12.7)		23 (29.1)	
Ranking order	1	4	3	6	2	5

Source: Own survey.
NB: [1] Refers to persons who answered the question (193).

The answers that donations were made out of, "thankfulness to the government" for their assistance already carried out, in the interests of, "improvements of relations with the local authorities", or were made as a response to a suggestion by governmental or party organizations, do not imply only the element of corruption and forced payments, but are rather intended too to prepare the way for the exertion of political influence on the authorities. Over 79% of all respondents chose one of these motives for making donations, a clear reference to the widespread existence of such objectives. Donations, whether demanded or voluntarily made, are as a result first of all a one-sided initiative that creates confidence, and is supposed to prepare the way for negotiations that promise success. In no way is a service at once in return automatically expected. Much rather it is intended that the willingness to make concessions to the donor should be boosted.

On the other hand, the cadres from administration and Party would like to take part in the apparent prosperity that the private sector promises. Many try to obtain financial donations from the private entrepreneurs, for example, in exchange for protection, information, state resources for production etc. In 1995 almost all of the entrepreneurs interviewed by us accordingly made donations of money to the local administration.

4. *Cognitive patterns, interests and preferences*

4.1. *Social morality and social obligations*

4.1.1. *Money and social morality*
In Confucian intellectual history, the search for money and wealth was considered to be a rather immoral form of behavior. The Chinese like the Vietnamese interpretation of Marxist-Leninist ideology confirms this view of matters. Not least the process of reform and the emergence out of that of market economy structures connected as they are to that process led, however, to a gradual transformation of attitudes. Nowadays, the striving for monetary goals and wealth is not as negatively evaluated as before the reform process. Above all, amongst youth the attaining of high income is considered to be an important aim in life in both countries. Entrepreneurs, in turn, form a social group, whose occupation by necessity has to be profit orientated. Our questions aim at the attitudes of this group towards money and to the linkages between money and morality.

Referring to China, Table 68 makes clear, that almost two thirds of the respondents assessed the statement, "As long as one does not break the law, all methods of making money are correct" as "false", something more than a quarter considered them to be "partially correct", and only a small percentage as "true". So, the absolute majority have clearly defined legal and moral boundaries. The result shows that most of the respondents interviewed were of the opinion that when people strive to make a profit, they have to respect not only the law, but rather too the societal morality. But the great majority recognize that such an attitude is not the usual societal standard. Chinese surveys too give reason to think that a phenomenon of societal commercialization exists.[168] Only 9.5% of the respondents interviewed were "satisfied" with morality. 30.9% were "not", 59.6% "only partly satisfied". The entrepreneurs too critically evaluated societal morality, and through that the social-psychological state of the society. Interestingly, our survey among cadres revealed that functionaries were still significantly more critical in this respect: 48.8% were as a matter of fact dissatisfied with the societal morality, 50.2% were dissatisfied to some extent, and merely 1% were satisfied.

With increasing commercialization the significance of money, wealth and monetary power increases. Table 68 demonstrates this: from it one can deduce that entrepreneurs in Zhejiang, in urban areas as well as large entrepreneurs, that is to say in spheres in which the process of commercialization has developed more rapidly, agree more strongly with this statement than other groups of respondents. Only between 57% and 59% of the entrepreneurs in Zhejiang held this statement to be false. While legally speaking it is literally true, it appears to be above moral standards. These standards were more strongly emphasized in the following spheres: in the countryside, in less developed regions, as well as by smaller entrepreneurs, our qualitative survey indicated. At any rate, what was implied by the response behavior was a transformation in values.

Table 68: Assess the following statement: "As long as one does not break the law, all methods of making money are correct" (China)

	Completely true		Partially true		Untrue	
	Numbers	%	Numbers	%	Numbers	%
Total	11	6.2	51	28.8	115	65.0
Zhejiang	5	7.2	24	34.8	40	58.0
Henan	3	5.0	17	28.3	40	66.7
Gansu	3	6.3	10	20.8	35	72.9
Urban areas	9	8.3	35	32.4	64	59.3
Rural areas	2	2.9	16	23.2	51	73.9
Large entrepreneurs	4	7.4	19	35.2	31	57.4
Small entrepreneurs	7	5.7	32	26.0	84	68.3

Source: Own survey.

[168] Zhang Youyu 1993.

The response behavior of the Vietnamese entrepreneurs basically differed from that in China. Only a low percentage evaluated this statement as "false", whereby the quota of rejection in rural areas and in respondents interviewed was the highest. Above all, in North Vietnam almost half of the respondents agreed with this statement "completely", and 45% at least "partly".

Table 69: Assess the following statement: "As long as one does not break the law, all methods of making money are correct" (Vietnam)

	Completely true	*Partially true*	*Untrue*
Hanoi	28	28	2
Tien Son	15	12	4
Danang	10	10	2
Duy Xuyen	1	8	1
Ho Chi Minh City	14	30	7
Thu Duc	10	12	8
Total	**78 (38.6)**	**100 (49.5)**	**24 (11.9)**
Urban areas	52 (39.7)	68 (51.9)	11 (8.4)
Rural areas	26 (36.6)	32 (45.1)	13 (1.3)
North Vietnam	43 (48.3)	40 (44.9)	6 (6.7)
Central Vietnam	11 (34.4)	18 (56.3)	3 (9.4)
South Vietnam	24 (29.6)	42 (51.9)	15 (18.5)

Source: Own survey.

Here, the interviews showed that the legality ("As long as one does not break the law") stood more strongly at the center of the response behavior. As long as this was safeguarded, "naturally" every (permitted) method was correct. Moralistic points of view appeared to play less of a role here than the prohibition forbidding the method in question which might be used.

The overwhelming majority of the respondents (China 83.1%, Vietnam 76.7%, see Tables 70 & 71) were of the opinion that greater wealth is **not** attained by illegitimate means or methods. This is not surprising. For one thing, entrepreneurs hardly want to attribute illegitimate behavior to themselves and their social group during the process of acquiring their assets; for another, entrepreneurs do not view themselves as having behaved in any way illegitimately, much rather as having utilized traditional methods in the interests of their business activity. The lack of legal security and the political structures, those concerned explained, make indispensable the use of such methods in the interests of friction-free business processes.

Table 70: Assess the following statement: "Greater wealth is normally attained by illegitimate methods" (China)

	True		Untrue	
	Numbers	*%*	*Numbers*	*%*
Total	*30*	*16.9*	*147*	*83.1*
Zhejiang	17	24.6	52	75.4
Henan	6	10.0	54	90.0
Gansu	7	14.6	41	85.4
Urban areas	22	20.4	86	79.6
Rural areas	8	11.6	61	88.4
Large entrepreneurs	12	22.2	42	77.8
Small entrepreneurs	18	14.6	105	85.4

Source: Own survey.

Table 71: Assess the following statement: "Greater wealth is normally attained by illegitimate methods" (Vietnam)

Hanoi	11
Tien Son	5
Danang	6
Duy Xuyen	
Ho Chi Minh City	15
Thu Duc	10
Total	**47 (23.3)**
Urban areas	32 (24.4)
Rural areas	15 (21.1)
North Vietnam	16 (18.0)
Central Vietnam	6 (18.8)
South Vietnam	25 (30.9)

Source: Own survey.

Interestingly, a relatively high percentage agreed with the statement "Greater wealth is normally attained through illegitimate methods": in South Vietnam (30.9%), in China in Zhejiang (24.6%) and the large entrepreneurs (22.2%), in both countries the entrepreneurs in the urban areas (China 29.4% , Vietnam 24.4%). Probes established that a section of the entrepreneurs concerned were of the opinion for one thing that such dishonest methods were required if one truly wanted to obtain great wealth. As examples of such methods, the respondents interviewed named the following: the construction of good relationships with functionaries; the instrumentalization of relatives in high-up political positions; or even bribery. Moreover, entrepreneurs do not relate "economic wealth" to themselves, but rather to functionaries and corrupt behavior. In general, the necessity of employing such methods can be traced back to the lack of legal security and the arbitrary behavior of functionaries and institutions.

4.1.2. *Social obligations: entrepreneur and wage-dependent employees*

The employees dependent on wages in private companies form a very heterogeneous category that in both countries includes the following groups of people:

- specialized technical and management staff from the state or collective sector with above-average salaries and other material extras (such as condominiums, their own cars, or luxury goods);
- relatives or members of the clan;
- friends and people with whom they are in *tong* relationships;
- members of the workforce whose employment is due to other relationships;
- people recruited for employment from the free market;
- migrant workers.

Depending on group affiliation the channels by which people find employment vary too. The major part of the local workforce is not recruited from the labor market but rather find employment due to relationships. These people can be classified as follows: firstly relatives and/or members of the clan; members of native place associations or groupings (from the same village, the same town/township, the same county), or people who were recommended by relatives, friends or other persons with whom relationships exist. Not only in urban areas, but also in rural areas the employment of migrant workers recruited from the labor market, is gaining in importance. Just like the state or collective sector, the private companies use the cheap labor of non-locals whom they can treat more rigidly than people to whom personal relationships exist. Unlike the latter, there are no social obligations of any kind with non-locals. The weightier company positions are given to people with relationships or local place residents; less important positions to people from the nearby surrounding area; and the poorer jobs to migrant workers. This heterogeneity amongst the wage-dependent employees necessarily brings with it at the same time, a different status that is determined by the relationships to the owner (relatives, members of the same village), ancestry or degree of work-related know-how.

Statistically seen, in 1998 in the Chinese private sector an average of 14.2 people were employed per company. Although meanwhile one can find private entrepreneurs with a number of thousands of employees, the average private company is relatively small. This is linked on the one hand to the private sector having a short history (being licensed only from the end of the 1970s), and as far as the employment of wage-dependent employees is concerned, for a long time the whole subject was not adequately resolved. On the other hand, surveys about Taiwan suggest that there too enterprises are relatively small. On Taiwan, at the end of the 1980s (calculated on the basis of adults) a company on average had eight wage-dependent employees. Hamilton explains this with the wish of Chinese people to own their own company and their conviction that, whoever is capable of doing so, should be able to found one. Precisely this factor characterizes the dynamic form of Taiwanese capitalism.[169] As a result, small companies possess too a cultural economic component it seems.

According to the Chinese 1% sample that we have already mentioned above, the employment situation in the middle in the 1990s appeared as follows:

Table 72: Employees in private companies according to the Chinese 1% Sample (1995)

Employees	8-10	10-20	20-50	50-100	>100	Average
Founding year (%)	28.7	28.9	26.3	9.4	6.7	18
End 1994 (%)	31.8	28.6	17.0	19.4	3.2	38

Source: Zhang, Li and Xie 1996: 147.

Table 73: Composition of the workforce (China, in %)

	1992	1994
Management	6.6	8.9
Technicians	4.1	8.8
Workers	89.3	82.3

Source: Zhang, Li and Xie 1996: 147.

The average numbers of the workforce are higher in the industrial sector (68.8 - 47.6) than in the agricultural (40.3) or in the service sector (18.8 - 40.0). As Tables 72 and 73 show, not only the size of the company workforce increases, but rather too the number of qualified employees. On the other hand, it needs to be taken into account that in both countries private entrepreneurs employ family members, who are not paid as employees dependent on wages. The seasonal workers as well, whose number is sometimes significantly above that of the regular workers, are not included in the official statistics of employment. So the true numbers of employees are significantly higher.

According to Chinese surveys, the employees in private companies in 1995 turned out to have had the following specifics:

* 85% were younger than 25.

---

[169] Hamilton 1997: 254–255.

- The majority of the workers before their job in the private sector at the time of the survey had been peasants (urban areas: 58.9%, rural areas: 87.7%) or unemployed (urban areas: 18.9%, rural areas: 8.4%).
- Management and technical personnel were primarily recruited from the public sector (state and collective sectors).
- The educational level of the employees was lower than in other sectors: 10.5% primary school level/illiterate (in comparison: state sector 5.3%, collective sector 8.5%, joint venture 4.8%). The percentage of people who had attended a university was relatively high (9%, in comparison: state sector 24.2%, collective sector 7.4%, joint venture 15.6%).This is due to larger private companies increasingly recruiting qualified, specialist personnel on the basis of special material benefits and higher salaries.[170]
- 36,3% of the employees apparently possessed a written employment contract.
- The annual average wages (1995) were stated as amounting to 3,572 Yuan, which would have meant an average monthly pay of 297 Yuan (in comparison: state sector companies, 239, collective sector 195, joint venture 376 Yuan).[171]

Table 74 makes clear how entrepreneurs classify their companies, their own positions, and the role of the employees. In that respect – unlike in Vietnam – none of the people interviewed were of the opinion that relations between employers and employees should be understood as purely economic ones ("Workers are waged and should work, accordingly"). According to locality and firm there were differences in the self-understanding of the company in the organization of work, and in the treatment of the staff. As our surveys show, patriarchal ideas of the company leadership are dominant just as they were before. About 98% of the respondent entrepreneurs declared that their company should be led like a family, which means on the one hand the entrepreneur takes responsibility for the welfare of the workforce; but on the other hand they expect the respect for the entrepreneur's authority, and that employees behave as if they were members of the family i.e. selfless commitment for the goals of the company. This paternalistic view of things achieved almost 100% consensus in Henan. In Gansu, in turn, more than a fifth were of the opinion that a company must be led "like an army", which entails strict maintenance of discipline, and acceptance of a hierarchical order. The latter could be the result of the fact that many of the respondents interviewed in the city of Baiyin in Gansu formerly had worked in a large, state sector company for non-ferrous, heavy metal. Ac-

---

[170] According to Chinese surveys, the percentage of university graduates who wanted to work in private firms, had by the end of the 1990s clearly increased. For graduates in 1998, it amounted to 15.0%, the highest percentage, which had been achieved in opinion surveys up till then (in comparison: in state firms 40.9%, in companies with foreign capital 44.1%), cf. *Zhongguo Gongshang Bao*, 24 April 1998.

[171] We shall examine the purely nominal character of higher pay below.

cording to the statements of those entrepreneurs, in the 1950s and 1960s, this firm was organized and administered along the lines of an army, a factor that had apparently lastingly influenced their company concept.

Table 74: Which of the following agreements do you agree with? (Multiple responses possible, China, only Henan und Gansu)

	Numbers	%
1. Workers are waged and should work accordingly	0	0.0
2. The entrepreneur has to lead his workforce like an army	11	10.3
3. A company is like a large family	96	89.7
Total	*107*	*100.0*

Source: Own survey.

Table 75: Which of the following agreements do you agree with? (Multiple responses possible, China, only Henan und Gansu)[172]

	Luohe	
	Numbers	%
1. Workers are waged and should work accordingly	0	0.0
2. The entrepreneur has to lead his workforce like an army	1	1.7
3. A company is like a large family	58	98.3
Total	*59*	*100.0*
	Baiyin	
	Numbers	%
1. Workers are waged and should work, accordingly	0	0.0
2. The entrepreneur has to lead his workforce like an army	10	20.8
3. A company is like a large family	38	79.2
Total	*48*	*100.0*

Source: Own survey.

A paternalistic company management entails at the same time that the relations between entrepreneurs and staff are not merely purely work-oriented ones rather at the same time private, personal relationship exist. According to a Chinese survey (1995), 25% of the workers interviewed in it stated that their employers paid visits to funeral services or weddings of the families concerned. 30% of the respondents obtained in these cases financial or material presents

---

[172] Since a second question for the second phase of the fieldwork, this question only refers to the respondents in Henan and Gansu.

from their employer.[173] The creation of a family ideology internal to the firm, of familial feelings of the employees towards the firm and its owner has its effect in creating identity and assisting performance, and therefore meets the needs of the entrepreneurs.

Reality diverges from the imaginary idea of the family. The overwhelming majority of the occupants come from the rural areas, and mostly work on a temporary basis in a private firm. Until 2002 a separate labor law for the private sector did not yet exist. Therefore, the negotiating position of the employees against the employers has been weak. The former are primarily interested in keeping their jobs, and for that they put up with difficult or problematic conditions of work. According to our survey only 36.3% of the workforce possessed any written work contract at all, 32.3% had made an oral agreement, and the others had no contract of any kind with their employer. In 66.2% of the contracts which were made in writing, the obligations and rights of the companies and employees were not clearly defined.[174] Certainly, one needs to differentiate in this matter, according to whether members of the clan or family relatives to whom social obligations exist are employed, or whether they are migrant workers from outside to whom no (paternalistic) obligations exist. The relationships of work in companies with a high percentage of migrant workers are rather exploitative and unstable. Where the opportunity is available, above all in the urban areas such employees have meanwhile in individual cases turned to the courts for redress when breaches of labor law had taken place.[175]

In Chinese (as in Vietnamese) private companies a traditional style of management still exists as it did before, under which – in the ideal case – authority is centralized, and paternalistic and caring behavior are combined together in order to maintain the authority of the entrepreneur, but at the same time the well-being and enthusiasm for work of their employees. As a matter of fact, the two factors authority and welfare come into conflict with one another and slide into an authoritarian style of entrepreneurial management.

The entrepreneur is "the helmsman at the head of the organization", always the patriarch at the peak of the work hierarchy. So, he cannot have two roles: either he exercises control or he withdraws.[176] The military comparison between leading a company and an army has not only found its place in the social-science literature (e.g. economist Dong Fureng speaks of the entrepreneur operating like an officer and fighter),[177] but also in the Chinese literature about entrepreneurs. The entrepreneur Wang Hai argued to the effect that in respect of the competitive battle and the deployment of one's own life, the market and the battlefield resemble each other and: "Already very early on I declared that the entrepreneur was as a result, to be equated with the generals of the war

---

[173] Zhang, Li and Xie 1996: 173.
[174] Heberer and Taubmann 1998: 183ff.
[175] Cf. Wei Yan 1999.
[176] Chan and Chiang 1994: 350.
[177] Cf. Dong Fureng 1998: 229.

years."[178] He Yang likewise came to the conclusion that precisely the complexity of the employment structure in private companies, the low level of training of the workforce and the lack of discipline associated with that, required military standards. But it was insufficient, he continued, only "to administer with toughness" (yan zhi) and not at the same time with "care and attention" (qing zhi). As a result, entrepreneurs had to love their employees and to take care of them, just like parents do their children. And only then would the administration of a company be good all-round. In this sense the military, the family oriented, and the educational-training style can be considered to be the three basic styles of Chinese company culture, and the combination of them as the most successful form of company management.[179]

In Vietnam, the private companies on average are smaller than in China. According to a Vietnamese survey (1995) the situation concerning employees was as follows:

Table 76: Employees in private companies according to a Vietnamese study (1995)

Employees	<10	10-50	50-100	100-200	>100	Average
% of the firms	66.3	29.3	3.0	0.7	0.7	7

Source: Dang Duc Dam 1997: 178.

Whereas in China less than a third of the companies that had less than ten employees, in Vietnam it was more than two-thirds. Only nearly 4% of the Vietnamese private companies employed more than 50 staff (cf. Table 76), in China it was at least 22.6% . But the Vietnamese data contained not only the limited companies (on average 53 employees per firm), but also the joint-stock companies (106), so that seen all in all the differences are not so drastic, even if Vietnam lags behind China in terms of reform development.[180]

In Vietnam the assessment of the role of the company and the relations between entrepreneurs and wage-dependent employees has taken a similar course to that in China. In Vietnam too, as far as the relations between companies and employees are concerned, the comparison with the family was named most often, whereby here too the entrepreneurs understood themselves as "a family father". As Table 77 makes clear, over 84% of the respondents interviewed had this kind of paternalistic view of matters perceiving the company not merely as a point of production with rationalized processes for the obtaining of a maximum profit. The position of the family father implies on the one hand the obedience of the family members (likewise that of the employees) towards him. Insofar, from the viewpoint of the entrepreneurs the position of the employers

---

[178] He Yang 1999, vol. 2: 446ff.
[179] Ibid.
[180] Dang Duc Dam 1997: 178.

differs from their legally defined situation. According to that, the employees possess in the final analysis no rights of their own, which exist for them independently of the employer in each case, rather depend for the most part on the entrepreneur. On the other hand, the entrepreneur has the ideal-typical obligation towards their employees of taking care of their well-being, and to look after them beyond the work in the company. This special relationship between companies and employees is demonstrated – according to the opinions of the entrepreneurs – for example in that the workforce are fed and accommodated free of charge.

The regional differences in the response behavior of the respondents interviewed were low. But one would have expected in North Vietnam a higher percentage of family ideology than in South Vietnam, since the North, historically seen, was more strongly marked by Confucianism and as a result considered to be rather family oriented. One should not overlook that in the South already under French rule a stronger commercialization had set in along Western lines.

Three-quarters of the respondents stressed that the relations between companies and employees could finally be reduced to the formula "work for pay" i.e. were shaped by rational and impersonal factors (cf. Table 77), a clear difference to China, where all respondents denied this statement. All things considered this large percentage shows that many entrepreneurs are aware that the economic aspect represents a central factor in the company processes. The relationships with the employees cannot be defined exclusively by the paternalistic angle. The worker has to do a job for which he or she (from the viewpoint of the entrepreneur) obtains an appropriate wage. In this answer a critical element may also be present, because many entrepreneurs evaluate the work performance (measured by wages) as too low.

The regional differences were conspicuously large, especially those between North Vietnam where only 67.4% agreed with this statement compared to 81.5% in South Vietnam. In the North, imbued as it is by communism, where the paternalistic-socialist viewpoint was predominant in private companies, and the social prestige of the workers in contrast to the South was relatively high, a lower percentage were of this opinion ("work for wages"). In turn In the South the elements of the market economy play a larger role, and economic considerations were of more weight. Almost the half of the respondents interviewed agreed with a military metaphor: 43.9% were of the opinion that a entrepreneur leads his firm like a general an army (cf. Table 77). In contrast to the family father, this image stresses the position of the entrepreneur as commander. The workforce complies with his directions and carry out their tasks with discipline. The competition in the market is perceived as a theatre of battle, where one has the best chances of victory when one follows a clear strategy with united forces, just like an army goes into combat and into battle in a purposeful way. The regional variations in the response behavior were here surprisingly low.

Table 77: Assess the following statements (Vietnam, multiple responses, percentages in brackets[1])

	Workers are waged and should work accordingly	The entrepreneur has to lead his workforce like an army	A company is like a large family: the entrepreneur = a family father	The company gives my life an important meaning
Hanoi	35	26	50	[Not asked]
Tien Son	25	13	24	
Danang	18	8	18	10
Duy Xuyen	9	4	10	8
Ho Chi Minh City	43	22	41	30
Thu Duc	23	14	27	11
Total	*153 (75.7)*	*87 (43.1)*	*170 (84.2)*	*59 (52.2% of 113 answers)*
Urban areas	96 (73.3)	56 (42.8)	109 (83.2)	40 (54.8)
Rural areas	57 (80.3)	31 (43.7)	61 (85.9)	19 (47.5)
North Vietnam	60 (67.4)	39 (43.8)	74 (83.1)	
Central Vietnam	27 (84.4)	12 (37.5)	28 (87.5)	18 (15.93)
South Vietnam	66 (81.5)	36 (44.4)	68 (83.95)	41 (50.6)

Source: Own survey.
NB: [1] Referring to persons who answered the question (202).

In both countries, the patriarchal-authoritarian family concept can be traced back to traditional ideas of the family. The family was hierarchically structured and there were no relationships of equality within it. Loyalty towards the family head and – transferred to business life – unpaid service and work performance characterize the relations of dependence. Precisely this family concept is what many Chinese and Vietnamese entrepreneurs still have in their heads, above all when a large part of the work force consists of members of the family or clan, or are persons who were found employment on the basis of relationships. Loyalty and selfless labor were required precisely in the context of proving loyalty. Over half of the respondents saw in their companies a purpose in life i.e. the company was not only understood simply as a means for obtaining a living but rather as life-fulfilling to a certain degree giving it a special meaning. Those who think in this way will commit themselves much more strongly and long-term than somebody who is only working in the private sector for purely material reasons. At the same time this answer reveals self-confidence: Vietnam is nominally still a socialist country, the private sector has only been legal for about 10 years, and in the policies publically proclaimed is considered to be an extension of the state sector, that is of secondary rank. Those who recognize in private sector occupations a degree of self-fulfillment, spotlight themselves in contrast to the general public and /or the collective and so belong to a minority. A private company may represent self-fulfillment and aim in life: in that one can certainly recognize an unambiguous committed declaration of belief in a non-socialist lifestyle.

In the urban areas the percentage of entrepreneurs who were of this opinion was higher (54.8%) than in the rural areas (47.5%), a finding linked to the stronger individualization in the urban areas.

The response behavior all in all indicates that the entrepreneurs already possess a relatively homogenous self-image (family father), and unambiguous ideas about the behavior of the workforce (performance-related wages). In contrast, as to the most important factors contributing to the employees' work morale (cf. Table 78) job security in respect of losing their job (at nearly 39%) was named most often. It was not a surprise that this answer appeared more often (41%) in the urban areas than in the rural areas at only 35%, because many rural members of the workforce as worker-peasants are still strongly bonded to their native place. Unemployment in these areas still offers the possibility of returning to the peasant family and with that a certain social safety net. For the unemployed in the urban areas this possibility as a rule does not exist.

Table 78: Assess the question: "What in your opinion is the most important factor contributing to the work morale of your employees?" (Vietnam, multiple responses in Central Vietnam; percentage in brackets[1])

	Appropriate income	The abilities of the employee to do their jobs	Long-term job security	Good relationships between employers and employees
Danang	10	3	9	11
Duy Xuyen	5	3	4	2
Ho Chi Minh City	15	2	21	13
Thu Duc	8	2	10	9
Total	*38 (33.6)*	*10 (8.8)*	*44 (38.9)*	*35 (31.0)*
Urban areas	25 (34.2)	5 (6.8)	30 (41.1)	24 (32.9)
Rural areas	13 (32.5)	5 (12.5)	14 (35.0)	11 (27.5)
Central Vietnam	15 (46.9)	6 (18.8)	13 (40.6)	13 (40.6)
South Vietnam	23 (28.4)	4 (4.9)	31 (38.3)	22 (27.2)

Source: Own survey.
NB: [1] Question was only posed in South and Central Vietnam.

From the point of view of the private entrepreneurs, how large the problem of unemployment appeared to be is shown by the possibility that an appropriate income was named not in first but rather only in second place (33.6%). The regional differences reflect the actual level of wages: where the wages were lower, the workforce were more satisfied with a lower income than for example in Ho Chi Minh City with its – in Vietnamese terms – relatively high levels of pay and high expectations concerning income. In Central Vietnam, this level was less strongly marked than in South Vietnam; accordingly around 47% of the Central Vietnamese entrepreneurs thought that an appropriate income was the main factor contributing to the morale of the employees. In contrast only 28.4% of the South Vietnamese entrepreneurs agreed with this statement. In South Vietnam and in Ho Chi Minh City, income is higher than anywhere else in the country. Good relationships between companies and employees were stated by nearly a third of the respondents interviewed (31. 0%) as important for work motivation. Here too there were significant regional differences. Whereas in Central Vietnam about 40% were of this opinion, agreement in the southern part of the country was lower (27.2%), which may in turn be associ- ated with the greater degree of economic rationality in the South. As far as obtaining work on the basis of competence of the workforce in each case is concerned, in the rural areas and in the more strongly rural region of Central Vietnam, more entrepreneurs agreed with such arrangements of labor than in urban areas. Such considerations may play a greater role due to personal rela- tionships and ties in the rural areas than in the urban areas.

As we shall make clear below, the majority of the entrepreneurs certainly declared their readiness to offer their workforce certain social benefits and better conditions at work. However, the reality of conditions of life and work of the staff in private companies resemble in many respects early capitalist labor relations. Most entrepreneurs explained this with still weak economic perform- ance, and the low degree of consolidation of their firms which did not permit them to offer the provision of social benefits.

But Chinese and our own surveys suggest that the relationships between en- trepreneurs and employees dependent on wages are still far removed from ra- tional interaction and social thinking. In that the following lines of conflict showed themselves:

- In the case of labor conflicts, entrepreneurs often use the means of imme- diate dismissal; channels for the solution of conflicts do not exist. Accord- ing to the statistics, 59.7% of those dismissed in this way had supposedly breached work discipline or insulted the boss, 24.2% had lost their appetite for work, and 8.1% of had not fulfilled their production quotas.
- A high degree of fluctuation (10%) exists; around 20% of those who fluc- tuate go to another private sector firm, 20% return to their villages, 7% make themselves self-employed. Our own surveys demonstrate the high degree of fluctuation. Employees from rural areas who work in companies in urban areas often stay away from work depending on their moods,

change their places of work without informing anybody, or return spontaneously to their native places.

- In some companies in Luohe (Henan) the workforce changed completely
  every three months. Work contracts were as a result of hardly any use, so
  argued the private entrepreneurs. Such a high degree of fluctuation is finally the result of poor treatment, of an enormous work pressure, of discrimination, lack of rights, isolation and estrangement; it corresponds to
  what the sociologist Albert O. Hirschman has termed *Exit* and represents
  the simplest form of resistance.[181]

- Common breaches of the rights of the employees (in the form of physical
  punishment, insults, or house arrest in the time outside of work). At any
  rate, 5.6% of the respondents interviewed stated that they had been insulted
  or physically beaten by entrepreneurs, 2.4% of the female employees that
  they had been sexually harassed. The employees defend themselves with
  forms of *collective action*: damaging machines and/or buildings, raw material and products, sloppiness, theft, etc.

- Although the provinces have since 1996 stipulated minimum wages for all
  forms of company ownership (also private companies), which have to be
  laid down in work contracts,[182] such contracts and stipulations in agreements – if they exist at all – are to be found in the urban areas, in the rural
  areas hardly at all. The employees are rarely informed about their rights.[183]

These elements as described for China are to be found in a similar form in Vietnamese private companies. Our surveys were confirmed by press reports, and
revealed that in the private sector over-long work times predominate (12–14
working hours with a seven-day working week), child labor is widespread, and
accidents in the workplace due to a lack of work protection are common.
Merely 40% of the employees in the non-state sector possessed work contracts
in 1996. When we subtract from that figure the one which relates to Vietnamese–foreign companies in which contracts are already standard, then one can
conclude that they hardly exist in private firms. According to a Vietnamese
survey in non-private companies firms in Ho Chi Minh City, 70% of the employees interviewed stated that they knew nothing about the labor law of their
country.[184]

In contrast to the native place workforce against whom private entrepreneurs
can only with difficulty display authoritarian attitudes due to local circumstances, migrant workers are often subject to discrimination in many forms. The
Chinese press reported mistreatments, physical and financial punishments,
sexual harassment and rapes, as well as massive breaches of work safety and

---

[181] Cf. Hirschman 1970.

[182] This is supposed to be controlled by the associations for those who are self-employed, but
due to the enormity of the task they are hopelessly over-extended by it.

[183] Zhang, Li and Xie 1996: 166-177; Dai Jianzhong 1996: 25-34.

[184] *Viet Nam News*, 13 August 1996.

labor law regulations, that de facto have up till now only been valid for public enterprises. Descriptions of the work situation in private companies resemble in many ways those existing in firms before the founding of the People's Republic. According to a Chinese survey, in 1995 81% of the employees lived in accommodation owned by the factory, which in most cases was cramped, dark, dirty and over-crowded with people (up to 10 persons in a small cramped space), and moreover even rented at extortionate prices. Measures relating to work safety such as protection from heat, dust, dangerous or toxic substances were for the most part unknown, and overtime was commonly not remunerated.[185] The temporary character of work (seasonal work), the prospects concerning income, the lack of possibilities for making comparisons, and the inactivity of the government have the cumulative effect that the majority of the workforce accept this state of affairs.

It often occurs that deposits *(daizi)* are required from the migrant workers; these are supposed to hinder them leaving their jobs as the mood takes them, but on the other hand form a kind of interest-free or low interest credit, which as a rule is then paid back only if the agreed period of labor is completed. A "breach of contract" i.e. the premature ending of the agreed period of work for whatever reasons generally results in the deposit being forfeited. While the demanding of such payments is officially forbidden as it was before, this practice is widely spread in companies with all forms of ownership, and above all in private companies it is hard to control. According to our surveys around 31% of all employees in companies in rural areas (private and township enterprises) had to pay a deposit before they commenced employment. 78% had to pay more than 500 Yuan, and a fifth more than 2,000 Yuan. The accumulation of capital by this method was, however, more common in private companies than in collective companies, because in the first access to credits was more difficult.[186]

In the existing work contracts, it is merely the obligations of the employees which were foregrounded. And only seldom was there any mention of rights. As a result, although work contracts were stipulated, in the urban areas they were hardly widespread, and in rural areas seldom. In total only in 36.3% of the firms did written work contracts exist, 32.3% according to their own statements had reached oral agreements, in a further third there were no agreements of any kind. In two-thirds of the "contracts" in turn neither rights nor obligations on either side were stipulated. Mostly, they were contracts about the deposit which regulated the expiry and repayment of deposit payments. Also in cases in which formal contracts of work were at hand, depending on the current matter at issue they were ignored, altered, or suspended. On the one hand, this may have something to do with the fact that up till now contracts have played no great role, and agreements generally reached orally; on the other hand it may be caused by

---

[185] Zhang, Li and Xie 1996: 173.
[186] Cf. Heberer/Taubmann 1998.

private entrepreneurs in the rural areas having just as little basic knowledge about contracts as their workforce, of whom many are illiterate.

In cases where firms had sales problems, wage payments were sometimes not made for months; indeed it is not seldom in new companies that the employees had to work without pay for so long until the company made a profit. Payments at the end of a quarter-year or first at the end of the year were widely spread.[187] Some larger flagship companies were an exception to this rule, mostly due to the public attention which they enjoy. For example, the owner of a factory manufacturing spirits in Pingle with 106 employees was considered to be an exemplary private entrepreneur at the level of province, who paid higher wages than the county's own spirits factory and had three kinds of work contracts:

(a)   for permanent members of the workforce (*zhengshigong*) with fixed additional allowances for medicinal and pension provision; those people obtained this status who had worked hard and in a disciplined way for more than three years;

(b)   contract workers; (*hetonggong*) newly taken on members of the workforce, who might be able to rise to category (a) obtained top-ups for medical treatment;

(c)   temporary workers (*linshigong*) without any additional allowances at all.

According to the Chinese 1% sample mentioned above the percentage of private companies that offer their employees social benefits was relatively large: already by the middle of the 1990s, 46.3% of all companies were supposedly offering sick pay or health insurance, 15.3% pension insurance, 22.9% life insurance policies, 12.4% top-up payments for flats. For those the percentage difference between urban and rural areas was not large, but indeed between the amounts being paid out.[188] In the framework of our own surveys, however, we hardly found one company which offered its employees social benefits, although during the interview a definite majority supported social benefits at least verbally:

---

[187] Ibid.
[188] Zhang, Li and Xie 1996.

Table 79: Should private entrepreneurs at least partially guarantee social benefits for their employees? (China)

	Agree	%	Disagree	%
Unemployment insurance	130	73.0	48	27.0
Pension insurance	153	86.0	25	14.0
Health insurance	170	95.5	8	4.5

Source: Own survey.

In reality things looked rather different. According to our surveys, in cases of industrial accidents only about 70% obtained pay; if they did get any at all, then it was reduced, and a quarter had to pay costs of treatment by themselves. Only 12.9% of the private companies paid for medical treatment. If provision for pensions existed at all, then solely for a few individuals, with specialized skills.

Even if the answers in Table 79 were only of a tactical nature (in order not to awake the impression of being an "exploiter"), the response behavior showed that the entrepreneurs were mostly aware of the necessity of social insurance, and felt that in principle there was a need for the state to take action.

As far as the question in Table 79 is concerned, there were regional differences, however. In the more developed Zhejiang, the biggest single group of the respondents interviewed agreed with the necessity for the introduction of social insurance payments. There the construction of a social insurance system had grown the most widely. Relations of employment were longer term and more stable than in Henan and Gansu, especially given that many of the workforce in the private sector had already abandoned agriculture and had become workers. These persons had already leased their land to other peasant families. In Henan and Gansu, in contrast, the majority of the workforce were still rooted in agriculture. As worker-peasants they were primarily employed as seasonal workers, and during the agricultural high season returned to their villages.

The differences of opinion between large and small companies in respect of social benefits were rather low. Large entrepreneurs (90.7%) agreed more often than small entrepreneurs (83.7%) with the necessity of pension insurance, probably because large companies have a greater interest in long-term relations of work.

Interestingly, a higher percentage of entrepreneurs in rural areas spoke for the introduction of social insurance payments. A reason for that might lay in the fact that 86.9% of the employees in rural firms stemmed from the same village, the same town/township or the same county as the entrepreneur and the most varying relationships existed between them. This may bring about a stronger feeling of responsibility on the part of the employers in rural areas. 75% of the employees in urban areas, in contrast, stemmed from other regions than the employer. These relations of work are less personalized and as a rule temporary in nature so that the willingness to take on the responsibility by the owner of the company is lower.

Table 80: Should private entrepreneurs at least partially guarantee social benefits for their employees? (China, in %)

	Zhejiang		Henan		Gansu	
	Agree	Dis-agree	Agree	Dis-agree	Agree	Dis-agree
Unemployment insurance	75.4	24.6	75.0	25.0	66.7	33.3
Pension insurance	92.8	7.2	85.0	15.0	79.2	20.8
Health insurance	100.0	0.0	95.0	5.0	89.6	10.4

Source: Own survey.

Table 81: Native place and place of job of the employees (China, in %)

	Location of company				
Place of residence	Large city	Middle-sized urban areas	County town	Town/ township	Village
in the same village	0.0	0.0	0.0	0.0	39.1
in the same town/township	0.0	0.0	0.0	10.7	17.4
in the same county	0.0	5.6	29.2	35.7	30.4
in the same city	0.0	38.9	45.8	42.9	0.0
in the same province	25.0	25.0	16.7	3.6	4.3
in a different province	75.0	30.6	8.3	7.1	8.7

Source: Zhang, Li and Xie 1996: 168.

The attitudes of entrepreneurs to social benefits depicted above deviate from the results of a Chinese study (1993). That survey arrived at the following results:

- In the case of industrial accidents 30.6% of the respondents obtained continuation of wage payments during the time of incapacity to work, 62.9% obtained partial continuation of payments, and 6.5% no pay of any kind. 23.5% of the respondents themselves had to pay the costs of medical treatment.
- In the case of illness 37.1% of the respondents supposedly received complete payments of wages, 18.5% partial, and 31.5% none at all. 12.9% of the respondents supposedly obtained the complete costs of medical treatments from their employers, 16.1% partially, and 53.2% not at all.
- In merely 3.2% of the companies surveyed were there apparently internal agreements in respect of a pension system for the employees.

Our own survey showed that company pension regulations had mostly been agreed only for leading employees with special know-how (managers and engineers). For the other employees there were no such regulations in any of the companies surveyed by us. In this matter one needs to take into account that the character of the relations of work at that time (peasant seasonal workers, high degree of fluctuation, the temporary character of job relations) made the introduction of social insurance for private companies significantly more difficult. For those employees who for the most part return once again to the agricultural sector, and perceive a job in the private sector only as a temporary possibility for earning some money, unemployment or pension insurance is of less interest than medical provision. Finally, as far as the wages are concerned, nominally the pay in more developed regions is partially higher than in public companies. But, as a matter of fact it is lower, since the social benefits that are paid by state companies (provision for ill health and retirement, subsidies for flats or kindergarten, as well as other additional payments) are not made and the work times are partially much longer.

It is not unusual for private entrepreneurs to have to pay higher wages in such regions in order to obtain a local workforce at all, or recruit employees from other localities who are cheaper, have fewer rights, and are less self-confident than the locals. In less developed regions, where the access to collective companies either does not exist at all or only to limited extent, private firms dominate, and the pay is to some extent lower than in comparable non-private companies.

The higher level of pay in private companies has the following causes:

(1)   the wage level in the private sector is determined according to the market. If private entrepreneurs pay too low wages, then only with difficulty can they find long-term and industrious employees;

(2)   since above all in the urban areas, a job in private companies is considered to be of less value than employment in a public company, entrepreneurs have to pay significantly higher salaries to qualified employees with the requisite know-how. Nevertheless, it is often not possible to bond the latter to a company in the long term. For example, the owner of a company for decorating material in Luohe reported that he had financed the studies of three employees at a technical college. However, all three did not return to his company after the completion of their studies, but rather had sought better paid jobs in the province of Guangdong. Four further graduates of technical colleges likewise left the company after only one year. As a result, entrepreneurs try to recruit top-flight employees for their company with top offers. The owner of the Xiaohesen Ltd. in Hangzhou had, for example, recruited from private companies his leading members of staff (young graduates of universities with Party membership) with the granting of condo-

miniums in Hangzhou, their own company cars, and monthly salaries amounting to about 10,000 Yuan.

The amount of pay depends as a rule on the status of an employee. Members of the workforce to whom personal relationships exist, or local employees obtain higher pay than migrant workers, employees with a contract more than temporary members of staff. The level of pay in the companies surveyed by us, generally, was between 300 to 500 Yuan per month. According to a survey by the Chinese Trade Union (1995), the average monthly level of pay of the workers in a private sector firm amounted to 291 Yuan, in joint venture companies 376 Yuan, in collective firms 195, and in private companies 239 Yuan.[189]

According to our survey only 22% of the migrant workers obtained monthly wages over 300 Yuan, in contrast 33% of the local ones. Only 17.1% of the temporary workers (mostly migrant labor) obtained more than 300 Yuan, whereas the figure for employees with contracts was 38.1%.[190] Higher salaries are paid to people with special skills in management and in technical spheres. For the most part they are specialists from state companies who are in retirement or are granted a leave. To some extent they are also university graduates who found the higher salaries in the private sector attractive.

In the labor-intensive, light industry companies it was mostly young women often only aged 20 to 22 from rural areas that obtained work. This was because younger people – or so the argumentation goes – work faster and more skillfully. In addition as a female entrepreneur in Sichuan described to us, at that age they only thought of earning money and were not rebellious. Work times often consisted of seven days in the week, and up to 16 hours daily labor is not rare. When people are unable to work or are ill, immediate dismissals are widespread, even if the case involved an industrial accident. Child labor is common above all in poorer regions. The conditions of work are reminiscent – as already mentioned – of early capitalist labor relations, and those in the rural collective firms often differ only little from those in private companies.

The rather hesitant attitude of the government which issues appeals and levels criticism, but has developed little ability to implement changes, strengthens one's impression that the political elite certainly tolerates the early capitalist relations in the interests of economic development, the promotion of rural private and collective business sectors, the reduction of poverty, and the manufacture of cheap products for exports. China appears in this respect to be a part of the "East Asian path" i.e. cynically to take for granted high social and human costs in the work sector in the interests of "development".

Although the setting-up of trade union and Party organizations in private companies has been propagated since years, in order to get a better grip on forms of exploitation and repression, by the end of the 1990s only a very low

---

[189] Ibid.: 166.
[190] Heberer and Taubmann 1998.

percentage of such groups had been set up. There, where they did exist, they were active rather in the interests of the entrepreneurs; the latter were either themselves the secretaries of the Party branch, or they had given the Party secretary a quiet, pleasant or highly paid job. In one case which we saw for ourselves, the Party secretary was working as a company gardener and, according to his own admission, saw his personal task as consisting of smothering discontent amongst the employees, so as to be able to guarantee a manufacturing process which ran without friction. He obtained a hefty bonus for carrying out these duties.

And according to a survey amongst employees in private sector firms, 54% were of the opinion that trade unions were merely responsible for the organization of cultural and sporting meetings, 23% thought their task was to help the entrepreneur in the organization of production, 15% could not name any function of the trade unions, and merely 8% thought that the unions should actually represent the interests of the employees. 71% of the respondents saw at the same time no sense in private firms setting up trade union committees. In reference to Party organizations, the results turned out to be similar: 55% saw their function in supporting the entrepreneurs and/or production, 19% could recognize no difference between Party members and other employees, 13% thought that their task was making propaganda for the Party, 5% held that they could communicate the opinions of the employees, and only 8% thought they should protect the interests of the workers.[191]

An organized movement in the private sector of employees dependent on wages against exploitation and repression does not yet exist. A lack of rights and the atomization of migrant workers above all , the possibility that "awkward" people can be sent packing at short notice without any legal sanctions occurring as a result, and the widely spread prejudices against such people have the effect that even moderate forms of protest and collective refusal are penalized by the entrepreneurs with immediate dismissal. Rural employees in private companies and migrant workers in rural areas remind one of social groupings whom the sociologist Mancur Olsen termed "forgotten groups" who "suffer in silence". He meant by that, groups which are not organized and without a lobby, that do not defend themselves collectively and are not organized on the basis of the community of interests.[192]

However, such a designation would, be all too over-simplifying. So, for example, migrant workers have formed informal native place associations, that operate as organizations representing interests and certainly do negotiate with entrepreneurs; where necessary they asserting with violence or threats of violence the concerns of the members of these groups. In places with a large concentration of migrant workers (as in the special economic zones) to some extent underground trade unions have come into being which offer their members a certain degree of protection, and are undoubtedly recognized by the

---

[191] Dai Jianzhong 1996: 32, 33.
[192] Olson 1985: 163, 164.

certain degree of protection, and are undoubtedly recognized by the entrepreneurs as negotiating partners, because they are able to channel conflicts.

But the intended center point of life of most migrants (native village and/or
township), the high degree of fluctuation, and *angst* concerning the loss of jobs
– often hard to come by – makes the organizing and representation of the interests of the employees in private sector firms more difficult. In urban areas on
the other hand, where there are more job vacancies available, it is less difficult
for organizations representing interests such as the native place associations to
offer protection and even to contribute to the finding of new jobs. Here there
are certainly new developments. In larger cities, groups of employees appear
(also from private sector firms as well as migrant workers) to be increasingly
taking legal steps to assert their rights against entrepreneurs or companies who
have infringed their labor or personal rights.[193]

This in turn supports Olson's thesis that first of all only small groups are in a
position to begin to join together and to defend themselves. On the other hand,
it has been demonstrated that the apparently "forgotten groups" without a doubt
display willingness to articulate and to take action for their rights, even if –
which is hardly surprising in the current political framework existing in China –
for the time being in informal structures. The criteria offered by the sociology
of organizations for organizational competence (lasting a long time, urgency,
and generality)[194] are lacking to some extent for the employees in private sector
firms because they are usually only employed on a temporary basis, they are
migrant workers, and they are mostly still attached to the social structures in
their native villages i.e. after some time they want to return to their native
places. The formation of hierarchies amongst the employees in this sector
makes it even more difficult to organize them.

The composition of the workforce (for the most part peasants) shows that
working in the private sector is for the most part a concern of peasants. Those
circles of persons which leave the villages and seek employment in this sector
are very often the most able and those with a certain level of education. On
average, they have attended a school for 8.8 years. This would be way above
the average in rural areas.[195] Our own surveys demonstrate that rural private
companies increasingly seek out their employees according to their level of
education.

4.1.3. *Social obligations: entrepreneur and government*
Unlike in Vietnam, a large majority of the entrepreneurs in China expressed
support for the notion that social benefits should at least to some extent be paid
by the employers.

---

[193] Bai Fang 1998: 25.
[194] Cf. amongst others von Winter 1997: 541, 542.
[195] Dai Jianzhong 1996: 28.

Table 82: Should the following social benefits be paid for at least partially by the employer? (China, in %)

	Agree	*Disagree*
Unemployment insurance	73.0	27.0
Pension insurance	86.4	24.0
Health insurance	95.5	4.5

Source: Own survey.

It seems very probable that entrepreneurs have a strongly developed sense of awareness about their social obligations. 84.2% of the respondents were of the opinion that entrepreneurs should take care not only of company management but rather of total societal and social questions too. Differences of opinion between regions, urban and rural areas, as well as between large and small entrepreneurs, were in this point low. Macro-societal components (such as education and training, provision of health care, environmental protection or road construction) in market economies are as a rule paid for by the government, and financed by taxes.

The lack of separation of functions between state and companies which even nowadays still exists, and the somewhat backward state of the taxation system in both countries have the effect that such social benefits often have to be paid for by the companies. State and collective sectors run kindergartens, schools and clinics for their employees. Firms are also supposed to contribute to combating poverty because the state does not possess sufficient means to subsidize them. Private entrepreneurs finance infrastructural projects, the construction of roads, the building of schools or cultural centers above all there where town/townships or villages are not in a position to do so.

Their motivation stems not only from their sense of community. Entrepreneurs attempt by means of such project financing to improve their image and social prestige. In terms of management science, however, the financing of such projects constitutes a not insignificant overloading for the company. A functioning, across-the-board, fiscal system and also the construction of a social security system would – in the sense of a cost calculation along Western management theory lines – entail a significant relief for private companies. But such a view of the situation ignores community obligations: just as they did in the past these play an important role in the consciousness of the population above all in rural areas but also in urban areas, and are associated with considerable social prestige.

Interestingly a Chinese survey amongst entrepreneurs and company directors of firms including all kinds of ownership structures, found that private entrepreneurs expressed more socially oriented views than the other groups. Asked about measures to be taken for employees made redundant, 20.7% of the private entrepreneurs (but only 18.4% of all respondents), answered that the companies themselves should find another job for them. Only 3.4% were of the opinion that the state was responsible for them (all respondents: 13.3%). However, 51.7% of the private entrepreneurs, in the spirit of a labor market favored the idea that employees who had been made redundant should themselves find a way out (all respondents 30.1%), whereby the state should take measures which would enable the transfer of the employees to the tertiary sector (51.7%, all respondents: 45.7%).

More than a quarter (27.6%, all respondents: 22.8%) were in favor of the companies ensuring a minimum income for those employees, nearly a quarter (24.1%, all respondents: 37.6%) thought that the state should bear that responsibility.[196] Above all state and collective sectors as well as companies with investment from abroad placed more emphasis in this respect on the state, whereas private entrepreneurs think more in market categories even if not fully neglecting social components.

Unlike in China, a significant percentage of the respondents interviewed in Vietnam rejected the idea of employers taking on social benefits, and understood this to be rather a task for governmental politics. Less than 50% of the respondents were of the opinion that entrepreneurs should at least partially take over the responsibility for unemployment and pension insurance contributions.

Table 83: Should the following social benefits be paid for by the employer at least partially? (Vietnam)

	Unemployment insurance		Pension insurance	
	Agree	Disagree	Agree	Disagree
Hanoi	22	25	33	18
Tien Son	3	27	5	25
Danang	11	8	12	7
Duy Xuyen	8		7	1
Ho Chi Minh City	21	29	20	30
Thu Duc	9	7	7	8
Total	**74 (43.5)**	**96 (56.5)**	**84 (48.6)**	**89 (51.4)**
Urban areas	54 (46.6)	62 (53.4)	65 (54.2)	55 (45.8)
Rural areas	20 (37.0)	34 (63.0)	19 (35.8)	34 (64.2)
North Vietnam	25 (32.5)	52 (67.5)	38 (46.9)	43 (53.1)
Central Vietnam	19 (70.4)	8 (29.6)	19 (70.4)	8 (29.6)
South Vietnam	30 (45.5)	36 (54.5)	27 (41.5)	38 (58.5)

Source: Own survey.

---

[196] Zhongguo qiyejia diaocha xitong 1997: 19.

Table 84: Should the following social benefits be paid for by the employer at least partially? (Vietnam)

	Health insurance	
	Agree	Disagree
Hanoi	50	5
Tien Son	16	14
Danang	20	2
Duy Xuyen	10	
Ho Chi Minh City	44	6
Thu Duc	29	
Total	**169 (86.2)**	**27 (13.8)**
Urban areas	114 (89.8)	13 (10.2)
Rural areas	55 (79.7)	14 (20.3)
North Vietnam	66 (77.6)	19 (22.4)
Central Vietnam	30 (93.8)	2 (6.2)
South Vietnam	73 (92.4)	6 (7.6)

Source: Own survey.

Unlike in China, only a low percentage of the entrepreneurs in rural areas declared themselves to be willing to make a financial contribution by themselves. That applies to health insurance just as it does to unemployment and pension insurance.[197] An important reason consists of the differences concerning the size of the company and capital endowment. The Vietnamese firms were mostly smaller and possessed less capital. As a result, the question of insurance contributions was seen by them as being rather utopian, and at present an unimaginably heavy burden.

In the rural areas, there is no social security from the state, but instead in contrast to the urban areas the family is regarded as a social safety net. Consequently the idea of including inhabitants of rural areas in public social security, which anyway is not very popular and is still not recognized as a social necessity or social obligation. This is indeed true too for China; but the better conditions offered by the companies there, may have initiated a re-think in respect of the question at least theoretically of social benefits.

Merely in the sphere of health insurance did the majority concur, even if with a lower percentage than the respondents in China. Along with the motives named for China which partially are also true for Vietnam, and with the obligations linked to the self-image of the family father (so our conversations re-

---

[197] This statement does not contradict the one above it about the greater degree of willingness of rural area entrepreneurs about social benefits; this is because it concerns only the higher contributions, whereas social benefits can also be brought about in other ways (e.g. free of charge accommodation and full board for the workers etc.).

vealed), self-interested considerations play a role too. A sick employee
achieves either less than usual or nothing for the firm. Their quick recovery is
therefore in the interests of the employer (insofar as they do not want to or are
able simply to fire the employee). Moreover health insurance releases the employer from the social obligation of themselves paying compensation or making
severance payments, and so contributes to a rationalizing of company processes.

Noticeable is here as for all the three insurance components, the high degree
of agreement amongst Central Vietnamese entrepreneurs, since it diverges from
those of the entrepreneurs in North Vietnam and South Vietnam. Whereas the
majority themselves rejected making a financial contribution to the pension and
unemployment insurance (56.5% und 51.4%), this proposal found much greater
support amongst the Central Vietnamese entrepreneurs (with in each case 70%),
and this although the private entrepreneurs in Central Vietnam are on average
in a worse position than their South Vietnamese equivalents. Amongst the three
regions surveyed, Central Vietnam is the poorest, so that here the greatest need
for social security appears to exist. Possibly as a result the entrepreneurs in
Central Vietnam are also the most willing themselves to pay a financial contribution.

**Table 85: Assess the following statement: "Entrepreneurs should take care
of the economic performance of their companies, social benefits are a matter for the state." (China)**

	Completely true		Partially true		Untrue	
	Numbers	%	Numbers	%	Numbers	%
Total	10	5.6	18	10.2	149	84.2
Zhejiang	5	7.2	7	10.1	57	82.6
Henan	3	5.0	5	8.3	52	86.7
Gansu	2	4.2	6	12.5	40	83.3
Urban areas	5	4.6	11	10.2	92	85.2
Rural areas	5	7.2	7	10.1	57	82.6
Large entrepre-neurs	4	7.4	7	13.0	43	79.6
Small entrepre-neurs	6	4.9	11	8.9	106	86.2

Source: Own survey.

That the entrepreneurs are definitely aware of their social obligations, and do
not want necessarily to call in the state is shown also by Table 86. In China
more than 80% of the respondents interviewed rejected the view that for social
matters the state was first of all responsible; after all were they not themselves
responsible too. The differences between regions, as well as urban and rural

areas were in this respect relatively low. Only larger entrepreneurs hoped for some relief from the state probably because they feared that due to the large number of employees there would be an over heavy burden through social costs, and believed that through the creation of jobs they had satisfactorily fulfilled their social obligations.

The attitudes in Vietnam differ only slightly from those in China. Here too the majority of the respondents interviewed acknowledged their social obligation: over a half rejected the statement, "The entrepreneurs should only look after the economic performance, the state is responsible for social benefits;" only a small percentage agreed with it completely.

Table 86: Assess the following statement: "Entrepreneurs should take care of the economic performance of their companies, social benefits are a matter for the state." (Vietnam)

	Completely true	Partially true	Untrue
Hanoi	3	16	36
Tien Son	3	11	17
Danang	3	8	11
Duy Xuyen	1	2	7
Ho Chi Minh City	6	19	26
Thu Duc	2	7	21
Total	**18 (9.0)**	**63 (31.7)**	**118 (59.3)**
Urban areas	12 (9.4)	43 (33.6)	73 (57.0)
Rural areas	6 (8.4)	20 (28.2)	45 (63.4)
North Vietnam	6 (7.0)	27 (31.4)	53 (61.6)
Central Vietnam	4 (12.5)	10 (31.25)	18 (56.25)
South Vietnam	8 (9.9)	26 (32.1)	47 (58.0)

Source: Own survey.

In contrast to China, nevertheless, a significantly higher percentage of the respondents (about 40%) were fully or partially of the opinion that social benefits were a task for the state whereby this viewpoint in the North, where the (communist) government had anyway performed this duty for decades, was more widespread. Also in rural areas, this point of view was found more often than in the urban areas. The moral obligation (already mentioned) towards the community is still more deeply rooted, and purely economic calculations predominate to a lesser extent. Insofar as private entrepreneurs enable the community to take part in their prosperity, their prestige grows and reduces administrative and individual envy. Such an obligation certainly does not represent a new phenomenon. As already mentioned, traditionally in peasant societies such as China and Vietnam fixed obligations exist towards the village communities: it is expected of fellow residents of a village and/or members of a clan who have managed to achieve prosperity that they share their wealth with the members of the respective reference group and/or the complete village, or support them with assistance. Even nowadays relatively little has changed in this moral obligation which Scott termed the *moral economy of the peasantry*.[198]

But this needs to be placed in relative terms because – when we take into account the answers "completely accurate" and "partially accurate" – something like the same percentage of the respondents interviewed spoke out at least partially for a social obligation (urban areas: 90.6%; rural areas: 91.6%). Only a small percentage of the respondents wanted to see the role of the private entrepreneur in the economy reduced. Consequently, the results from both countries in principle contradict the allegation that private entrepreneurs were nothing more than "capitalist exploiters" who only thought of their profits. Much rather feelings of responsibility towards society are expressed in the results. The entrepreneurs perceive themselves to be part of society who are obligated to behave in a socially appropriate way. There may also be present here an implied desire for actively shaping the society; this is indicated too by the wish expressed later in this work on the part of the entrepreneurs that they wish to function as role models for society.

Our question as to whether social benefits could only then be offered and the working conditions improved when the entrepreneurs earned well, did not find a majority in either country. An absolute majority of the respondents interviewed in China and Vietnam were of the opinion that the time was already ripe for employees' working conditions and social benefits to be improved (Vietnam: 61.3%, China: 52.0%) and only a low percentage (Vietnam: 7.5%, China 18.6%) argued that this was still too early due to the current turnover of the company. At any rate almost a third (Vietnam: 31.2%, China 29.4%) regarded the conditions for those changes as only partially existent, and favored a step-by-step implementation. In both countries the willingness of the entrepreneurs in the urban areas was more strongly marked than in the urban areas. In Vietnam the regional differences were sometimes considerable. In the North, socialized in a socialist manner, only 54.7% were for improvements irrespective of the amount of orders at the respective firms, in the South contrastingly it was 67.9%. This may be the result of the weaker development of companies in the North, possibly in some cases the greater pressure in the South on entrepreneurs for self-legitimation.

4.1.4. *Attitudes towards income differences*
Growing disparities in income might become a source of social dissatisfaction if the gap between rich and poor were to develop all too far apart. This set of problems may contain an especially explosive power in countries such as China and Vietnam – in which egalitarian ideas firstly possess a certain tradition, and furthermore have been fed for decades by socialist ideology and propaganda.

---

[198] Scott 1976.

The entrepreneurs form a stratum whose income in recent years has risen the most and they form the core of the "nouveau riche".

At the beginning of the 1990s in China, there were apparently around three million "nouveau riche", a large number of them entrepreneurs.[199] According to a Chinese survey, private entrepreneurs in 1998 had a monthly income of 16,800 Yuan, eight times the average wages of manager of the most different types of companies (average wage: 2,160 Yuan). But only about 10.7% of the entrepreneurs interviewed were of the opinion that their income had been too "high". 68% held it to be average (zhongdeng), 21.4% even for low.[200] According to our survey what people stated about their own incomes (which with certainty were given as significantly lower than they really were) was as follows:

Table 87: Annual income (1995) of the entrepreneurs surveyed (China, in Yuan)

	Number	%
10.000 - 20.000	90	51.4
>20.000 – 50.000	46	26.3
>50.000 – 100.000	24	13.7
>100.000 – 200.000	8	4.6
>500.000	5	2.9
Total	*175*	*100.0*

Source: Own survey.

Our survey of 203 functionaries at the Central Party School in Beijing in 1996 found that those officials earned much less:

---

[199] Cf. *Zhongguo Gongshang Bao*, 26 October 1999.
[200] Zhongguo qiyejia diaocha xitong 1998a: 7, 8.

Table 88: Annual income (1995) of respondent cadres (China, in Yuan)

	Number	%
5,000 – 10,000	119	58.6
>10,001 – 30,000	79	38.9
>30,000 – 50,000	4	2.0
> 50,000 – 100,000	1	0.5
> 100,000	0	0
Total	203	100.0

Source: Own survey.

Whereas half of the functionaries had a yearly income of less than 10,000 Yuan, not a single entrepreneur was to be found in this income category. Quite to the contrary, almost a quarter of the entrepreneurs had an income of more than 50,000 Yuan, which amongst the cadres interviewed was only within the grasp of a single leading functionary.

Such high incomes make the entrepreneurs the leading earners in the country, but create on the other hand envy and dissatisfaction with income disparities amongst the population and the functionaries. As a result, 37.3% of the respondents interviewed declared themselves to be dissatisfied with the distribution of income, only five (2.5%) were satisfied with it, the rest (60.2%) were moderately satisfied. This dissatisfaction with the growing polarization of income has been reflected too in the Party's discussion. So we wanted to find out how the entrepreneurs assess this factor which directly concerns them and their political legitimation.

In China, the absolute majority of the respondents (88.7%) agreed that disparities between rich and poor exist as the inevitable product of natural forces in a society. This may at first be unexpected, since egalitarian incomes have for decades been considered in the People's Republic to be a fundamental social goal. A process of rethinking commenced here first in the course of the reforms and the construction of market economic structures.

Primarily in more developed economic regions and regions stamped more strongly by market economics such as Zhejiang, but also amongst entrepreneurs in urban areas or larger entrepreneurs, many have grasped that people possess different capabilities and skills and create different amounts of achievement; differences of income are in the final analysis also the outcome of these differences. In contrast, in rural areas, and in Henan and Gansu where agriculture still plays a dominant role, such market-oriented, economic attitudes were still not part of the mindset of a section of the entrepreneurs. Traditionally egalitarian values, (such as the ideal of equal distribution of income) still stamp the attitudes of many entrepreneurs. Since entrepreneurs, as stated, count amongst the leading earners in China, their consent to the normality of income

the leading earners in China, their consent to the normality of income disparities also entails that they would like to legitimate the normality and rationality
of their own high income.

On the other hand, the growth of income disparities has turned out to be ever
increasingly a social problem. According to a Chinese survey of 1,867 people
(mid-1990s), only 7.1% of the respondents were satisfied with the distribution
of income at that time.[201] If the income differences developed all too far apart,
this could lead to social instability and conflicts. Consequently, the Party leadership has endeavored to stem this trend. A social regulation dating from the
1980s attempted to stipulate that the income of private entrepreneurs should not
exceed by 1,000% the average wage of employees.

But actually, the average income of entrepreneurs as determined by the Chinese 1% sample (1995) had already in 1992 mounted to approximately 50,000
Yuan annually, that of the workers in 1995, however, only 3,572 Yuan.[202]
Based on those figures, entrepreneurs would have earned on average 14 times
what a wage-dependent employee received. However, such figures should, only
be used as trend values, since entrepreneurs do not divulge their real income
and here a figure valid for 1992 had been compared with one for 1995.

What is significant in that is that while, indeed, most of the respondents interviewed in comparison had achieved more prosperity in contrast to the non-
entrepreneurial population, the degree of dissatisfaction with the current income distribution amongst the entrepreneurs is at the same time relatively high.
Only 33.3% of the respondents interviewed declared themselves to be satisfied
with it, 49.2% "not completely satisfied", and 17.5% "dissatisfied". Many entrepreneurs at the same time showed themselves indignant about the phenomenon of dishonest acquisition of wealth. In Zhejiang, entrepreneurs often declared that managers of companies in rural areas could become rich more
quickly and simply, because they had the possibility (illegally) to transfer collective property into their private control.

The growing income disparities which have helped to increase social dissatisfaction is detrimental to the interests of the entrepreneurs, because these interests have been identified in the consciousness of a wide swathe of the population with new social relations based on exploitation. As a result, most of the
respondents interviewed by us were part of a consensus that the development of
income should be more strongly controlled by the state.

But the regional differences of opinion were relatively large in this matter. In
Zhejiang about 50% of the entrepreneurs were against government regulation,
in Henan about 80% in favor. This may too be causally related to with the already mentioned business culture of each province. In Zhejiang, an entrepreneurial tradition exists which is oriented towards performance and achievement.
Many renowned, foreign ethnic Chinese originated or originate from this prov-

---

[201] Statement of the Commission for the Reform of the Economic Structure in Beijing, 1 March
1996.
[202] Zhang, Li and Xie 1996: 173.

ince. So market-oriented thinking possesses deeper roots here. In Henan which
is strongly stamped by agricultural egalitarianism quiet the opposite is the case,
given that the industrial base is still decidedly thin. In contrast to Zhejiang, the
entrepreneurial stratum has not played much of a role in historical terms.

Right up until the 1980s the province was a hotbed of collectivist models.
Henan was the forerunner of the collective movement in the middle of the
1950s, during the "Great Leap Forward" (1958-60) and in the Cultural Revolution. In 1957 the first People's Commune came into being (Xinxiang), and all
of the collectivist mass movements of the Mao era were carried out here with
particular rigidity.[203] In the 1980s, new "communist" villages came into being
as counter-models of the supposed "new capitalism".[204] The differences between urban areas and rural areas as well as between large and small entrepreneurs in turn can be derived from the already mentioned element amongst larger and/or urban entrepreneurs that is better informed about the market economy.

More than a third of the respondents interviewed (38.4%) did not, however,
agree with the negative assessment of growing income disparities.

It should be emphasized that many entrepreneurs appear to have placed their
confidence in market economic mechanisms in respect of distribution of income. According to Western economic theories and the practical experiences of
market economics in Western societies, market mechanisms do not automatically lead to an optimal income distribution. Much rather attempts are made to
regulate the income distribution by means of different economic levers for
instance those of a fiscal political nature.

In developing countries (e.g. in Latin America), it has been shown that massive social conflicts may occur if the distribution of income is not regulated on
the part of the government. Our interviews indicate, nevertheless, that governmental interventions tend to be rejected because through them further negative
implications for society are feared, and furthermore, increasing income is not
automatically brought into association with social conflicts.

Most of the respondents interviewed by us positively estimated the future
development of income distribution. More than two-thirds were of the opinion
that larger income disparities had only been a transitory phenomenon in the
course of economic development. More than a quarter held this statement,
however, to be inaccurate (cf. Table 90). This is associated with the entrepreneurs' hope for an increase in the total social wealth given the growth of the
private sector and economic development in general. As a result, they (the
entrepreneurs) regarded themselves only as role models and pioneers of a general development which finally would be advantageous for everyone. On the
other hand, they envisaged that the phenomenon of over-proportionally high
income should be put into a relative context in terms of time. They also take

---

[203] On that: Heberer and Jakobi 2002.
[204] Cf. Heberer 1997b.

issue with the solution offered by the Party according to which first of all a part of the society becomes prosperous which implies a temporary expansion of economic differences.

Table 89: The increase of social income disparities causes envy and conflict between people, and so the government should regulate the development of income more (China)

	Correct		Incorrect	
	Number	*%*	*Number*	*%*
Total	*109*	*61.6*	*68*	*38.4*
Zhejiang	34	49.3	35	50.7
Henan	48	80.0	12	20.0
Gansu	27	56.25	21	43.75
Urban areas	62	57.4	46	42.6
Rural areas	47	68.1	22	31.9
Large entrepreneurs	29	53.7	25	46.3
Small entrepreneurs	80	65.0	43	35.0

Source: Own survey.

Table 90: The increase of income distribution is a temporary phenomenon in the process of economic development (China)

	Correct		Incorrect	
	Number	*%*	*Number*	*%*
Total	*126*	*71.2*	*51*	*28.8*
Zhejiang	42	60.9	27	39.1
Henan	52	86.7	8	13.3
Gansu	32	66.7	16	33.3
Urban areas	78	72.2	30	27.8
Rural areas	48	69.6	21	30.4
Large entrepreneurs	36	66.7	18	33.3
Small entrepreneurs	90	73.2	33	26.8

Source: Own survey.

Regional differences of opinion were in some questions considerable. 39.1% of the respondents interviewed in Zhejiang, but only 13.3% of those in Henan, did not agree with the statement that increasing differences in income were only a temporary phenomenon. In Henan our probes showed that the view that first of all part of the society and after that everybody should become prosperous had assumed more significance in the mindset of the respondents. More so than in

Zhejiang and Gansu, entrepreneurs there hoped that after a period of expansion of income disparities, there would be a return to egalitarian distribution.

Especially in Zhejiang it was clear to many entrepreneurs that market-oriented economic relations were inextricably intertwined with income distribution because – as one entrepreneur formulated it – there are "different capacities for achievement and varying chances in the market." Just as in China (97.2%) so too in Vietnam did the entrepreneurs agree with the statement that income should depend on performance and people's own initiative.

In Vietnam, there was a significantly lower number who were of the opinion that this process was merely a temporary phenomenon. Whereas the contrast between the urban and rural areas was minimal, in regional terms the response behavior diverged from one another. In the North over 50% of the respondents interviewed held income disparities to be a temporary phenomenon and hoped that after that there would be a return to egalitarian relations, whereas in Central and South Vietnam only 37.5% and 39.5%, respectively, shared this opinion. Socialist socialization too is reflected in the response behavior in the North.

If one takes the communist ideology, which was officially propagated as the measure for official values decades long before the introduction of market-oriented reforms, what we found suggests that in process here is a transformation of values. That applies particularly to the question which is central from the communist viewpoint of rich and poor. Whereas the communists demanded that wealth be equally divided, almost 75% of the respondents interviewed accepted the difference between poor and rich in the society as something quite natural.

Table 91: It is natural that in every society a difference between rich and poor exists (Vietnam)

Hanoi	49
Tien Son	28
Danang	17
Duy Xuyen	7
Ho Chi Minh City	35
Thu Duc	15
Total	**151 (74.8)**
Urban areas	101 (77.1)
Rural areas	50 (70.4)
North Vietnam	77 (86.5)
Central Vietnam	24 (75.0)
South Vietnam	50 (61.7)

Source: Own survey.

According to socialist theory, wealth and poverty are not natural facts of life, but are rather exploited by people through people. The communist should struggle against exploitation and through the elimination of class differences facilitate an equal distribution of wealth. Private entrepreneurs in contrast – as the argumentation goes – create their own wealth and contribute objectively to the income inequality; as a result they would rather tend to regard differences of income as a natural phenomenon of all societies. What appears unusual in the response behavior is the large difference between South (61.7%) and North Vietnam (86.5%) concerning the acceptance of the income disparities as "natural".

Probes established that the existence of such income disparities in the North is increasingly accepted through the build-up of strong, market-economic relations, whereas entrepreneurs in the South do not simply accept or complain about this difference, but often are of the opinion that they could personally change them through their own efforts.

It became clear that entrepreneurs in both countries had been pioneers of a transformation of values in the sense that they perceive money, earning money, achievement and income disparities pragmatically and not ideologically. In societies, which were stamped for a long time by low-level agriculture and communism with a corresponding flattening of income between the different groups of the population, and in which wealth had appeared dubious, the introduction of market-oriented economic sectors changed the attitudes towards income differences as well as concerning poverty and wealth.

The market economy necessarily brings out such disparities. Such a transformation of values has taken place, however, not only within entrepreneurial strata but rather also in the total population. Whereas we have already documented the situation in China elsewhere,[205] as an example this will be elucidated for Vietnam. According to a survey carried out by the Institute of Psychology in Hanoi (1992), 77.4% of the respondents classified the difference between rich and poor as natural. A similar survey in areas with an ethnic minority in Vietnam came to a comparable result with around 70% acceptance.[206]

As far as the ideas about companies are concerned, traditional concepts are still widely spread (patriarchal ideas). But this does not extend to social security. Here, there is room for improvement, also in the sphere of social awareness. While the majority pay lip service to the necessity of social protection for the employees, in reality this is not put into practice. In this respect state regulation is needed, because without the state the establishing of a social security system is hardly feasible.

---

[205] Heberer and Taubmann 1998: 347ff.

[206] Conversation with Vu Cong, deputy director of the Institute of Psychology, Hanoi, 15 January 1997; unpublished report about the reaction of ethnic minorities to the market economy, Hanoi 1994. Interestingly about half of the ethnic minorities interviewed mentioned personal flexibility as an important ability in order to achieve wealth.

4.2. *The entrepreneurs' goals in life*

The goals in life formulated by us in the survey can be sub-divided into *societal-related* (contribution to socialist developments likewise contribution to the society, and being a social role model), *material* (higher income), *familial* (better future for their own children, happy families), and *individual* goals in life (self-fulfillment, economic freedom, enjoyment of current life, and higher social position). These goals were shaped through the present social situation as well as through traditional ideas.

The majority of the respondents named as their first goal in life "making a contribution to society". This result can be considered from two angles. On the one hand it says that entrepreneurs have the self-confidence to believe that they could make such a contribution. On the other hand, an attitude was revealed which one would rather classify as traditional. Because in a traditional world-view, the individual was subordinate to the community i.e. the individual should be subordinated to the interests of the community.

Table 92: How do you assess the importance of the following goals in life for your life? (China)

	Very important		Average		Unimportant	
	Number	%	Number	%	Number	%
1. Making a contribution to socialist development	142	80.2	34	19.2	1	0.6
2. Higher income	61	34.5	91	51.4	25	14.1
3. Higher social position	37	20.9	74	41.8	66	37.3
4. Making a contribution to society	157	88.7	20	11.3	0	0.0
5. Better future for one's own children	139	78.5	28	15.8	10	5.6
6. Economic freedom	96	54.2	68	38.4	13	7.3
7. Enjoyment of current life	10	5.6	91	51.4	76	42.9
8. Being a social role model	54	30.5	66	37.3	57	32.2
9. A happy family	151	85.3	20	11.3	6	3.4
10. Self-fulfillment	127	71.8	47	26.6	3	1.7

Source: Own survey.

This rather traditional attitude was more markedly present in the province of Henan (96.7%) than in Zhejiang (84.1%) and Gansu (85.4%). And this corresponded with our view of the matter already set down elsewhere, that traditional, societal-related styles of thought in Henan are much more strongly developed than in most other provinces.[207] As far as "making a contribution to Socialist development" or "being a social role model" goes, Henan displays a significantly higher percentage than both the other provinces. Social relations play a more significant role in Henan than they do in other regions.

A categorization according to the mean value and the order of priority gives the following breakdown:

Table 93: How do you assess the importance of the following goals in life for your life? (China)

	mean value	order of priority
1. Making a contribution to society	1.11	1
2. A happy family	1.18	2
3. Making a contribution to socialist development	1.20	3
4. Better future for one's own children	1.27	4
5. Self-fulfillment	1.30	5
6. Economic freedom	1.53	6
7. Higher income	1.80	7
8. Being a social role model	2.02	8
9. Higher social position	2.16	9
10. Enjoyment of current life	2.37	10

Source: Own survey.

Our analysis suggests that traditional attitudes amongst entrepreneurs in rural areas (94.2%) were more strongly marked than amongst urban ones (85.2%). A further, societal-related element is to be found in the leading group in the response behavior concerning goals in life: making a contribution to socialist development was classified as the third most important goal in life. On the one hand the agreement to this question may be marked by the general ideological trend (the respondents do not want to be labeled as "anti-socialist" and/or cannot express themselves in an "anti-socialist") i.e. they do not wish to express themselves in contradiction to the state. At any rate, around a fifth of the respondents did not attribute great significance to this goal, however. On the other hand, as our probes showed, this aim was symbolically interpreted due to the internalized equating of nation, Party and political system ("socialism"): to make a contribution to socialist development is considered to be an achievement for the modernization of China. Here too, there were regionally striking differences, whereby amongst all socially related statements, Henan was at the top. Whereas in the more developed Zhejiang, 29% of the respondents classi-

---

[207] Cf. on that Heberer and Jakobi 2002.

fied the contribution to socialist development as not quite so important, for 91.7% of the respondents in Henan and 79.2% of those in Gansu it possessed a high value. But probes established here that when people ticked this goal in life, considerations based on political correctness ("one simply has to tick that"), played a not insignificant role.

Being a social role model only came in eighth place in the list of life goals, which was surprising. Merely 30.5% of the respondents claimed that they wanted to be such a role model. This is unexpected because right up to the present day the Party and the media very much emphasize these role models and "social role models" play an important role in everyday propaganda. Entrepreneurs, the interviews show, do not identify with the traditional role models propagated by the Party.

Entrepreneurs want to be shining examples but not in the interests of the Party, rather role models of market-oriented, economic development, which in the opinions of many does not necessarily mean "social role model" in the traditional meaning. Contrastingly, in rural areas the exemplary function was more strongly identified with Deng Xiaoping's idea of "role model through becoming wealthy" i.e. with the idea of acquiring wealth and in this way having the effect on the population of being a role model. This explains why more entrepreneurs in rural (33.3%) than urban areas (28.7%) found it important to be a role model. Here too, the community orientation in Henan was strongly reflected, since 43.3% held this personal role model function to be "very important" (Zhejiang: 24.6%; Gansu: 22.9%).

Family and children play a central role in the life of most Chinese people. The desire for a happy family scored second highest, the desire for a better future for their children in fourth place. Individuals are traditionally subordinated to the family, too. The continuity of this idea finds expression accordingly in the response behavior. Over 85% of the respondents interviewed classified family happiness as very important, whereby regional differences were low.

In rural areas the percentage (92.8%) was still higher than in the urban areas (80.6%).[208] Here, not only the stronger roots in the traditions in the countryside played a role, but rather too the rapid changes in the attitudes of the population in urban areas through modernization processes and social transformation. The speedy increase in divorce rates in urban areas likewise contributes to the erosion of family values.

Parental duties to set in motion good prospects in the future for their children through qualified training, plays a central role in the traditional thinking of the Chinese. Although 78.5% of the respondents agreed with this psychological goal, more than a fifth of the entrepreneurs were of the opinion that their chil-

---

[208] This corresponds with the results of a survey by Heberer and Taubmann amongst the employees of firms in rural areas from 1993–94. According to that 83.2% of the respondents assessed familial happiness as "very important", 10.4% as "important", whereas for 62.6% of the respondents the future of their children was "very important", for 19.6% "important". Cf. Heberer and Taubmann 1998: 349f.

dren should shape their own future and themselves achieve something in life. They thought too that it is sufficient when the parents make possible average starting chances in life. Above all, children are not to be "spoilt" i.e. educated in a luxurious and idle way of life. Here too, entrepreneurial considerations play a role, because a string of respondents interviewed held the opinion that habituation to wealth, luxury and idleness would be a bad precondition for their successors in the companies. They thought it required much rather the spirit of "hard struggle" and a simple life in order to be able to lead a firm successfully.

The individual goal in life *self-fulfillment* received a higher placing: 71.8% of the respondents interviewed thought it to be very important. Entrepreneurship and market processes in which the entrepreneurs behave as individuals, automatically lead to a stronger emphasis on individual goals and ideas. The element of self-realization is the expression of individualism and, in principle, stands in strong contrast to those traditional values regarded as "socialist", but also traditional attitudes (stronger emphasis on collective and community interests).

At the same time, in the response behavior one finds an apparently conflict-free coupling of individual and community interests: on the one hand the majority of the entrepreneurs want to make a contribution to society, on the other hand the element of self-realization is valued very highly. Asked about their respective entrepreneurial philosophies, however, a clearly individualistic attitude became apparent, sign of an increasing process of individualization associated with the privatization process. To illustrate that, here are two examples out of many and ones which could certainly be added to with the use of examples from Vietnam: Wan De'an (50), manufacturer of shoe molds declared:

> Being an entrepreneur is like stairs: step for step upwards. My view is directed upwards and forwards. Two stages are important in that. Firstly, the government's policies which is moving in my direction and corresponds for the most part with my ideas, and secondly, the development of my company. Here everything runs satisfactorily, unlike in the state companies. In contrast to the state companies, my employees receive their pay regularly. For that reason alone you find my entrepreneurial philosophy: a good entrepreneur is one who makes money and not losses i.e. who leads and steers his company well. My ideals? I want to become a millionaire, yes, or even a multi-millionaire.[209]

The food manufacturer Shi Dongmin (34) opined:

> We entrepreneurs should have high social prestige. We achieve a lot and great things for society. In that we do everything ourselves and alone. The government only needs to provide a good political framework, we sort everything else out ourselves. What are my entrepreneurial goals? An ever larger company.[210]

---

[209] Conversation on 9 October 1996 in Luohe.
[210] Conversation on 9 October 1996 in Luohe.

As a result, there appears to be some supporting evidence for Norbert Elias's thesis that, "individuals form a society and every society is one made up of individuals," that development processes are necessarily accompanied by processes of individualization that can neither be hindered by governments nor by social groupings.[211]

Although economic freedom represents an indispensable precondition for entrepreneurial activity, only 54.2% of the respondents interviewed classified this factor as very important. Probes established that an excessive amount of economic freedom was regarded as problematic because through that uncontrolled phenomena came into being and society could find itself in "disorder" *(luan)*. On the other hand social and individual goals in life are assessed more highly than a term regarded by many as abstract i.e. "freedom": apparently for Chinese entrepreneurs it does not possess the positive meaning which is attributed to it in Western society.

A higher income is only in seventh place as a goal in life. This result appears first of all to contradict the aim of private companies that of profit maximization. Firstly, it is worth bearing in mind here, that striving for material interests was always negatively assessed in the Chinese tradition of thought. In the Mao era too, such endeavors were classified as capitalist. The influence of traditional-egalitarian thought on the present day should not be underestimated. Secondly, a possible explanation would be that entrepreneurs do not see higher income as a target but rather as an instrument. During the interviews in Zhejiang province, many entrepreneurs expressed the idea that money was not so important, whereby the proverb was quoted a number of times that one comes into the world without money and one cannot take it to one's grave.

A third factor may be that private entrepreneurs, as a rule, have already achieved a very high income, and so further increases in earnings do not count amongst the prioritized goals in life. This is true primarily of large entrepreneurs and more developed regions, less for smaller entrepreneurs and less developed regions. As a result, 39.8% of the small, but only 22% of the large entrepreneurs declared the acquiring of higher income to be a prioritized target. And in less developed regions as well, this goal was assessed in percentage terms as more important. Seen all in all, material values (here: higher income) do indeed definitely play a role when one takes into account for example that only 14% of the respondents regarded this factor as unimportant. Also due to reasons of social standing and political sensitivities, the financial element was not foregrounded by the entrepreneurs. For the final item in the list, "enjoyment of present life", it is still too early under the conditions of the beginnings of entrepreneurship and the daily struggle for entrepreneurial survival. This point which fits in with the ideas of Western leisure societies, moreover contradicts traditional Chinese concepts of what life is about.

---

[211] Cf. Elias 1991.

The differences between the regions surveyed, between urban and rural areas, as well as large and small entrepreneurs were relatively small. Material goals in life (income) were for urban areas and – as mentioned before – more important for small entrepreneurs than for people who live in rural areas, for whom life goals based on moral and social obligations appear to be much closer to heart due to their stronger reference to community (village and clan). The same applies as well to Henan province, which is strongly influenced agriculturally.

A relatively small percentage of the respondents (20.9%) evaluated a higher social position as particularly important. The differences in opinion between entrepreneurs in urban and rural areas as well as between large and small entrepreneurs were in this respect not very large. A higher percentage of entrepreneurs in Henan (26.7%) and Gansu (20.8%) held this to be important for their life than in Zhejiang (15.9%). The element of reaching a higher social position and the increased social prestige associated with that was for a long time connected with political ascent and the world of functionaries. Consequently, there is still a certain reluctance to propagate entrepreneurship as a new, alternative social ladder. Furthermore, openly foregrounding such an intention is negatively assessed socially. Due to that one may be able to explain the low percentage of those who said that rising socially was not one of their priority targets in life. On the other hand, only a little more than a third of the respondents stated that this goal was for them completely unimportant.

In all conversations entrepreneurs made clear that increasing their social prestige was very important to them. This finding was underlined by other results from our survey, for example, that 88.2% of the respondents stated they would very much like to become deputies of the People's Congresses. In this response behavior, the ambivalent political situation in which entrepreneurs find themselves was reflected: on the one hand they try to preserve a certain distance to politics, on the other hand they are interested in an improvement of their social position. With the downgrading of this element in their life targets some of the respondents wanted to make clear that they take care, first of all, of their business and have less concern about their own social position. And although in the economic sphere wide-ranging liberties have indeed already established themselves, freedom in the political domain exists only in a limited way; political controls as they did before play an important role. For that reason too, the element of social position is a sensitive topic, since it is always linked to political ambitions. As a result entrepreneurs only admit unwillingly that they are interested in reaching a higher social position.

The attitudes of the entrepreneurs to capital and with that to material interests are complemented by the following question:

Table 94: If you had a large sum of money at your disposal, what would you do with it? (China, three answers possible)

	Number	%[1]
1. Invest in my own firm	171	96.6
2. Better education for children	118	66.7
3. Expenditure for improving social relationships	14	7.9
4. Buying a car	6	3.4
5. Traveling inland /abroad	7	4.0
6. Retiring	1	0.6
7. Donations for social purposes	134	75.7
8. Purchasing a house	7	4.0
9. Investing the money	12	6.8
10. Own further education	16	9.0
11. Provision for old age	39	22.0
12. Others	6	3.4

Source: Own survey.
NB: [1] refers to respondents who answered the questions (177).

Entrepreneurial investments (investment in their own firm) are in first place because without investment no company can develop; the company represents the income basis of an entrepreneur. Immediately after that follows a social target, namely donations for social purposes (the combating of poverty, assistance when catastrophes have occurred, village development, building roads, etc.).[212] Only in third place came a family-related goal (education of their children). Elements relating to individuals were only named by a small percentage, but almost a quarter apparently were thinking of their retirement. Interestingly, many entrepreneurs argued that building up their own company likewise represented a contribution to social development, since through that not only did more taxation flow to the government and new jobs created, but in addition, the financial prerequisites for making donations to social causes were brought about.

In Vietnam too, the central position of family-related values was confirmed by the assessment of life goals. As uppermost aim, a happy family was named most commonly (95%), followed by a better future for their own children (93%) (cf. Table 95). None of the respondents classified both these aims as less important. Regional differences were minimal, whereby these aims were even more important in rural areas than in urban areas.

---

[212] For assistance after the catastrophe in the flooded areas in the Yangtze river area (1998), private entrepreneurs donated alone via the nationwide Association of Industry and Commerce about 850 m Yuan, cf. *China Daily*, 28 September 1998.

As further very important goals in life the following were named: making a contribution to building up their country (about 73%) likewise the society (50%). Contributing to the development and modernization of Vietnam is an expression of widely spread patriotism. But the nation is regarded as primary, society as secondary. The emphasis on the role of the nation manifested itself in percentage terms more strongly in the responses of the entrepreneurs in rural areas than in those in the urban areas, however. In the urban areas, the nation appears to have lost significance at least to some extent as opposed to other values. It is hardly surprising that these patriotic thoughts were stronger in the North than in the South. The North regards itself not only as the sanctuary and guardian of the nation; through the socialist education, the war and the victory over the USA, the North was much more strongly sensitized to the needs of the nation than the South, which even nowadays many North Vietnamese accuse of a certain "Americanism". At the same time, the percentage of those who saw the commitment to their own country as less important was extremely low.

At the same time, the way in which respondents assign functions to themselves indicates self-confidence: entrepreneurs are and see themselves as being in a position to be able to contribute to the goals of modernization and to play a part in shaping it. With that they assume for themselves a definite place in society and do not any longer regard themselves as a marginalized group.

A life goal is not an inspiration present in everyday life, but rather a long-term orientation, which to a greater or lesser extent directly gears people's own behavior. As a rule people work actively towards achieving a life goal, instead of merely passively waiting for its realization. Insofar, the percentage share of private entrepreneurs who hold it to be very important to be a role model for society at 35% should certainly be assessed as high, given that only 20.8% regard the exemplary function as less important.

A role model raises himself or herself up above the mass of the population. As a result to regard oneself as a role model, demonstrates a large degree of self-confidence and belief in one's own abilities. Role models want to make changes. They are not satisfied with the status quo which is incomplete because most people do not resemble the role model and do not possess his or her qualities. In that many people emulate the role model, the status quo is overcome and a process of positive development is started. Private entrepreneurs as role models thereby make similarly high moral demands from themselves as the earlier Communist cadres did. One needs to bear in mind that Vietnamese communism was marked historically by an emphasis on people behaving as moral role models (thoroughly in the Confucian tradition). From the viewpoint of their moral-ethical self-image, the private entrepreneurs represent in a certain way competition to the communist cadres, whose moral weight has suffered serious damage precisely through the corruption endemic in Vietnam.

Table 95: How do you assess the importance of the following goals in life for your life? (Vietnam)[213]

	Very important		Average		Unimportant	
	Number	%	Number	%	Number	%
1. Making a contribution to the development of the country	144	72.7	52	26.3	2	1.0
2. Higher income	125	62.8	69	34.7	5	2.5
3. Higher social position	25	12.7	84	42.6	88	44.7
4. Making a contribution to society	100	50.0	96	48.0	4	2.0
5. Better future for one's own children	185	93.0	14	7.0	0	0.0
6. Economic freedom	133	67.9	55	28.1	8	4.1
7. Enjoyment of current life	18	9.1	105	53.3	74	37.6
8. Being a social role model	69	35.1	87	44.2	41	20.8
9. A happy family	189	95.0	10	5.0	0	0.0
10. Individual happiness	55	28.1	92	47.0	49	25.0

Source: Own survey.

In rural areas this exemplary function is stronger than in the urban areas, because here private sector activity is much more likely to guarantee social ascent than in the urban areas, and at the same time possesses a *pull* function i.e. engenders emulation processes. Role models are more important in less developed regions such as Central Vietnam (precisely for the *pull* effect).

Table 95 indicates further just how important – in contrast to China – the element of economic freedom of decision is regarded. Only an insignificantly low minority (4.1%) classified this element as less important. This is hardly surprising, since the private sector is dependent on economic activity which is as unconstrained as possible. Even if this concept of freedom cannot be equated with liberal Western or laissez-faire ideas, because it has been molded by other historical, political and cultural experiences and backgrounds, economic freedom in Vietnam entails carrying out one's business relatively uninfluenced by interventions on the part of government bureaucracies. At any rate, 67% classified this goal in life as very important, whereby the percentage in urban areas (70%) exceeded that in rural areas (63.8%). Surprisingly, there was no differ-

---

[213] According with the wish of our Vietnamese partners, we deviated from the original questionnaire and changed two questions: instead of asking about self-fulfillment, we asked about individual happiness; instead of a contribution to communist development, about a contribution to the construction of the nation.

ence between North and South Vietnam. The private sector operating according to the rules of a market economy has to and wants to develop itself freely, irrespective of whether or not it is doing so on socialist or market-economic terrain. Only Central Vietnam diverges to some extent, whereby the number of those who classified economic freedom as less important is still overall equally low.

In contrast to China, in Vietnam nearly 63% characterized higher incomes and higher standards of living as very important goals in life, whereas only 2.5% of these classified them as less important. Compared with the question of the major motive for founding their companies, (to which only 9% replied in terms of a higher income), material motives appear to have gained in importance in the course of entrepreneurial activity. The material success of private sector operations – private entrepreneurs earn above average incomes – may have strengthened the desire for higher salaries.

As in China, in Vietnam too merely 12.7% of the respondents interviewed stated that for them reaching a higher social position was an important goal in life. Seen in absolute terms, this number may appear to be low, but the goal does not represent in itself a value. Such a social rise is at present indivisible from a higher income, high standards of living, power and influence. A social rise is only achievable by means of an economic one, and so the former is subordinated to the latter. Entrepreneurs in rural areas regard this goal as more important than those in urban areas, precisely because there are – as we have emphasized above – fewer chances of upward social mobility in rural areas than in urban areas. In North Vietnam, the proportion of those who hold upward social mobility to be very important is the lowest, possibly because a higher social position in that region has up till now for the most part only been reachable via Party membership. In the response behavior, one needs in general to take into account that the wish for upward social mobility is seldom expressed openly, but instead rather guardedly. An entrepreneur in Ho Chi Minh City pointed out that his colleagues indeed harbored ambitions concerning rising socially, but social conventions forbade all too open expressions of such intentions.

Only 9% of the respondents held the enjoyment of one's current life to be very important, and so this appears to be hardly meaningful as a goal in life in Vietnam too. An exception to this was in Central Vietnam (32.3%) which in contrast to North and South Vietnam appear to be rather hedonistically disposed. 28.1% of the respondents assessed their own personal happiness as a very important goal in life which shows a clear trend towards individualism. In the urban areas which have undergone a more rapid social transformation than the rural regions, 30.2% gave this answer compared to 24.3% in the latter. There are relatively large differences between the three regions. In North Vietnam every third person emphasized their own personal happiness, in South Vietnam only every fourth, and in Central Vietnam merely every fifth.

In the sphere of life goals, we can note that there is a change in the direction of stressing the individual: a significant proportion of the entrepreneurs interviewed assessed self-realization or individual happiness as an important goal in life. During the interviews the respondents let it be known that their life-goals had changed in the last ten years. As a rule they confirmed such a transformation both in material and immaterial domains.

The formerly highly regarded ideal of reference to the social collective did not achieve undivided agreement amongst all entrepreneurs. Within Vietnam above all amongst entrepreneurs in rural areas, there is an apparently weaker sense of social responsibility than amongst the urban ones. The statement of a paper manufacturer in Tien Son district was characteristic: when he founded the firm, there was annoyance in his native place since the manufacture polluted the water, and his company received preferential treatment concerning electricity, which the remaining inhabitants of the village lacked due to the general shortage of energy. Meanwhile the people there had got used to it, was his answer to the question about he had responded to the annoyance. He saw no obligation to bring about less pollution of the water. Only after specific questions, did he claim to want to construct a pond to store the water outflow. He stated that unfortunately he was not yet in a position to solve this problem.

4.3. *Attitudes to the market economy*

On the one hand, private companies form a central plank of market economy relations, on the other hand, the existence and development of the private sector presupposes relations as in a market economy. So, it is almost self-evident that the absolute majority of the respondents spoke in favor of such relations. In China, almost 80% held the statement, "The market economy assists economic development" to be accurate, more than a fifth found it to be partially accurate, and nobody thought it inaccurate.

That around one fifth expressed only qualified support is linked to the specific ideas of "socialist market economy" and current uncertainties about the development of the private sector. In this question too, regional differences showed themselves. Respondents from Henan and Gansu agreed more often than those in the province of Zhejiang (more developed in terms of the market economy), with the general formulation about the advantages of the market economy.

A range of entrepreneurs elaborated on their (only) qualified support after they had answered the question to the effect that economic development had not only been influenced by mechanisms of the market economy, but also through other factors (such as the government's economic policies, the human capital available, the natural resources, etc.). The market economy, they stated, need not automatically lead to economic development. Moreover, there was still no complete market economy system in China, which has still got a mixed and transitional economy, they argued.

The companies experience at the same time the negative effects of the market economy (such as fluctuations of the state of the economy, competition, unemployment). In Zhejiang, where market economic relations were the strongest amongst all three regions surveyed, the respondents we interviewed articulated the problems associated with the consequences of the market economy that they had experienced as negative.

In Gansu and Henan where the private sector was still less developed, firstly the ideas in images concerning the "market economy" were much more nebulous. Secondly, it is seen as a panacea and, thirdly, the private sector appeared to be a vehicle for the rapid acquisition of money. In Gansu, many entrepreneurs declared that they would like to orientate themselves to the market economic role models such as Shenzhen. They thought that there the framework conditions for the market economy were better and Shenzen had demonstrated that and how market economic relations could lead to rapid business developments.

Entrepreneurs in urban areas (85.2%) agreed more often than those in rural areas (71%) with this statement (market economy promotes economic development). In the countryside, there were stronger reservations concerning the market economy, when understood as purely an economic phenomenon, because the moral element of social behavior (as a result of that definition) retreats into the background, so entrepreneurs argued. There, the market economy was more perceived as an anti-social economic system, which accelerates the erosion of local communities.

There were hardly any variations of opinion between large and small entrepreneurs, an indication that the evaluation of market economy is rather to be viewed as a regional factor and has less to do with the size of the firm.

Table 96: Assess the following statement "The market economy assists economic development" (China)

	Completely true		Partially true		Untrue	
	Number	%	Number	%	Number	%
Zhejiang	42	60.9	27	39.1	0	0.0
Henan	53	88.3	7	11.7	0	0.0
Gansu	46	95.8	2	4.2	0	0.0
Urban areas	92	85.2	16	14.8	0	0.0
Rural areas	49	71.0	20	29.0	0	0.0
Large entre-preneurs	43	79.6	11	20.4	0	0.0
Small entre-preneurs	98	79.7	25	20.3	0	0.0

Source: Own research.

A Chinese survey (1993) amongst 1,428 people in Shanghai suggests that only a relatively low percentage of the non-entrepreneurial population appear to share the attitudes of private entrepreneurs towards the market economy. Only 40.6% of the respondent held the statement which was to be assessed (in Table 96) to be accurate, 39% for partially true, 19.6% did not have an opinion, and 0.8% held it to be inaccurate.[214]

Here too indeed, a basically positive assessment of the market economy was expressed. But this is on the one hand more strongly limited because the interests of the non-entrepreneurs are less closely linked to the market economy, on the other hand the level of knowledge about the market economy amongst large sections of the population still appears to be relatively low. Almost a fifth, however, did not wish to express themselves on this matter.

In Vietnam the results looked similar with a relatively low geographical dispersion, whereby here too, as in China, nobody fully contradicted this view of matters. That the market economy is characterized as assisting development is consensus amongst the entrepreneurs in both countries. But, in North Vietnam and in rural areas stronger reservations were articulated, whereby negative aspects of the market economy and social consequences were named as major factors.

Table 97: Assess the following statement: "The market economy assists economic development" (Vietnam)

	Completely true	Partially true	Untrue
Hanoi	48	9	
Tien Son	25	6	
Danang	21	1	
Duy Xuyen	9	1	
Ho Chi Minh City	44	6	
Thu Duc	26	4	
Total	**173 (86.5)**	**27 (13.5)**	
Urban areas	113 (87.6)	16 (12.4)	
Rural areas	60 (84.5)	11 (15.5)	
North Vietnam	73 (83.0)	15 (17.0)	
Central Vietnam	30 (93.8)	2 (6.3)	
South Vietnam	70 (87.5)	10 (12.5)	

Source: Own research.

Because we wanted to find out the general ideas of entrepreneurs expressed in a more precise way, we asked for an assessment of the differences between socialist and capitalist market economies. However, in Vietnam our cooperation partner deleted this question from the questionnaire, so that the following explanations refer only to China.

---

[214] Zhuanxing shiqi Shanghai shimin shehui xintai diaocha he duice yanjiu 1994: 19-25.

Merely 4% held the opinion that both forms of the market economy were identical. 22.6% held it to be partially true, and 73.4% for inaccurate. The "Chinese" form of the market economy was defined by the Party leadership as a socialist market economy. This definition is decided on a political basis, whereby "socialist" stands for the leadership of the CP. In the socialist form of the market economy, the Party is supposed, at one and the same time, to direct and control the market economy. Almost three-quarters were aware of this formal differentiation at least to a certain extent. Our probes established that the following variations were regarded as basic differences to the capitalist market economy; the element of direction and regulation (through the state and the Party); and the dominance of the state sector as well as the political system in which the market economy functions in China. At any rate, it has to be said that more than a quarter agreed at least partially with this statement. In Gansu, in the rural areas and amongst large entrepreneurs, this figure even rose in each case above 30%. Agreement, although partial, contained not only the thought that the laws of the market economy are the same everywhere, even if in China there is an attempt by the state more markedly to limit it. They contain at the same time a critical element in the sense that those factors which were always considered to be negative elements in the capitalist market economy have had the same effect in China as under capitalism (unemployment, anarchy, companies going out of business, corruption, white-collar crime, etc.).

Table 98: Assess the following statement: Income should be geared to economic and personal achievements (China)

	True		Untrue	
	Number	*%*	*Number*	*%*
Total	*171*	*96.6*	*6*	*3.4*
Zhejiang	67	97.1	2	2.9
Henan	60	100.0	0	0.0
Gansu	44	91.7	4	8.3
Urban areas	103	95.4	5	4.6
Rural areas	68	98.6	1	1.4
Large entrepreneurs	53	98.1	1	1.9
Small entrepreneurs	119	96.7	4	3.3

Source: Own research.

Amongst the basic principles of the market economy can be counted the principle of achievement. It states that income should be geared to performance or achievement, whereby we have combined the personal with the economic (company) results. And being an entrepreneur is based precisely on this double achievement. 96.6% of the entrepreneurs whom we surveyed held that to be correct for China too; merely 3.4% held a different opinion. So the principle of achievement is of significance for entrepreneurs because for one thing it justifies their income. Many declared their high income to be the result of a corresponding performance and the entrepreneurial risk factor. Additionally this principle is valid in companies in order for them to be able to survive against the competition in the market.

The differences in opinion between urban areas and rural areas as well as between large and small entrepreneurs were relatively low, an indication that in this respect there is a large area of agreement between almost all entrepreneurs.

This result corresponded for the most part to that in Vietnam, here too with low geographical variations. According to the ideas of the Chinese elite, the state sector should continue to play a leading role in the economy. Only just under a fifth agreed, four-fifths rejected this completely or partially.

Table 99: Assess the following statement: "The development of state-owned companies should have priority above that of private companies" (China)

	Completely true		Partially true		Untrue	
	Number	%	Number	%	Number	%
Total	37	20.9	64	36.2	76	42.9
Zhejiang	5	7.2	31	44.9	33	47.8
Henan	17	28.3	21	35.0	22	36.7
Gansu	15	31.3	12	25.0	21	43.8
Urban areas	26	24.1	36	33.3	46	42.6
Rural areas	11	15.9	28	40.6	30	43.5
Large entrepreneurs	4	7.4	22	40.7	28	51.9
Small entrepreneurs	33	26.8	41	33.3	49	39.8

Source: Own research.

There was, nevertheless, a relatively high percentage that agreed fully or partially with this statement (above all in Gansu and Henan, in the urban areas, and amongst small entrepreneurs) and this was for a number of reasons. For one thing, many of the respondents did not want publicly to subordinate the state sector, given that the hierarchy (i.e. the private sector subordinate to the state sector) was still the official political line, a reason why "partially accurate" was so often ticked. Secondly, entrepreneurs in those two provinces (Gansu and Henan), in urban areas as well as small companies are dependent in terms of orders on state-owned companies many times over. More than two-thirds of the respondents interviewed claimed that their most important way to obtain raw materials was the public sector (state and collective companies), and three-quarters stated that their main customers were likewise from this sector. So their own success depended to a significant degree on the development of the state sector.

This showed that the state sector and the private sector could not be treated as domains separated from one another. The Chinese, like the Vietnamese economy is characterized nowadays by a significantly hermaphroditic nature. In this the socialist and market economic elements co-exist in the wake of extensive privatization from below combined with the simultaneous retention of a large state sector alongside market economic elements. Consequently the private sector does not stand alone in opposition to the state sector; instead both forms of the economy are connected in many ways and complement each other. Close economic inter-connections exist between them; these lead, for example, to the swapping of orders between firms in the two sectors. The extensive inter-connections turn out to be mutually advantageous: they increase the operational flexibility of the state sector, and facilitate its adaptation to market economic circumstances. At the same time, private entrepreneurs obtain access to modern technology, capital and relatively stable markets. Implicitly the fate of a section of the private sector depends on the further development of the state sector.

But there are clear regional differences. While the commercial dependence on the state sector is more significant in Zhejiang than in Henan and Gansu, at the same time the agreement with the developmental priority for entrepreneur companies was at its lowest. This may for one thing depend on the fact that the state sector was in the latter two still very much dominant, the private entrepreneurs were as a result to a higher degree dependent on public sector, whereas in Zhejiang the possibilities of alternative business relationships outside of the state sector were greater.

Moreover, state and collective companies merged together. As probes demonstrated, for private companies in Zhejiang the collective sector in the shape of companies in rural areas played a more important role, whereas in Henan and Gansu it was rather state firms with which commercial relations existed.

But as Chinese surveys stressed private entrepreneurs are especially skeptical about firms in the state sector and their reform. In respect of the solution of the problems of state sector firms in the coming years, a survey (1997) found 67.9% of the private entrepreneurs interviewed, but only 45.3% of the surveyed company bosses in companies with other forms of ownership structures, had only a little or even no confidence in such measures.[215]

In Vietnam, a larger percentage contradicted the view that the state sector in terms of development should be granted priority, and a significantly lower number agreed with this statement.

---

[215] Zhongguo qiyejia diaocha xitong 1997: 13.

Table 100: Assess the following statement: "The development of state-owned companies should have priority above that of private companies" (Vietnam)

	Completely true	*Partially true*	*Untrue*
Hanoi	1	9	45
Tien Son	1	11	17
Danang	1	7	13
Duy Xuyen	1	8	
Ho Chi Minh City	8	23	19
Thu Duc	6	10	14
Total	**18 (9.3)**	**68 (35.1)**	**108 (55.7)**
Urban areas	10 (7.9)	39 (31.0)	77 (61.1)
Rural areas	8 (11.7)	29 (42.6)	31 (45.6)
North Vietnam	2 (2.4)	20 (23.8)	62 (73.8)
Central Vietnam	2 (6.7)	15 (50.0)	13 (43.3)
South Vietnam	14 (17.5)	33 (41.3)	33 (41.3)

Source: Own research.

Here, there were significant geographical differences. In North Vietnam almost three-quarters of the respondents expressed opposition to prioritizing the state sector. Entrepreneurs comprehend such preferential treatment as a direct threat to the private sector and through that to their company. On the other hand, in the final analysis development of firms and their expansion depends on the private sector receiving non-discriminatory treatment.

In contrast in the South, where entrepreneurs are mostly both more self-confident and experienced than in the North, the question of priority apparently did not play so big a role. One entrepreneur argued that it could only be advantageous to the development of the private sector, if too the state sector developed. In rural areas, the question about priority was not of great relevance, because there the state sector in the form of manufacturing companies hardly exists any more.

The dependence of the private sector on the state and collective companies is much less in Vietnam than it is in China, whereby there are differences, however, between the North and the South.

Whereas in China two-thirds were dependent on the supplies from the non-private sector and three-quarters on the customers from it, the corresponding figures for Vietnam were in each case only a little more than a third. And this percentage was considerably influenced by North Vietnam with its dominant state sector, because in Central and South Vietnam the percentage of suppliers from the state sector was in each case under 5%, and for the customers under 7% and 6%, respectively. Whereas Chinese private companies were more strongly inter-connected with other private companies in the spheres of supply and sales (in each case over 50%), the share in Vietnam (between 38% and 43%) was definitely lower.

That the market economy is not only positively evaluated by the entrepreneurs is made clear by the following table:

Table 101: Assess the following statement "Market economy leads to many social problems (such as unemployment, white-collar crime, corruption)" (China)

	Completely true		Partially true		Untrue	
	Number	%	Number	%	Number	%
Total	43	24.3	66	37.3	68	38.4
Zhejiang	3	4.3	26	37.7	40	58.0
Henan	20	33.3	26	43.3	14	23.3
Gansu	20	41.7	14	29.2	14	29.2
Urban areas	24	22.2	42	38.9	42	38.9
Rural areas	19	27.5	24	34.8	26	37.7
Large entrepreneurs	6	11.1	20	37.0	28	51.9
Small entrepreneurs	37	30.1	46	37.4	40	32.5

Source: Own research.

As Table 101 shows, there is a split of opinion. In their own interests entrepreneurs did not want to see the market economy too negatively assessed, precisely because their firm is a part of this market economy. But it is interesting that this question was answered on the one hand in Zhejiang and Henan and Gansu on the other completely differently. Only a very low percentage in Zhejiang perceived negative aspects, whereas in both the other provinces a third and over 40% respectively held this opinion.

As the probes shows, the market economy in Zhejiang functions very well with a flourishing, private entrepreneurial strata combined at the same time with an extensive opening to foreign countries has the effect of a different, more economically oriented viewpoint. In both the other provinces by contrast the market economy is still significantly restricted by the authorities and traditional concepts of society and social behavior are stronger; in those areas social and moral developments as well as negative trends play a more important role in the assessment of the market economy.

In Vietnam about the same number (in percentage terms) as in China agreed with the view that the market economy leads to many problems, too. But the percentage in South Vietnam was some points higher than in North and Central Vietnam. Some entrepreneurs explained this with the multiplicity of social problems (prostitution, substance abuse, corruption), problems which, while they are to be found throughout the country, in Ho Chi Minh City were particularly conspicuous. The respondents' behavior indicates at the same time that the assessment of the linkage between market economy and social problems is judged as being more serious by the Vietnamese entrepreneurs than in China. Whereas in China almost 40% contradicted this viewpoint, in Vietnam it was only 21%. Here too, in North Vietnam noticeably more contradicted (30.2%) than in South Vietnam (8.8%) which appears to confirm the hypothesis that special social problems are to be found there.

Table 102: Assess the following statement: "Market economy leads to many social problems (such as unemployment, white-collar crime, corruption)" (Vietnam)

	Completely true	*Partially true*	*Untrue*
Hanoi	12	23	21
Tien Son	7	18	5
Danang	5	9	7
Duy Xuyen	1	7	2
Ho Chi Minh City	14	35	1
Thu Duc	7	17	6
Total	**46 (23.4)**	**109 (55.3)**	**42 (21.3)**
Urban areas	31 (24.4)	67 (52.8)	29 (22.8)
Rural areas	15 (21.4)	42 (60.0)	13 (18.6)
North Vietnam	19 (22.1)	41 (47.7)	26 (30.2)
Central Vietnam	6 (19.4)	16 (51.6)	9 (29.0)
South Vietnam	21 (26.3)	52 (65.0)	7 (8.8)

Source: Own research.

The response behavior in both countries certainly allows the interpretation here too, that an ambivalent assessment of the market economy is relatively widespread. Many entrepreneurs, while they indeed favor expansion of the market economy, do not want a market-oriented society which is exposed to unhindered market forces and could lead to many social problems, even finally to instability.

5. *Political and participative basic attitudes*

5.1. *Comprehension of politics*

Diagram 20: Which of the following statements about politics could you agree with most? Politics…. (China)

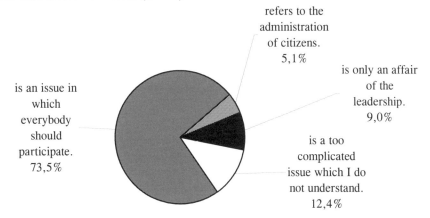

Source: Own research.

The question about comprehension of politics was also deleted from the questionnaire in Vietnam, so that the following analysis only refers to China. Diagram 20 makes clear what entrepreneurs understand by the term politics. Four statements for assessment were presented that referred for the most part to participative themes. Almost three-quarters of the respondents agreed with the statement that politics was a matter in which everybody should participate; only a low percentage thought that politics was merely an affair to do with the political elite, or that they wanted to remain distant from politics on grounds of it being "too complicated".

Almost three-quarters saw in politics the possibility of participation, apparently meaningful and necessary involvement, which is why one should have a hand in its shaping. Only around a quarter wanted to have nothing to do with politics, either because political activity was basically considered to be too risky, based on their historical experiences (the Cultural Revolution and other political movements), or because they saw in it no possibilities to personally shape it themselves. The great interest in politics and participation which was expressed here was surprising insofar as private entrepreneurs are often regarded as apolitical and in their behavior as purely clientele-oriented.

In the qualitative interviews it was shown that the majority of entrepreneurs have grasped that they cannot only operate on a clientele basis, but rather that they have to shape politics in that they take part in negotiations with the government (likewise the Party or the authorities); additionally they have to organize, to represent their own interests, to bring their interests in common into the political process, and also have to achieve something inside the political institutions (the Party, the People's Congresses and the Political Consultative Conferences). In this way politics was not understood only as a power process, but rather too as something open to being shaped.

The difference between Henan on one side, and Zhejiang and Gansu on the other side is noticeable. In Henan around 86% voted for the participative element; in the two other provinces it was between 60% and 70%. The qualitative interviews showed that many entrepreneurs from Gansu equate politics with that of the central government, but given the geographical distance only saw a few possibilities for participating and shaping the "big" political arena. In Zhejiang the high degree of commercialization was apparently responsible for many entrepreneurs declaring that owing to the intensive nature of work no time remained for politics. An example of that was the owner of the firm Xiaohesen in Hangzhou who explicitly criticized other entrepreneurs who were very active politically and took part as representatives in the People's Congresses or the Political Consultative Conferences. Through their political contacts they came into contact with important politicians, and this was reflected in the attaining of considerable business profits. In a sequence of cases such entrepreneurs were said to have become arrogant, and because of that had got into conflict situations with other officials. This had a negative affect on their company, he stated. As a result he thought it better to remain distant from politics. He went on that he himself was not interested in working as a political deputy (in the institutions just mentioned), his goal was much rather rational management of his company. His politics consisted of creating jobs and the introduction of social benefits for his staff. In the last analysis this entrepreneur was involved in a political process even if his concept of politics was different i.e. non-clientelistic and indeed a rather socially orientated one.

The differences of opinion between urban and rural areas, as well as large and small entrepreneurs are not very big, above all with the background of a greater degree of knowledge in the urban areas. Large entrepreneurs were less interested in participation than smaller ones, which was explained by probes: larger entrepreneurs often perceived in political participation a time problem and expressed stronger concerns respecting the meddling by Party or government in business activities.

5.2. *Attitudes to political participation*

Huntington and Nelson once termed participation a *hallmark* of political modernization.[216] The terms means first of all participation, the taking part or cooperation by members of a group in matters which mutually concern them. In the

---

[216] Huntington and Nelson 1976: 1.

family, at the place of work, in club or associations, in the economy, in politics, in many areas of life there are possibilities for participation.

So, the term is in no way bound only to political decision-making. Individual forms of social participation certainly take place in the economy, too. Further illustrations of that are the collaboration in markets or entrepreneurial activity, both of which can be evaluated as forms of individual (socio-economic) participation. Often, the latter creates the preconditions for political participation. In this context, we want to concentrate on the term participation in the political sphere, whereby politics refers to the structures of relations between the state and social groups, to the interaction between these groups, as well as the decisions and establishing of frameworks for an organized functioning social existence in the political fabric of the state. But there are varying forms in differing societies. The "Western" notion of participation is closely associated with institutional and direct participation, whereby political participation in the final analysis means that individuals or groups *intervene* for the purposes of maintaining or altering matters of public interest, in order to influence decisions (political output) or to bring into being realities in public. Such a term orientates itself on democratically conceived societies.

This concept implied in the term participation needs to be differentiated. One needs to note the following: the bonding to democratic institutions and views of the world; the conscious collaboration of citizens in the processes of forming opinions and decision-making; the direct assertion of policies in the form of *pressure groups*; the active intervention in matters of public concern; and the conscious changes to the society or social emancipation as a goal. All of these factors restrict the term participation to specific political structures and framework conditions. Such a narrowing down prevents an analysis of participation, its forms and goals in the non-democratically conceived countries of East Asia. But participation does indeed exist too in China and Vietnam; but it assumes other forms and different means of influencing the *output* of politics. Its goal is not so much direct social emancipation, but rather striving to find solutions or modifications to immediate everyday or life issues.

In that I start out with the following minimal definition for the term *political participation:* members of a group take part in the regulation of matters of common concern in the society and/or their sub-groups (of that society). This can take place institutionally and/or directly or indirectly, non-violently or violently, legally or illegally. All activities through which individuals or groups of individuals make their intentions clear and influence political *output* directly or indirectly have to be assessed as participation. Such a minimal consensus for the determination of political participation applies equally to Western and East Asian, to democratic or non-democratic, to agricultural and as well as to industrial countries.

As I have already made clear above, direct and active interventions, the work as a *pressure group* which in a Western context is taken for granted, do not correspond to the traditions of political cultures in East Asia. In the two countries which I treat here, direct interventions in political matters or the attempt to exercise political pressure are rather dangerous.

Informal and indirect actions, the inclusion and corporatist bonding-in of groups through the Party and state, *bargaining*, negotiating behind the scenes, but also the somewhat unconscious *collective action*, the joint unconscious activities of social players (e.g. of entrepreneurial strata) can have some influence on political output. On the *individual level* the upshot is that *Guanxi* and corruption are among other things forms of participation, both in a positive and in a negative sense.[217]

Above, we have already shown in which ways entrepreneurs can exert influence on local politics. In that, stronger informal forms (by means of networks, *Guanxi*, or corruption as well) stand at the center. Beyond that, however, one should not overlook formal and organized forms (through membership of parties, in People's Congresses, Political Consultative Conferences or associations representing entrepreneurs). The two complement each other and are for the most part indispensable for the purposes of ensuring company activities run without friction. As a result, what is at issue as far as the entrepreneurs are concerned, is also not a fundamental interest in politics as such; the latter is much rather a necessary component of entrepreneurial activity.

The view that entrepreneurs were only slightly interested in politics was also challenged by another question. 78.5% of the respondents were namely of the opinion that entrepreneurs should not only be interested in company affairs, but rather too should concern themselves with politics. Only 2.8 % of the respondents interviewed thought that politics was just a matter for politicians, 18.6% held this view to be "partially accurate" (cf. Table 103). The absolute majority of the entrepreneurs we interviewed also saw politics as a sphere in which they had to involve themselves. The question "Do you sometimes discuss important affairs of your country with friends or acquaintances?" was assented to by 84.2% of the respondents interviewed. This confirmed too that entrepreneurs are by no means only interested in their companies, and also cannot be so, because political developments and decisions directly affect their business activity. Out of that results a significant degree of interest on the part of many entrepreneurs in exerting political influence.

As a result, the Chinese entrepreneurs are certainly not only agents of economic development, but also agents of societal change and political participation. Numerous entrepreneurs declared that they had not only founded a company due to expectations of profit making, but rather as well to prove that the private sector could be more efficient than state and collective companies. Behind this argumentation too exists a political attitude: the positive evaluation of market economy elements as opposed to state-directed ones as part of a centrally planned, state dominated economy.

---

[217] More detail on this set of problems: Heberer 1997a.

Geographically based differences of opinion confirm the information given above.

Table 103: Entrepreneurs should not be concerned with political affairs, but rather only questions to do with business. Politics is the business of politicians. (China)

	Completely true		Partially true		Untrue	
	Number	%	Number	%	Number	%
Total	5	2.8	33	18.6	139	78.5
Zhejiang	4	5.8	17	24.6	48	69.6
Henan	0	0.0	8	13.3	52	86.7
Gansu	1	2.1	8	16.7	39	81.3
Urban areas	1	0.9	18	16.7	89	82.4
Rural areas	4	5.8	15	21.7	50	72.5
Large entrepreneurs	2	3.7	11	20.4	41	75.9
Small entrepreneurs	3	2.4	22	17.9	98	79.7

Source: Own research.

In contrast to managers of state and collective companies, private entrepreneurs assume a position which is still politically subordinate. The former are almost without exceptions Party members with the corresponding social and political relationships and enjoy a higher political and social prestige, especially in view of the fact that, in spite of legal equality, state companies are regarded as being of primary importance just as they were before. Table 104 shows that most of the entrepreneurs (68.9%) are trying to achieve a political positioning in which they are given treatment equal to that accorded to the managers of state and collective companies, and the former want to collaborate in political decision-making. Many entrepreneurs argued that the private sector was – in terms of the national economy – the most dynamic sector and contributed significantly to economic development (more than a third of the GDP). In spite of the economic meaning of the private sector, the political significance and the political possibilities of influence of the entrepreneurs had not changed appropriately. They argued that it was about time that they were given equal ranking to the managers of state and collective companies.

The difficult framework conditions of their work awake in the entrepreneurs the understandable desire for participation in a discussion about economic-political decisions by the government, in order that they be able to exert a certain influence on the socio-political environment surrounding their business operations. Even general political questions were no longer seen exclusively as the affair of the Party or the state. Consequently, only a very small percentage or the respondents we interviewed wanted to separate themselves from political participation. Those with reservations ("partially accurate") made up in contrast a significant percentage. The reasons for that were very different: some saw in the request for equality (with managers from the state and collective companies) a kind of hubris, others had – during the Cultural Revolution or in other political movements – accumulated negative experiences with politics and political activity, others in turn feared restrictions in the time available for their business work, or perceived politics to be a sensitive affair with which politicians acting on their behalf should concern themselves.

Some of the respondents we interviewed had earlier lost their jobs for political reasons and/or been imprisoned. But all of these doubters held political participation by entrepreneurs to be necessary, for one thing in the interests of the group.

Differences in response behavior between the areas surveyed were low on this question; significant deviations showed themselves, however, between entrepreneurs in urban and rural areas. One can see from Table 104 that entrepreneurs in urban areas possess a stronger participative interest than those in rural areas. Cities are the political centers of a region in which too most of the companies in the state sector are to be found. Entrepreneurs in urban areas have on the one hand easier access to political information; on the other hand due to the local dominance of the state sector, they tended to be marginalized in political terms.

In contrast with managers of companies in the state sector, private entrepreneurs in urban areas often have fewer possibilities of influencing political decisions. Entrepreneurs in rural areas, in turn, are more strongly bound into local networks and believe themselves to be able to realize their interests better with the help of *Guanxi*. Furthermore, private entrepreneurs in rural areas move socially in completely different surroundings. At the level of municipality and county, the private sector in many areas plays a leading role. In contrast to entrepreneurs in urban areas, the private entrepreneurs in rural areas were not so markedly restricted by the local authorities in political questions, but rather were often given equal treatment to that received by the managers of collective companies in rural areas. Private entrepreneurs are often too at the same time township or village cadres. Under such circumstances, such entrepreneurs are already relatively influential in political terms, at least on the local level.

A relatively high percentage of larger entrepreneurs (33.3%) agreed only partially with the statement that private entrepreneurs should participate in economic-political decisions just as the managers of state and collective companies do. For one thing, larger entrepreneurs argued, this had not been possible for them due to structural differences. They went on that the managers (of state and collective companies) were state employees and cadres, they in contrast as self-employed were subjected to completely different work processes. Others maintained that this was not realistic at that particular juncture, since private entrepreneurs were politically still discriminated against despite all improvements. The owner of the firm Jinyi in Hangzhou mentioned, for example, that although he had made a major donation towards the carrying-out of an international sports meeting, he had not been invited to the opening festivities. This made clear to him that entrepreneurs were still not given equal treatment. At the same time, one should not attach exaggerated importance to such statements; almost unanimously the larger entrepreneurs agreed with the position of equal treatment for entrepreneurs and managers.

Table 104: Private entrepreneurs should participate actively in economic-political decisions just as the managers of state and collective companies do (China)

	Completely true		Partially true		Untrue	
	Number	%	Number	%	Number	%
Total	122	68.9	52	29.4	3	1.7
Zhejiang	47	68.1	20	29.0	2	2.9
Henan	42	70.0	18	30.0	0	0.0
Gansu	33	68.8	14	29.2	1	2.1
Urban areas	81	75.0	24	22.2	3	2.8
Rural areas	41	59.4	28	40.6	0	0.0
Large entrepreneurs	35	64.8	18	33.3	1	1.9
Small entrepreneurs	87	70.7	34	27.6	2	1.6

Source: Own research.

In contrast to China, where more than three-quarters of the respondents did not agree with the statement that private entrepreneurs should concern themselves only with business but not political questions, in Vietnam it was only 40% who rejected it. Over 13% approved this statement. So it can be seen that although a significant number, openly expressed their interest in participating in political questions, half of the respondents we interviewed agreed only with reservations. Politics was apparently understood as a much more sensitive field for involvement than in China, with the consequence that a significant number appeared to have withdrawn from politics. Unlike in China, the participative element, however, appeared to be stronger in the rural areas.

Table 105: Entrepreneurs should not be concerned with political affairs, but rather only questions to do with business. Politics is the business of politicians (Vietnam)

	Completely true	*Partially true*	*Untrue*
Hanoi	4	31	22
Tien Son	3	13	15
Danang	6	8	8
Duy Xuyen	1	2	7
Ho Chi Minh City	8	26	15
Thu Duc	5	15	10
Total	**27 (13.6)**	**95 (47.7)**	**77 (38.7)**
Urban areas	18 (14.1)	65 (50.8)	45 (35.2)
Rural areas	9 (12.7)	30 (42.3)	32 (45.1)
North Vietnam	7 (8.0)	44 (50.0)	37 (42.0)
Central Vietnam	7 (21.9)	10 (31.3)	15 (46.9)
South Vietnam	13 (16.5)	41 (51.9)	25 (31.6)

Source: Own research.

That at any rate 86.4% agreed with the participative element completely or at least partially, should lead us to think that participation represents for entrepreneurs too an important element in their activities. One of the reasons may lie in the difficult framework conditions surrounding activities in the private sector. Political participation might open the possibility of exerting influence on these conditions. That is shown by the high number of politically interested in the Central Vietnamese region, which is the one least developed. At nearly 47% the figure is markedly higher than that in the most developed region (South Vietnam) with "only" 31.6%. The development conditions are at their most difficult in Central Vietnam, and the policy of providing assistance for the private sector kicked in there comparatively late and rather hesitantly.

For a long time the collective companies were favorized above the firms in the private sector. Even nowadays, the idea of the collective companies still possesses political supporters – but in a form similar to the Ltd. or joint stock company. Contrastingly, in South Vietnam the development conditions for the private sector are much more favorable, so that there appears to exist less of a necessity to seek possibilities of exerting political influence on the framework conditions. But it would be false from that to conclude that there is a general political disinterest in South Vietnam.

Interestingly, in the rural areas a larger percentage stated there to be a necessity to concern themselves with politics. Possibly this indicates that the degree of political resignation in the rural areas is still somewhat less than in the urban areas. The recognition of this necessity was at the same time much the largest in the North. In that region 92% showed themselves to be generally or partially interested in political participation. Their socialist socialization had perhaps shaped the participative interest in the North to a special extent.

The political interest became even more apparent, when one touched on the question of the economic-political sphere, which of course directly affects the interests of the private entrepreneurs (cf. Table 106). Only a tiny minority of 3% rejected a "very active" discussion of economic political decisions with the government. Almost 70% agreed completely with such discussions and the rest partially.

Table 106: Private entrepreneurs like the managers of state and collective companies should take part actively in the economic-political decision-making of the government (Vietnam)

	Completely true	*Partially true*	*Untrue*
Hanoi	40	16	1
Tien Son	20	10	1
Danang	14	8	
Duy Xuyen	8	2	
Ho Chi Minh City	32	16	1
Thu Duc	25	5	
Total	**139 (69.9)**	**57 (28.6)**	**3 (1.5)**
Urban areas	86 (66.7)	40 (31.0)	2 (2.3)
Rural areas	59 (84.3)	17 (24.3)	1 (1.4)
North Vietnam	60 (69.0)	26 (30.0)	2 (1.0)
Central Vietnam	22 (68.8)	10 (31.2)	
South Vietnam	57 (71.3)	21 (26.3)	1 (2.4)

Source: Own research.

Hereby, economic policies are no longer regarded simply as a bundle of economic measures that people should accept without criticism. Much rather it is a field for discussion. It can be put into question or in extreme cases even rejected.

The private entrepreneurs who were formerly politically marginalized found themselves called on to express themselves in a central sphere of politics, namely that of economic policies. They made the demand to be allowed to pass judgments on the government (and through that implicitly on the Party). Politics is no longer a sacrosanct domain, but rather is subordinated to the discussion too of those who formally were not involved in bringing it into being.

Such an attitude too is the expression of an increased degree of self-confidence amongst the private entrepreneurs, whose economic success is apparent in contrast to the decaying state and collective companies. On the other hand, specific local factors play an important role. Where the framework for development in the private sector for a long time has been rather poor, there has been a greater need for the right to have a say or at least to take part in discussions about economic policies. Correspondingly, 18% more rural than urban private entrepreneurs demanded a right to discussions.

A section of the respondents we interviewed expressed political ideas which contradicted the official ideology. Some were of the opinion that such far-reaching economic changes, like those now occurring in Vietnam, would in the long run lead to the dominance of capitalist elements, to a further political lib-eralization and opening of the country, and finally to the introduction of a multi-party system. This development they viewed as a natural indeed even inevitable process.

The statement by an entrepreneur in Danang illustrated this thoroughly widespread point of view. To express his ideas he used the well-known Viet-namese play 'The soul of Truong Ba and the skin of the pork-seller', in which a sales assistant borrows the soul of an intellectual, in order to be able to live with it; but this does not work out, since the two do not fit together. Just as little – so this entrepreneur thought – do communism and capitalism fit together.

Every society possesses a self-regulatory mechanism, he argued, which leads to the resolution of such contradictions. Likewise in Vietnam one day too communism and capitalism (through the victory of the latter) will be separated. Although everybody, including the authorities, knew that this corresponded to reality, hardly anyone had dared to say it openly, he declared.

He continued, that a (capitalist) revolution was brewing up, which would basically be different from the East European varieties: "If the Asians and the Vietnamese wanted to carry out such a revolution, then they would do it qui-etly, internally, they work behind the scenes; it is not on the surface like the Europeans in Eastern Europe and in the Soviet Union." One should not believe only what could see on the surface, that is superficial.

This entrepreneur hoped very much – like others too –for political changes. He opined that out of our survey political proposals could be formulated for the Vietnamese government. He responded to our probe as to whether there could be problems for him arising from this, by stating that he had already made pro-visions for that eventuality. Furthermore, he added with a certain idealism, that one had to be prepared to accept losses when one strove for something better.[218]

Despite his confidence, the respondent was not free of a certain degree of skepticism in which along with his personal experiences indeed too the year-long, communist propaganda with its demonization of the private sector was reflected. He doubted that the private entrepreneurs would be able to retain in a capitalist system their current "romantic ideas", for example the desire to do

---

[218] The respondents were conscious of the fact that such statements could lead to unpleasant consequences for themselves. Another entrepreneur opined that he should not say too much other-wise he would end up in jail. In response to our probe as to whether this danger in fact really ex-isted, he responded affirmatively. In the course of the interview, this entrepreneur, just like others, himself started a political discussion without any prompting. Another respondent declared that he was happy finally to be able to speak openly with someone. During none of those conversations was a representative of the authorities or our Vietnamese cooperation partners present.

good for another person. He held it to be possible that the entrepreneurs in capitalism would only earn their money "without heart", whereby they would be exclusively interested in their own profit.

Some entrepreneurs in Danang openly expressed their dissatisfaction that the state and the Party did not appropriately honor them although they as entrepreneurs would willingly contribute significantly to the solution of the main problems of developing their nation. They accused the Party of restricting the economic development of the country insofar as it had permitted the growth of private companies only up to a certain relatively low level.

Bach Minh Son, the owner of a large company in Hanoi even declared explicitly that a change in the political system was required, in order to enable a further development of the private sector. He even recorded this opinion on our questionnaire although it was known to him that the questionnaire would remain in the hands of our cooperation partners in Hanoi. He did not have any anxiety that his answers could lead to any negative consequences for him.

A further question in the context of political participation referred to participation in the People's Counciles (assemblies). The People's Counciles constitute according to the prevailing opinion a representative organ of the population, and open at least theoretically not only the chance of membership in the Party and in mass organizations but also possibilities of political participation. But they offer nominal rather than true possibilities of having some influence on processes and proceedings. Although the representatives there possess prestige, over half of the respondents (55%) did not want to be active in that function, even if they had the possibility. Only 8% would be prepared gladly to take on this work. In the rural areas this percentage was somewhat higher, here too indeed for reasons of social ascent, whereas in contrast, for entrepreneurs in urban areas social ascent via politics is less attractive.

The role of being a representative (at the People's Counciles) counts for more in the rural areas than it does in the cities, and is at the same time associated with a greater degree of potential for exerting influence and acquiring relationships. Since the competition in the cities is mostly stronger than in the rural areas, the factor of amount of time invested may also play a role here: someone who has to be involved in their own company, has less time left over for political activity.

Table 107: If you had the chance to be voted as a representative of the People's Councils (Vietnam)

	Very gladly	Quite gladly	Not very gladly	No answer
Hanoi	4	19	31	4
Tien Son	4	14	13	
Danang		8	14	
Duy Xuyen		7	3	
Ho Chi Minh City	4	17	29	1
Thu Duc	4	7	19	
Total	**16 (8.1)**	**72 (36.6)**	**109 (55.3)**	**5**
Urban areas	8 (6.3)	44 (34.9)	74 (58.7)	
Rural areas	8 (11.3)	28 (39.4)	35 (49.3)	
North Vietnam	8 (9.4)	33 (38.8)	44 (51.8)	
Central Vietnam	0 (0.0)	15 (46.9)	17 (53.1)	
South Vietnam	8 (10.0)	24 (30.0)	48 (60.0)	

Source: Own research.

The opinion was widespread (not only amongst entrepreneurs) that political activity in the People's Councils does not constitute any high degree of political participation, since important matters anyway were decided by the party or at least decided de facto, and in many respects the Councils were left merely with the function of acclamation. Precisely because of those reasons many respondents in Danang and to some extent in Ho Chi Minh City too classified the possibilities for political action in the People's Councils as relatively low. Even the sole private entrepreneur (a banker) who was a member of the People's Councils in Quang Nam–Danang confirmed the restricted political opportunities available to him. Some entrepreneurs dubbed the People's Councils as "stage comedies" since the People's Councils do not possess and powers of their own to make decisions and the actual decisions themselves are made by the authorities (or the Party). Here the widespread rejection of political involvement too manifested itself, a result of experiences which people have had since the re-unification.

However, in this matter one should not overlook the fact that involvement in the People's Councils does offer certain possibilities of influence. The banker mentioned was active in the local Committee for Budget and Economy of the People's Councils whereas the other representatives from business in that committee were managers from state-owned companies. In this way it is at any rate possible to create a hearing for the specific concerns of the private sector in local politics. Furthermore such activity facilitates the establishing of contacts with politically influential persons at the local level (e.g. from the People Council, the National Front or the CPV.[219]

In order to become a deputy in a People's Council, as a rule membership of the Party is required or at least protection through Party organizations. But only a limited section of the entrepreneurial stratum fulfills this precondition. As a result the rejection of this institution amongst the entrepreneurs is relatively large. In conversations we had, many of them declared that their interest in becoming a deputy was at that time minimal, due to the low chances that they had to become one. The fact that private entrepreneurs are politically still not completely accepted indeed plays a role in the response behavior. There is – as shown above – within the CPV leadership a strong grouping, just as there was before who are suspicious of the private sector. Due to the ideological-political situation that has not yet been clarified, a section of the entrepreneurial stratum came to the conclusion that it would be better not to get involved politically – even if this were in the framework of the existing system. And that entails finally not being a candidate for the People's Council.

But clear regional differences exist. What is conspicuous is that in North Vietnam there is a 0% greater readiness (almost 10% more) – when one adds together the answers "quite gladly" and "very gladly" added together– than in the South. This willingness might be based on various factors: in South Vietnam the private sector is better developed than anywhere else in the country. The greater amount of private sector competition has forced a stronger concentration on the business sphere. In North Vietnam and post-1975 in all of Vietnam, the regime was of a mobilizing-authoritarian nature; it mobilized the population politically in order to achieve a particular goal (e.g. victory in the Vietnam war). That mobilization took place in the context of the Communist Party (membership), various mass organizations as well as "democratic" institutions such as the People's Council at the different levels of the political system, whereby all candidates and delegates were required to have CPV membership – at least until a few years ago.

Political activity so long as it took place in the spirit of socialism is not only desired but rather the duty of citizens. The mobilization led to a nominal willingness to participate politically e.g. as a delegate to the People's Council, which due to the longer tradition of socialism in North Vietnam is more important than in the southern part of the country. Weaker development of market economic structures and a greater degree of socialist molding and traces as well as interventions in the economy characterize North Vietnam in contrast to the South. As a result in the northern part of the land the work of a deputy was

---

[219] Conversation with Thieu, Danang, 13 January 1997. One of the larger private entrepreneurs of Danang was a friend of the banker: the former made use of his personal relationship with the deputy in order to obtain illegally from the City a number of pieces of real estate close to Danang Airport. The real estate was transferred to him for a small amount of money by deed of gift, and had meanwhile increased in value three-fold; conversation with the entrepreneur, Danang, 1 January 1997.

more strongly perceived as a path to facilitating the realization of economic ideas.

The results in Danang were very surprising where not a single one of the respondents was prepared "very gladly" to become a deputy. The victorious North Vietnamese established the system of the People's Councils after 1975 throughout the country. Due to that, reservations may have existed amongst the population of South Vietnam, because the wounds of the war have certainly not yet been healed. During our interviews in South and Central Vietnam, the distrust of the North Vietnamese was noticeably widespread. As an example an entrepreneur in South Vietnam who had served as an officer in the former South Vietnamese armed forces, refused to answer our questions at first. After he had declared himself available for an informal conversation, neither notes could be taken, nor political questions posed. In the course of the conversation he made his anger about the North Vietnamese very clear.

The most common answer to the question about reasons why the respondents did not want to become deputies, was the response "no skill" (56%). In second place followed with the same number of respondents in each case (22%) were the answers "no interest" and "other reasons". Amongst the latter a lack of time was particularly significant.

Table 108: Reason if answer "Not very gladly" (Vietnam)

	No interest	*No skill*	*Others*	*No answer*
Hanoi	8	16	8	
Tien Son	3	6	4	
Danang	3	7	3	1
Duy Xuyen		3		
Ho Chi Minh City	7	17	5	
Thu Duc	3	12	4	
Total	**24 (22.0)**	**61 (56.0)**	**24 (22.0)**	**1**
Urban areas	18 (24.3)	40 (54.1)	16 (21.6)	
Rural areas	6 (17.1)	21 (60.0)	8 (22.9)	
North Vietnam	11 (24.4)	22 (48.9)	12 (26.7)	
Central Vietnam	3 (17.6)	10 (58.8)	3 (17.6)	
South Vietnam	10 (20.8)	29 (60.4)	9 (18.8)	

Source: Own research.

On the one hand the answer "no skill" for sure reflected accurately the attitudes of a section of the respondents. An entrepreneur from Danang commented on that that the work as a representative required specific knowledge e.g. of the existing laws, which amongst different population groups like the workers or the peasants was not available.[220]

On the other hand this "modest" answer (i.e. one possesses as a humble person too few skills in order to take on such a high post so full of responsibility as that of a deputy) made it possible to avoid a difficult question. The state, characterized by its mobilizing-socialist nature required political participation, but it is unclear whether this also applied to a politically marginalized group i.e. the private entrepreneurs. People withdraw from the obligation in an elegant style and manner by the unsuspicious reference to one's own inability. They needed to behave differently with the response "no interest" through which one would run the danger of being classified as apolitical i.e. not a socialist person and with that as a potential opponent of communism.

Interestingly, the low interest among the respondents in Vietnam was basically different from the interest amongst Chinese entrepreneurs. There, almost half of them answered concerning their readiness to be deputy "very" and almost four-fifth "quite gladly" or "very gladly". Only about 12% showed no special interest.

Diagram 21: If you had the possibility of being voted into the People's Congress, would you do that gladly? (China in %)

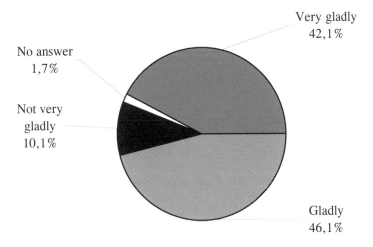

Source: Own research.

For Chinese entrepreneurs, a post as deputy offers political protection, influence and access to the political, economic and intellectual elites of the respective levels. In Vietnam in contrast entrepreneurs tended to be marginalized and

---

[220] Interview Danang, 2 January 1997.

not put up as candidates. Moreover the institution People's Congress in China has been involved in a process of remodeling for some years. The Congress is supposed obtain expanded rights concerning having a say, making decisions and scrutiny, and with that a greater degree of political power. As a result, so numerous interviews showed, it appeared to many entrepreneurs that participation in People's Congress is a possibility of exerting influence and the assertion of the interests of entrepreneurship. In the middle of the 1990s in a district of Hebei province, 82% of the entrepreneurs with capital of over 1 m Yuan were said to be in public office of some kind. They were either deputies in the People's Congresses or occupied leading position in those institutions, or were top members of the Communist Youth League or the Women's Federation.[221]

5.3. Attitudes concerning the role of the Communist Party and of the state in the reconstruction towards market economy

The processes of reform and privatization have changed the role of the Party and the state in both countries. In this context we wanted to know how entrepreneurs assess these roles. Since these are very sensitive fields of interest, the questions had to be formulated rather indirectly. However, we were compelled to delete individual questions in Vietnam or reformulate them.

As can be seen in Table 109, nearly all of the respondents in China preferred strong leadership in order to get to grips with current social problems. This is not surprising, since a weak leadership certainly would hardly be in a position to have at its disposal the necessary powers to resolve social problems. This question was, as a result, rather conceived as a peg for an assessment of authoritarianism, since direct questions about the evaluation of authoritarian structures would not as such have been acceptable. In the qualitative interviews it became clear that "strong" was associated with leadership qualities and authority and the solution of these problems was not expected from a different political system or from a state under the rule of law, but rather from a "strong personality". But here there were subtle differences in the response behavior. The majority were of the opinion, fully in the spirit of the theory of neo-authoritarianism, that only a charismatic leadership personality could fundamentally change the political development of China. The robust leadership desired by the entrepreneurs should be in a position to implement market economic and social changes favorable for private entrepreneurs, as well as to bring about social transformation.

All respondents rejected a return to an autocratic system similar to that of the Mao era. But a rapid transformation to a democratic society based on the rule of law was also hardly a realistic option. However, a significant number hoped that a strong leadership would bring about the preconditions for increasing freedom and democracy.

---

[221] Yang Long 1998: 92/93.

A relatively higher percentage of the respondents in Zhejiang (11.6%) and the larger entrepreneurs (11.1%) only agreed partially with this statement (the necessity of a strong political leadership). Amongst both those groups of respondents the attitude that it was less a "strong" than a "qualified" and "liberal" leadership that was required, was definitely more marked than in Henan and Gansu likewise amongst small entrepreneurs. Strength alone, the former groups thought, still does not solve any problems; moreover all too much strength (in an authoritarian sense) would lead as well to more interventions in the private sector.

Table 109: In order to overcome present-day social problems and difficulties caused by economic development, a strong political leadership is required (China)

	Completely true		*Partially true*		*Untrue*	
	Number	*%*	*Number*	*%*	*Number*	*%*
Total	*165*	*93.2*	*12*	*6.8*	*0*	*0.0*
Zhejiang	61	88.4	8	11.6	0	0.0
Henan	57	95.0	3	5.0	0	0.0
Gansu	47	97.9	1	2.1	0	0.0
Urban areas	101	93.5	7	6.5	0	0.0
Rural areas	64	92.8	5	7.2	0	0.0
Large entrepreneurs	48	88.9	6	11.1	0	0.0
Small entrepreneurs	117	95.1	6	4.9	0	0.0

Source: Own research.

Over 70% of the entrepreneurs surveyed held the opinion that the state's ability to function should be strengthened under the conditions of market economic reconstruction. This too is hardly surprising. Market economies require the balancing out and regulation of the inequalities and disparities associated with market economic structures. The state is required to set the guidelines for the framework and the appropriate regulatory structures. An absolute majority of the entrepreneurs certainly recognized this (cf. Table 110). But, the further the market economic relations in a region had developed, so the more entrepreneurs declared themselves to be *against* a strengthening of the state's functions.

Apparently what they required was not a state providing social order and control, but an ordo-liberal one, which intervenes less in matters to do with the market and private economics, rather setting instead the framework conditions. This was shown too by our probes. Numerous entrepreneurs, above all in Zhejiang, thought that in the course of a functioning market economy many task areas for which the state was responsible could be transferred to the market (such as the distribution of raw materials and products, the fixing of production prices, etc). This explains why, particularly in Zhejiang, a large proportion of the entrepreneurs (50.7%) spoke against giving further power to state-controlled functions. Unlike in Gansu and Henan, where the market economic reconstruction has not yet grown so far, the local authorities had been required to take over countless economic functions and the companies were more dependent on the state. Above all larger entrepreneurs, who were more markedly dependent on the market, objected to strengthening interventions by the state, whereas the contrast between urban and rural areas in this respect was rather minimal.

It is conspicuous that only a small percentage (1.1%) assessed as inaccurate the underlying statement that forms the basis of the one in Table 111. Above all in Zhejiang, to a limited extent as well in Henan and Gansu, a larger group of respondents (in Zhejiang more than half) were of the opinion that this statement was only partially accurate. Our probes established that entrepreneurs only to a limited extend were of the opinion that the functions of state should be strengthened. Much rather it is their opinion that the macro-economic steering functions and the social tasks should be reinforced, but not interventions in the economy. Here what was needed was a definite reduction. 80.8% of the respondents were of the opinion that the government was only responsible for the macro-economic sphere and ought not to intervene in company processes, above all in the sphere of the private sector (cf. Table 112). Most of the respondents voted against state intervention and for company autonomy. Strengthening state functions as a rule referred to macro-economic steering tasks.

Table 110: Under conditions of market economic relations the function of the state has to be strengthened (China)

	Completely true		Partially true		Untrue	
	Number	%	Number	%	Number	%
Total	124	70.1	51	28.8	2	1.1
Zhejiang	32	46.4	35	50.7	2	2.9
Henan	49	81.7	11	18.3	0	0.0
Gansu	43	89.6	5	10.4	0	0.0
Urban areas	77	71.3	30	27.8	1	0.9
Rural areas	47	68.1	21	30.4	1	1.4
Large entrepreneurs	32	59.3	22	40.7	0	0.0
Small entrepreneurs	92	74.8	29	23.6	2	1.6

Source: Own research.

Table 111: The state should only be responsible for macro-economic direction; company processes should be a matter for the entrepreneurs (China)

	Completely true		Partially true		Untrue	
	Number	%	Number	%	Number	%
Total	143	80.8	26	14.7	8	4.5
Zhejiang	54	78.3	12	17.4	3	4.3
Henan	50	83.3	8	13.3	2	3.3
Gansu	39	81.25	6	12.5	3	6.25
Urban areas	87	80.6	16	14.8	5	4.6
Rural areas	56	81.2	10	14.5	3	4.3
Large entrepreneurs	47	87.0	6	11.1	1	1.9
Small entrepreneurs	96	78.0	20	16.3	7	5.7

Source: Own research.

Table 112 makes clear what role private entrepreneurs attribute to the CP in the course of market economic changes. More than two-thirds of the respondents agreed with the statement that the Party should in the course of market economic development exercise a "role model function". Almost 30% only partially agreed with this statement. Probes established that a large number of those who were in favor were of the opinion that the Party should be a role model in the sense that it should support and promote the further development of market economic relations and with that the private sector. Party politics and ideology should be coordinated towards this development. A smaller number understood by the statement to be assessed that the Party *members* should orientate themselves to market economic principles and act more strongly in a market economic way in the sense of working as in an entrepreneurial role. Above all, entrepreneurs in Zhejiang and larger entrepreneurs perceived this statement as not being completely correct.

But here one needs to differentiate the response behavior. A significant part of the larger employers regarded themselves as "role models". The Party, they thought, could not itself be an entrepreneurial role model, but rather, at the most create better framework conditions for entrepreneurs. This view of matters was also in Zhejiang an important strand of opinion. Entrepreneurs in rural areas, in turn, understood the Party to be more a balancing element that should not be allowed to lose this function by being too involved in the market economy; it possesses equalizing functions and gets rid of accompanying negative phenomena. In Henan and Gansu, the idea that the CP has a balancing role as the political counterparts to potential, market economic anarchy was still more clearly marked. The role model function was in those areas understood in this sense above all. The question was consciously kept relatively general, because such a question about the Party might be understood as a sensitive one, and secondly, there was more room to maneuver within the interpretative framework offered by qualitative interviews supported by the guidelines.

Some entrepreneurs, principally those with higher levels of education, pointed out a further important element: for a long time there had not been a division of function between the Party and the state. The Party boss of an administrative level was, as a rule, also the head of the administration of that level. The Party was in the final analysis an institution organized along monopolistic lines. In the course of the reform process, the functions of the Party became more limited, and the significance of the governmental level increased. This group of respondents emphasized that the CP should primarily take care of steering the macro-social sphere, the total social balance as well as internal matters to do with the Party and the shaping of political ideology. According to the ideas of the CP itself, the main function of the Party should be realized not as being an organizational-institutional one, but rather in the form of political-ideological leadership. So, if one talks about the role model function of the Party under market economic conditions, then the role model function should in the end be reduced to the area of tasks just named.

Table 112: Assess the statement: "In the development of the market economy the CP should exercise a role model function." (China)

	Completely true		Partially true		Untrue	
	Number	%	Number	%	Number	%
Total	123	69.5	52	29.4	2	1.1
Zhejiang	30	43.5	37	53.6	2	2.9
Henan	53	88.3	7	11.7	0	0.0
Gansu	40	83.3	8	16.7	0	0.0
Urban areas	79	73.1	27	25.0	2	1.9
Rural areas	44	63.8	25	36.2	0	0.0
Large entrepreneurs	32	59.3	22	40.7	0	0.0
Small entrepreneurs	91	74.0	30	24.4	2	1.6

Source: Own research.

The question as to the exemplary function corresponded with the one about the assessment of the Party's work (cf. Table 113), since the role model function is always measured by the reality of practical activity, too. Almost three-quarters of the respondents stated that they were either only partially, or not at all satisfied with the work of the Party.

This result was surprising insofar as, despite the presence of an official representative from the administration, the absolute majority of the respondents declared themselves to be not at all or not fully satisfied by the Party's work. In that one should take into account that many of the respondents, due to reasons of caution, decided on the more moderate answer ("only partially satisfied"), rather than for "not satisfied".[222]

The dissatisfaction was directed primarily against all forms of corruption, but then too against the orthodoxy of many functionaries, who even now discriminate against the private sector. And in the third place against the inflexibility respecting market economic organization and processes. Numerous entrepreneurs complained that the Party functionaries do not protect their interests, but rather the opposite i.e. they damage them. Beyond this, the private sector, they thought, is promoted due to practical considerations, on the other hand the entrepreneurs as a social stratum are still not accepted on ideological grounds. On this point, many of the respondents referred to the resolution by the Party leadership, which exists as it did in the past, that entrepreneurs are not allowed to enter the Party. The entrepreneurs are often referred to in the media controlled by the Party as "exploiters", too.

Table 113: How do you assess the work of the Party? (China)

	Satisfied		Only partially satisfied		Not satisfied		No answer	
	Number	%	Number	%	Number	%	Number	%
Total	46	26.0	94	53.1	32	18.1	5	2.8
Zhejiang	11	15.9	42	60.9	12	17.4	4	5.8
Henan	22	36.7	26	43.3	12	20.0	0	0.0
Gansu	13	27.1	26	54.2	8	16.7	1	2.1
Urban areas	31	28.7	59	54.6	17	15.7	1	0.9
Rural areas	15	21.7	35	50.7	15	21.7	4	5.8
Large entrepreneurs	8	14.8	30	55.6	12	22.2	4	7.4
Small entrepreneurs	38	30.9	64	52.0	20	16.3	1	0.8

Source: Own research.

The dissatisfaction was strongest in Zhejiang with the most highly developed market economic relations. One can ascertain as a tendency: the more developed the market economic structures in a region were and the larger the entrepreneurs, so the clearer would be the criticism that the entrepreneurs made of the work of the Party, because here the contradiction was particularly striking between on the one hand the development of market-economic and entrepreneurial differentiation, and political monopolization on the other hand. In He-

---

[222] Unofficially numerous respondents admitted this.

nan and Gansu, the inter-connections between Party and entrepreneurs were moreover **politically** denser than in Zhejiang, because there the hegemony of the Party i.e. the element which locally controls everything, was still much more powerful than in Zhejiang. In rural regions, above all in less developed areas, the interfering by the bureaucracy in entrepreneurial matters is considerable, an important reason why the entrepreneurs in rural areas are even more dissatisfied with the work of the Party than are those in the urban areas.

Almost three-quarters of the respondents were not satisfied with the Party's work or only partially satisfied, or refused (in five cases) to answer. All in all, this creates a picture of relatively widespread criticism of the work of the CP. The government came off much better from the same question, above all in Henan and Zhejiang (dissatisfied in total: 14.0%; partially satisfied: 43.3%) than did the Party. Interestingly, our survey of cadres at the Central Party School found that there 97.0% were not satisfied with the Party (39.8%) or only partially satisfied (57.2%). The assessment of the work of the administrational government was definitely similar (35.8% not, 61.7% partially satisfied). This appears to indicate that the dissatisfaction amongst Party functionaries is much higher than amongst entrepreneurs. This dissatisfaction was intensified still more through their own material life situation. Merely 2.5% of the cadres declared themselves to be satisfied with the distribution of income in the country as a whole, and less than a third (32.3%) with their housing situation. Only 1.5% expressed satisfaction with public security and safety, and 19.9% with medical provision. In contrast, of the entrepreneurs whom we surveyed, 62.4% had nothing against their housing situation, 44.4% nothing against the medical provision, 33.7% the distribution of income, and 29.8% the state of public order.

As mentioned, in Vietnam political questions could only be put in a limited way. The following questions had to be deleted from our questionnaire there: that concerning the exemplary role of the Party, the work of the Party as well as the general situation in Vietnam. Nevertheless, from those questions that remained one can draw conclusions about the political attitudes of the entrepreneurs. Tables 114 and 115 describe the attitudes of the Vietnamese entrepreneurs towards the state and its duties. In Vietnam, the percentage of the entrepreneurs surveyed who wanted to see the function of the state strengthened was lower than in China, although here too over 62% desired stronger state control over the market economy and only a low percentage (3.6%) spoke against that. Significantly higher than in China, however, was that proportion that wanted to have stronger **political** leadership. This proportion in Vietnam exceeded in turn the percentage of those who spoke for an expansion of state functions.

Table 114: Under market economic relations, the function of the state has to be strengthened (Vietnam)

	Completely true	Partially true	Untrue
Hanoi	28	23	5
Tien Son	21	10	
Danang	12	7	1
Duy Xuyen	10		
Ho Chi Minh City	27	22	1
Thu Duc	25	5	
Total	**123 (62.4)**	**67 (34.0)**	**7 (3.6)**
Urban areas	67 (53.2)	52 (41.3)	7 (5.5)
Rural areas	56 (78.9)	15 (21.1)	
North Vietnam	49 (56.3)	33 (37.9)	5 (5.8)
Central Vietnam	22 (73.3)	7 (23.3)	1 (3.3)
South Vietnam	52 (65.0)	27 (33.8)	1 (1.2)

Source: Own research.

Table 115: A stronger political leadership is required in order to overcome the current social problems and difficulties caused by economic development (Vietnam)

	Completely true	Partially true	Untrue
Hanoi	11	33	8
Tien Son	12	17	
Danang	8	10	3
Duy Xuyen	6	3	1
Ho Chi Minh City	17	29	3
Thu Duc	20	7	3
Total	**74 (38.7)**	**99 (51.8)**	**18 (9.4)**
Urban areas	36 (29.5)	72 (59.0)	14 (11.5)
Rural areas	38 (55.1)	27 (39.1)	4 (5.8)
North Vietnam	23 (28.4)	50 (61.7)	8 (9.9)
Central Vietnam	14 (45.2)	13 (41.9)	4 (12.9)
South Vietnam	37 (46.8)	36 (45.6)	6 (7.6)

Source: Own research.

In principle, what one can read into that, is the attitude that the state should be "strong" in its direction of economic matters, but reduce its political powers. As a result, control likewise strength apparently does not signify direct governmental control over the private entrepreneurs, which would undoubtedly inevitably lead to an even stronger restriction of entrepreneurial freedom to decide. Al-

most 78% agreed in turn with the statement that the government should not
intervene in internal company processes (cf. Table 116).

**Table 116: The state should only be responsible for macro-economic direc-
tion; company processes should be a matter for the entrepreneurs (Vietnam)**

	Completely true	Partially true	Untrue
Hanoi	47	6	3
Tien Son	25	6	
Danang	18	3	1
Duy Xuyen	7	2	1
Ho Chi Minh City	36	12	1
Thu Duc	21	8	1
Total	**154 (77.8)**	**37 (18.7)**	**7 (3.5)**
Urban areas	101 (79.6)	21 (16.5)	5 (3.9)
Rural areas	53 (74.7)	16 (22.5)	2 (2.8)
North Vietnam	72 (82.8)	12 (13.8)	3 (3.4)
Central Vietnam	25 (78.1)	5 (15.6)	2 (6.3)
South Vietnam	57 (72.2)	20 (25.3)	2 (2.5)

Source: Own research.

What is meant by control, primarily – so the interviews revealed – is a legal
framework that one can rely on during commercial transactions. The task of the
government would be then to introduce a certain degree of stability into the
framework conditions of the private sector by strengthening the rule of law in
that sphere.

Moreover it should be noted that the private entrepreneurs correspondingly
displayed great interest in information about the legal system in the mass media:
70% of the respondents in Vietnam spoke of their above-average interest and a
further 26% an average degree of interest (cf. on that theme Table 120 and the
corresponding interpretation).

Characteristic for the Vietnamese (as with the Chinese) Communism is the
stress on the exemplary function of the cadres, who are supposed to set an example for the society to emulate through behavior that is beyond moral re-
proach. At any rate, four out of five of the respondents thought that the functionaries had to play an exemplary role under the conditions of a market economy, too.

Table 117: Assess the statement: "Under the conditions of a market economy the functionaries should exercise a role model function" (Vietnam)[223]

	Completely true	*Partially true*	*Untrue*
Hanoi	38	16	2
Tien Son	19	11	1
Danang	20		
Duy Xuyen	9	1	
Ho Chi Minh City	45	5	
Thu Duc	28	2	
Total	**159 (80.7)**	**35 (17.8)**	**3 (1.5)**
Urban areas	103 (81.7)	21 (16.7)	2 (1.6)
Rural areas	56 (78.9)	14 (19.7)	1 (1.4)
North Vietnam	57 (65.5)	27 (31.0)	3 (3.5)
Central Vietnam	29 (96.7)	1 (3.3)	
South Vietnam	73 (91.3)	7 (8.7)	

Source: Own research.

Whereas there were no major divergences between the response behavior in urban and rural areas, in Vietnam considerable regional differences existed. In North Vietnam only around two-thirds agreed with this statement, but almost everybody in South Vietnam and Central Vietnam. The higher the percentage, so one may assume, the higher the degree of dissatisfaction and the desire associated with it that the Party officials should behave in a "role model" manner.

One can ascertain from this that entrepreneurs are certainly interested in politics, political participation, and playing a role in the political organization of society. But it is true to say that their political interest is first of all based on their entrepreneurial occupation i.e. is about the sphere of economic policies. Tables 118 and 119 make this clear too according to both of which 80% of the respondents in both countries possessed a great deal of interest in information about economic policies. Moreover, the entrepreneurs surveyed took great heed of reform policies and their continuation (about 80% in both countries). The entrepreneurial activity depends on those policies and every change in politics takes its effect on the private sector.

In general there were significant agreements in both countries on the question about interest in media information. Only the interest in Vietnam in social questions was lower, indeed because the Vietnamese press reports on social questions in a more limited way than does the Chinese press. The interest in political information was not particularly marked. As our probes showed, most of the respondents associated with such information abstract political or theoretical texts as well as information about politicians in their country.

---

[223] Since unlike in China no questions about the party were permitted, the questions for Vietnam were reformulated.

As far as the interest in reform policies goes, the regional differences and those between urban and rural areas in China were rather low. It was different in Vietnam: there politics had lead to greater progress in the development of the private sector in the urban areas than in rural areas. This is expressed among other things in the larger number of firms in the private sector and was reflected too in the varying response behavior: whereas the interest in urban areas in information about reform policies of the government at 75.6% was already very high, in the rural areas at 84.5% was even exceeded by 9%. The regional differences between the answers supports this interpretation: in North Vietnam the interest at 82% was the strongest, whereas 74.7% in South Vietnam expressed corresponding interest.

This higher percentage in total made it clear that they considered the reform was in no sense completed, but rather still very much in process. In the South, the interest was slightly less; this could be seen in conjunction with the entrepreneurs there being very much more autonomous, operating more in a network-oriented way, and therefore somewhat less dependent on the political climate than those in the North. In North Vietnam, the hope for changes were more focused on governmental policies.

Table 118: In which information in the media do you have an interest? (China in %)

	Great interest	*Average interest*	*No/ low interest*
1. Social problems	53.7	41.2	5.1
2. Economic policies	79.7	17.5	2.8
3. Reform policies	81.4	16.9	1.7
4. Political information	45.2	39.0	15.8
5. Market information	78.5	18.6	2.8
6. Culture, Sport	28.8	54.2	16.9
7. Everyday life	10.7	48.0	41.2

Source: Own research.

The reform policies characterize the general, political climate in the country, and the element of legal security is a decisive factor for commercial activity based on the rule of law. As a result, this element represents a central theme for entrepreneurs not only in the relations with the administration, but also in the economic interaction with other business units. 70% of the respondents accordingly expressed information about the legal system in the mass media. In that the wish too may also be contained for a greater degree of legal transparency, and for the publication of regulations that are often internal and remain unpublished.

Table 119: In which information in the media do you have an interest? (Vietnam, in %)

	Great interest	Average interest	No/ low interest
1. Social problems	27.5	63.3	9.2
2. Economic policies	82.9	14.6	2.5
3. Reform policies	78.8	19.7	1.5
4. Political information	42.1	52.8	10.1
5. Market information	79.0	18.5	2.5
6. Culture, Sport	21.2	64.7	14.1
7. Everyday life	19.1	55.3	15.6
8. Law	70.0	26.0	4.0

Source: Own research.

The regional differences in the response behavior indicate a greater need for information concerning the legal system, in North Vietnam and – even more so – in Central Vietnam. In both regions, a legal tradition with a codified, civil law system is lacking to a greater extent than in South Vietnam. Central Vietnam is considered to be a hotbed of (Confucian) tradition; legal decisions were traditionally pronounced through the mandarin. The law was insofar of a personal nature and only to a very limited degree offered legal protection to individuals. North Vietnam is furthermore stamped by a socialist tradition, in which legal safeguards for individuals in the Western spirit are likewise foreign. The southern part of the country is in this respect different: the basis for a legal system and a Western tradition of thought were already laid down during the French colonial era, and further developed during the epoch of the Republic of South Vietnam under American influence. The Western tradition of thought is here certainly much more widespread and more strongly integrated into practice. Consequently, the need for information about the legal system in the South was apparently less than in other regions. On top of that comes the fact that the majority of foreign investments take place in Ho Chi Minh City, as a result of which an additional pressure exists in the direction of increasing the scope of the legal system.

The interest in legal questions was in rural areas even more striking than in urban areas. This may be related to the lack of possibilities to inform oneself in rural areas compared to urban areas, so that a greater need for information predominates. The arbitrariness of local authorities, above all in rural areas, has in recent years intensified the demand for legal safeguards amongst the rural population.

Table 120: In which information in the media do you have an interest? (Vietnam)

	Legal system		
	Great interest	*Average interest*	*No/ low interest*
Hanoi	44	11	2
Tien Son	21	9	1
Danang	16	6	
Duy Xuyen	9	1	
Ho Chi Minh City	28	19	3
Thu Duc	22	6	2
Total	**140 (70.0)**	**52 (26.0)**	**8 (4.0)**
Urban areas	88 (68.2)	36 (27.9)	5 (3.9)
Rural areas	52 (73.2)	16 (22.6)	3 (4.2)
North Vietnam	65 (73.9)	20 (22.7)	3 (3.4)
Central Vietnam	25 (78.1)	7 (21.9)	
South Vietnam	50 (62.5)	25 (31.3)	5 (6.2)

Source: Own research.

After the unrest in Thai Binh mentioned above, the calls for a strengthening of rights in public life has become louder. This is a call for a law which restricts the power of local authorities, and that would enable their behavior to be controlled. The dissatisfaction is directed above all against embezzlement in the financial sphere, the arbitrary demands for taxes and payments, or the confiscation of real estate and agricultural land suitable for growing.

PART THREE: THEORETICAL IMPLICATIONS AND CONCLUSIONS

1. *Summary of the most important conclusions:*
Group profile of the entrepreneurs

In general, it has been ascertained that the private sector and entrepreneurship have developed further in China than in Vietnam. This has to do primarily with political constellations and symbols and less with economic or cultural factors. There were differences not only in respect of the acceptance, the political ideological assessment and support, but rather too in respect of the distribution of lines of business, the size of firms, their equipping with capital and the educational level of the entrepreneurs.

Our interviews suggest that private entrepreneurs in China despite all their problems were more satisfied with the economic and political situation than in Vietnam. In China 26.4% declared themselves to be satisfied, and 64.6% more or less satisfied with the latter; in Vietnam contrastingly, 28.8% showed themselves to be unsatisfied or somewhat unsatisfied, 54.5% more or less satisfied and only 17.0% satisfied. When we condense the most important results of our surveys and interviews, we can note first of all significant similarities but also considerable differences between the two countries, which deconstruct the idea of a unified development. When assessing the result, however, it must be taken into account that significant differences existed between the regions as well as between urban and rural areas. And in Vietnam major variations were to be seen in the response behavior between North and South Vietnam, in which the different socialization processes were expressed, whereas the answers in China in comparison may be characterized as partially more homogenous.

The following points represent the core outcomes of our research work:

1) *Privatization: a spontaneous non-strategic process that originated in rural areas.*

In both countries the privatization set in as a spontaneous process, whose starting points were rural areas and the peasants. Along with the economic crises in both countries and the widespread rural poverty before the start of the reform process still other factors played a role: the strong desire of the peasants for private property and familial management; a certain degree of autonomy of the peasantry in respect of the state; the lack of integration of the rural population in the state's social welfare network; and (on the part of the political elite) the toleration and ideological acceptance of private employment, so far as they ruled out at least at the beginning the employment of employees dependent on pay (and with that exploitation). But, the authorizing of private sector occupations turned out to be a veritable Pandora's box, because these in effect inevitably brought with them employees dependent on pay.

The political elite could more easily tolerate private sector activities on the part of peasants at first, because the peasantry was not understood to be principal actors in socialist re-organization (in contrast to the industrial proletariat). The primary goal in both countries was industrialization and nationalization in urban areas, whereas the agricultural sphere – at least so the predominant views ran – in the course of the industrialization would indeed inevitably more and more decrease in significance. The urban areas and the urban economy, above all the large industrial firms, were considered in all socialist countries to be the decisive sector for the dominance of the socialist economy. The leaderships of both countries could therefore tolerate processes of liberalization and privatization that emanated from the rural areas, because they appeared not to limit the real power basis of the CP (industry and the urban areas).[1] Milanovic draws our attention to – ideologically perceived – declining classes like the peasantry with their tendency to private small-scale ownership, that were simply not viewed as a threat to power.[2]

2) The heterogeneity of the entrepreneurial stratum

The Chinese or Vietnamese entrepreneurs do not exist as such. Sweeping generalizations like "Confucian entrepreneur" and others, characterized by Thomas Menkhoff as "the orientalization of the Chinese entrepreneur",[3] are out of place.

The entrepreneurs do not form a unified homogenous group. There are very different categories such as large middle and small-sized entrepreneurs, successful and unsuccessful, or – as our research showed – entrepreneurs who moved on a scale between the poles active-optimistic and passive-pessimistic.[4] There are entrepreneurs who came out of the local Party or government bureaucracy (origin: "cadre") and who possessed a high level of relationships, and those without such relationships. It was exactly the interweaving of the strata of functionaries and entrepreneurs that contributed to the process of economization of politics and with that to the development of the private sector.

Werner Sombart divided entrepreneurs into the "powerful" and the "smart": the first originated from the stratum of civil servants and could base themselves on that potential power which was at their disposal due to their earlier positions (cultural capital, relationships and networks); the latter appear as "conquerors" and base themselves for the most part on trader-entrepreneurial potential.[5] There are as mentioned in part II, *push* entrepreneurs who have made them-

---

[1] See too Milanovic 1989: 66f.

[2] Ibid.: 67.

[3] Menkhoff 1999.

[4] On the different types of entrepreneurs Cf. too Fröhlich and Pichler 1988.

[5] Cf. Sombart 1909: 730ff. and 1987, 1. Volume, 2. Half volume: 839. But here there are diverse in-between and mixed forms.

selves self-employed because they were dissatisfied with the working conditions in their earlier company, and *pull* entrepreneurs who are attracted by the
entrepreneurial effect and its social and financial possibilities, and who consequently gave up their jobs.[6]

We can subdivide too according to the reason for commencing self-
employed occupations as follows: (a) *the use of market chances and market
incentives* (above all in urban areas and in more developed regions); (b) *due to
blocked chances of ascent* (self-employment as an alternative path for upward
mobility); (c) *advantages in opportunity* (privileges and social relationships) by
members of the political elite and sub-elite (above all at the local level); or (d)
survival strategies (unemployed, pensioners).[7] Li Fang in turn differentiates
between three types of entrepreneurs: people competent in rural areas (*neng-
ren*), speculators in urban areas (*daoye*), and persons from the government
administration who "dived into the sea" (*xia hai*) i.e. have made themselves
self-employed.[8] Such a classification appears to be strongly molded by negative
stereotypes, however, because their effect is to lump different things together
and equate entrepreneurs in urban areas to some extent with speculators. And
finally, the social stratification too within the entrepreneurial strata should not
be overlooked.

A categorization could also take place according to sectors or origins: stemming from familial-entrepreneurial origins; from political-administrative relationships; or from the economic environment (private companies or commercial
administration). Those who privately leased or bought a state or collective
company had as a rule a different relationship to his or her property than the
founder of a new company. They would in the former case endeavor to squeeze
out of the leased company the largest profit possible and to obtain further subsidies from the state, whereas in the latter case the entrepreneur themselves
have created their possession i.e. the firm. Each of the named groups has their
own status which as amongst owners is influenced by success in business, level
of education, social relationships, and (above all in rural areas) achievements
for the community (job creation, financing of public projects, raising the local
living standards). Moreover, there are cultural, regional and ethnic specific
factors that make a typification according to nation difficult.

3) *Heterogeneous social background*

Heterogeneity also shows itself in differing origins. Unlike in the private individual sector, or in trade, new entrepreneurial personalities in the industrial
sphere in China and Vietnam do not hail from the lower class, but rather for the
most part from local sub-elites (former managers in state or collective compa-

---

[6] On this differentiation: Amit and Muller 1996.
[7] Similarly: Li Fang 1998: 87, 88.
[8] Ibid.: 58.

nies, Party functionaries in rural areas), the sphere of the local elite (relatives of cadres), the lower middle-class (skilled workers, purchasers or sellers in state or collective companies, successful individual entrepreneurs), and partially too from politically "marginal groups" who are excluded from social ascent (former "class enemies" and their family members).

This contradicts the view expressed by Western social scientists that robbers and pirates represent the "original" model of entrepreneur.[9] It is only a partially accurate perception that in the post-socialist societies, talented individuals from the lower classes often became rich in the transition from a planned economy to a market-oriented one, and that acquisition certainly not only in a legal way, whereby the formation of assets often took place through the private acquisition of state-owned assets.[10] Such persons are often to be found in trade, in the individual economy or the shadow business sector. But the smallest sized areas of the economy, that of individual trading and the shadow sector have both to be understood as a training ground for the training of larger private entrepreneurs.

Making comparisons within one nation shows that in situations of an economic, social and value transformation, members of the upper class (also the local one) work as entrepreneurs. This is because firstly they are able to grasp the nature of the transformation due to their knowledge of society, secondly they want to maintain their traditional roles in spite of the transformation, and thirdly due to their thoroughly market-oriented, economic activity.[11] In China and Vietnam these are the functionaries and their families, who contribute in this way to social change and the process of economization within politics. In a very pragmatic way Janos Kornai described the cadre privatization with the benefits of hindsight.

> How will a historian of economics ... view the privatization in 2100? It will appear fully irrelevant to him who stole how much money during the privatization... They will much rather ascertain that within a very short period of time a socialist society based on collective property was transformed into a society based on private property.[12]

Basically, the new entrepreneurs are a combination of people with professional as well as social capital. The majority belonged earlier to upper or middle social strata. The origins of the entrepreneur in China and Vietnam resemble those of the new business class in the former Soviet Union and Eastern Europe. In the latter they stem mostly from the informal sector (*self-employment* and/or shadow economy), the younger and more able sections of the nomenklatura, previous directors of state companies or the economic technical intelligentsia.[13] Concerning the genesis of an entrepreneurial stratum, there are it seems paral-

---

[9] Along these lines e.g. Sombart 1987: 2. Volume, 1. Half volume: 25–26.
[10] Cf. e.g. Sievert 1993: 237.
[11] Hoselitz 1963.
[12] Kornai 1998: 36.
[13] Silverman and Yanowitch 1997: 114, 115; Roth 1997: 195,196.

lels between the social changes in China and Vietnam with the processes of transformation in the former Soviet Union. The parallels exist insofar as, for example, the nomenklatura/cadres did not possess financial capital but instead social capital that resulted from their earlier positions and relationships, and could use these for their new functions as entrepreneurs. In this way they try to compensate for their loss of political power; and such a loss took place more markedly in Eastern Europe and the former Soviet Union than in China and Vietnam as yet. Ivan Szelenyi's survey of 3,000 entrepreneurs in five East European countries showed that 90% of the self-employed entrepreneurs stemmed from the ranks of directors of state companies.[14] It is politically important that the switch by functionaries into the ranks of the entrepreneurs fundamentally changed their value and goal orientation. They are seldom still oriented to ideology and collectivism, but rather now as entrepreneurs, in the final analysis that is market-economy oriented. Otherwise they would fundamentally have to negate themselves and their entreprencurial impact.

4) *Strong ties and weak ties*

The often idealized "networks" or the "family orientation" do not form a homogenous characteristic of Chinese or Vietnamese entrepreneurs, because these base themselves during their operations according to the matter at hand on either in tendency strong and/or in tendency weak relationships. While *strong ties* such as kinship relationships indeed play a very important role in the life of most entrepreneurs, at the same time we have ascertained in both countries three differing attitudes amongst entrepreneurs: (a) kinship or clan-oriented, (b) partnership-oriented (outside of kinship categories) and (c) individually-oriented entrepreneurs.

Here too there are differences between urban and rural areas. In urban areas kinship plays less of a role in business life than in rural areas. The same applies to networks: a section of the entrepreneurs base themselves on networks and have to for reasons of access to markets, information and raw materials; a second set do this sometimes; a third seldom according to the specific business and market conditions. The myth of the "Chinese" or "Vietnamese" entrepreneur is correspondingly weakened.

5) *Motivation*

A central factor in the decision to choose to be an entrepreneur was the desire for greater independence and personal responsibility, through which finally the desire finds expression for greater individual freedom but also for social free space. But this percentage was higher in more developed regions in which the wish for a higher income and an improvement of living conditions was clearly

---

[14] Cf. Roth 1997: 196 and 197; Szelenyi 1995.

reflected. In people's reflections on their decision to choose occupational independence, other factors were also involved such as access to capital, the availability of useful relationships (for instance to functionaries) and market opportunities. Self-fulfillment was considered one of the most important goals in life (in each case over 70%).

6) *Guanxi relationships and access to cadre networks as important starting and strategic capital.*

Guanxi, social relationships, remain important and indispensable above all due to the legal insecurity and the socio-political monopoly position of the Party and with that of the functionaries. Relationships to cadres represent social capital that makes it considerably easier for the entrepreneurs to carry out their occupations. As a result it is not surprising that most of the entrepreneurs in Chinese urban areas stem from the ranks of functionaries (administration and company management). Even in the rural areas, this set was the second most common group (concerning origins) with in first place people of peasant descent. And about 40% of fathers of the entrepreneurs surveyed were likewise cadres.

In Vietnam this percentage was much lower, however, due to stronger restrictions. For groups handicapped by a negative social evaluation, entrepreneurship still appeared there to represent an important path to upward social mobility, at the same time entrepreneurial family experience representing important socio-economic capital. An example is that the parents of 25% of all respondents had earlier possessed their own company. Above all in South and Central Vietnam the percentage was particularly high from families of former "class enemies" (members of the old regime, and "capitalists") as well as ethnic Chinese. This demonstrates too that entrepreneurship is the most effective way to integrate people who exist outside of the economy, or are the victims of obstructed opportunities for upward social mobility.

7) *Conceptions of companies*

Conceptions of companies are influenced by traditional-paternalistic ideas. Over 80% wanted their firm to be run like a "large family" in which the "father" (entrepreneur) takes care of his employees, and the personnel work with selfless dedication for the company. In Vietnamese society stamped as it is by military thinking, almost half of the respondents described the relations between entrepreneurs and employees with a military metaphor ("the entrepreneur manages the company like a general").

8) *Entrepreneurs as protagonists of market economy relations*

The great majority advocates the assertion of market economic structures and the freedom for economic development as the precondition for modernization. They thought that entrepreneurs were social role models and pioneers. At the same time social obligations are recognized for the most part in relation to communities to which a player belongs or to which they feel an obligation. This supports the hypothesis that entrepreneurship represents not only an economic role but also rather a social one. The role of the family remains dominant vis-à-vis the society, however.

9) *Entrepreneurs and the political system*

First of all one should take into account that entrepreneurs become ever more indispensable for the system. They have been developing increasingly to being the most important employers and tax payers, create a growing number of jobs, possess the greatest power of innovation, and stamp the new economic and entrepreneurial culture in a sustained way. Moreover, close inter-relationships exist with the local authorities that cause high costs however (i.e. due to corruption, the payment of "donations"). Without good relationships most entrepreneurs hold that their work would be very difficult.

A high percentage expressed themselves critically about the way of working of the Party and the local governments. In both countries only a quarter of the respondents declared themselves to be satisfied with the work of the Party. This was said to be bureaucratic, inefficient and hindered the company's work. The criticism of the political system and of too little freedom to make economic decisions was expressed more strongly in Vietnam than in China. Significantly more entrepreneurs perceived there the present conditions as a transition to a post-socialist society, also to some extent to a more democratic system. The dissatisfaction with the current political fluctuations in the Party leadership may favor this tendency. Chinese entrepreneurs spoke more clearly than those in Vietnam for a strong political leadership (93%), but wanted from the latter the installation of greater legal security, more liberties and rights.

10) *Interests in participation and shaping politics*

All in all our surveys showed that the new entrepreneurs are not only interested in processes of social and political transformation, but actively attempt rather to affect them. Entrepreneurs certainly do not understand themselves to be only economic players but rather at the same time political ones; this was documented not only by the high degree of interest in politics but also through the desire for political participation. But politics was understood less in the sense of the creation of alternative or parallel structures than as the possibility of shaping public policy in the framework of the existing relations. Above all larger entrepreneurs with a higher level of education intended as well to bring about long-term alterations of business conditions. In each case over 70% regarded the establishing of legal security and participation as a necessity.

But in China a considerably higher percentage were of the opinion that entrepreneurs had to be politically active. This referred less to individual involvement than to the formation of entrepreneurial networks and interest communities. An absolute majority in both countries favored the formation of non-statutory associations representing entrepreneurs even if these were obligated primarily to co-operate with Party and state. At any rate more than a third were of the opinion in both countries that such associations should have the role of being lobby and interest organizations vis-à-vis the state. All in all one can ascertain that private entrepreneurs are politically interested if too their greatest concern is the relationship between policies affecting the private sector. Entrepreneurs appear through their organizations to be increasingly an interest group going beyond individual interests and actions, whereby the functions of those groups are no longer restricted to measures for self-protection but rather ever more they advocate group interests and negotiate politically. Our surveys confirm Chinese studies suggesting that it is firstly the more highly educated and politically experienced who make political demands, and urge a stable political status quo as well as locally the implementation of the policies decided on by the central or regional elites.

11) *Transformation of power structures*

Under the influence of the market economy and the process of privatization, one may note that in both countries a transformation of power structures at the local level has already taken place affecting the Party and government institutions equally. This is due to the economic success of the entrepreneurs eroding the power of the Party and the government that are no longer ideologically anchored. Entrepreneurs need help and political protection in a complex political environment in which an uncompromising support of the private sector is lacking. Amongst the different ways of inducing such protection may be counted:

-   Membership of the CP. Whether forbidden or not private entrepreneurs manage to gain entry into the Party at the local level. While one cannot specify precise numbers,[15] observations in the course of our fieldwork indicate that joining the Party is relatively widespread at the local level. These memberships may occur on the basis of personal relationships but are also quite simply purchased.

---

[15] Indeed 19 of the 100 small entrepreneurs interviewed by Kurths in Vietnam were party members, but this figure cannot be classified according to company form. In Kurths' sample there were seven private firms and three Ltd.s, whereas the rest were mostly individual or family companies. Cf. Kurths' 1997: 170.

-   Networks in the sense of friendship or kinship relationships to cadres in the Party or administrations are organized on a reciprocal basis. The private entrepreneurs are aware of the significance of close personal relationships in the incomplete, market economic system with its partial political control of key resources. Accordingly, the overwhelming majority of the entrepreneurs we surveyed regarded networks of relationships as important for their business activities.
-   Bribery of cadres in the Party and administrations. Successful private sector activity enables the allocation of a new key resource, namely money, despite the incomplete realization of a market economic system. With its help entrepreneurs have no difficulty in obtaining access to cadres in Party and administration important for their business activity.

Corruption inside the Party and administration has meanwhile reached endemic proportions and withstands all campaigns against it. Even radical measures right up to the death penalty have not been able to change anything as yet.[16]

With the means named above private entrepreneurs exercise de facto political power and influence economic and political decisions at the local level.

12) Entrepreneurs as "agents of change"

Carroll stated that by setting up a company an entrepreneur already became an *agent of social changes*,[17] whereby he meant that the emergence of entrepreneurs fundamentally changed societies. In principle our work has confirmed that. According to our results, the following trend is clearly to be seen: the expansion of the private sector has led in both countries to extensive changes stamped by regionally specific factors. Those changes started a process which originating in an economic sub-system has affected other sub-systems such as society and politics in an unenvisaged way. This unplanned and extensive proc-

---

[16] On this e.g. Weggel 1997a: 126f.; Weggel 1997b: 218. The continual warnings of the Party appear meanwhile to have degenerated into a ritual in view of the failure of the measures taken; the population appear to grant scant credence to those warnings. From the viewpoint of the party, corruption represents not only an ideological and political danger based on the fact that the politically marginalized population group of the private entrepreneurs is now in a position to exercise a limited degree of influence. Rather they have a directly, destabilizing effect if the disadvantaged population groups actively defend themselve The unrest e.g. in the Vietnamese area Thai Binh 1997 is a drastic example since this region is said to have a particularly revolutionary tradition. Insofar as the CPV's legitimation to rule is still partially derived from its revolutionary victory, the Party of course observe the development in the "Nurseries of revolution" with particular attention. Often these regions cannot be counted amongst those which have profited from the market economic reforms: "The conditions of life of part of the population, especially in a number of former revolutionary and resistance bases ... , remain very hard;" so runs the report of the Central Committee to the 8th National Congress, Cf. the Communist Party of Vietnam 1996: 20. On the events in Thai Binh, see too the semi-official inquiry report by Nguyen Anh and Vu 1997 as well as reports of the news agencies Reuter, AFP and dpa.

[17] Carroll 1965: 3.

ess i.e. the economization of society and politics is increasingly gaining in dynamism. On of the driving forces of this transformation are – whether desired or not – strata of private entrepreneurs. Their occupation molds their lives, and their altered behavior coupled with the transformation of their attitudes takes its effect on the social environment and bring about changes in it. This process multiplies itself at the micro-level since in many places it takes place along parallel lines – even if to a different degree. Here one needs to take into account that the processes of pluralization and autonomization are proceeding more rapidly in regions with stronger market economic orientation (Hangzhou, Ho Chi Minh City) than in less developed or more strongly egalitarian regions (Luohe, Hanoi).

The Party as well is subject to pressures to change itself caused by economic development. This is because many Party members work as entrepreneurs and insofar pursue economic interests which are diametrically opposed to the original goals of both the dominant parties. Here economic and political interests merge bringing about an intensifying erosion of the predominant ideology and a greater degree of political pragmatism. Amongst the political elites of both countries, apparently widespread recognition accorded to market economic principles contributes to these processes.

13) *Entrepreneurs as a social group*

Insofar as entrepreneurs differ from other groups through lifestyle, behavior, consciousness, other groups' (e.g. cadres) appraisal of them etc., one can speak of the formation of a new social stratum. The successful and larger private entrepreneurs possess a striking group consciousness that can be clearly differentiated from other social groups, to some extent as well from smaller or less successful private entrepreneurs. The former group is aware of its economic importance and is not shy of articulating its interest in having a say in economic political decisions. Although at least isolated general political interests exist which go beyond that even going as far as the desire to set up a multi-party system and possibilities of direct political activities, the entrepreneurs understandably do not openly formulate such opinions.

Due to their ever-increasing economic significance the private entrepreneurs have developed into an independent social group from which pressure for political change stems. From the viewpoint of some entrepreneurs this development is of an inevitable nature and the necessary consequence of the introduction of market economic structures. Socialist and market economy are more and more regarded as being incompatible.

Direct articulation of their own interests exists for the entrepreneurs first of all in the shape of entrepreneurial associations whose political influence is concentrated at the moment on the formulation of economic-political proposals and bills for legislation. These proposals are taken seriously and are implemented in business policies at the local and central levels. The possibilities of political activity in the framework of a mandate as a deputy of People's Congresses or People's Councils are theoretically possible but in practice much restricted. Yet, officially accepted since the 16th Party Congress, private entrepreneurs meanwhile have access to Party membership.

Of course, the social transformation brought about by the dynamism of economic development has not been restricted to private entrepreneurs but has spread as well to other social groups. But the entrepreneurs are situated at the center of this process of transformation and require our special attention.

2. The transformative potential of entrepreneurs as the precondition for strategy formation

The results of our survey demonstrate that privatization and the formation of an entrepreneurial stratum associated with that should not only be understood as a process either primarily economic or one of economic policy. It implies at the same time elements of pluralization and with that democratization because it

- creates and strengthens personal responsibility and societal participation;
- helps to reduce the element of direct governmental intervention in economic processes [18],
- contributes to the privatization of societal life, since more and more societal spheres (education, housing, training, welfare matters, birth control, ideological and political questions) are no longer decided by the state but instead by families and individuals;
- makes the society and the individuals within it more autonomous vis-à-vis the state and in this way furthers pluralization;
- strengthens business elites against political ones;
- spreads the viewpoint that successful privatization increasingly requires the strengthening of the legal system i.e. the safeguarding of rights[19], freedom of occupation, contract and associations.[20] In this way this process furthers the development of a legal system.

Basically, the private sector differs structurally from the state sector:

> The public sector is defined through power and compulsion ..., whereas the private sector is defined by freedom and with that privacy and individuality,

---

[18] The social psychologist Hans-Christian Röglin (1991) explicitly pointed out that the furthering of private property promotes the destruction of bureaucratic systems.

[19] Sombart 1987, 1. Volume, 2. Half volume: 460ff., refers to the development of civil law through European entrepreneurship.

[20] The renowned Chinese economist Dong Fureng argued that the market economy requires regulation through law. Official interventions also had to be put a stop to. The bottom line was that, "Democracy is a necessary requirement for the market economy," in: *Bei Yue Fang*, 9/98: 8.

and that as a consequence the growth of each sector has to take place at the cost of the other.[21]

Through the privatization process the role of the state is not simply weakened but much rather the sphere of state duties is re-situated into other domains (the creation of framework conditions for the existence and development of the private sector as well as a legal frame, questions of labor law among, etc.). Through rights of personal decision-making and in participatory processes of the private sector, new societal forms of participation come into being and with that a new distribution of rights. Vanhanen accordingly established that under such conditions new political and economic structures emerge as an expression of a new distribution of power.[22] Successful privatization and a successful market economy based on it bring about a significant potential pressure in the direction of democratization,[23] even if the current characteristic of the transformative process is not towards democratization but rather in the pluralization of society.[24]

In order to sketch the social field of action: entrepreneurship makes possible a higher degree of autonomy, freedom of decision, independence and personal responsibility, but implies at the same time a leadership function as well. This field of activity takes place nonetheless in a dense social structure of relationships. Entrepreneurs are not bound into the usual *unity (Danwei)* structures, rather they move within the market despite all the bureaucratic restrictions. There they can reach independent decisions i.e. they possess a greater degree of *social space*. This space also creates a specific economic point of view, and makes the entrepreneur per se an actor who more or less consciously attempts to expand his or her space. If the state restricts the freedom of the entrepreneurs, the economic results in the market deteriorate and lead to a weakening of economic growth. Consequently, the body responsible for economic policies, the state, is in principle not interested in all too strong such restrictions.

Furthermore, entrepreneurs and the maintenance of company assets associated with them strengthen the market, market processes, market regulations and competition. They contribute to the breaking up of monopolistic market structures, and assist in the acceptance of market economic "rules of play" amongst the population and bureaucracy, factors which in turn help to expand the entrepreneurial framework conditions.[25] At the same time entrepreneurs operate as

---

[21] Barber 1997: 42.

[22] Vanhanen 1990: 3. Cf. also Dorraj 1994: 179ff.; Cowling 1995: 170ff.; Bahgat 1993. Dahl argued explicitly that modern democracy was the precondition for a market economy, Cf. Dahl 1992: 82/83.

[23] See on that: Berger 1993.

[24] The market economy is in principle the precondition for a civil society because this requires autonomous citizens, who are not dependent alone on governmental money. But the market economy does not mean in itself either democracy or democratization, because the latter pre-supposes a functioning *civil society*.

[25] Cf.. Lageman, Friedrich and Döhrn 1994: 27, 28.

interest groups who organize themselves in associations to further their interests (such as entrepreneurial associations), and form networks in order to assert common interests vis-à-vis the bureaucracy and in politics. Insofar the collective activities of entrepreneurship are to be found in these organizations.

The transformative potential consists for the most part in the following factors:

- Entrepreneurs set in motion first of all a dynamic economic *process*. Through economic novelties they bring into being processes of social change. Specifically in relation to China this entails elements such as behavior appropriate for the market that differs fundamentally from the economic and management behavior of state sector companies, willingness to take risks and outperform, as well as diverging behavior for the assertion of their own economic and social interests.

- They contribute to the building up of a market system and to the assertion of market oriented thinking.

- The impact of their activity leads to a clearer division between state and economy.

- Without a doubt, entrepreneurs are not and cannot be merely profit-oriented. Non-monetary incentives (psychic profits) also play a role (e.g. recognition in society). Above all the realization of economic duties requires at the same time social and political involvement, and with that the influencing of political input and output.

- Safeguards and minimization of risks make the creation of social relationships and networks necessary. In the last analysis they require a legal framework, the manufacturing of social and political contacts as well as organization in associations representing their interests in order to have a stronger basis for negotiation vis-à-vis the state, and to be able to assert and bring about framework conditions favorable for themselves. In this way entrepreneurs can play the role of protagonists of a legal system. Two mechanisms are in this respect thinkable: on the one hand the use of *Guanxi* relationships, networks and patterns of patronage, on the other hand pressure for the development of the legal system. So long as – above all under imperfect market conditions – no functioning legal system has been established and the entrepreneurs possess no confidence in legal institutions, the relationships mechanisms will remain of prime importance. But rational, reliable business activity cannot in the long term be based on relationships alone, because these contain the element of insecurity and arbitrariness. The development of property and entrepreneurship requires in the end legal safeguards, the formalizing and institutionalization of law. The private sector and entrepreneurship require, as I have already outlined above, legal stipulations and control mechanisms and with that juridical safeguarding. They demand new institutions, further the expansion of market-oriented relations, assist the development of a non-state financed sector etc.

• Entrepreneurship makes possible a high degree of freedom, individualism, independence and personal responsibility. Entrepreneurs are active less in structures connected to the state than in the market. As a result they possess greater independence and a larger, societal space. Precisely this stamps their economic thinking too and their urge to expand this space in the economic, social and political spheres, in which entrepreneurs necessarily have to operate. the upshot is that they possess the function of players who first of all expand their own frames of action, and through that the space for maneuver and action of the society in general vis-à-vis the state.

• The impact of the entrepreneurs leads to changes in the social structures.

• Specific consumer behavior also stamps the transformation of values and behavior.

• They break through routine patterns and in this way alter more than just values, but rather institutions too.

At the same time as bearers of functions the entrepreneurs exercise "power". By power we understand not only the potential for implementation of their own will (as Max Weber or Amitai Etzioni argue), rather – in the spirit of Parsons – it is a power of implementation which might not only be based on violence and force but also on persuasion and consensus.[26]

In this sense power must be grasped much more as a process of interaction and not as a mere vertical mechanism of implementation. Accordingly, private entrepreneurs may exercise power on the basis of the following factors: their activities in a social system and their participation in the shaping of social order; their pretial status (assets which can be used for purposes of political influence); their networks of relationships; their cultural (local prestige); or political capital (integration in political institutions e.g. Party, People's Congresses) as well as through the associations representing their interests which do not function as *pressure groups* but rather create political input through social relationships and networks. Through that, private entrepreneurs certainly also have the effect of being *renewers of society* and *change agents*.[27] Due to this function they are considered to be *social deviants* much more in Vietnam than in China, because they contribute to changes of the existing structures, institutions and attitudes, and with that potentially threaten the system.[28] Confucianism had already recognized this and as a result – as shown above – business people and manual workers were classified at the lowest point of the social hierarchy.

---

[26] Cf.. on that Parsons 1967. Kaplan 1964 formulated power correspondingly as "the ability of one person or group of persons to influence the behavior of others, that is, to change the probabilities that others will respond in certain ways to specified stimuli."

[27] Broehl 1978: 1.

[28] Cf.. on that also Hoselitz 1969: 38ff.

On the other hand entrepreneurs also have an effect as indirect agents of change because their impact leads to an alteration of the social structure, to a clearer division between state and the economy, and in the long term to a strengthening of the legal system, given that entrepreneurs endeavor increasingly to achieve upwards social mobility. In place of what were at first simple laws governing business, in recent years more differentiated legal regulations such as laws of trade, contract and company have been passed.[29] The differentiation in the sphere of commercial law increasingly furthers the discussions about safeguarding societal and also political laws and obligations in the society as a whole.

In general one can state the following as the socio-political aims of private entrepreneurs in China and Vietnam:

- the desire for political and economic security as well as legal safeguards;
- the rejection of predominance and preference given to structures of state ownership and allocation;
- the aversion to permanent attempts by the state and the Party to intervene in business processes.

Entrepreneurship also entails and requires as a result the unrestricted self-fulfillment of individuals, power to make decisions and rights of disposal (of personal property) which are likewise unrestricted, and a more open and competition-oriented economy and society. The desire for a free flow of information in the interests of companies (economic and market information) promotes at the same time the wish for information in other spheres too (socio-political).[30]

The lower degree of dependence of the private sector on the state can be made clear by a simple example: a Chinese survey about the thinking of entrepreneurs and managers in companies with different forms of ownership found – certainly not surprisingly – the following percentages in response to the question as to whether they paid much attention to the appraisal of their work by higher organs of administration (affirmative answers per group):

Managers of state companies	*67.3%*
Managers of collective companies	*54.3%*
Managers of companies with foreign capital	*39.7%*
Private entrepreneurs	*0.0%*

As this makes clear, entrepreneurs possess a greater degree of economic and political independence. They elude control by the Party or they impact (as members) in the Party, and contribute to its alteration by bringing in deviant opinions and attitudes as well as through the deployment of their pretial status.

---

[29] See for example *Renmin Ribao*, 15 August 1998.
[30] On that: Sullivan 1994.

Since no alternative political structures exist, in the interests of their personal business activities they seek co-operation with Party institutions (membership, relationships, corruption).

But the desire both for societal stability in the interests of their companies and for individual freedom in order to make decisions in the interests of their "business idea",[31] stands in the long term in contradiction to the monopolistic claims of the CP. This renders entrepreneurs *potentially* hostile. One should not understand this oppositional element as open opposition or confrontation – this would be perilous under the circumstances of an authoritarian state – rather incorporates all factors which help to alter the existing system in its basic structures i.e. to contribute to a further opening and pluralization or to a transformation of values in the direction of opening, pluralization and individualization. Vaclav Havel summarized all of that as, "where the real intentions of life cross those borders which the intentions of the system have forced on them."[32] With that he expanded the term opposition to informal and individual ways of behaving as well.

Róna-Tas differentiated between the *erosion of socialism* that set in with the authorization of small companies run by individuals, and the *transition from socialism* as the result of the formation of modern private enterprises.[33] This differentiation characterizes the variation between the first phase of spontaneous privatization marked as it is by the spontaneous expansion of informal business activity in the spheres of small traders and crafts, and the second phase in which the entrepreneurs emerge who acquire social power through capital and occupational know-how. In this phase the private sector is put on the same level as the state sector. Such a dualism, however, does not explain how this transformation takes place and who its bearers are. As a result it appears to me that a differentiation is meaningful based more strongly on actors and the potential for change of those actors:

---

[31] The term stems from Sombart 1909: 708.
[32] Havel 1990: 44.
[33] Róna-Tas 1994.

Diagram 22: Potential of the private sector

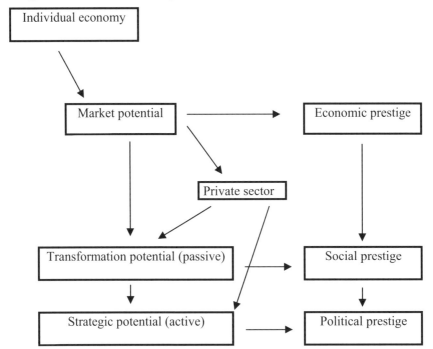

Diagram 22 classifies three dimensions of potential for change. In the first stage the individual sector leads to an expansion of market economic relations, out of which then larger private entrepreneurs emerge too. Successful operations in the market create economic prestige. The impact of the larger entrepreneurs in society alters institutions and values and contributes to an economization of the society, preconditions for the transformation potential that alters the society. This potential ensures for the entrepreneurs social prestige. Their economic and social roles permit the entrepreneurs to make an entry into the political market: interests in common will be pursued and organizationally ensured e.g. legal safeguards, and political equality. Through the formation of community and organizing themselves, strategic potential comes into being which at the same time leads to an increase in the political prestige of the entrepreneurs.

The potential explained in this section as *agents of change,* the responsibility for oneself and self-reliance, the expansion of societal space in which the entrepreneurs operate, the desire for legal safeguards and the growing power potential, in the last analysis the transforming potential, all form the basis for the strategic planning and strategic action of entrepreneurs as a social group.

3. *Entrepreneurs as a social group*

3.1. *The societal volume of capital as strategy capital*

As rigid Marxism would have it, private entrepreneurs count as capitalists and with that as exploiters. Such a classification no longer finds majority support in present-day China because entrepreneurs represent *social necessities*. If the (economic) crisis is to be turned round, the development of such an entrepreneurial stratum is required. The requisites and necessities of development demand as a result a different interpretation of entrepreneurship, a factor that the Chinese leadership has certainly comprehended. The position in Vietnam is somewhat different. There, the private entrepreneurs are still perceived in an ideological sense more as a negative factor in "capitalistic" terms. While the official terminology avoids an unambiguous classification (e.g. as "exploiters" or "capitalists"), because the entrepreneurial stratum is likewise urgently needed, that is likewise represents a social necessity. However, in descriptions of the economic system and development, they are only seldom mentioned. An unmistakable difference between the two countries lies in the ideological acceptance of private entrepreneurship up till now.

Although as I have shown above, in both countries the private entrepreneurial stratum is in no way a homogenous phenomenon, in terms of Bourdieu's analysis one can recognize common positioning. Firstly, there is the commonality of **economic capital** in the form of entrepreneurial ownership, company assets, real estate as well as an above average income resulting from company profits, a factor concerning capital that needs no further elucidation.

The second point is more difficult and concerns the description of **cultural capital** because there is no unified level of education of entrepreneurship. But the level of education of the entrepreneurs in both countries lay above that of the total populations. Education influences values, attitudes and Weltanschauung, promotes at the same time curiosity and innovative behavior and with that the desire for more extensive freedom of thought and action, which in turn furthers strivings for political liberalization.[34]

Part of the cultural capital is at the same time internalized patterns of thought and behavior as well as corresponding states of mind, but also knowledge determined by culture that contributes to the classification of procedures and processes. Since the term culture can only be defined with difficulty, it is helpful too to speak of **cognitive capital**.[35] Cognitive capital in this sense includes among other things knowledge of law or political resolutions.

As far as **social capital** is concerned, there are major differences between the entrepreneurs. An earlier post as functionary or the fact of parents, spouses, siblings, or friends having been functionaries, Party membership, or good rela-

---

[34] Cf. on that Kerr, Dunlop, Harbison and Myers 1994.
[35] Along these lines Zschoch 1998: 202, 203.

tionships to functionaries represent important elements of social capital, and are applicable to a large section of the entrepreneurial strata. A central component of social capital are the *Guanxi* relationships, which can be activated via personal relationships or networks. Something that should not be underestimated for the inception of a social group, is the consciousness created not only by common experiences in the process of becoming a entrepreneur, but also the problems of companies. The biographies of entrepreneurs show that the path to becoming a private entrepreneur for a major part of the persons concerned was a very stony one. In addition the shared experiences of problems in common concerning the development of their companies (shortage of capital, corruption, bureaucracy) contributes to an intensification of the degree of identification.[36]

Furthermore, the shared pattern of life (behavior, tastes) i.e. lifestyle is also of significance and includes what sociology terms *conspicuous consumption* (demonstrative consuming). Such a life-style generates symbolic differences and forms a "proper language".[37] It symbolizes membership of a particular stratum or group, and is a symbol of delimitation vis-à-vis others who do not belong to the group, and the entrepreneurs put it on display as an icon of their entrepreneurial achievements. The possession of one's own house or a condominium as well as certain brands of automobiles e.g. limousines, the consumption of expensive, mostly imported brands of alcohol (French cognac, American whiskey) and cigarettes, the wearing of renowned foreign brands of watches, the installation of expensive consumer goods, to some extent luxuriously fitted homes, the symbolic collecting of prestigious and expensive kinds of alcohol (in glass showcases in their living-rooms visible for all visitors), regular visits to expensive restaurants and karaoke bars, to some extent attractive, young girl-friends are recognized components of such a life-style and identify those concerned as a part of the new entrepreneurial stratum. The visiting of exclusive sports and golf areas, fitness studios or swimming pools can also be counted as part of this phenomenon. According to a survey carried out by the Chinese People's University (1996), half of what the entrepreneurs in Beijing spent, went on amusements in expensive hotels and restaurants, karaoke or other bars.[38]

But such visits do not serve only personal uplift, but rather are to a great extent social investments (e.g. for business friends or functionaries important for business). An entrepreneur whom we asked about his collection of prestigious brands of alcohol declared:

> Actually, I don't like any alcoholic drinks. But I need them for social intercourse... When I stockpile and am in a position to stockpile big name alcoholic drinks, then this is an indication of my social status.[39]

---

[36] Cf. on that Heberer 2001.

[37] Bourdieu 1998: 23, 24.

[38] Li Tongwen 1998: 260.

[39] Conversation on 6 October 1996 in Luohe.

The purchase of foreign luxury cars is a demonstrative way of displaying their wealth. The largest and most expensive car in Luohe was driven not by the city's Party secretary but rather a private entrepreneur. Over and over again, the population marveled at his limousine, which was evaluated as an expression of his success. A private entrepreneur in Ho Chi Minh City had acquired from Germany a Mercedes Benz of the most sophisticated kind, despite the immense import tax. In both countries, however, there were strong regional variations in consumer behavior. In East China and South Vietnam where anyway people achieved the highest incomes and their life-styles appeared more open and elegant, luxury was more clearly put on display than in the other regions. A growing number of Chinese entrepreneurs have in the meantime been sending their children to expensive private schools in their respective countries (so-called "schools for aristocrats", *guizu xuexiao*), and even to an increasing extent to ones in Western countries.

But consumer behavior and life-style are subject to processes of permanent change. In the 1980s, televisions, fridges, washing machines, and video recorders were important status symbols and signs of at least modest prosperity. In the first half of the 1990s, they were replaced by music systems and air-conditioning as well as video cameras; in the second half of the 1990s by mobile phones, computers, automobiles, comfortable condominiums and luxurious fittings for residential spaces.[40]

According to our own survey, 94.4% of the Chinese and 96% of the Vietnamese entrepreneurs possessed at least one house of their own. About a third of the Vietnamese and a significant proportion of the Chinese entrepreneurs listed still further properties as belonging to them. Over half of the respondents in China (58.5%) possessed more than 100 meters square of residential space, 13.5% of them more than 200 and 5.1% more than 300 meters square. A Chinese survey in 1993 found even higher figures. According to that 37% of the families of entrepreneurs in urban areas and 39.1% in rural areas possessed more than 200 meters square of residential space, whereby the average in urban areas was 148.1 and in rural areas 166.8 meters square. According to statistics for the total population, the average residential space in urban areas (1993) was thought to be 7.5 and in rural areas 21.0 meters square. For every 100 families of entrepreneurs in 1993, there were 38 private cars (average value: 65,000 Yuan), 55 motorbikes, 140 telephones and 15 computers, in contrast to normal households with no private cars, 6.3 (urban areas) correspondingly 4.9 (rural areas) motorbikes. In that year the families of Chinese entrepreneurs spent 600 Yuan every month on food, 235 Yuan on clothes, 300 Yuan for maintenance of relationships and 50 Yuan for recreational activities; for families of non-entrepreneurs in urban areas these figures (1995) amounted to 147 Yuan (for food), 39.9 Yuan (clothing) and 5.8 Yuan (for recreational activities).[41]

---

[40] For more detail on patterns of living of the urban middle classes see Duan Yiping 1999.
[41] Zhang, Xie and Li 1994: 146ff.; *Zhongguo tongji nianjian* 1995: 289ff.

According to the Chinese 1% sample (1995), the families of 37.1% of the entrepreneurs spent for their living costs per month more than 2,000 Yuan, 28.4% between 1,000 and 2,000 Yuan, a quarter less than 1,000 Yuan. Almost 10% simply didn't answer the question at all. In the same year, the average monthly income of families in urban areas amounted to 324 Yuan, in rural areas 132 Yuan. Private entrepreneurs earn, as I have shown above, more than any other group in the society, with an income way above the average. Their expenditure is correspondingly high and its general size reflects their unmistakably higher standard of living, especially, when one takes into account that the figures given by the entrepreneurs were generally lower than they really are. Whereas a Chinese survey ascertained that 10.9% of the private entrepreneurs spend more than 5,000 Yuan per month, 4% per month even over 10,000 Yuan,[42] our sample contrastingly established the following results:

Table 121: Monthly expenditure (1995) of the cadres and entrepreneurs surveyed (China, in Yuan)

	Entrepreneurs		Cadres	
	Number	%	Number	%
< 500	21	12.0	14	6.9
> 500 – 1,000	50	28.6	112	55.2
> 1,000 - 3,000	86	49.1	73	36.0
> 3,000 - 6,000	12	6.9	4	2.0
> 6,000	6	3.4	0	0.0
Total	175	100.0	203	100.0

Source: Own research.

Almost two-thirds of the cadres (62.1%), but only 40.6% of the entrepreneurs stated that in 1995 they had spent per month less than 1,000 Yuan. But 38% of the functionaries and almost 60% of the entrepreneurs declared they had spent more. Even if the expenditure side may be considerably understated, a comparison with the officially issued expenditure statistics makes clear the difference to the average population. In statistical terms, inhabitants of urban areas (1995) spent an average of 295 Yuan per head, those of rural areas 178 Yuan. While functionaries constitute a group with above average high income and expenditure, those were far exceeded by the entrepreneurs, however.

At a lower level a similar development has taken place in Vietnam. Whereas the national income per head (1996) lay at (US) $250 on average, almost 40% of the respondents earned in 1995 from their occupations as entrepreneurs alone an income of at least (US) $2,000 per head.

The actual amounts may lie considerably higher, because (as most of the respondents in both countries declared) income represents a sensitive theme; as a

---

[42] Zhang, Li and Xie 1996: 161; *Zhongguo tongji nianjian* 1996: 281.

result in response to the corresponding questions lower amounts are deliberately stated. 84.5% of the entrepreneurs spent according to their own answers annually more than (US) $1,200, and 46% even more than 2,200.

But not every entrepreneur pursues this pattern of living, and the directors of larger state sector companies also follow a partially similar life-style. This demonstrative consumption varies as well between urban and rural areas, and between regions. On the other hand, this style of consuming also impacts on other social groups, because this life-style takes on a role model function for young people as well as for functionaries, the individually employed, and others. Achieving such a life-style becomes for ever more people the sought-after goal that can only be reached through entrepreneurial activity. And by means of the expectations of profits that they imagine to be associated with it, or in effect as a substitute through corruption and speculation.

In still other ways too *conspicuous consumption* has its effect in shaping people's way of life: in the form of eating together in expensive restaurants this consumer behavior promotes group consciousness (shared meals in the company of befriended entrepreneurs who can regularly afford such banquets) as well as the formation of networks amongst entrepreneurs. *Gastro politics* serves to manufacture relationships to functionaries and other important contact persons for the sphere of business. Gastro politics too belongs to the way of life of entrepreneurs who have to spend a considerable part of their profits on hospitality; at the same time, however, it stamps the ideas of "guests" of group behavior as well as the status classification of the entrepreneurs. As a result it has the effect of forming values and a "social language".[43] Brand awareness in life-style and the frequenting of certain restaurants and amusement firms serves the symbolic display of wealth less than they document success in business, self-confidence in status, and with that upwards social mobility. In a study of the banqueting behavior of entrepreneurs in the special economic zone Shenzhen (China), Wang Gan describes how the hierarchical barriers between functionaries and private entrepreneurs evaporate in the social space provided by restaurants:

> It is their [the entrepreneurs'] place where they have authority and prestige. They often know the restaurateur, or some waiters and waitresses. They know how to order and how to ear some rarity. Principles and rules permeating the place are different from those in bureaucratic sphere: you have to pay high prices to get in, and you have to pay much more to come again and again and get familiar with the environment. The overarching theme is not power but wealth. Therefore, the hierarchical relationships between the hosts and the guests can be transformed into more or less equalized ones. The service as well as the themes of money hegemony contribute to the transformation. ... *Conspicuous consumption* enables them to forge a high-class identity shared by them and their guests.[44]

---

[43] Chang 1977.
[44] Wang Gan 1998: 15.

The possession of capital assets and education, the access to functionaries and with that to resources, the manufacture of entrepreneurial networks, the membership of associations representing entrepreneurs, the virtually common interests (such as the necessity of making a profit, economic freedoms, the market economy, increasing legal safeguards, social recognition and upwards social mobility) as well as gradual commonalities and similarities in ways of life and life-style point to the existence of a probable class in the spirit of Bourdieu. But we cannot conclude from that that what we are observing is already a political player with common interests. Much rather, what is at issue is the representation of a closeness within a social space so that we are at least able to refer to the existence of groups and elements of a group consciousness.

Finally **symbolic capital** in the form of reputation, prestige and social status plays an important role for the formation of the identity of the entrepreneurial strata. At this point the results of our survey gain in relevance. In response to our questions to the entrepreneurs about the assessment of the economic, social and political positions of different professional and functionary groups, *in economic terms* the private entrepreneurs in both countries attributed to themselves leading positions. The level of assessment in China was, however, higher than in Vietnam, which may be based on the higher incomes on average, the greater stability of incomes and the larger amounts of company assets.

Table 122: Economic position of groups of professions

China	Vietnam
1. Private entrepreneur	1. Private entrepreneur
2. Manager state firms	2. Manager state firms
3. Manager rural firms	3. Cadre (central)
4. Individually employed	4. Individually employed
5. Scientist/ technician	5. Scientist/technician
6. Cadre (central)	6. Manager rural firms
7. Local cadre	7. Local cadre
8. Worker private sector	8. Worker in state firms
9. Worker in state firms	9. Worker private sector
10. Peasant	10. Peasant

Source: own research.
NB: 1=highest value, 10= lowest.

While the result in both countries are similar, it is noticeable that the respondents in China classified cadres on the central level lower than in Chinese surveys in the 1980s, and lower than the Vietnamese entrepreneurs. Above all in both countries the local cadres were classified in economic terms hardly higher than workers.

This allows one to conclude that the functionaries in terms of income all in all cannot keep up with the entrepreneurs. On the other hand the table demon-

strates the increased self-confidence of the entrepreneurial strata. The combination of an uncertain future for the state sector companies with at the same time
partially higher pay in some sectors of the private sector has had the effect in
China that the workforce in private sector firms are placed higher than those in
the state sector companies. The workers who in the past were privileged now
come at the bottom of the economic league table along with the peasantry.

In social terms the entrepreneurs attributed to themselves a middle position,
whereby the classification in China was already rather at the upper middle level.
This appears to make clear that in their self-perception they want socially as
well to rise into the upper class. Private entrepreneurs who according to Chinese surveys in the 1980s were continually to be found in the lower third have
apparently achieved upwards social mobility, whereas the small entrepreneurs
(individually employed) are as they were before not particularly respected socially.

Table 123: Social position of groups of professions

China	Vietnam
1. Cadre (central)	1. Cadre (central)
2. Scientist/ technician	2. Manager state firms
3. Manager state firms	3. Scientist/ technician
4. Private entrepreneur	4. Local cadre
5. Local cadre	5. Private entrepreneur
6. Manager rural firms	6. Manager rural firms
7. Worker in state firms	7. Worker in state firms
8. Individually employed	8. Individually employed
9. Worker private sector	9. Worker private sector
10. Peasant	10. Peasant

Source: Own research.

In the results for this table there were clear differences between large and small
entrepreneurs. Larger ones attributed to themselves after the central level cadres
(average value: 2.6) the second highest degree of social prestige (3.6), the
smaller ones only rank 6 (4.4). In rural areas entrepreneurs placed themselves
likewise socially higher (place 3, average value: 3.3) than in urban areas (5/3.7).

Whereas the regional differences in China were rather low, they were evident in Vietnam. The technical intelligentsia (scientists and technicians)
occupied second place in North Vietnam (urban and rural areas), where the
Party had always emphasized the role of science; in Ho Chi Minh City in
contrast only rank 4.

In political terms the entrepreneurs classified themselves in the middle, in
Vietnam rather the lower middle. These placings underline their increasing
prestige because Chinese surveys of the early 1990s showed the entrepreneurs
viewed politically still to be at the bottom of the scale.

Table 124: Political position of groups of professions

China	Vietnam
1. Cadre (central)	1. Cadre (central)
2. Local cadre	2. Manager state firms
3. Manager state firms	3. Local cadre
4. Manager rural firms	4. Scientist/ technician
5. Scientist/ technician	5. Manager rural firms
6. Private entrepreneur	6. Worker in state firms
7. Worker in state firms	7. Private entrepreneur
8. Individually employed	8. Individually employed
9. Worker private sector	9. Worker private sector
10. Peasant	10. Peasant

Source: own research.

Political prestige is also the expression of authority as well as competences of power and decision-making, which are concentrated in the hands of the central as well as the local functionaries. Following immediately after, came the managers of larger, state sector companies, who in the political life of Vietnam still play an important role more so than in China. In Hanoi, strongly stamped by socialist structures, the role of employees in the state sector was placed higher than in the rural areas or in Central Vietnam or South Vietnam. Private entrepreneurs appraised their own political influence in both countries as still rather low, although politically seen entrepreneurial self-confidence in China appeared to be somewhat higher than in Vietnam, where private entrepreneurs still categorized themselves lower than workers in the state sector.

To summarize the results show that private entrepreneurs in both countries perceive their economic capital and with that their economic position as superior, and view themselves economically as the top social stratum (or class). The constancy of these factors in all parts of the land that we surveyed, as well as in urban and rural areas, indicates that in this respect a relatively homogenous consciousness already exists amongst the entrepreneurs. Private entrepreneurs also classified themselves in social terms relatively highly, in China even higher than the local functionaries on whom they are dependent in principle. This also reveals something about the evaluation of these functionaries in public opinion. Only in political terms do the entrepreneurs in both countries perceive themselves as being an average or marginal factor, at least in respect of participation in visible political life and the possibilities for shaping events and circumstances resulting from that.

For elite status, the assessment by other social groups is also important. Our survey of cadres, which posed questions about the same set of categories (1 – 10) as those in tables 122 – 124, showed that 80.7% attributed top ranking to the entrepreneurs concerning economic matters. With an average score of 1.5, the private entrepreneurs lay clearly above managers of collective enterprises in rural areas (2.6) and the individually employed (3.8).

In terms of social prestige, they were ranked sixth (average value: 5.3) and likewise concerning politics (6.0), in each case lower than functionaries at the central and local levels, the managers of state or collective companies, and the scientific-technical specialists. Whereas the economic assessment made by cadres and entrepreneurs in respect of ranking and average values was identical, entrepreneurs assessed themselves in social terms somewhat higher (rank 4, average value: 3.5) and politically about the same (rank 6, average value: 5.8). At any rate 15.8% of the cadres i.e. every sixth one declared that they would become private entrepreneurs if they were given the chance of making such a decision. However, while 61%, wanted to remain cadres, 27.6% emphasized their willingness to switch into business in the event of such a new possibility of choice. More than a third were, it seems, dissatisfied with the option of being a cadre, more than every second one of them would like to move into the private sector. This indicates that the private sector increasingly represents an important, career alternative for functionaries. This latter factor is associated with the private sector enabling people to improve their social and political prestige; entrepreneurs in this respect too have become part of the middle class. A further answer given by the functionaries appears to show that the percentage of those who would like to become entrepreneurs is actually higher. A large part of them do not have at their disposal the financial prerequisites to do so, hence they did not express such a desire: about a third (33.7%) would, if they came into possession of a large sum of money, invest this money in any case in their own company. Only providing for their retirement (46.5%) and the education of their children (69.8%) achieved higher scores. That entrepreneurs are not – as has been claimed for a long time – recruited primarily from lower social strata, is also indicated that 11% of the functionaries we surveyed stated to have entrepreneurs in their families. And successful entrepreneurial activity in the private sector within their family impacts too on the consciousness and the actions of the functionaries concerned.

Chinese surveys have also suggested the growing prestige of private entrepreneurs. A survey of 2,599 people in the second half of 1999 concerning their appraisal of 69 professions (in which 100 points represents the highest, 20 the lowest valuation of prestige) resulted in private entrepreneurs attaining rank 25 with 78.6. In a corresponding survey in 1987 private entrepreneurs received 67.6 points. In each case the age group 16–35 evaluated entrepreneurs the highest. In response to the question about their career desires, becoming private entrepreneurs occupied third place in the age group 16– 45, amongst those aged over 46 fourth place.[45]

---

[45] Xu 2000.

The entrepreneurial strata do not already constitute an "economic bourgeoisie" in the Western sense of the term.[46] The question that is always posed in this context is whether from the new entrepreneurial strata a middle class will emerge which might become the bearer of economic or political changes and with that at the same time bearer of a process of democratization.[47] The "Aristotelian middle class" is desired as one may observe. In general it can be stated that the Chinese and Vietnamese entrepreneurial strata are still in *status nascendi* (process of emerging). The characteristics of traditional middle classes e.g. their solid embedding in the societal structures of power, prestige and income, are still in a state of fluctuation.

Some economic theoreticians as a result hold the view that most owners of private companies are not yet entrepreneurs in the real meaning of the word, given that they are still stamped by the consciousness stemming from their origins mostly from a peasant background: it is argued they cannot adequately orientate themselves to the market since the members of the workforce stem for the most part from the circles of their relatives, friends and acquaintances, and illegal machinations (transactions involving speculation, tax withholding) are widespread, they argue. In addition, great anxiety about changes in the political climate predominates amongst the entrepreneurs. As a result profits are consumed rather than productively invested.[48]

But these elements are connected to a significant degree with the systemic uncertainty in which private entrepreneurs are forced to move. Restrictions and bureaucratic hindrances limit the willingness to invest and take risks. Viewed economically, one can certainly already speak of entrepreneurs. And these entrepreneurs have already developed a plurality of interests and activities that go beyond the purely economic, and in this way flow into a general strategy. This refers, as mentioned above, to the formation of organizations representing their interests (entrepreneurial associations) and entrepreneurial networks, to participatory interests in political institutions (parties, People's Congresses and People's Consultative Conferences), but at the same time refers to the coming into being of a special life-style, and to symbolic consumption which is already recognizable amongst the entrepreneurial strata, and finally is an expression of inequality between groups of people.

---

[46] The term economic bourgeoisie – unlike the term entrepreneur – refers to a social class, to which apart from the entrepreneurs owners of capital belong Cf. Schumann 1992: 19.

[47] On that: Glassman 1997: 105ff.

[48] Gao and Chi 1996: 118ff.

4. *Summary: Entrepreneurs as a "strategic group"*

The categorization of entrepreneurs as a "class" or "middle strata" appears to be problematic, due to the heterogeneity of its composition and interests as well as the imprecision of definition. But there are – in the spirit of Bourdieu – a range of commonalities both existing and some in formation which point to the existence of a *potential social group*, to be exact the forms of capital already mentioned: *economic capital* (in the form of higher income as well as company assets); *cognitive capital* (entrepreneurial competencies and knowledge of management); *symbolic capital* (entrepreneurial impetus and interests, striving for social prestige); *social capital* (the existence of relationships and networks in the interests of business procedures free of friction, for the safeguarding of profit opportunities or for the purposes of protection; what tend to be common-alities respecting life-style); and *organizational capital* (membership in state-controlled or semi-controlled organizations representing their interests). There is a tendency for entrepreneurs to strive as well for *political capital* (member-ship of the Party or in state institutions, formal or informal participation in the interests of molding the framework conditions for entrepreneurs).

As a result we can term entrepreneurs first of all a quasi group i.e. as a social group, which indeed displays common interests and specific forms of behavior, but apparently still does not pursue a conscious strategy for the assertion and implementation of its interests.[49] But such a classification would not go far enough. Processes and developmental tendencies have already taken place that go beyond the quasi group. Amongst these one may count not only organization in associations, even if these are state controlled, but also the articulation of interests in specific newspapers and magazines at the central[50] as well as the regional, and to some extent already at the local level. In addition people have been striving to create new associations independent of the bureaucracy or to find a wider hearing in the media (radio and TV).

Amongst these factors going beyond the quasi group one should note too or-ganized network meetings of entrepreneurs. Above all in the larger cities of East China, such meetings have the function of strengthening group conscious-ness. An example of this trend was the "Forum of Chinese entrepreneurs at the end of the 20th century", which met at the end of the 1990s in Beijing; this was a network through which entrepreneurs met together every Sunday evening in the *Xin Dadu* hotel, listened together to a lecture, after which they exchanged ideas in conversation and so strengthened their linkages and co-operation. To

---

[49] Cf. Dahrendorf 1959: 179ff.; Mayer 1977; Holthus and Schams 1987: 283.

[50] The following newspapers and magazines have the biggest circulation: *Zhongguo Gongshang Bao* (Newspaper for Industry and Trade), which in two issues per week as its main focus reports on the development of the private sector and about entrepreneurs (The editor is the National Bureau for the Administration of Industry and Commerce), as well as the monthly *Zhongguo Qiyejia* (Chinese entrepreneur), a glossy published by the same publisher responsible for the daily *Jingji Ribao* (Business daily) with articles about Chinese entrepreneurial personalities.

these meetings they invited each time representatives of the media so that relationships to journalists could be intensified.[51] Amongst the activities which promote group consciousness, one may furthermore include the setting-up of their own foundations which among other things organize and finance scientific meetings (international ones too) concerning private sector and market economics as well as corresponding publications of books (some in English).[52] While that development in Vietnam up till now has been less in evidence, the trend in this direction is developing along the same lines.

As I elucidated in Part 1, the term *strategic group* is thus actually the one most suitable to characterize the phenomenon of entrepreneurship as a social group in present day China and Vietnam. I named five preconditions that are characteristic of strategic groups:

- they possess an important function for political development and political transformation of a society;
- they appear as an organized interest group with political negotiating power;
- they work "strategically" in the sense named above and possess strategic abilities for assertion and implementation of their interests that can take place formally and informally;
- the organizations representing their interests possess strategic knowledge, strategic planning and the capacity to carry out this planning;
- the patterns of behavior and attitudes of group members impact socially to shape and change values.

These five criteria make clear that entrepreneurs are not only a *collective agent* but rather a *collective symbol* as well. Keller classified three levels of the latter: the *cognitive* (specialized prowess and knowledge), the *moral* (values and attitudes), and the *expressive* level (emotions, forms of behavior).[53] Entrepreneurs impact in this way as role models for the society and individuals, as well as role models and people of whom much is hoped. On the one hand they act collectively through their organizations representing their interests, but on the other hand stand symbolically for economic authority, professionalism, bearers of economic decisions, entrepreneurial success, wealth and a specific lifestyle.

The symbolic includes as well particular moral expectations (employer, helping with social welfare, social behavior), ideas concerning values and social order. The creation of such a symbolic character can be made clear by a concrete example: at the end of 1999 an entrepreneur wrote in the Party magazine that the entrepreneur of the 21st century would have to be at one and the same time politician (*zhengzhijia*), thinker (*sixiangjia*) and artist (*yishujia*). Politician because their work is indivisibly associated with politics in the sense

---

[51] Zhongguo Gongshang Bao, 12 November 1999.

[52] E.g. the foundation set up by private entrepreneurs on Hainan *Hainan (China) Foundation for Reform and Development Research.*

[53] Keller 1963: 154.

of the political and legal framework conditions which they have to actively impact on and help to shape; thinker because the development of a company depends upon their philosophy, artist because they have to encounter other people with understanding and empathy.[54] Here as in so many press contributions written by entrepreneurs, the universal, strategic and exemplary aspects of entrepreneurship are foregrounded, and with that they polish up a social role model. This is also part of the strategy of strategic groups. The term strategic group contains along with strategic actions the element too of strategic symbolism (i.e. the entrepreneur as symbol for a particular way of behaving and specific values).

While the symbolic manifests itself in the role model character, the pattern of behavior, lifestyle and in social actions, and only becomes socially effective when their role model nature becomes accepted, the levels of symbols named above are at the same time important premises for social acceptance and upwards social mobility. Collective action and symbolic action move hand and hand in that. These factors do not depend on the symbolism and actions of individual entrepreneurs. Entrepreneurs can much rather only then act collectively and symbolically, and exert influence when they are organized (e.g. in associations). Insofar they also do not act as a class but rather are organized in the form of associations.

Furthermore they make their impact in the shape of *collective action* i.e. as individual players whereby the sum of their informal, non-organized, and non-coordinated actions has an effect that makes changes. As a result the existence of an entrepreneurial stratum leads to an increase of social space as opposed to state-controlled space. Where there are no entrepreneurs, the state of necessity has to appear as an entrepreneurial actor. Entrepreneurial impact thereby brings about a reduction of state control over the economy. This is intensified through the existence of networks that also which have also to be understood as mechanisms of direction independent of the state. Besides active shaping and altering of events and circumstances, there exists in addition an informal framework correspondingly an informal space in which a social infrastructure for transformation forms. This affects in the case of China and Vietnam, for instance, the emergence of market economic structures which are promoted by entrepreneurs *as a position*, namely through entrepreneurial actions. A successful market economy creates, as we know, the economic preconditions for and pressure in the direction of democratization.

Successful means here, that a state exists capable of taking action, so as to consciously drive the development on. That development in turn indeed is required to keep within acceptable limits the engendering of what would be otherwise all too serious spatial and stratum-type inequalities, and at the same time bring economic and social advantages for the absolute majority of the total population (South Korea and Taiwan are examples of this). Secondly, entrepre-

---

[54] Wei Jiafu 1999.

neurs bring about transformations through their patterns of life in that they contribute to the changes of attitudes and values (e.g. in respect of prosperity, wealth, property, luxury, but also concerning elements like competition, economic freedoms, innovation, and market behavior), of structures (organizations representing their interests, public income structure at the local level, labor market, legal institutions).

They impact as trendsetters and role models concerning taste. Attitudes and values are indeed not individual characteristics, but rather are primarily formed and altered through interactive processes inside groups. During the concluding workshop for this research project, the director of our Chinese partnership institute, Cao Yuanzheng, declared correspondingly that the most important role of the private sector consisted of the function, "to transform the thinking, the ideas and values of people."[55]

At the same time, a central indicator of entrepreneurs, namely innovation, is not only an economic action, but rather also has something to do with social change with the re-evaluation of values.[56] Re-evaluation of values means that the entreprencur interprets values differently and with that puts in question old patterns of thinking. This transformative side of entrepreneurs as *potential and strategic players producing change* has been for the most part overlooked in the relevant literature. Thirdly, entrepreneurs use their economic capital to expand their social and political capital e.g. through donations (strategic philanthropy) in the interests of matters of public concern, or in that they manufacture and develop *Guanxi* to functionaries both individually and through networks. The strategic use of *Guanxi*, networks, alliances as well as negotiating processes in the strategic interests of entrepreneurs as a group has to be grasped as a part of the strategy planning. The interest of the absolute majority of the entrepreneurs in the creation of a non-state, controlled organization representing their interests makes clear the desire for a stronger and more independent voice in the shaping of policies. And finally, the work of entrepreneurs in formal structures is an important means to influence policies. As we have described above, there is not only an above average percentage of entrepreneurs who are Party members. The desire to join the Party, have a seat in Parliament or in the People's Consultative Conferences is widespread.

The growing proportion of Party members amongst the private entrepreneurs and the attempt to integrate this group into the activities of the Party, will accelerate the ideological and organizational reshaping of the Party. This is because here a group with directed economic interests exists that at the same time is enthusiastic about participation, while possessing significant potential economic power; one can safely predict that they will exert a decisive influence on the future shaping of policies.

---

[55] Cao Yuanzheng on 14 May 1999 in Duisburg.
[56] Cf. on that also Groys 1999: 63ff.

As I mentioned in Part I, in 1994 the Party leadership had already pointed out that the purchase of political office, of votes, and of functionaries by private entrepreneurs in rural areas was assuming ever more serious forms, whereby these phenomena had already begun to spread into the urban areas. The leadership argued that ever increasingly private entrepreneurs had recognized, that business and politics could not be separated from one another.[57] One of the largest private entrepreneurs summarized this in the formulation, "Entrepreneurs in China have to be politicians; if they do not understand how to be political, they will fail."[58]

But not all entrepreneurs are equally active, and not all of them impact strategically. Amongst the strategically active section of the entrepreneurial stratum are to be found as a rule the larger, more significant and more educated entrepreneurs who moreover take on public functions and operate as "intelligent key players".[59] This segment of entrepreneurial strata is more self-confident than smaller entrepreneurs, above all when the former stem from upper strata. More self-confident people behave more pro-actively and exert themselves more strategically for their interests. It is this group too that makes up the core of a *strategic elite*, possesses leadership qualities, and is beginning to stand out from the collective strategic group of the entrepreneurs as recognized spokespersons and representatives. People who stem from lower strata, small entrepreneurs or such like, who have already at some time in their lives committed misdemeanors condemned politically or socially , often display angst or reservations about becoming involved politically or socially, and try to behave in a politically conformist manner.

Chinese studies underline that the smaller individually employed tend rather to view politics as something negative ("Politics is an evil thing" or "Politics is a matter for a small minority"), than private entrepreneurs. The former group tends as well to be more politically indifferent.

Entrepreneurs exercise power and influence not only through individual but also through collective behavior not only in the market but also in political life. This takes place economically, for instance, through decisions concerning investments, locations, production and employment. These decisions in turn influence the political framework conditions and with that political decisions at the local or regional level; and they exercise power and influence too in both the social and political spheres: socially through donor and (financial) support behavior; politically through networks, relationships, participation in institutions, and corruption too. This can be exercised individually or collectively (e.g. through associations or organizations representing their interests). Larger entrepreneurs in turn are mostly holders of political office. In authoritarian societies such as China and Vietnam where active collective behavior, above all in the

---

[57] Lu Yusha 1994: 4-5.
[58] Tyson and Tyson 1995: 54.
[59] Jahns 1999.

political sphere is a sensitive question and quickly meets with distrust, collective political actions by entrepreneurs always represent only the second best decision.

Strategies in no way automatically pose the power question and are not only pursued in the interests of political power. As the response behavior of the entrepreneurs showed, we need to differentiate different strategies: *growth strategies* (in the interests of growth of the group and/or their organizations), *business strategies* (to assert market and business interests), *stability strategies* (in the interests of societal or group stabilization), *political defense strategies* (to ward off disadvantages), *political offensive strategies* (for the formal and/or informal assertion of interests), or *combinations of different strategies*.

Since the choice of strategy in each case depends on the specific circumstances, one cannot ascertain any consistent and uniform behavior of the entrepreneurs as a group. Strategies and strategic goals are much more likely to vary. Furthermore, entrepreneurs do not only act in a socially positive way. The *symbiotic clientelism*,[60] i.e. the alliance between cadres and entrepreneurs in the interests of mutual, dyadic benefit through which the entrepreneur obtains access to resources and profit opportunities, and at the same time protection against both administrative arbitrariness and the soft interpretation of regulations, changes nothing in this transformative function. A entrepreneur who plays host to a tax official in order to gain a tax reduction, ensures for himself through that not only a higher or any profit at all, which he may reinvest, rather he changes as well the behavior of the officer in question which is advantageous for them both, contributing in this way in turn to the development of the company. Moreover, this should be comprehended as a part of the negotiating process between bureaucracy and entrepreneurs that manufactures – if too through corruption – a compromise and consensus. The political costs of such corruption, while contributing to the destabilization of the entire system, do not change anything of the informal, transforming function of the entrepreneur, however.

And finally, the change from dependent to symbiotic clientelism is a clear signal of the shifting position of entrepreneurs in China and Vietnam.

Seen in political terms, it appears to be premature to speak already of unambiguous "strategic behavior" by the entrepreneurs because such action would have to be politically goal-directed and pursued in an organized way. But if we fall back on the organizational strategy of *strategic management* through which entrepreneurs seek the control of relationships through co-operation and political activities in order to obtain competitive advantages (cf. Part I, Chapter 6), the term strategy becomes more tangible. Co-operations and agreements with other entrepreneurs, the establishing and mobilizing of relationships and networks and political activities inside formal institutions (Party, People's Congresses among others) all serve the goal of, as effectively as possible, exerting influence on the framework conditions, and to shape the

---

[60] Wank 1995: 52.

346 PART THREE: IMPLICATIONS AND CONCLUSIONS

influence on the framework conditions, and to shape the situation of the entrepreneurs and their firms to their best possible advantage.

Furthermore, fully in the spirit of Bourdieu, strategic behavior is indeed
thoroughly goal-directed, but does not necessarily have to be a calculated pursuit of a goal consciously exploring every detail. It may very well pursue goals
that are objective and are rather unconsciously perceived, which "do not necessarily have to be the subjectively sought-after goals". Bourdieu termed this
strategy a "soft, relative determinism".[61]

The analysis in the previous paragraphs applies to the political space,
whereby the organizing of controls represents at present a central strategic goal.
The organizational means for the establishing of those controls are the already
existing associations that, in the framework of the guidelines of the Party and
the state, cautiously formulate economic-political goals at the local and national
levels. One may list among these demands such as that made by the Association for Private Enterprises (which is subordinate to the Bureau for the Administration of Industry and Commerce) that it has to become an "independent juridical person", and not be under the influence of any section of the authorities;
it should become instead a purely interest representing organization for private
entrepreneurs.[62] Along these lines, the associations which are subordinate to the
Bureau for the Administration of Industry and Commerce are working towards
becoming autonomous associations representing the interests of the entrepreneurs i.e. "independent juridical persons and social associations".[63] Membership of it should be voluntary.[64]

Up till now entrepreneurs in China and Vietnam, while they do not possess
independent organizations representing their interests, have also been able to
express their interests through the associations however corporatist as well as
through informal channels.[65] But in the meantime, an astonishing experiment
has come into being: in some regions of the province Guangdong, entrepreneurs as early as 1993 were allowed to found self-administered "guilds" (min-
jian qiyejia gonghui) on an experimental basis. The membership in these guilds
is voluntary; the managing boards are not stipulated by the bureaucracy but
rather voted in by the members. These organizations are supposed to attend to
the interests of the entrepreneurs, and take part in negotiations as appropriate
with Party and the authorities.[66]

---

[61] Cf. Bourdieu 1992: 114f. and 1993: 113.
[62] Cf. for example *Zhongguo Gongshang Bao*, 20 November 1998.
[63] Ibid.
[64] Zhongguo Gongshang Bao, 19 March 1999.
[65] On that in more detail: Heberer 1996.
[66] Qin Nanyang 1999: 106ff.

4.1. *Group cohesion*

There are only initial attempts of group cohesion, among other things because the composition of the entrepreneurial stratum is still viewed by the individual entrepreneurs as too heterogeneous (from size of company, degree of education, extent of production, equipping with capital, and regional linkages). A large entrepreneur in Shanghai who wrote his Ph.D. in the USA, and who exports high technology products may at first sight have little in common with a peasant entrepreneur who in a distant region of West China has members of his clan manufacture baskets for the local market.

But the group cohesion that is still in an imperfect state is also an expression of the fact that the private sectors were only legalized again little more than a decade ago in both China and Vietnam, and the fluctuation is still relatively large. But compulsory membership in associations controlled by the state has contributed to strengthening the group cohesion and solidarity amongst the entrepreneurs, because it implies at least symbolically a community of interests and promotes the exchange of information amongst each other. A certain degree of identity and group consciousness also came to the surface in the course of our interviews. As an illustration entrepreneurs in China and Vietnam spoke of "us" when they referred to entrepreneurs in general. They also did not want to be lumped together with the individually employed whom they regarded as economically and socially inferior ("disputatious street vendors"), whereas they themselves gave the impression of being entrepreneurs, and assumed in economic and social terms an important position in the economy.

The group consciousness also came to light in the delimitation from other social groups, above all vis-à-vis the peasantry, but also in relation to the functionaries on other levels. Proud of their (the entrepreneurs') own achievements, expressions of this consciousness are the self-assessment by a large section of the entrepreneurs that they were social role models and increasingly the self-appraisal as an "elite".

Our survey indicated as a result that the private entrepreneurs have already begun to form themselves into a social group of their own with a marked self- and group consciousness; in that the private entrepreneurs who manage large companies have a stronger group consciousness than small entrepreneurs. Often they represent the private sector in associations and organizations (such as in China the *Association of Industry and Commerce* or in Vietnam in the *Union Association of Industry and Commerce*).

There is a trend towards strong unified organizations representing their interests. In China the Association of Industry and Commerce has crystallized ever more as the strongest, most politically powerful organization which more than the others is fired by the interests of those it represents. For some years they have insisted that they be recognized as an independent, juridical person (*faren*) after which they will be able to operate as an independent association on behalf of entrepreneurs i.e. no longer needing a guarantor organization which acts as their patron, and exerts control over them. It would then exist as a non-profit NGO. This is still not settled but the front formed by the opponents of such a move is crumbling. Consequently one may expect that in the next few years a relatively autonomous entrepreneurial association will come into being.[67]

A growing group consciousness may be noted too in Vietnam. Although the entrepreneurs from Ho Chi Minh City and Danang were reluctant for understandable reasons to speak of a class of private entrepreneurs, they emphasized nevertheless that the entrepreneurs form a social group who differed clearly from other groups in the society.[68] Interestingly in response to the question about the criteria for this demarcation as a group, they did not name in first place a high income and material prosperity, but rather a higher level of training and special skills. They argued that not everyone was in a position to become a successful entrepreneur. They denied that the peasantry in particular had the necessary skills especially mental flexibility.

The low opinion of other social groups expresses a certain pride and self-confidence on the part of the entrepreneurs. Both were evident too in the self-appraisal of economic skills already mentioned, in which the private entrepreneurs awarded themselves the highest marks.[69] A relatively high percentage of the entrepreneurs were even self-confident enough to regard themselves as having an exemplary function for the society. Up till then only the Vietnamese Communist Party and their members had pretensions to such a function.

Relatively common exchanges of experience strengthen such a group consciousness. A noteworthy section of the respondents in both countries met on a weekly basis to have discussions with other private entrepreneurs, almost a half of them took part in a number of such discussions every month. The discussion of similar experiences and problems strengthens the perception of commonalities amongst the entrepreneurs. It promotes and stabilizes the formation of a "we feeling", and plays a role in the delimitation from other social groups.

The existence of what are sometimes different interests (competition), ideas of goals or strategies (such as the partial use of *guanxi* or corruption) does not alter the feeling of belonging to a group. This is because a shared *basic interest* amongst them can be assumed: in economic freedom (market and attaining profits), in societal stability and development, as well as orderly framework conditions (legal and political safeguards). And this basic interest determines too the formulation of strategy. Precisely this formulation and assertion of common interests in an organized form makes the entrepreneurial stratum into a

---

[67] Conversations on 27 September 1996 and 30 September 1998 in Beijing. Also relevant is Chen Qingtai 1995.

[68] An entrepreneur in Danang on the other hand used the term "new social movement", in order to characterize private entrepreneurs. He indicated with that description that he thought the current development was still in motion, and in his opinion had still not led to the formation of a permanently structured social order.

[69] This matched the appraisal by others as in the evaluation by the cadres whom we surveyed, who likewise gave the private entrepreneurs the highest grades for their economic skills.

strategic group. As a result the entrepreneurs in both countries are well on the way to becoming such a strategic group, if too, the development in China is already further advanced than in Vietnam due to fewer political restrictions.

4.2. *Group aims*

The term "strategy" implies that a group attempts to implement group aims according to a plan or spontaneously. As a result, the question is raised how far the term "strategic" applies to entrepreneurship in both countries. Olson questioned for example whether groups can truly be said to spontaneously pursue collective group aims. He holds it to be something of an exception when people altruistically put their own individual interests into abeyance, so as to pursue collective interests, and argues that it requires instead incentives or the application of compulsion to form organizations representing their interests.[70] The developments in China and Vietnam appear to support his view. Entrepreneurship came into being first of all spontaneously and as a deviation from official policies. The attaining of profits, if possible quickly, in an environment which made long-term commercial trading appear uncertain furthered conformity to the conditions of the political framework, the requirement to prioritize *Guanxi* and networks, and the lone fighter mentality of the entrepreneurs. This picture will appear somewhat different, however, if the process nature of the development of the entrepreneurs is made clear.

The history of the rebirth of private entrepreneurship can be divided into the following stages: (a) existence as a shadow economy, (b) striving for acceptance, (c) substitution of political controls through economic ones,[71] and (d) legal safeguards and equality. Existence as a shadow economy has already been discarded, acceptance consolidated, noticeable progress made in the replacement of political controls through economic ones and in legal safeguards. As a result, it is at present the factors of legal security, political participation and political equality (access to membership of the CP), which form the current collective aims, which private entrepreneurs have a common interest in reaching.

The ability of the group to organize themselves, which is the precondition for effective organization in associations representing their interests, presupposes three key elements: *continuity* of pursuit of interests (in order to be able to reach a goal at all), the *urgency* of the realization of interests and the *commonality* of interests. The reality of organizations of entrepreneurs in associations representing their interests is an expression of group consciousness, or it will further (so far as compulsory membership predominates) the formation of such a group consciousness.

---

[70] Olson 1985: 1ff.

[71] As an illustration of this at a conference about the economic administration of the private sector, it was explicitly stated that the era of political control was over, and in future economic control would be foregrounded instead. Cf. among others *Zhongguo Gongshang Bao*, 23 October 1998.

Our interviews suggest that entrepreneurs through these organizations also pursue in continual work the goal of realizing common interests and aims.[72] In this sense of the word, the element of ability to organize is strengthened by the following factors:

(a)   Through compulsory organization in quasi-state organization controlled by the administrating authorities. Through them, entrepreneurs are embedded in trans-entrepreneurial structures, out of which new networks, co-operations and sources of information result. At the same time, at least for a section of the entrepreneurship a common identity arises out of that: the knowledge of common interests and the necessity to take action as well as the awareness that organizations representing their interests are necessary, but such which are not directed and controlled by the state, but are rather administered by themselves.

(b)   Recognition accorded by the state to the private sector, its legal equality and ideological acceptance, and finally its economic success have promoted the self-confidence of the entrepreneurs. Furthermore, (in China more than Vietnam), mobilizing work has been commenced, which attempts through the media and different institutional channels to raise social and political prestige.

(c)   The continual interventions of local authorities in the work of entrepreneurs, the high degree of corruption, the discrepancy between the policies of support, decided on by central and province governments, contrasted with partially rigid behavior of local bureaucracies cause high costs which do long-term damage to the development of individual firms. "Arbitrariness can not be overcome in the long-term by individual actions," an entrepreneur declared. The cumulative effect of political acceptance (at the central level), economic and social necessity (the private sector is indispensable for reasons of dynamism, employment and fiscal politics), as well as the entrepreneurial self-confidence that likewise promotes the process of organizing. Many entrepreneurs have recognized that organization cannot be restricted merely to consultation i.e. the function of communicating economic-political opinions to the authorities. What is required rather is lobbying and the influencing of economic and legal policies in the interests of the entrepreneurs.

Precisely this last point can be demonstrated with an example. At the meeting of the national People's Congress and the national Political Consultative Conference in China (March 1998), numerous deputies from the private entrepreneurial stratum voted for a change in the constitution which would entail that in it the private sector be given equality. This was justified with the benefits that this sector brings to the economy and employment as a whole, as well as for the increases in export performance and currency inflow. At the same time, the

---

[72] On that von Winter 1997.

setting up of an "Office for the private sector" was proposed, which would not only re-evaluate the position of this sector in the administrative apparatus, but would also improve the possibilities of the use of this department to assert their interests. An entrepreneur, deputy of the national People's Congress, declared to me:

> For years we have worked towards the goal of having the private sector recognized as being of equal status, and having this equality laid down in the constitution. This is for us an important goal whose realization would bring with it a certain amount of political and legal security. Mostly, in the framework of the Association of Industry and Commerce and in many conversation with the United Front Department of the Central Committee of the CCP (responsible for that association: comment by the author) we have worked to convince people.
>
> When we do that, we always agree beforehand who, how and where we should put forward our arguments. Our work as deputies enables us to have access to political leaders and to influential personalities, and gives us the possibility of putting forward our views, to explain them and to ask for support. That is both the Chinese and our way of doing politics. It allows us to realize our goals gradually and to participate in politics to further our interests.[73]

Not only the state level but also the Party are the targets of the entrepreneurs. In a contribution published in the *Zhongguo Gongshang Bao* entrepreneurs repeatedly make the case that their interests had to be represented even in the CP itself. In an article with the title "We want representatives in the Party", which was distributed by the national news agency Xinhua, it was stated that the economic significance (of the private sector) in the total national strategy required such a step. The argumentation was backed up ideologically. "It is the policies of reform and openness introduced by the Party, which have given us everything that we have achieved today. Only when we move forward with the Party will the path become ever broader."[74]

4.3. *Law, legislation and organized anarchy: strategic groups as players in the legal domain*

The transition from planned to a "socialist market economy" requires changes in legal ideas and the law in the sense that, "the legislator (has to provide) the participants in the market a transparent shape."[75] The market and the players in it (to some extent new actors), have arisen through it, need new regulatory patterns in order to reduce damage caused by friction and a loss of social order. Business law (that pertaining to companies, stock holders, contract, shares,

---

[73] The conversation took place in July 1999 in private, the interviewee asked me not to name him.
[74] Zhongguo Gongshang Bao, 21 November 1997.
[75] Heuser 1999: 375.

labor, etc.) had to be rewritten, and with the expansion of market relations an increasing differentiation within the law came about.

According to Robert Heuser, five transitions are characteristic for this process on the level of legal culture: (a) the transition from norms of habit to legal norms, (b) from traditional obligations to a catalogue of laws and obligations, (c) from avoidance of trials to their acceptance, (d) from disciplining in order to achieve governmental goals to individual legal protection, and (e) from "instrumentality" (in the meaning of "class interests") to "political bonding", and from the "masses as object to forms of participation".[76] Responsible for this alteration is the path dependency of the political leadership. The market economy and opening required new rules of social order and play. If the private sector is to develop, then it has to be legally safeguarded and protected. Political safeguards have to be substituted by legal ones, the texts of the law have to be made capable of implementation through institutionalized law. The linkages to the world market and the globalization of business require an increasing adaptation to international legal norms and standards. Entrepreneurs are not the sole players but those who, most of all, are interested in a sound and solid business law, because otherwise their companies are not in a position to consolidate. As a result, no articles on the private sector lack the concept of legal safeguards.

The emergence of entrepreneurial strata has, at the same time, brought about a further change of legal culture: whereas until well into the 1990s the juridical subject in the legislation of both countries was rather the company as an institution,[77] not the individual owner or entrepreneur with their rights of property. In the meantime, above all in China, it has been recognized that the entrepreneurs themselves have to become a legal subject so as effectively to protect them and their business activity, and to hinder the *exit* of private entrepreneurs from economic life. That is to say it is no longer corporate business law that is at issue, but rather increasingly business law concerning individuals. And that is precisely the prior stage to discussion about individual rights.

In the last two decades in China and Vietnam indeed a multiplicity of laws have been passed, so many as to make them hardly manageable. But, these laws possess a double function: beyond the protective function they indicate the endeavors of the state to control in future the private sector through legal instruments and not by means of arbitrary decisions. Law means in this sense not justice but rather legal controllability. Exactly that is what is meant in Vietnam by the concept, "exerting state power by means of law" (*nha nuoc phap quyen*) as opposed to the rule of law.[78] The former implies the exertion of the existing Party domination with the help of legislation and law in order to restrict the arbitrariness of government; the latter stands for the legal state in which every

---

[76] Ibid.: 471/472.
[77] Cf. on that among others Jayasuriya 1996.
[78] On that also: Herno 1998: 10.

form of political dominance is formally subordinate to law. It is worth noting that the Chinese amendment to the constitution in 1999 similarly introduced the concept of, "governing the country with the help of the law" [*yi fa zhi guo*].[79]

Without a doubt, in China and Vietnam concepts different from Western ideas of legal rule exist: one could tersely summarize this difference as rule of law and rule through law. Governing the country with the help of the laws is in both China and Vietnam a paraphrase for the role of the law in the state. This function is not interpreted in the sense of a legal state, but rather in the sense of directing society and state through the law. With that law takes on more the role of an instrument of discipline, and moves away from the regulating of the rights of individuals vis-à-vis the state and the protection against governmental arbitrariness. Recently, in China this interpretation has been questioned. A legal theoretician has elucidated that *yi fa zhi guo* means limiting the power of the state and of the bearers of state power (whether institutions of individuals) through law. This was, he argued, the most important link in the chain of this definition of the term.[80]

The director of the political science institute at the Central Party School in Hanoi also interpreted the principle of rule through law divergently from the predominant interpretation: for him this principle meant that the citizens could do everything that is stated in the legislation.[81] This reading implies in principle that the right guaranteed by the constitution should also be implemented in the form of laws which among other things would contain the freedoms of speech and assembly, associations (clubs, organizations etc.) and demonstration.

The role of law and legislation in authoritarian, one-party states has been for long neglected in social sciences because it was assumed that law was controlled by the political elite anyway, and merely possessed a legitimizing function for the rulers. This may have been accurate about the China of the Mao era, but in the course of the reforms a significant change took place. China is the country in which, since the 1980s, the most laws have been passed. At the same time, a differentiation of the legal system took place, among other things through a differentiation of the jurisdiction and the licensing of lawyers. The organ that passes laws, the national People's Congress, was able to expand its power to affect legislation and its competencies. This has been shown, for example, in rejections or far-reaching alterations to official motions in recent years, or by the large number of no's during votes. The increasing fragmentation of decision-making procedures and processes is based on the growing pluralization of the society, the clearer division between Party and state, the representation of new interest groups in the People's Congresses at all levels, and the new political culture amongst the deputies. Societal differentiation and pluralization manifest themselves also in the attitudes and behavior of the depu-

---

[79] Zhonghua Renmin Gongheguo xianfa 1999: 48.
[80] Ma Xinlan 1998.
[81] Conversation with Ho Van Thong on 15 March 1996 in Hanoi.

ties who go about their duties more self-confidently, increasingly oriented to interest groups, and less obligated to the Party.

Through the transfer of important, older Party leaders into the leadership of the national People's Congress, its functions were thereby strengthened given that these transferred persons constructed in and through the national People's Congress a new political arena. The fragmentation of power also led all in all to positive re-evaluations of the People's Congresses. The process of differentiation in the society and the duties of Party and state have had the effect that the People's Congresses have been granted increasingly greater competences in those spheres in which the Party leadership is considered to be *systemically secondary*. Among these may be counted legislation, so long as it does not impact *contra-systemically* i.e. is not directed against Party rule. While the Party leadership at least reserves for itself the ultimate right of decision, it has recently permitted *moderate dissension*.

This reinforces once again our original thesis that state and Party represent less a *structure* than a *process*. This process nature consists of neither Party nor State Council nor national People's Congress constituting a unit in themselves; rather they can be deconstructed in vertical (regional, local) and horizontal structures (Party, State Council, National People's Congress, etc.), which exist in an interactive process with one another and are subject to permanent change (What is valid for the People's Congress applies as well to the Political Consultative Conference, moreover).

Correspondingly, Tanner speaks of three *arenas* in the legislative procedure: People's Congress, State Council and Party leadership whereby the Political Consultative Conferences without a doubt should be regarded as the coalition partner of the People's Congresses, because they can operate relatively independently, are less controlled and possess merely a consultative function; on the other hand they should be and are integrated into decision-making processes as organs of consultation. Tanner refers in his appraisal to the "*garbage can*" model put forward by Cohen, Olsen and March according to which complex organizations represent at times a form of *organized anarchy*.

They suggest that organized anarchy exists when the relevant organizations are unclear about their target priorities and target hierarchies, and have inefficient, decision-making systems. This is because clear rules and procedures for reaching a decision are not in place. As a result, uncertainty about decisions reigns amongst the participating players, and that makes decisions very unpredictable. They continue their analysis with a third point, that the actors most responsible for decisions are not clearly and regularly involved in decisions. Tanner compares the Chinese legislative process with this organized anarchy because the differentiation of the societal system dissolves vertical, decision-making procedures into interactive and negotiating processes, and has scattered power and decision processes.[82]

---

[82] Tanner 1999: 28ff. For more on the *Garbage Can Theory* see Cohen, March and Olsen 1972.

This hypothesis appears to be confirmed in practice. Let us examine for example, how the process of representing interests of entrepreneurs takes place in legislation. *Zhongguo Gongshang Bao* with a regular weekly issue about the "non-public" (private) sector that announces in a sub-heading that it is the "voice" of entrepreneurs has reported about a "law for the protection of business rights and interests" for the private sector, which entrepreneurs introduced as a motion through the Association of Industry and Commerce at the meeting of the National Political Consultative Conference in spring 1998.

This motion contained a tactically skilled argumentation: the Association of Industry and Commerce (not generally the entrepreneurs!) was of the opinion that the non-public sector which had been declared to be an important part of the socialist market economy (at the last conference of the CCP), had now developed to such a degree that political support alone was no longer sufficient. It required beyond the latter legal safeguards as well. Otherwise it would be difficult to implement the policies resolved (by the Party) in a "determined" way that would "maintain stability".

Consequently, the property and assets of those concerned would have to be legally protected. Through interventions contravening the laws the further "healthy" development of this sector would be negatively affected. The constitution had protected up till now only public property but not that of the private sector. The motion went on that, happily the city of Guangzhou (capital of Guangdong province) had already decreed a corresponding legal regulation through which autonomous management, intellectual products, investments, rights concerning appointing staff, imports and exports, and rights to do with assets, property and other matters had been safeguarded, and these should now be transposed onto the national level.[83]

An institution close to the Party would implement this in procedural terms: The Association of Industry and Commerce, which in turn is under the aegis of the United Front Department of the CCP, were to be given the task of introducing a motion at a central institution (Political Consultative Conference) that possessed considerable (consultative) weight. Private entrepreneurs and the private sector were not mentioned by name in the motion. The article pointed out that it was a motion originating from the Association of Industry and Commerce, which was concerned with nothing more than the legal safeguarding of the Party leadership's resolution for the non-state sector to be given equal rights; precisely because this – so the argument went – was in the interests of the economy.

Since legal novelties always require a long process of consultation, the implementation is made easier if a tangible "prototype" exists already. This was the case in the South Chinese metropolis Guangzhou. If we follow this genesis further, one can ascertain that after the 15th Party Congress (which had passed a resolution calling for the public and non-public sector to be put on equal foot-

---

[83] Zhongguo Gongshang Bao, 6 March 1998.

ing), that the Association of Industry and Commerce at the suggestion of private entrepreneurs had introduced a motion at the Political Consultative Conference of Guangzhou city. This motion had proposed equal status for the private and state sector, had given reasons for it and then gained the support of the majority of deputies. The motion that was passed was then sent to the city parliament (People's Congress), after conversations had taken place between representatives of the Political Consultative Conference, the leading political figures in the city, and the Association of Industry and Commerce. The United Front Department (responsible to the Party's committee of the city) was also persuaded during this process, and prepared an appropriate resolution for said Party's committee of Guangzhou. The latter organ and the leadership of the city in parallel procedures then approved this document.

After the declaration by the 15th Congress of the CCP that the private sector was a part of the socialist sector, from the viewpoint of the central leadership, first of all of Guangzhou city had taken this statement as a justification to decree a "regulation for the protection of the rights of the private entrepreneurs",[84] that was primarily concerned with the safeguarding of legally defined rights, of property, of assets, of independent organization of companies, as well as protection against administrative arbitrariness. But such protective rights strengthen simultaneously the societal and political position of the private entrepreneurs, and protect them from governmental interference. This took place in a first step, not at a relatively abstract national or province level, but rather at that of a city, which is significantly closer in political terms to entrepreneurs. This measure was so successful that the organized private entrepreneurship in the province then proposed corresponding legal safeguards at the province level and finally negotiated this to a conclusion with the government of the province.

In July 1999, a corresponding regulation came into force valid throughout the province.[85] The resolution of the capital of the province, Guangzhou, was thereby transferred through the same procedure to the province of Guangdong. So Guangdong became the first province to introduce special measures for the legal protection of private entrepreneurs.[86]

In a similar way 32 deputies in the province Fujian in 1999 put forward a motion at the national People's Congress, which proposed the preparation of a "law for entrepreneurs" *(qiyejiafa)*.[87]

This procedure demonstrates that organized and strategic politics carried out by the associations representing their interests does indeed exist and – because this was an action, which concerned the total interests of all entrepreneurs, and not partial interest ("equality under the law") – also constitutes strategic politics of

---

[84] Zhongguo Gongshang Bao, 31 October 1997.

[85] Zhongguo Gongshang Bao, 9 July 1999.

[86] Li (2000) explains why Guangdong plays a pioneer role in legal matter She suggests among other things that it is due to economic interests (foreign investments) and the proximity of Hong Kong.

[87] Qu 2000:39.

the entrepreneurs in the interests of the entire social group. Such an interaction between formal and informal influences, and the merging of interests in different arenas certainly appears to confirm Tanner's thesis about organized anarchy.

Diagram 23 makes clear the interaction in this process between entrepreneurs and the institutions participating at the central level.

Diagram 23: Options of the institutionalized impact of entrepreneurs and their interest association

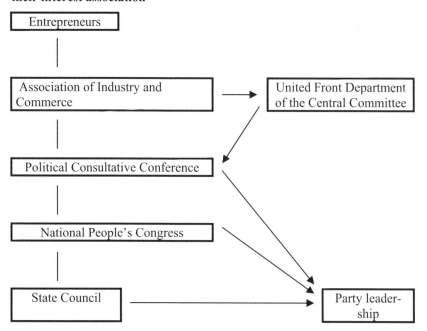

A further example of conscious and strategic collective action is the policy of petitions. *Zhongguo Gongshang Bao* reported e.g. about petitions produced by deputies (entrepreneurs) of the Political Consultative Conference at their conference in spring 1998. Besides a re-formulation of existing regulations (valid for the private sector), petitions were handed in which demanded more rights for the acquisition of foreign capital, the matter of company flotations on the share market, or the appointment of members of the workforce. Others called for the setting up of special "departments for small and middle-sized enterprises", which in future would be responsible for the administration of the private sector. These should work out the policies, guidelines, laws and legal regulations for this sector, and take care of the following: the safeguarding of its rights and their respecting; obtaining credits; provision of information and further training; advertising their products; the working through and solution of problems; the direction and administration of organizations representing their interests; and the regulation of relations to the state and collective sector.

Such a department would – unlike the Association of Industry and Commerce – be responsible exclusively for the private entrepreneurs and could, as a result, be used by the entrepreneurial strata in order to assert better their interests with and through bureaucratic levels of government, and to optimize negotiating capacities vis-à-vis the bureaucracy. Other entrepreneurs also urged the founding of Party organizations in companies and the admission of more entrepreneurs to the Party (Motto: "To strengthen the work of the Party in companies").[88]

Such a proposal won the support of a section of the entrepreneurs because a corresponding resolution would achieve the following: firstly facilitate the admission of entrepreneurs into the Party which is – as it was before – not permitted (even if widely practiced); entrepreneurs would be more strongly integrated into Party networks; and thirdly, the private sector could also politically legitimate itself and improve its image.

Similarly, in 2002 deputies of the Association of Industry and Commerce to the National People's Congress (private entrepreneurs) submitted petitions to the Congress demanding more legal and equal rights for entrepreneurs ("market economy is law economy"). They argued that entrepreneurs needed more trust, because they were "Patriots" who linked the interests of their enterprises and their personal interests to the interests of the nation.[89]

In Vietnam, this process has been less clearly documented, but the entrepreneurs and their associations endeavor to place their proposals and criticisms more prominently in the media. Here too, legal safeguards, the safeguarding of rights and equal footing with state-owned companies are still in the foreground. More strongly than in China, the "government" and the organizations representing their interests have been explicitly accused of neglecting the private sector and discriminating against it.[90]

After the 8th Party Congress (1996), the deputy chairman of the Vietnamese Chamber of Industry and Commerce declared in an interview with the magazine *Dien Dan Doanh Nghiep* (Weekly Business Forum), that for the first time a representative of his organization had been allowed to take part as a delegate at a Party Congress. He stated that this indicated the growing role of the Chambers of Industry and Commerce. He had been very active there, he continued, working for increased state support of small and middle-sized enterprises (mostly private firms), and proposed that the organization he worked for should be entrusted with this duty. Happily, the number of members of the *business community* in the Central Committee had increased.[91]

---

[88] Zhongguo Gongshang Bao, 20 March 1998.

[89] *Zhongguo Gongshang Bao* 7 and 8 March 2002.

[90] Cf. e.g. *Viet Nam News* 6 August 1996 and 13 March 1997; *The Saigon Times*, 2 -8 March 1996: 25.

[91] *Viet Nam News*, 20 July 1996.

Already in advance of the conference, organizations representing their interests like the *Hanoi Union Association of Industry and Commerce* had called on the conference through petitions and the press to grant the private sector a stronger role. The general secretary of the organization went on record as saying that their goal was fundamentally to alter the attitude of Party and government towards the private sector. Prejudices against the private sector, such as that it was based on exploitation, had to be abandoned. Without the private sector, modernization would hardly be imaginable.[92]

All in all, out of the present set of factors, it has emerged that entrepreneurs primarily endeavor to achieve an expansion and safeguarding of their business rights as well as a stabilization of their commercial activities.

Precisely in the interests of reducing insecurity and the minimization of transaction costs, they are concerned to strengthen their rights and legal security. At present this determines as well their political activity. There is nothing unusual about this, because the companies form the basis of their livelihood for every entrepreneur. A Chinese survey amongst them, as to which worry plagued them most, found out that their main concern was the (continuing) existence of the company, in second place came the irksome problem of *Guanxi* relationships (*guanxi mafan*), and in third place they named corruption.[93] This shows that the existence of these endemic problems in the system are in no way viewed as part of "Chinese entrepreneurial culture", but are rather perceived as an enormous burden.

4.4. *Conclusion: Entrepreneurs as a strategic group and political change*

From the expositions above, it follows that entrepreneurs, so far as they act as members of associations representing their interests, demonstrate that they understand themselves at least partially as an interest group which co-ordinates and agrees on its actions, that is to all intents and purposes pursues shared political goals.

But the concrete actions of the entrepreneurs cannot be prognosticated because they are determined by situation. Vanhanen put forward the hypothesis that democratization took place under conditions in which power resources were so widely spread that no group was any longer in the position to hold back its competitors or to maintain its hegemony.[94]

This thesis certainly has its justification. Referring to China and Vietnam, we can extend it by stating that the entrepreneurs without a doubt strive to obtain more power resources for themselves, even if first of all they do this in the economic sphere. Since access to economic resources is partially still controlled by political elites, it is a strategically necessary maneuver to obtain increased

---

[92] *Vietnam Investment Review*, 10 – 16 June 1996: 13, 18.

[93] *Zhongguo Qiyejia* (China's Entrepreneur), 9/1999: 78.

[94] Vanhanen and Kimber 1994: 63ff.

access to political power resources. This is not a political agenda of the entrepreneur, but rather in the last analysis in their economic interests.

Viewed politically, entrepreneurs are still relatively powerless, even if their
political influence has increased significantly, above all at the local level. They
lack as well the element of will to change the system, so that they do not constitute a player actively working for democratization. But, as I showed in Part I,
the entrepreneurial strata displays the characteristics of a *potential elite*. In
economic terms, they represent not an average group but rather a leading one,
as far as income and local economic power are concerned. I attributed this
potential elite status to them, because their leading economic role is being recognized more and more, because they help to shape the norms and values of the
society, influence changes in economic, social and political structures as well as
stratification in society, and contribute to changes of the framework of the social system.

But what does political transformation actually mean? Gabriel Almond understands by it that, "a political system develops capacities which it did not
possess before." He argues, that basic changes of the political culture and structure are associated with such a transformation.[95] The strategic group approach
contributes in this sense by naming the players beyond the state, who through
their strategic actions develop such capacities.

Although the activities of the entrepreneurs still cannot be termed system-
changing strategies, nevertheless they are ones which influence politics and
structures groups so that one can certainly speak of *strategic action*. At the
same time, it appears to be appropriate to differentiate the term strategic action.
One can subdivide along the lines of, "strategies for maintaining power and/or
expanding power,"[96] whereby this can be made more precise in the sense of a
goal orientation, namely a distinction between (a) *system changing strategies,*
which aim for a fundamental alteration of structures as a precondition for the
assertion of interests; (b) *participative strategies* which intend a greater degree
of participation and possibilities for shaping circumstances and conditions; and
(c) *status quo maintaining* or *restorative strategies* which for the purposes of
particular interests oppose structural changes or wish to restore traditional relations.

Entrepreneurs in China and Vietnam pursue at present participative strategies. But strategic refers not only to actions, but rather as well to the strategic
significance for political developments of a society (such as processes of reform, conflict, transformation or transition).

One should not conclude from the characterization of the entrepreneurs as a
"strategic group" that entrepreneurial strata are in a position to initiate a democratization process by themselves. Such a development depends much rather on

---

[95] Almond 1970: 216.
[96] Korff 1992: 4ff.

the distribution of power between different social groups. So, a coalition with other social actors is necessary in any case.

The strategic element consists finally of entrepreneurs being able to involve themselves in the change process in a goal-directed manner through their associations, and being able as important players to support or hold back the transformation independently of the direction of the developments of change. Not only the size of entrepreneurial strata, but rather its ability to form coalitions as well, and above all the nature of their interests defines their political functionality. At the beginning, I pointed out that entrepreneurs as an *active political element* assume an ambivalent middle position: they will not be interested in a transformation of the political system so long as the current political setup does not deprive them of acceptance, integration and with that a certain degree of participation. A majority of them support political (not systemic) change, because corruption and restrictions through bureaucracy limit their entrepreneurial development and cause to some extent high costs.

As coalition partner for the entrepreneurs, another strategic group appears to be available, namely the Party cadres. Our survey of cadres at the Central Party School in Beijing brought to light a range of commonalities, which make a coalition appear not unrealistic:

1. *Economic orientation*

More than a quarter of the functionaries surveyed wanted most of all to switch to working for a company, almost a quarter to become themselves private entrepreneurs. In the case that they had access to a large sum of money, around a third would invest this money as capital.

2. *Dissatisfaction with life situation in material terms*

In their dissatisfaction with low income, unsatisfactory health care and with the housing situation, it became apparent that functionaries no longer count among the materially most privileged.

3. *Dissatisfaction with the situation in the country*

Corruption, the decay of social morality and public security as well as dissatisfaction with the work of the Party and governments belong to the core factors that in the long term might bring about a loss of confidence on the part of the cadres in Party and system.

4. *Increasing individualism*

Almost all functionaries (94.4%) declared that their families possessed top priority for them, and about 90% were concerned with the education of their

children as the second most important factor. Almost half declared personal
self-fulfillment to be their most important aim in life.

5. Acceptance of the market economy

Absolute majorities spoke for a market economy, support for the private sector,
and against prioritizing state sector companies. Disparities of income and income growth based on performance were widely accepted. Similarly as with
the entrepreneurs, the cadres surveyed were also for the market economy in the
sense of economic freedom of management, but against a *market society* in
which all societal relations are subordinated to the market.

6. Support for private entrepreneurial interests

More than two-third of the cadres surveyed thought that entrepreneurs should
be concerned with politics. A third favored involving them on a wide basis in
political decisions, almost half at least partially. Only a fifth rejected this. 85%
declared that private entrepreneurs should decide autonomously about their
companies, and that the state ought not to intervene there. They stated that the
private sector should not be limited. More than two-thirds (68.7%) voted for the
licensing of an independent entrepreneurial association.

However, one should not conclude that the functionaries represent a homogenous stratum that would press for changes to the political system. Neither
a majority of the functionaries nor the private entrepreneurs want a system
change. Both agree that this would necessarily lead to instability, and all social
groups and strata in China fear social instability. Here it is not only the Cultural
Revolution that has an after-effect as a negative example. The growing prosperity of a majority of the population, economic, societal and political pluralization
have also led to the costs of a change of system being envisaged as more expensive than the present one, which despite everything does move and react
relatively flexibly to fluctuations.

Consequently, at present the question of system change through shock ther-
apy or a collapse of the system is not relevant, but rather through gradual alterations with parallel acceptance of change potentials and the formation of new
system capacities, if and insofar as they are useful to some extent for economi-
cal and social development. In this respect Hirschman's statement appears to be
confirmed that a transformation of organizations and institutions is only
achievable through gradual processes of development.[97]
Our study has confirmed the impression that a large section of the younger
functionaries are thoroughly open for a gradual reconstruction of the political
system, so long as the country and its population "modernize" and no major
crises appear on the scene. Sun, Li and Shen write explicitly of a coalition for

---

[97] Hirschman 1970.

stability between political and economic elites.[98] Given the circumstances of such a coalition for stability, entrepreneurs apparently are regarded more and more as one of the strategic groups that should play a central role in this reconstruction. Precisely in this spirit, one can predict a coalition of functionaries and entrepreneurs. But how entrepreneurs concretely act will depend on the tangible situation in each case and a specific cost-benefit analysis, given that this strategic group constitutes just *one* player that only in linkages with other strategic groups can impact in a system-transforming manner.

---

[98] Sun, Li and Shen 1999: 18, 19.

REFERENCES

AFP 28 August 1997: "Up to Five Officials Killed in Farmers Unrest in Northern Vietnam"
AFP 4 September 1997: "Thai Binh Officials Accused of Corruption Probed"
Albach, Horst (1997), "Eine lebendige Theorie der Unternehmung", in: *Frankfurter Allgemeine Zeitung*, 11 November
Aldrich, Howard/Zimmer, Catherine, (1986), "Entrepreneurship through Social Networks", in: Sexton/Smilor: 3-23
Almond, Gabriel A. (1970), "Politische Systeme und politischer Wandel", in: Zapf, W.: 211-227
Amit, Raphael/Muller, Eitan, (1996), "'Push'- und 'Pull'-Unternehmertum", in: *Zeitschrift für Klein- und Mittelunternehmen*, 2, Bd. 44: 90-103
Annerstedt, Jan/Vu Cao Dam (1990), *Vietnam's Industrial Rehabilitation. The Mobilization of Technology and Science for Industrial Innovation and Economic Growth in the Period 1975-93* (unpublished manuscript)
Asiaweek, Hong Kong
Axelsson, B./Easton, G. (1992), eds., *Industrial Networks: A New View of Reality*, London (Routledge)
Bahgat, Gawdat (1993), "Privatization and Democratization in the Arab World: Is There a Connection?", in: *The Journal of Social, Political & Economic Studies*, 4: 427-444
Bai Nanfeng et al. (1993), Gaige de shehui chengshouli yanjiu (Forschung über die gesellschaftliche Belastungsfähigkeit der Reform), in: *Guanli Shijie* (Managementwelt), 5: 189-198
Baiyin tongji nianjian (Baiyin Statistical Yearbook) (1995), Baiyin (Baiyin shi tongjiju)
Barber, Benjamin R. (1997), "Zivile Gesellschaft. Ansätze für die Wiederbelebung einer starken Demokratie", in: *Lettre*, Heft 39: 42-45
Barmè, Geremie R. (1999), *Time's Arrows: Imaginative Pasts and Nostalgic Futures*. Paper presented at the International Conference "Was the Chinese Revolution really necessary? Interpreting 50 years of the People's Republic of China", Hamburg, September 23-25
Barth, Frederik (1967), "On the Study of Social Change", in: *American Anthropologist*, 6: 661-669
Becker, Bert/Rüland, Jürgen/Werz, Nikolaus (1999), *Mythos Mittelschichten. Zur Wiederkehr eines Paradigmas der Demokratieforschung*, Bonn (Bouvier)
Bell, Daniel A./Brown, David/Jayasuriya, Kanishka/Jones, David M. (1995), eds., *Towards Illiberal Democracy in Pacific Asia*, Houndmills, Basingstoke, London (Palgrave/Macmillan)
Beresford, Melanie (1989), *National Unification and Economic Development in Vietnam*, New York (Palgrave)
Berger, Brigitte (1991a), *The Culture of Entrepreneurship*, San Francisco, ICS Press
Berger, Brigitte (1991b), "The Culture of Modern Entrepreneurship", in: Berger, B. (1991a): 13-32
Berger, Peter L. (1993), "The Uncertain Triumph of Democratic Capitalism", in: *Diamond, Larry/Plattner, Marc F.*, eds., *Capitalism, Socialism, and Democracy Revisited*, Baltimore, London (John's Hopkins University Press): 1-10
Berner, Erhard (1991), *Strategische Cliquen und Proto-Klassen*, Working Paper No.158 des Forschungsschwerpunkts Entwicklungssoziologie an der Universität Bielefeld, Bielefeld (University of Bielefeld)
Berner, Erhard (2001), "Kollektive Strategien, Herrschaft und Widerstand: Zur Relevanz einer Theorie Strategischer Gruppen in der Entwicklungssoziologie", in: Schrader, Heiko/Kaiser, Markus, Korff, Rüdiger, eds., *Markt, Kultur und Gesellschaft: Zur Aktualität von 25 Jahren Entwicklungsforschung*, Hamburg (LIT): 113-132
Birley, Sue (1985), "The Role of Networks in the Entrepreneurial Process", in: *Journal of Business Venturing*, 1: 107-117
Birley, Sue (1996), "Start-up", in: Burns, Paul/Dewhurst, Jim, eds., *Small Business and Entrepreneurship*, Houndmills, Basingstoke, London (Palgrave/Macmillan): 20-39
Birley, Sue/MacMillan, Ian C. (1995), eds., *International Entrepreneurship*, London, New York (Thompson Business Press)

Birley, Sue/MacMillan, Ian C. (1997), eds., *Entrepreneurship in a Global Context*, London, New York (Routledge)

Blecher, Marc/Shue, Vivienne (2001), "Into Leather: State-led Development and the Private sector in Xinji", in: *The China Quarterly*, June: 368-393

Boissevain, Jeremy (1997), "Small European Entrepreneurs", in: Rutten, M./Upadhya, C.: 301-323

Boudre-Gröger, Joachim (1993), "Vietnam - noch ein asiatischer Tiger?", in: *Vierteljahresberichte der Friedrich Ebert-Stiftung*, 134: 403-411

Bourdieu, Pierre (1987), *Die feinen Unterschiede. Kritik der gesellschaftlichen Urteilskraft*, Frankfurt/M. (Suhrkamp)

Bourdieu, Pierre (1992), *Rede und Antwort*, Frankfurt/M. (Suhrkamp)

Bourdieu, Pierre (1993), *Soziologische Fragen*, Frankfurt/M. (Suhrkamp)

Bourdieu, Pierre (1997), *Der Tote packt den Lebenden*, Hamburg (VSA Verlag)

Bourdieu, Pierre (1998), *Praktische Vernunft. Zur Theorie des Handelns*, Frankfurt/M. (Suhrkamp)

Bowen II, J. Ray/Rose, David C. (1998), "On the Absence of Privately Owned, Publicly Traded Corporations in China: The Kirby Puzzle", in: *The Journal of Asian Studies*, 2: 442-452

Broehl, Wayne G. (1978), *The Village Entrepreneur. Change Agents in India's Rural Development*, Cambridge/Mass., London (Harvard University Press)

Brown, David/Jones, David M. (1995), "Democratization and the Myth of the Liberalizing Middle Classes", in: Bell/Brown/Jayasuriya/Jones: 78-106

Brusatti, Alois (1979), "Der Individualismus als Geistige Grundlage des Europäischen Unternehmers", in: *Zeitschrift für Unternehmensgeschichte*, 3: 3-11

Bruun, Ole (1995), "Political Hierarchy and Private Entrepreneurship in a Chinese Neighborhood", in: Walder, Andrew G., ed., *The Waning of the Communist State. Economic Origin of Political Decline in China and Hungary*, Berkeley, Los Angeles, London (University of California Press): 184-212

Bun, Chan Kwok/Ngoh, Claire Chiang See (1994), *Stepping Out. The Making of Chinese Entrepreneurs*, New York, London et al. (Pearson Education I.D.)

Bundesstelle für Außenhandelsinformation (o. J.), *Vietnam. Aktuelle Wirtschaftsübersicht*, Köln, Berlin [1993]

Bundesstelle für Außenhandelsinformationen BfAI (1995), *Vietnamesischer Privatsektor weitet sich aus*, 15 September

Bürklin, Wilhelm P. (1993), *Die vier Kleinen Tiger, die pazifische Herausforderung. Hongkong, Singapur, Südkorea, Taiwan*, München (Langen-Müller)

Burns, Paul/Dewhurst, Jim (1996), eds., *Small Business and Entrepreneurship*, Houndmills, Basingstoke, London (Palgrave/Macmillan)

Business Club (1993), ed., *Various Forms of Business. Experiences and Activities*, Hanoi

Carley, Kathleen M. (1999), "On the Evolution of Social and Organizational Networks", in: Andrews, Steven B./Knoke, David, eds., *Networks in and Around Organizations. Research in the Sociology of Organizations*, vol. 16, Stamford, Connecticut: 3-30

Carroll, John J. (1965), *The Filipino Manufacturing Entrepreneur. Agent and Product of Change*, Ithaca (Cornell University Press)

Carsrud, Alan L./Olm, Kenneth W./Eddy, George G. (1986), "Entrepreneurship. Research in Quest of a Paradigm", in: Sexton/Smiler: 367-378

Casson, Markl (1982), *The Entrepreneur*, Oxford (Robertson)

Chang, K.C. (1977), ed., *Food in Chinese Culture. Anthropological and Historical Perspectives*, New Haven (Yale University Press)

Chen Dongqi/Qin Hai (1997), "Zhongguo dalu jingji zhidu zhi bianqian" (Change of the Economic System in Mainland China), in: *Zhongguo Shehui Kexueyuan Yanjiusheng Xueyuan Bao* (Journal of the Post-doctoral Institute of the Chinese Academy of Social Sciences), 4: 24-40

Chen Jianpo (1995), "Xiangzheng qiye de chanqun jiegou ji qi dui ziyuan peizhi xiaoliu de yingxiang" (Impact of rural enterprise ownership structure on the efficiency of resource distribution), in: *Jingji Yanjiu* (Economic Studies) 9: 24-32

Chen Jinluo/Wu Chongze/Yang Henggen/Duoji Cairang (1998), eds., *Shetuan guanli gongzuo* (Administration of social associations), Beijing (Zhongguo shehui chubanshe)

Chen Qingtai (1995), ed., *Shanghui fazhan yu zhidu guifan* (Development of Chambers of Commerce and Organizational Regulations), Beijing (Zhongguo jingji chubanshe)

Chen Xiwen (1993), "Jiegou biange yu buju tiaozheng: xiangzhen qiye fazhan de xin jieduan" (Structural transformation and locational regulation: new development phase of rural enterprises); in: *Nongye Jingji Wenti* (Problems of Agriculture), 1: 31-38

Cheng Guoxia (1998), "Guanyu wo guo zhongchan jieceng de sikao" (Considerations on the middle strata of our country), in: *Tongji Yu Juece* (Statistics and Decision), 9: 23/24

Cheng Yan/Sun Yaoyuan (1996), "Lun Zhongguo qiyejia de shuangzhongxing" (On the Ambiguity of Chinese entrepreneurs), in: *Caijing Wenti Yanjiu* (Studies on problems of financial and economic science), 12: 42-44

Christiansen, Flemming (1993), "Zhang Jian's Bianfa Pingyi - A Place for Gradual Reform in Late Imperial and Early Republican China?", in: Radtke, Kurt W./Saich, Tony, eds., *China's Modernisation. Westernisation and Acculturation*, Stuttgart (Franz Steiner): 40-57

Cima, Ronald J. (1989), "Vietnam's Economic Reform. Approaching the 1990s", in: *Asian Survey*, 8: 786-799

Civil Code (1996), *The Civil Code of the Socialist Republic of Vietnam*, Hanoi (The Gioi Publishers)

Codagnone, Cristiano (1995), "New Entrepreneurs: Continuity or Change in Russian Economy and Society?", in: Bruno Gracelli, ed., *Social Change and Modernization*, Berlin, New York (Walter de Gruyter): 63-82

Cohen, Margot (2000), "A Glimmer of Hope", in: *Far Eastern Economic Review*, 8 June: 76

Cohen, Margot (2002), "New Entrepreneurs", in: *Far Eastern Economic Review*, 9 May: 44

Cohen, Michael/March, James G./Olsen, Johan P. (1972*), "A Garbage Can Model of Organizational Choice"*, in: *Administrative Science Quarterly*, 1: 1-26

Cole, Arthur H. (1959), *Business Enterprise in its Social Setting*, Cambridge/Mass. (Replica Books)

Coleman, William D. (1988), *Business and Politics. A Study of Collective Action*, Kingston and Montreal (McGill- Queen's University Press)

Communist Party of Vietnam (1996), ed., *VIIIth National Congress. Documents*, Hanoi (The Gioi Publishers)

Cowling, Keith (1995), "Reflections on the Privatisation Issue", in: Chang, Ha-Joon/Nolan, Peter, eds., *The Transformation of the Communist Economies*, Houndmills, Basingstoke (St. Martin's Press/Macmillan): 162-176

Croissant, Aurel/Faust Jörg (1999), "Mittelschichten und Systemwechsel in Mexiko und Südkorea", in: Becker, Bert/Rüland, Jürgen/Werz, Nikolaus: 120-159

Cui, Zhiyuan (1997), "Privatization and the Consolidation of Democratic Regimes: An Analysis and an Alternative", in: *Journal of International Affairs*, No.2: 675-692

Dahl, Robert A. (1992), "Why Free Markets are not Enough", in: *Journal of Democracy*, 3: 82-89

Dahrendorf, Ralf (1959), *Class and Class Conflict in Industrial Society*, Stanford (Stanford University Press)

Dai Bingyuan/Wan Anpei (1998), "Zhongguo zhongchan jieceng de xianzhuang tedian ji fazhan taishi jianxi" (Short analysis of the current situation and development of China's middle stratum), in: *Caizheng Yanjiu* (Financial Studies), 9: 59-61

Dai Jianzhong (1996), "Siying qiye gugong ji laozi guanxi diaocha baogao" (Report on the relationship between employees and employers in private enterprises), in: *Shehuixue Yanjiu* (Sociological Studies), 6: 25-34

Dang Duc Dam (1997), *Vietnam's Macro Economy and Types of Enterprises. The Current Position and Future Prospects*, Hanoi (The Gioi Publishers)

Dang Phong/Le Van Cuong (1999), "Economic Transition in Vietnam: Origins and Roadmap", in: *Vietnamese Studies*, 3: 87-101

Dao Cong Tien (1999), "Trao doi mot so van de lien quan den nhan thuc ve tang lop doanh nghiep (Some problems regarding the perceiption of an entrepreneurial stratum), in: *Tap chi Xa hoi hoc* (Sociological Review), 1: 17-22

Diamond, Larry (1992), ed., *The Democratic Revolution. Struggles for Freedom and Pluralism in the Developing World*, New York (Freedom House)

Diehl, M. (1993), *Systemtransformation in Vietnam. Liberalisierungserfolge - Stabilisierungsprobleme*, Kiel (Institut für Weltwirtschaft)

Dietz, Raimund (1993), "Eigentum und Privatisierung aus systemtheoretischer Sicht. Ein Beitrag zur Theorie der Transformation", Sonderdruck, Wien (WIIW)

Dinh Qu (1993), "Vietnam's Policy Reforms and Its Future", in: *Journal of Contemporary Asia*, 4: 532-553

Do Duc Dinh (1993), "Vietnam's Economic Renovation toward the Market Mechanism", in: *Journal of Southeast Asian Business*, 3: 17-33

Do Minh Cuong (1996*), Einige Probleme der Wirtschaft des Volkes oder der 'unstrukturierte Sektor' in Vietnam*, Paper delivered at the DED Regional Conference Asia, Hanoi 25-28 October

Dodsworth, John R./Spitäller, E./Braulke, Michael et al. (1996), *Vietnam. Transition to a Market Economy*, Washington, D.C. (IMF)

Dong Fureng (1998), "Qiyejia yu shichang jingji" (Entrepreneurs and Market Economy), in: *Zhongguo qiyejia diaocha xitong* 1998a: 229-233

Dong Wonmo (1991), "The Democratization of South Korea: What Role Does the Middle Class Play?", in: *Korean Observer*, 2: 257-282

Dorraj, Manochehr (1994), "Privatization, Democratization and Development in the Third World. Lessons of a Turbulent Decade", in: *Journal of Developing Societies*, vol. X: 173-185.

dpa 25 July 1997: "Worst Unrest in Years Spreads to Other Northern Vietnam Provinces"

Dreitzel, Hans P. (1962), *Elitebegriff und Sozialstruktur. Eine soziologische Begriffsanalyse*, Stuttgart (Enke)

Duan Yiping (1999), *Gaoji hui. Zhongguo chengshi zhongchan jieceng xiezhen* (Superior grey. The truth about China's urban middle stratum), Beijing (Zhongguo qingnian chubanshe)

Duc Luong (1997), "On Quality Improvement of Grassroots Party Organizations", in: *Tap Chi Cong San*, April 19-21 (FBIS)

Duong Ngoc (2002), "Vietnamese Private Economy. Results and Limitations" in: *Vietnam Economic Review*, 5: 23-25.

"Economic Reform in Vietnam - Achievements and Prospects" (1994), ed. by Central Institute for Economic Management and Swedish International Development Authority, Hanoi (policy paper)

Economic Sectors in Vietnam (1992), *Situation, Tendency and Solutions*, Hanoi (The Gioi Publishers)

Economist Intelligence Unit (1993a), *Country Report Vietnam 1993*, 1st, 2nd, 3rd quarter (3 volumes), London

Economist Intelligence Unit (1993b), *Country Profile Vietnam 1993/94*, London

Elias, Norbert (1991), *Die Gesellschaft der Individuen*, Frankfurt/M. (Suhrkamp)

Endruweit, Günter (1986), *Elite und Entwicklung*, Frankfurt/M., New York (Europäische Hochschulschriftenreihe 22)

Eucken, Walter (1968), *Grundsätze der Wirtschaftspolitik*, Tübingen, Zürich (Mohr/Siebeck)

Evers, Hans-Dieter (1974), *The Role of Professionals in Social and Political Change*. Department of Sociology, University of Singapore, Singapore

Evers, Hans-Dieter (1997), "Macht und Einfluss in der Entwicklungspolitik. Neue Ansätze zur Theorie Strategischer Gruppen", in: *Entwicklung und Zusammenarbeit*, 1: 15-17

Evers, Hans-Dieter (1999), *Globale Macht: Zur Theorie strategischer Gruppen*. Working Paper No 322 des Forschungsschwerpunkts Entwicklungssoziologie an der Universität Bielefeld, Bielefeld

Evers, Hans-Dieter/Gerke, Solvay (1999*), Globale Märkte und symbolischer Konsum: Visionen von Modernität in Südostasien*, Working Paper No. 314, Sociology of Development Research Centre, Bielefeld (University of Bielefeld)

Evers, Hans-Dieter/Schiel, Tilman (1988) *Strategische Gruppen. Vergleichende Studien zu Staat, Bürokratie und Klassenbildung in der Dritten Welt*, Berlin (Dietrich Reimer)

Fan Gang (1993), "Shuanggui guodu yu shuanggui tiaokong" (Double track transition and double track control), in: *Jingji Yanjiu*, 11: 3-9

Fang, Bay (1998), "New Class Struggle, Lawsuits Serve Interests of the Masses - and Beijing", in: *Far Eastern Economic Review*, 19 March: 24-25

Far Eastern Economic Review, Hong Kong

Fei, Xiaotong *(1992), From the Soil: The Foundations of Chinese Society,* Berkeley et al. (University of California Press)

Feng Tongqing (1993), "1992-1993 nian Zhongguo zhigong zhuangkuang de fenxi yu yuce" (Analysis and Prospects of the situation of labor-force 1992-1993), in: *Shehuixue Yanjiu,* 3: 14-24

Fforde, Adam (1991), "The Successful Commercialization of a Neo-Stalinist Economic System. Vietnam 1979-1989", in: Forbes, Dean K. et al., eds., *Doi Moi. Vietnam's Renovation Policy and Performance,* Canberra (The Australian National University)

Fforde, Adam (1993), "The Political Economy of Reform in Vietnam. Some Reflections"; in: Ljunggren, B., ed.: 293-326

Fforde, Adam (1995), *Vietnam: Economic Commentary and Analysis: A Bi-Annual Appraisal of the Vietnamese Economy,* Canberra (Aduki)

Fforde, Adam (1997), ed., *Doi Moi. Ten Years after the 1986 Party Congress,* Canberra (The Australian National University)

Fforde, Adam/de Vylder, Stefan de (1996a), "Vietnam", in: *From Centrally Planned to Market Economies: The Asian Approach,* vol. 3, Lao PDR, Myanmar and Vietnam, Hongkong, Oxford, New York (Oxford University Press)

Fforde, Adam/Vylder, Stefan de (1996b), *From Plan to Market. The Economic Transition in Vietnam,* Boulder (Westview Press)

Fiedler, Katrin (2000), Wirtschaftsethik in China am Fallbeispiel von Shanghaier Protestanten, Hamburg (Institut für Asienkunde)

Frances, Jennifer/Levacic, Rosalind/Mitchell, Jeremy/Thompson, Grahame (1991), "Introduction", in: Thompson/Frances/Levacic/Mitchell: 1-19

Friedrich-Ebert-Stiftung (1998), ed., *Informeller Sektor: internationale Erfahrungen und Praxis in Vietnam im Transformationsprozess,* Hanoi

Fritsche, Klaus (1991), "Die Herrschaft der Partei bleibt unangetastet. Zu den Grenzen vietnamesischer Reformpolitik", in: *Südostasien Informationen,* 4: 4/5

Fröhlich, Erwin/Pichler, J. Hanns (1988), *Werte und Typen mittelständischer Unternehmer,* Berlin (Dunker und Humblot)

Fundamental Laws and Regulations of Vietnam (1993), Hanoi (The Gioi Publishers)

Gabler (1984) *Wirtschaftslexikon,* 11. Auflage, Wiesbaden (Th. Gabler Verlag)

Galaskiewicz, Joseph/Zaheer, Akbar (1999), "Networks of Competitive Advantage", in: Andrews, Steven B./Knoke, David, eds., *Networks in and Around Organizations. Research in the Sociology of Organizations,* vol. 16, Stamford, Connecticut (JAI Press): 237-262

Gansu nianjian (Jahrbuch Gansus) (1996), Beijing (Zhongguo tongji chubanshe)

Gao Shangquan/Chi Fulin (1996), eds., *The Development of China's Nongovernmentally and Privately Operated Economy,* Beijing (Foreign Languages Press)

Gates, Hill (1996), *China's Motor. A Thousand Years of Petty Capitalism,* Ithaca, London (Cornell University Press)

General Statistical Office (1996a), *Kinh Te - Xa Hoi Viet Nam, 10 Nam Doi Moi (1986-1995)* (Impetus and Present Situation of Vietnam's Society and Economy after ten Years of Doi Moi), Hanoi Statistical Publishers)

General Statistical Office (1996b), *Nien Giam Thong Ke 1996* (Statistisches Jahrbuch 1996)*,* Hanoi (Statistical Publishers)

Gerke, Solvay (1995), *Symbolic Consumption and the Indonesian Middle Class,* Working Paper No. 233, Sociology of Development Research Centre, Bielefeld (University of Bielefeld)

Gerschenkron, Alexander (1968), *Continuity in History and Other Essays,* Cambridge/Mass. (Belkamp Press)

Geti gongshanghu, siying qiye shouru zhuangkuang diaocha (1996) (Investigation on the Income situation of individual and private enterprises), internal report published by the Chinese Bureau for the Administration of Industry and Commerce, Beijing

Geti siying jingji fazhan zhuangkuang (1995) (Economic development situation of the individual and private economy, ed. by Guojia gongshang guanliju yanjiuzu, Beijing (internal report)

Giddens, Anthony (1979), *Die Klassenstruktur fortgeschrittener Gesellschaften,* Frankfurt/M. (Suhrkamp)

Glade, William P. (1967), "Approaches to a Theory of Entrepreneurial Formation", in: *Explorations in Entrepreneurial History*, 4, ser. 2: 245-259

Glaeßner, Gert-Joachim (1992), "Vergleichende Analyse kommunistischer Systeme"; in: Berg-Schlosser, Dirk/Müller-Rommel, Ferdinand, eds., *Vergleichende Politikwissenschaft. Ein einführendes Studienhandbuch*, Opladen (Westdeutscher Verlag): 213-239

Glassman, Ronald M. (1997), *The New Middle Class and Democracy in Global Perspective*, Houndmills, London, Basingstoke (St. Martin's Press)

Gongren Ribao (Worker's Daily), Beijing

Gongshang xingzheng guanli tongji huibian (1989-01) (Collection of Statistics of the Administration of Industry and Commerce), Beijing (Guojia gongshang xingzheng guanliju bangongshi) (various years)

Gonshanglian (1996), ed., *Guanyu gongshanglian fazhan huiyuan jianli zuzhi qingkuang de tongbao* (Report on the development of membership and organization of the Association of Industry and Commerce), 6

Goodman, David (1999), "The New Middle Class", in: Goldman, Merle/MacFarquhar, Roderick, eds., *The Paradox of China's Post-Mao Reforms*, Cambridge/Mass. (Harvard University Press): 241-261

Grabher, Gernot (1993), ed., *The Embedded Firm. On the Socioeconomics of Industrial Networks*, London, New York (Routledge)

Grabher, Gernot/Stark, David (1997), eds., *Restructuring Networks in Post-Socialism*, Oxford et al. (Oxford University Press)

Granovetter, Mark S. (1973), "The Strength of Weak Ties", in: *American Journal of Sociology*, 68 (May, 13): 1360-1380

Greenfield, Sidney M./Strickon, Arnold (1981), "A New Paradigm for the Study of Entrepreneurship and Social Change", in: *Economic Development and Cultural Change*, 3 (2): 467-499

Großheim, Martin (1997), *North Vietnamesische Dorfgemeinschaften. Kontinuität und Wandel*, Hamburg (Mitteilungen des Instituts für Asienkunde)

Groys, Boris (1999), *Über das Neue. Versuch einer Kulturökonomie*, Frankfurt/M. (Fischer)

Güldner, Matthias (1992), "Was ist kapitalistischer Sozialismus?", in: *Blätter des IZ3W* (Third World Information Centre), Sept.-Okt., Nr. 184: 3-6

Guo Zhenying (1993), "Guanyu wo guo suoyouzhi jiegou de jige wenti" (Some problems of Chinese ownership structure), in: *Jingji Yanjiu*, 5: 3-9

Guthrie, Douglas (1998), "The Declining Significance of Guanxi in China's Economic Transition", in: *The China Quarterly*, June: 254-282

Ha Huy Thanh/Bui Tat Thang (1999), "Socio-Economic Developments in Industrialization - Modernization Process and Some Problems Arising for Economic Theoretical Work", in: *Vietnam Social Sciences*, 3: 16-23

Haferkamp, Hans/Smelser, Neil J. (1992), eds., *Social Change and Modernity*, Berkeley, Los Angeles, Oxford (The University of California Press)

Hagen, Everett E. (1970), "Traditionalismus, Statusverlust, Innovation", in: Zapf, W.: 351-361

Hamilton, Gary G. (1997), "Organization and Market Processes in Taiwan's Capitalist Economy", in: Orru, M./Biggart, N.W./Hamilton G.G.: 237-293

Hamilton, Gary G. (1998), "Culture and Organization in Taiwan's Market Economy", in: Hefner, Robert W.: 41-77

Hangzhou tongji nianjian (Hangzhou statistical yearbook) (1995), Beijing (Zhongguo tongji chubanshe)

Hao Yunhong (2000), "Qiyejia jili: zhidu jili xingshi jili yu jili xingshi" (The motivation of enterprises: Systemic motivation, formal motivation and forms of motivation), in : *Jingjixuejia* (Economist), 2: 25-29

Havel, Vaclav (1990), *Versuch, in der Wahrheit zu leben*, Reinbek (rororo)

Hayami, Yujiro/Kawagoe, Toshihiko (1993), *The Agrarian Origins of Commerce and Industry*, New York, Basingstoke (MacMillan Press/St. Martin's Press)

He Yang (1999), ed., *Zhongguo siying gongsi yunchouxue* (Research on Chinese private companies), 2 vols., Lanzhou (Lanzhou daxue chubanshe)

He Yiting (2001), ed., *Xuexi Jiang Zemin 'qi yi' jianghua fudao wenda* (Supporting material for the study of Jiang Zemin's 'July 1st speech), Beijing (Dangjian duwu chubanshe/Yanjiu chubanshe)

He Zhenguo (1997), ed., *Shehuizhuyi yu siying jingji* (Socialism and private economy), Changsha (Hunan renmin chubanshe)

Hebel, Jutta/Schucher, Günter (1993), "Sozialer Wandel in der Volksrepublik China", in: *Aus Politik und Zeitgeschichte*, 51: 27-36

Hebel, Jutta/Schucher, Günter (1999), eds., Der chinesische Arbeitsmarkt. Strukturen, Probleme, Perspektiven, Hamburg (Mitteilungen des Instituts für Asienkunde)

Heberer, Thomas (1989), *Die Rolle des Individualsektors für Arbeitsmarkt und Stadtwirtschaft in der Volksrepublik China*, Bremen (Bremer Beiträge zur Geographie und Raumplanung 18)

Heberer, Thomas (1991), *Korruption in China. Analyse eines Politischen, Ökonomischen und Sozialen Problems*, Opladen (Westdeutscher Verlag)

Heberer, Thomas (1994), ed., *Yaogun Yinyue: Jugend-, Subkultur und Rockmusik in China. Politische und gesellschaftliche Hintergründe eines neuen Phänomens*, Hamburg, Münster (LIT)

Heberer, Thomas (1996), "Die Rolle von Interessenvereinigungen in autoritären Systemen: Das Beispiel Volksrepublik China", in: *Politische Vierteljahresschrift*, Heft 2: 277-297

Heberer, Thomas (1997a), "Wandlungsprozesse, Partizipation und Geschlechterverhältnis in Ostasien", in: Heberer, Thomas/Vogel, Kerstin K., eds., *Frauen-Los!? Politische Partizipation von Frauen in Ostasien*, Hamburg (LIT): 40-77

Heberer, Thomas (1997b), "Das 'kommunistische' Musterdorf Nanjie in der Provinz Henan. Eine sozio-religiöse Interpretation", in: *Internationales Asienforum*, 4: 287-318

Heberer, Thomas (1998), "Nordkorea zwischen Skylla und Charybdis: Beharrungsversuche und wachsender Druck von unten", in: Köllner, Patrick, ed., *Korea 1998. Politik, Wirtschaft, Gesellschaft*, Hamburg (Institut für Asienkunde): 281-312

Heberer, Thomas (1999a), *Erwerbstätigkeit im Privatsektor: Self-Employment, Unternehmertum und Vergessene Gruppen*, in: Hebel, J./Schucher, G.: 151-176

Heberer, Thomas (1999b), *Entrepreneurs as Social Actors. Privatization and Social Change in China and Vietnam.* Duisburg Working Papers on East Asian Studies, 21, Duisburg

Heberer, Thomas (2001a), "Der Funktionsmythos vom Neuen Unternehmer. Unternehmerbiographien zwischen sozialem Mythos und Individualität", in: Roetz, Heiner/Schilling, Ines-Susanne/Neder, Christine, eds., *China and her Biographical Dimensions. Commemorative Essays for Helmut Martin*, Wiesbaden (Harrassowitz): 535-552

Heberer, Thomas (2001b), *Unternehmer als strategische Gruppen: Zur sozialen und politischen Funktion von Unternehmern in China und Vietnam*, Hamburg (Institut für Asienkunde)

Heberer, Thomas (2002), *The role of private entrepreneurship for social and political change in the People's Republic of China and Vietnam*, in: Menkhoff/Gerke:100-128

Heberer, Thomas (2003), *Ethnic Entrepreneurs between Market Behavior, Social Morality and Ethnic Obligations. The Impact of Ethnic Entrepreneurship on Social Change and Ethnicity: A Case Study Among the Yi in Liangshan Autonomous Prefecture in China* (unpublished manuscript)

Heberer, Thomas/Jakobi, Sabine (2002), *Henan as a model: from hegemonism to fragmentism*, in: John Fitzgerald, ed., Rethinking China's Provinces, London, New York (Routledge): 89-124

Heberer, Thomas/Kohl, Arno (1999), "Privatisierungsprozesse in Vietnam und ihre soziopolitischen Konsequenzen", in: Vu, Duy Tu/Will, Gerhard, eds., *Vietnams neue Position in Südostasien*, Hamburg (Institut für Asienkunde): 157-204

Heberer, Thomas/Kohl, Arno/Tuong Lai/Nguyen Duc Vinh (1999), *Aspects of Private Sector Development in Vietnam.* Duisburg Working Papers on East Asian Studies, 24, Duisburg

Heberer, Thomas/Taubmann, Wolfgang (1998), *Chinas Ländliche Gesellschaft im Umbruch. Urbanisierung und sozio-ökonomischer Wandel auf dem Lande*, Opladen (Westdeutscher Verlag)

Hefner, Robert W. (1998), ed., *Market Cultures. Society and Morality in the New Asian Capitalisms*, Boulder, Oxford (Allen&Unwin)

Heilmann, Sebastian (2000), *Die Politik der Wirtschaftsreformen in China und Rußland*, Hamburg (Mitteilungen des Inst. für Asienkunde)

Heilmann, Sebastian/Hellwege, Christiane/Hsü, Urban (1996), "Verbände in der VR China: Eine Bestandsaufnahme", in: *China aktuell*, November: 1064-1070.

Heinemann, Klaus (1987a), *Soziologie Wirtschaftlichen Handelns. Kölner Zeitschrift für Soziologie und Sozialpsychologie*, Sonderheft 28

Heinemann, Klaus (1987b), "Soziologie des Geldes", in: ders. (1987a): 322-338

Heinen, Edmund (1987), *Unternehmenskultur*, München, Wien (Oldenbourg-Verlag)

Heinz, Wolfgang S. (1999), "Mittelschichten: ein zentraler Akteur im Demokratisierungsprozeß?", in: Becker, Bert/Rüland, Jürgen/Werz, Nikolaus: 266-271

Hemlin, Maud/Ramamurthy, Bhargavi/Ronnas, Per (1998), *The Anatomy and Dynamics of Small Scale Private Manufacturing in Vietnam*, Working Paper No. 236, Stockholm School of Economics, Stockholm

Henan tongji nianjian (Statistisches Jahrbuch Henans) (1996), Beijing (Zhongguo tongji chubanshe)

Henderson, Jeffrey (1993), "The Role of the State in the Economic Transformation of East Asia", in: Dixon, Chris/Drakakis-Smith, David, eds., *Economic and Social Development in Pacific Asia*, London, New York (Routledge): 85-114

Herno, Rolf (1998), *State-Private Business Interaction in Vietnam: State Management of Network Capitalism*. Paper presented to the 50th Annual Meeting of the Association of Asian Studies, Washington, D.C., March 26-29, 1998

Herrmann-Pillath, Carsten (1993), "Kulturell geprägte Wirtschaftsdynamik und politischer Wandel in China", in: *Aus Politik und Zeitgeschichte*, 51: 3-13

Herrmann-Pillath, Carsten (1995), *Wirtschaftsintegration in China. Ökonomische, politische und gesellschaftliche Perspektiven der Beziehungen zwischen Taiwan und der Volksrepublik China. Eine empirische Untersuchung*, Bonn (Friedrich-Ebert Stiftung)

Heuser, Robert (1999*), Einführung in die chinesische Rechtskultur*, Hamburg (Institut für Asienkunde)

Hiebert, Murray (1993), *Vietnam Notebook*, Hongkong (Review Publ. Co.)

Hirata, Mitsuko/Okumura, Akihiro (1995), "Networking and Entrepreneurship in Japan", in: Birley/MacMillan: 109-123

Hirschman, Albert O. (1967), *Die Strategie der wirtschaftlichen Entwicklung*, Stuttgart (Fischer)

Hirschman, Albert O. (1970), *Exit, Voice, and Loyalty. Responses to Decline in Firms, Organizations, and States*, Cambridge/Mass. (Harvard University Press)

Hirschman, Albert O. (1982), *Shifting Involvements. Private Interests and Public Action*, Oxford (Robertson)

Hoang Kim Giao (1993), ed., *Kinh te ngoai quoc doanh va chan dung mot so nha doanh nghiep Viet Nam*, Hanoi (The Gioi Publishers)

Hoang Pham (1996), "Smuggling Continues Unabated"; in: *Vietnam Courier* 7-13 January: 9

Hoang Phuoc Hiep/Bergling, Per/Nguyen Minh Man/Boström, Viola et al., *An Introduction to the Vietnamese Legal System*, (policy paper)

Holthus, Manfred/Shams, Rasul (1987), "Anpassungspolitik und Interessengruppen in Entwicklungsländern", in: *Hamburger Jahrbuch für Wirtschafts- und Gesellschaftspolitik*, 32: 275-289

Horstmann, Alexander (1997), *Mittelschichten in Südostasien: Gedankliche Konstruktion oder Empirische Wirklichkeit*, Working Paper No. 285, Sociology of Development Research Centre, Bielefeld (University of Bielefeld)

Hoselitz, Bert F. (1963), "Entrepreneurship and Traditional Elites", in: *Explorations in Entrepreneurial History*, 1: 36-49

Hoselitz, Bert F. (1969), *Wirtschaftliches Wachstum und Sozialer Wandel*, Berlin (Duncker&Humblot)

Hsiao, Hsin-Huang M./Koo, Hagen (1997), "The Middle Classes and Democratization," in: Diamond, Larry/Plattner, Marc F./Chi, Yun-han/Tien, Hung-mao, eds., *Consolidating the Third Wave Democracies. Themes and Perspectives*, Baltimore, London (The John Hopkins University Press): 312-333

Hsiao, Hsin-Huang Michael (1993), ed., *Discovery of the Middle Classes in East Asia*, Taipei (Inst. of Ethnology, Academia Sinica)

Hu Deqiao (1994), "Suoyouquan zhidu gaige de tupoxing jinzhan" (Dthe decisive development of ownership reform), in: *Gaige* (Reform), 4

Hu Tui et al. (1992), *Zhongguo xian jieduan siying jingji wenti yanjiu* (Studies on current issues of China's private economy), Hangzhou (Zhejiang renmin chubanshe)

Hu Yuemin/Zhu Ya (1996), "Siying jingji de fazhan yu Zhongguo shehui jiegou bianqian" (Development of private economy and China's change of social structure), in: *Changbai Luncong* (Changbai Analyses), 6: 38-40

Huang Rutong (1994), "Siying jingji lilun zuotanhui zongshu" (Overview on a conference on the theory of private economy), in: *Jingjixue Dongtai* (Economic Trends), 5: 26-27

Huang Weiding (1997), *Zhongguo de yinxing jingji* (China's Shadow Economy), Beijing (Zhongguo shangye chubanshe)

Huntington, Samuel P. (1968), *Political Order in Changing Societies*, New Haven, London (Yale University Press)

Huntington, Samuel P./Nelson, Joan M. (1976), *No Easy Choice. Political Participation in Developing Countries*, Cambridge/Mass., London (Harvard University Press)

Huy, Nguyen Van/Nghia, Tran Van (1996), "Government Policies and State-Owned Enterprise Reform", in: Yuen/Freeman/Huynh: 38-62

Hy Van Luong (1998), "Engendered Entrepreneurship. Ideologies and Political-Economic Transformation in a Northern Vietnamese Center of Ceramics Production", in: Hefner, R.W.: 290-314

Hy Van Luong/Unger, Jonathan (1998), "Wealth, Power, and Poverty in the Transition to Market Economies: The Process of Socio-Economic Differentiation in Rural China and Northern Vietnam", in: *The China Journal*, July: 61-93

Ivory, Paul (1994), "Social Origins of Entrepreneurship in Early Reform China", in: Schak, David: 39-59

Jahn, Olaf (1996), "Die Macht in Hanoi bleibt in der Hand der alten Männer", in: *Die Welt*, 2 July

Jahns, Christopher (1999), *Integriertes strategisches Management. Neue Perspektiven zur Theorie und Praxis des strategischen Managements*, Sternenfels (Verlag Wiss.&Praxis)

Jamann, Wolfgang/Menkhoff, Thomas (1988), *"Make big profits with a small capital": Die Rolle der Privatwirtschaft und des "informellen Sektors" für die urbane Entwicklung der VR China*, München (Minerva Publications)

Jayasuriya, Kanishka (1995), "The Political Economy of Democratization", in: Bell/Brown/Jayasuriya/Jones: 107-133

Jayasuriya, Kanishka (1996), "The Rule of Law and Capitalism in East Asia", in: *The Pacific Review*, 3: 367-388

Jayasuriya, Kanishka (1999), ed., *Law, Capitalism and Power in Asia. The Rule of Law and Legal Institutions*, London, New York (Routledge)

Jeong, Yeonsik (1998), *Interest Representation in Socialist Market Economies: A Comparative Study of Civil Society in China and Vietnam* (Diss.), Ann Arbor (UMI)

Ji Xiaonan/Liu Ningjin (1993), "1992-1993 nian ganbu renshi zhidu gaige zhuangtai de fenxi yu yuce" (Analysis and prospects of the reform of the cadre and personnel syste, 1992-1993), in: *1992-1993 nian Zhongguo: shehui xingshi fenxi yu yuce* (1992-1993 China: Analysis and prospects of the social situation), Beijing (Zhongguo shehui kexue chubanshe): 148-175

Jia Ting/Wang Dekuan/Tang Baoling (1987), "Dui Liaoning siren qiye de diaocha yu sikao" (Investigation and analysis of private enterprises in Liaoning), in: *Shehuixue Yanjiu*, 6: 28-32

Jiang Liu/Lu Xueyi et al. (1993), *1992-1993 nian Zhongguo: shehui xingshi fenxi yu yuce* (1992-1993 China: Analysis and prospects of the social situation), Beijing (Zhongguo shehui kexue chubanshe)

Jingji Yanjiu (Economic Studies), Beijing

Johnson, Dale L. (1982a), *Class & Social Development. A New Theory of the Middle Class*, Beverly Hills, London, New Delhi (Sage Publications)

Johnson, Dale L. (1982b), "Class Relations and the Middle Classes", in: Johnson, D.L. (1982a): 87-108

Johnson, Dale L. (1982c), "The Social Unity and Fractionalization of the Middle Class", in: Johnson, D.L. (1982a): 179-202

Johnston, Russell/Lawrence, Paul R. (1991), "Beyond Vertical Integration – The Rise of the Value-Adding Partnership", in: Thompson/Frances/Levacic/Mitchell: 193-202

Jones, David M. (1997), *Political Development in Political Asia*, Cambridge, Oxford, Malden (Polity Press)

Jones, David M. (1998), "Democratization, Civil Society, and Illiberal Middle Class Culture in Pacific Asia", in: *Comparative Politics*, January: 147-170

Kao Cheng-shu (1991), "'Personal Trust' in the Large Businesses in Taiwan: A Traditional Foundation for Contemporary Economic Activities", in: Hamilton, Gary, ed*., Business Networks and Economic Development in East and Southeast Asia*, Hongkong (Center of Asian Studies): 234-273

Kaplan, Abraham (1964), "Power in Perspective", in: Kahn, Robert/Boulding, Elise, eds*., Power and Conflict in Organizations*, London (Tavistock): 11-32

Keller, Suzanne (1963), *Beyond the Ruling Class. Strategic Elites in Modern Society*, New York (Random House)

Kelliher, Daniel (1992), *Peasant Power in China. The Era of Rural Reorm*, 1979-89, New Haven (Yale University Press)

Kent, Calvin A. (1984a), "The Rediscovery of the Entrepreneur", in: Kent, C.A. (1984b): 1-20

Kent, Calvin A. (1984b), ed., *The Environment for Entrepreneurship*, Lexington, Toronto (Heat)

Kerbo, Harald R. (1996), *Social Stratification and Inequality. Class Conflict in Historical and Comparative Perspective*, New York, St. Louis, San Francisco et al. (McGraw-Hill)

Kerkvliet, Benedict, (1993), *State - Village Relations in Vietnam. Contested Cooperatives and Collectivization*, Clayton (Centre of Southeast Asian Studies, Working Paper 85)

Kerkvliet, Benedict J. Tria/Porter, Doug J. (1995), eds., *Vietnam's Rural Transformation*, Boulder, Oxford (Westview/ Institute of Southeast Asian Studies)

Kerkvliet, Benedict J.T./Selden, Mark (1998), "Agrarian Transformations in China and Vietnam", in: *The China Journal*, July: 37-59

Kerkvliet, Benedict/Chan, Anita/Unger, Jonathan (1998), "Comparing the Chinese and Vietnamese Reforms: An Introduction", in: *The China Journal,* July: 1-7

Kerr, Clark/Dunlop, John T./Harbison, Frederick H./Myers, Charles A. (1994), "Industrialism and Industrial Man", in: Grusky, D., ed*., Social Stratification. Class, Race, and Gender in Sociological Perspective*, Boulder (Westview): 659-669

Kilby, Peter (1971), ed., *Entrepreneurship and Economic Development*, New York, London (The Free Press)

Kim Diep (1998), "Private Businesses Increasing", in: *Vietnam Courier Business,* 1-3 July

Kim Oanh (1996), "Capital Investment for Infrastructure"; in: *Vietnam Economic News,* No. 46: 22/23

Kim, Kyong-Dong (1976), "Political Factors in the Formation of the Entrepreneurial Elite in South Korea", in: *Asian Survey*, 5: 465-477

Kipnis, Andrew B. (1997), *Producing Guanxi. Sentiment, Self, and Subculture in a North China Village*, Durham, London (Duke University Press)

Kirzner, Israel M. (1978), *Wettbewerb und Unternehmertum*, Tübingen (Mohr-Verlag)

Kirzner, Izrael (1983), *Perception, Opportunity, and Profit: Studies in the Theory of Entrepreneurship*, Chicago (Univ. of Chicago Press)

Kirzner, Izrael (1985), *Discovery and the Capitalist Process*, Chicago (Univ. of Chicago Press)

Kirzner, Izrael M. (1989), *Discovery, Capitalism, and Distributive Justice*, Oxford, New York (Blackwell)

Knappe, Eberhard (1998), "Schritte zu einer neuen Gesellschaftsform. Die Umwandlung von Staatsbetrieben in Kapitalgesellschaften", in: *Südostasien*, 3: 9-10

Knoke, David/Kuklinski, James H. (1991), "Network Analysis: Basic Concepts", in: Thompson/Frances/Levacic/Mitchell: 173-182

Kohn, Melvin L./Slomczynski, Kazimierz M. et al. (1997), "Social Structure and Personality under Conditions of Radical Social Change: A Comparative Analysis of Poland and Ukraine", in*: American Sociological Review*, August: 614-638

Kokko, Ari/Sjöholm, Fredrik (1997), *Small, Medium, or Large? Some Scenarios for the Role of the State in the Era of Industrialization and Modernization*. Papers of the European Institute of Japanese Studies, Stockholm School of Economics, Stockholm

Kolderie, Ted (1990), "The Two Different Concepts of Privatization", in: Gayle/Goodrich: 24-34

Kolko, Gabriel (1997), *Vietnam. Anatomy of a Peace*, London, New York (Routledge)

Koo, Hagen (1991), "Middle Classes, Democratization, and Class Formation", in: *Theory and Society*, 20: 485-509

Koop, Michael J./Nunnenkamp, Peter (1994), "Die Transformationskrise in Mittel- und Osteuropa. Ursachen und Auswege", in: *Die Weltwirtschaft*, 1: 67-91

Korff, Rüdiger (1992), *Macht der Symbole; Symbole der Macht. Zur symbolischen Dimension strategischer Gruppen. Working Paper No. 166 des Forschungsschwerpunkts Entwicklungssoziologie an der Universität Bielefeld*, Bielefeld (University of Bielefeld)

Kornai, Janos (1998), "Warum ist es mit der sozialistischen Wirtschaft vorbei, Professor Kornai? Ein Interview mit Krisztina Koenen", in: *Frankfurter Allgemeine Magazin*, 2 January: 36-37

Korte, Hermann/Schäfers, Bernhard (1992), eds., *Einführung in Hauptbegriffe der Soziologie*, Opladen (Leske&Budrich)

Kraemer, Klaus (1997), *Der Markt der Gesellschaft. Zu einer soziologischen Theorie der Marktvergesellschaftung*, Opladen (Westdeutscher Verlag)

Kraus, Willy (1989), *Unternehmerschaft in der Volksrepublik China. Wiederbelebung zwischen Ideologie und Pragmatismus*; Hamburg (Institut für Asienkunde)

Kurths, Kristina (1997), *Private Kleinbetriebe in Vietnam. Rahmenbedingungen und Hemmnisse ihrer Entwicklung*, Saarbrücken (Verlag für Entwicklungspolitik)

Lageman, Bernhard/Friedrich, Werner/Döhrn, Werner/Brüstle, Alena/Heyl, Norbert/Puxi, Marco/Welter, Friederike (1994), *Aufbau mittelständischer Strukturen in Polen, Ungarn, der Tschechischen Republik und der Slowakischen Republik. Untersuchungen des Rheinisch-Westfälischen Instituts für Wirtschaftsforschung*, Heft 11, Essen

Lam Dieu Huy/Vo Sang Xuan Lan/Vo Sang Xuan Hoang (1994), *Comment aider les petites et moyennes enterprises?*, Ho Chi Minh Ville (Societe d'Etudes et de Conseil ECO)

Lan Ye (1993), *Zhongguo zhengfu da cai yuan* (The comprehensive reduction of China's government personnel), Chongqing (Chongqing daxue chubanshe)

Lardy, Nicholas (1994), *China in the World Economy*, London (Institute for International Economies)

Lavoie, Don (1991), "The Discovery and Interpretation of Profit Opportunities: Culture and the Kirznerian Entrepreneur", in: Berger, B. (1991a): 33-52

Le Dang Doanh (1990), "Economic Renovation and Some Social Problems in Vietnam", in: *Sociological Review*, 4: 3-8 (in Vietnamese)

Le Dang Doanh (1999), "Ten Years of doi moi: Where is Vietnam's Economy?", in: *Vietnamese Studies*, 2: 5-42

Le Huu Tang (1997), "On Social Equity", in: *Vietnam Social Sciences*, 3: 15-21

Le Ngoc Hung/Rondinelli, Dennis A. (1993), "Small Business Development and Economic Transformation in Vietnam", in: *Journal of Asian Business*, 4: 1-23

Le Quang Thuong (1996), *Mot so van de xay dung Dang ve to chuc trong giai doan hien nay*, Hanoi (The Gioi Publishers)

Le Van Sinh (1996): "On Becoming a more Diversified Countryside. Some Obeservations on Socio-Economic Changes in two Northern Vietnamese Villages", Paper presented at the III. Euroviet-Conference, 2-4 July

Le Viet Duc (1999), "Vietnam's Industry: 15 Years of Renovation (1986-2000)", in: *Vietnamese Studies,* 2: 125-138

Lee, Edmond (1991), "A bourgeois alternative? The Shanghai arguments for a Chinese capitalism: the 1920s and the 1980s", in: Brantly Womack, ed., *Contemporary Chinese Politics in Historical Perspective*, Cambridge, New York et al. (Cambridge University Press): 90-126

Leipziger, D.M. (1992), *Awakening the Market. Vietnam's Economic Transition*, Washington, D.C. (World Bank Discussion Papers 157), World Bank

Lepekhin, Vladimir A. (1999), "Stratification in Present-Day Russia and the New Middle-Class", in: *Sociological Research*, vol. 38., no. 3: 20-35

Lett, Denise P. (1998), *In Pursuit of Status. The Making of South Korea's "New" Urban Middle Class*, Cambridge/Mass., London (Harvard University Press)

Li Chengrui (1997), "Dangqian jingji chengfenlei he suoyouzhi goucheng de tongji wenti" (Statistical problems of current economic categories and ownership structure), in: *Jingji Yanjiu*, 7: 63-67

Li Dezhi/Li Jing (1996), "Wo guo qiyejia xianzhuang fenxi yu zhiyehua qiyejia peiyu jizhi yanjiu" (Analysis of the current situation of entrepreneurs in our country and studies on mechanisms for professionalization and training of entrepreneurs), in: *Qiye Guanli*, 5: 30-31

Li Ding/Bao Yujun (2000), eds., *Zhongguo siying jingji nianjian 2000* (Yearbook 2000 of China's private economy), Beijing (Huawen chubanshe)

Li Fang (1998), *The Social Organization of Entrepreneurship: The Rise of Private Firms in China* (Diss.), Ann Arbor (UMI)

Li Gang (1999), "Rang qiyejia chengwei yizhong zhiye" (Let entrepreneurship become a profession), in: *Zhongguo Qiyejia*, July: 49

Li Junjie (1997), "Guanyu qiyejia zhiyehua de sikao" (Considerations on professionalization of entrepreneurs), in: *Zhongnan Minzu Xueyuan Xuebao* (Journal of the Central-South Nationalities Institute), 4: 127-129

Li Lulu (1995), "Shehui ziben yu siying qiyejia - Zhongguo shehui jiegou zhuangxing de techu dongli" (Social capital and private entrepreneurs - specific driving-force of social structure change in China), in: *Shehuixue Yanjiu*, 6: 46-58

Li Lulu (1996), "Siying qiyejia de shehui jiegou" (The social structure of private entrepreneurs), in: Zhang/Li/Xie: 100-108

Li Lulu (1998a), "Xiang shichang guodu zhong de siying qiye" (Private enterprises in transition to market), in: *Shehuixue Yanjiu*, 6: 85-102

Li Lulu (1998b), *Zhuanxing shehui zhong de siying qiyezhu* (Private entrepreneurs in the transformation society), Beijing (Zhongguo renmin daxue chubanshe)

Li Peilin/Wang Chunguang (1993), *Xin shehui jiegou de shengchang dian. Xiangzhen qiye shehui jiaohuan lun* (The emerging of new social structures. On social exchange of rural enterprises), Jinan (Shandong renmin chubanshe)

Li Tongwen (1998), ed., *Zhongguo minsheng baogao. Zhongguo shehui ge jieceng de xianzhuang yu weilai* (Report on China's people's welfare. Situation and future of all strata in China), Beijing (Jinyu chubanshe)

Li Xinchun et al. (2002), "Qiyejia jingshen, qiyejia nengli yu qiye chengzhang" (Entrepreneurial spirit, entrepreneurial capabilities, and the growing of enterprises), in: *Jingji Yanjiu*, 1: 89-92

Li Xinxin (1994), "Xi woguo siying jingji fazhan zhong de tedian he wenti" (Analysis of characteristics and problems of China's private economy), in: *Zhongguo siying jingji yanjiu wenji* (Collection of essays on research on China's private economy), Shanghai (internal publication)

Li Yining (1993), "Gufenzhi: shehuizhuyi shichang jingji weiguan jichu de chongxin gouzao" (Shareholding company: Transformation of the micro-economic foundation of socialist market economy), in: *Beijing Jingji Liaowang* (Beijing Economic Overview), 2: 3-8

Li, Linda Chelan (2000), "The 'Rule of Law' Policy in Guangdong: Continuity or Departure? Meaning, Significance and Processes", in: *The China Quarterly*, March: 199-220

Liang Chuanyun (1990), *Zhongguo siren qiye jingying guanli zhinan* (Introduction into the management of Chinese private enterprises), Beijing (Beijing daxue chubanshe)

Liang Liping (2001), "Zhongguo qiyejia duiwu chengzhang yu fazhan toushi" (A perspective review on the process of Chinese Entrepreneurs Growing up, in: *Shehuixue Yanjiu*, 6: 96-108

Liang Xiaosheng (1997), *Zhongguo shehui ge jieceng fenxi* (Analysis of all strata of Chinese society), Beijing (Jingji ribao chubanshe)

"Liaoning sheng siying jingji fazhan de yi er san" (1994) (1, 2, 3 of the development of private economy in Liaoning province), in: *Zhongguo siying jingji yanjiu wenji* (Collection of essays on research on China's private economy), Shanghai (internal publication)

Light, Ivan (1987), "Unternehmer und Unternehmertum ethnischer Gruppen", in: Heinemann, K. (1987a): 193-215

Liljeström, Rita/Lindskog, Eva/Nguyen Van Ang/Vuong Xuan Tinh (1998), *Profit and Poverty in Rural Vietnam. Winners and Losers of a Dismantled Revolution*, Richmond (Curzon Press)

Lin Houchun (1991), "Bashi niandai Zhongguo nongmin jieceng fenhua shixi" (Analysis of peasants stratification in China in the 80es), in: *Shehuixue* (Sociology), 6: 63-68

Lin Yifu/Shen Minggao (1992), "Lun gufenzhi yu guoying dazhong qiye gaige" (Analysis on shareholding companies and the reform of state-owned mittel and large enterprises), in: *Jingji Yanjiu*, 9: 48-53

Lipset, Seymour M. (1959), "Some Social Requisites of Democracy: Economic Development and Political Legitimation", in: *American Political Science Review*, 33 (1): 69-105

Lipset, Seymour M. (1962), *Soziologie der Demokratie*, Neuwied, Berlin (Luchterhand)

Lipset, Seymour M. (1981), *Political Man. The Social Bases of Politics*, Baltimore (John Hopkins University Press)

Lissjutkina, Larissa (1997), "Die 'neureichen Russen': Zur Typologie der Unternehmerschaft", in: Sterbling, Anton/Zipprian, Heinz, eds., *Max Weber und Osteuropa*, Hamburg (Krämer): 67-180

Litvack, Jennie I./Rondinelli, Dennis A. (1999), eds., *Market Reform in Vietnam. Building Institutions for Development*, Westport, London (Quorum)

Liu Jianyi (1992), Geti siying jingji jichu zhishi shouce (Handbook of basic knowledge on individual and private economy), Beijing (Huawen chubanshe)

Liu Jixing (1992), "Wo guo de fei gongyouzhi qiyejia qunti jiben xianzhuang fenxi" (Analysis of the situation of entrepreneurs in non-state ownership sector of our country), in: *Shehuixue Yanjiu*, 6: 13-20

Liu Long (1986),ed., *Zhongguo xian jieduan geti jingji yanjiu* (Current Chinese research on private economy), Beijing (Renmin chubanshe)

Liu Yingjie (1994), "Siying jingji fazhan zhong de xin wenti he xin tedian" (Nee characteristics and new problems in the process of developing private economy), in: *Zhongguo siying jingji yanjiu wenji* (Collection of essays on research on China's private economy), Shanghai (internal publication)

Liu Yong (1997), *Zhongguo qiye shounao* (Chinese Entrepreneurs), Zhuhai (Zhuhai chubanshe)

Liu Zhicai (1998), *21 shiji qiyejia* (Entrepreneurs of the 21st Century), Beijing (Zhongguo jingji chubanshe)

Liu, Alan P. (1992), "The 'Wenzhou Model' of Development and China's Modernization", in: *Asian Survey*, 8: 696-711

Liu, Yia-Ling (1992), "Reform From Below. The Private Economy and Local Politics in the Rural Industrialization of Wenzhou"; in: *China Quarterly*, June: 293-316

Ljunggren, Björn (1993), ed., *The Challenge of Reform in Indochina*, o.O. (Harvard Studies in International Development)

Löwenthal, Richard (1963), "Staatsfunktionen und Staatsform in den Entwicklungsländern", in: ders., *Die Demokratie im Wandel der Gesellschaft*, Berlin (Colloquium): 164-192

Lu Jianhua (1993), "1992 shehui ge jieceng dui shehui xingshi de jiben kanfa" (Basic views of various social strata on the social situation in 1992), in: *Shehuixue Yanjiu*, 3: 5-13

Lu Mei (1999), "Zhongchan jieji de gainian ji lilun huigu" (Concepts on middle class and review of theoretical approaches), in: *Nantong Shizhuan Xuebao* (Journal of Nantong Pedagogical College), 3: 44-48

Lu Xueyi (2002), *Dangdai Zhongguo shehui jieceng yanjiu baogao* (Research report on China's contemporary social strata), Beijing (Shehui kexue wenxian chubanshe)

Lu Yusha (1994), "Xin zibenjia de zhengzhi yaoqiu" (Political demands of the new Capitalists), in: *Dangdai* (Present Time), Hongkong, 6: 4-5

Luohe tongji nianjian (Luohe Statistical Yearbook) (1995), Beijing (Zhongguo tongji chubanshe)

Luu Hong Minh (1999), "About Some Factors Affecting Social Stratification in Present-Day Vietnam", in: *Vietnam Social Sciences*, 5: 25-30

Ma Deyong (1999), "Zhuanxing shehui zhong de zhongjian jieceng" (The middle stratum in the transformation society), in: *Shehui* (Society), 9: 18-19

Ma Hong (1992), "Jianli shehuizhuyi shichang jingji xin tizhi" (Building a new system of socialist market economy, in: *Jingji Yanjiu*, 11: 3-9

Ma Xinlan (1998), "Yi fa zhi guo guanjian shi yi fa zhi quan" (The key link of 'to rule the country by law' is 'to rule the power by law'), in: *Zhongguo Gongshang Bao*, 8 December

Malarney, Shaun Kingsley (1998), "State Stigma, Family Prestige, and the Development of Commerce in the Red River Delta of Vietnam", in: Hefner, R.W.: 268-289

Malik, Rashid Abdur (1996), *Entrepreneurship in China: A Tianjin Case Study* (Diss.), Ann Arbor (UMI)

"Market Economy and Socialist Orientation" (1999), in: *Vietnam Social Sciences*, 5, S.74-94

Marr, David G. (1981), *Vietnamese Tradition on Trial 1920-45*, Berkeley, Los Angeles, London (Univ. of California Press)

Marr, David (1995), *Zwischen Marx und Markt. Eine kritische Bilanz der wirtschaftlichen, politischen und kulturellen Entwicklung Vietnams seit 1975*, Berlin (Deutsch-Vietnamesische Gesellschaft)

Martinelli, Alberto (1994), "Entrepreneurship and Management", in: Smelser, Neil/Swedberg, Richard, eds., *The Handbook of Economic Sociology*, New York (Princeton University Press): 476-503

Mayer, Adrian C. (1977), "The Significance of Quasi-Groups in the Study of Complex Societies", in: Leinhardt, Samuel, ed., *Social Networks. A Developing Paradigm*, New York, San Francisco, London (Academic Press): 293-318

McCarty, Adam (1992), ed., *Vietnam Data Bank, 1976-91*, Canberra (National Centre for Development Studies)

McCormick, Barrett L. (1998), "Political Change in China and Vietnam: Coping with the Consequences of Economic Reform", in: *The China Journal*, 40, July: 121-143

McMillan, John/Naughton, Barry (1996), eds., *Reforming Asian Socialism. The Growth of Market Institutions*, Ann Arbor (The University of Michigan Press)

Menkhoff, Thomas (1999), *The Impact of the New Asian Realism on Chinese Business Networks in Asia-Pacific*. Paper presented at the International Conference on "Crisis Management - Chinese Entrepreneurs and Business Networks in Southeast Asia", Bonn, May: 28-30

Menkhoff, Thomas/Gerke, Solvay (2002), eds., *Chinese Entrepreneurship and Asian Buisness Networks*, London and New York (RoutledgeCurzon)

Mi Jianing/Gao Dexiang (1997), "Qiyejia jieceng de shehuixue hanyi" (The sociological meaning of an entrepreneurial stratum), in: *Shehuixue Yanjiu*, 4: 42-47

Milanovic, Branko (1989), *Liberalization and Entrepreneurship. Dynamics of Reform in Socialism and Capitalism*, Armonk, London (Sharpe)

Minh Son (1997), "I Quit Job over Bribes Shame", in: *Vietnam Economic Times*, Nr. 35: 23/24

Moore, Barrington (1974), *Soziale Ursprünge von Diktatur und Demokratie*, Frankfurt/M. (Suhrkamp)

Murray, Geoffrey (1997), *Vietnam: Dawn of a New Market*, New York (St. Martins Press)

Nan Lin (1999), "Building a Network Theory of Social Capital", in: *Connections*, 1: 28-51

Nationale Politische Akademie Ho Chi Minh/Friedrich-Ebert-Stiftung (1997), Hanoi, eds., *Studie "Förderpolitik für die Klein- und Mittelunternehmen in Vietnam"*

Naughton, Barry (1996), "Distinctive Features of Economic Reform in China and Vietnam", in: McMillan, J./Naughton, B: 273-296

Nee, Victor (1989), "Peasant Entrepreneurship and the Politics of Regulation in China", in: Nee, Victor/Stark, David., eds., *Remaking the Economic Institutions of Socialism: China and Eastern Europe*, Stanford (Stanford University Press): 169-207

Nee, Victor (1996), "The Emergence of a Market Society: Changing Mechanisms of Stratification in China", in: *American Journal of Sociology*, 4: 908-949

Neelsen, John P. (1988), "Strategische Gruppen, Klassenbildung und Staat in der Peripherie. Eine Kritik des Bielefelder Ansatzes", in: *Kölner Zeitschrift für Soziologie und Sozialpsychologie*, 40: 284-315

Neelsen, John P. (1989), „Determinismus", "Teleologie", "Mystifizierung"? Zum Empirismus des Konzepts der strategischen Gruppen. Eine Duplik", in: *Kölner Zeitschrift für Soziologie und Sozialpsychologie*, 41: 555-562

Nevitt, Christopher Earle (1996), "Private Business Associations in China: Evidence of Civil Society or Local State Power", in: *The China Journal*, July: 25-43

Ng, Chee Yuen/Freeman, Nick J./Huynh, Frank H. (1996), eds., *State-Owned Enterprise Reform in Vietnam. Lessons from Asia*, Singapore (Inst. for Southeast Asian Studies)

Ngo Vinh Long (1991), "Ungeeignete Kollektive. Staatliche Reform und die Entwicklung auf dem Lande", in: *Südostasien Informationen*, 4: 18-21

Nguyen Anh Binh/Vu Kiem (1997), "What are the Causes of the Complicated Events in Thai Binh Province?", in: *Nhan Dan* 8, 9, 10 and 11 September

Nguyen Chuoc (1997), "Cultural Identity in Business", in: *Vietnam Social Sciences*, 4: 59-62

Nguyen Dang Thanh (1997), "Requirements of Political Leadership in the Socialist-Oriented Market Economy in Vietnam", in: *Vietnam Social Sciences*, 3: 3-8

Nguyen Dinh Nam/Tran Anh Tuan (1992/93), ed., *Making Investments in Ho Chi Minh Ville*, Ho Chi Minh Ville

Nguyen Dinh Phan (1996), "The Development of Small and Medium Scale Enterprises", in: *Vietnam's Socio-Economic Development*, 8: 3-12

Nguyen Dinh Tai (1996), "The Equitisation of the State Enterprises", in: *Vietnam's Socio-Economic Development*, 8: 42-49

Nguyen Duc Vinh (1999), "Overview of Non-State Small and Medium-Sized Enterprises in Vietnam", in: Heberer/Kohl/Tuong/Nguyen: 15-21

Nguyen Hai Huu/Nguyen Huu Ninh (1996), "The Policy Promoting Development of the Small and Medium Enterprises", in: *Vietnam's Socio-Economic Development*, 8: 13-21

Nguyen Minh Tu (*1996), Erste Diskussion über den unstrukturierten Wirtschaftssektor in Vietnam, Beitrag zur DED-Regionalkonferenz Asien*, Hanoi 25-28 October

Nguyen Ngoc Bich (1994), "Vietnam im Wandel", in: *Südostasien Informationen*, 1: 19-23

Nguyen Ngoc Tri (1991), "Factors of Social Environment Influencing Students Today", in: *Sociological Review* 3: 48-52 (in Vietnamese)

Nguyen Tri Khiem (1996), "Policy Reform and the Microeconomic Environment in the Agricultural Sector", in: Suiwah Leung, ed., *Vietnam Assessment. Creating a Sound Investment Climate*, Singapore (Institute of Southeast Asian Studies): 21-41

Nguyen van Thanh/Tran Thi Tuyet Mai (1993), "Rural Employment Creation in Vietnam: Present Situation and Solutions", in: The Development Strategy Institute of the State Planning Committee/The Rural Development Institute of the Chinese Academy of Social Sciences/Stockholm School of Economics, eds., *Rural Development: An Exchange of Chinese and Vietnamese Experiences*, Hanoi (policy paper)

Nguyen Xuan Oanh (1991), "Vietnam's Economic Reforms. Shifting to the Market", in: *Indochina Report*, Jan.-March: 1-15

Nien giam thong ke (Statistical Yearbook) 1997 (1998), Hanoi (Statistical Publishing House)

Nohria, N./Eccles, R. G. (1992), eds., *Networks and Organisations: Structure, Form and Action*, Cambridge/Mass. (Harvard University Press)

Nolan, Peter/Dong Furen (1990), eds., *Market Forces in China. Competition and Small Business, the Wenzhou Debate*, London (Zed Books)

Nugent, Nicholas (1996), *Vietnam. The Second Revolution*, Brighton (InPrint)

Odgaard, Ole (1990/91), "Inadequate and Inaccurate Chinese Statistics: The Case of Private Rural Enterprises", in: China Information, 3: 29-38

Odgaard, Ole (1992a), "Entrepreneurs and Elite Transformation in Rural China", in: *The Australian Journal of Chinese Affairs*, July: 89-108

Odgaard, Ole (1992b), *Private Enterprises in Rural China*, Aldershot (Avebury)

OECD (1992), *Technology and the Economy. The Key Relationships*, Paris

Oesterdiekhoff, Georg W. (1993), *Unternehmerisches Handeln und gesellschaftliche Entwicklung. Eine Theorie unternehmerischer Institutionen und Handlungsstrukturen*, Opladen (Westdeutscher Verlag)

Oi, Jean (1989), *State and Peasant in Contemporary China: The Political Economy of Village Government*, Berkeley (Univ. of California Press)

Olson, Mancur (1985), *Die Logik kollektiven Handelns. Kollektivgüter und die Theorie der Gruppen*, Tübingen. (Mohr)

Organisation for Economic Co-Operation and Development [OECD] (1996), ed., *Privatisation in Asia, Europe and Latin America*, Paris

Orru, Marco/Biggart, Nicole W./Hamilton, Gary G. (1997*)*, *The Economic Organization of East Asian Capitalism*, Thousand Oaks, London, New Delhi (Sage)

Pan Gang (1997), "Cong 'you yi buchong' dao 'zhongyao zucheng bufen'" (From 'useful supplement' to 'important element'), in: *Renmin Ribao*, 14 November

Parris, Kristen (1996), "Private Entrepreneurs as Citizens: From Leninism to Corporatism", in: *China Information*: 3-4 und 1-28

Parry, Simon/Tien Thanh (1997), "Cleaning Up", in: *Vietnam Economic Times*, No 35: 21

Parsons, Talcott (1963), "On the Concept of Influence", in: *Public Opinion Quarterly*, No 1: 37-82

Parsons, Talcott (1967), "On the Concept of Political Power", in: ders., *Sociological Theory and Modern Society*, New York, London (The Free Press): 297-354

Parsons, Talcott (1970), "Das Problem des Strukturwandels: eine theoretische Skizze", in: Zapf, W: 35-54

Pearson, Margaret M. (1997), *China's New Businesss Elite. The Political Consequence of Economic Reform*, Berkeley et al. (Univ. of California Press)

Pei Minxin (1991), *When Reform Becomes Revolution. Regime Transition in China and the Soviet Union, 1979-90*, Ann Arbor, Cambridge/Mass (Diss.) (UMI)

Pei Minxin (1994), "The Puzzle of East Asian Exceptionalism", in: *Journal of Democracy*, 4: 90-103

Pei Minxin (1998*)*, "Chinese Civic Associations. An Empirical Analysis", in: *Modern China*, 3: 285-318

Pettigrew, Andrew/Ferlie, Ewan/McKee, Lorna (1992*)*, *Shaping Strategic Change. Making Change in Large Organizations*, London, Newbury Park, New Delhi (Sage)

Pfeifer, Claudia (1990), "Bis zum Kater unter den Tigern ist es noch weit. Ergebnisse und Probleme einer sozialistischen Entwicklungsstrategie in Vietnam", in: *Südostasien Informationen*, 4: 8-11

Pfeifer, Claudia (1991), *Konfuzius und Marx am roten Fluß. Vietnamesische Reformkonzepte nach 1975*, Bad Honnef (Horleman)

Pfennig, Werner (1999), "Anmerkungen und Fragen zu Mittelschichten", in: Becker, Bert/Rüland, Jürgen/Werz, Nikolaus: 272-282

Pham Ngoc Kiem (2002), "Role of Private Economic Sector in Vietnam´s Economic Development", in *Vietnam Economic Review*, 5: 18-22.

Pham Quang Huan (1998), "Solution for the State-Owned Enterprise Reform", in: *Vietnam's Socio-Economic Development*, 14: 3-9

Pham Van Pho (1992), "Economic Reform and Entrepreneurship Development in Vietnam", in: *Public Enterprise*, 1-2: 78-84

Pham Xuan Nam (1997), *Culture and Development*, Hanoi (Social Sciences Publications)

Political Report of the Central Committee to the Eight National Congress (1996), in: *Vietnam Social Sciences*, 4: 103-120

Porter, Gareth (1993), *Vietnam. The Politics of Bureaucratic Socialism*, Ithaca, London (Cornell University Press)

Powell, Walter W./Smith-Doerr, Laurel (1994), "Networks and Economic Life", in: Smelser, Neil/Swedberg, Richard, eds., *The Handbook of Economic Sociology*, Princeton, New York (Princeton University Press): 368-402

Probert, J./Young, S.D. (1995), *The Vietnamese Road to Capitalism. Decentralization, de facto Privatization, and the Limits to Piecemeal Reform*. Paper prepared for the conference "Vietnam - Reform and Transformation", Center for Pacific and Asia Studies, Stockholm University, 31 August - 1 September

Protest (1997), *Protest in Rural Vietnam Prompts Official Probe*, Reuter 13 June

Putterman, Louis (1995), "The Role of Ownership and Property Rights in China's Economic Transition", in: *The China Quarterly*, No. 144 (December): 1047-1064

Qin Nanyang (1999), "Lun siying qiyezhu de zhengzhi canyu" (Political Participation of private entrepreneurs), in: Zhang/Ming: 103-117

Qin Shaoxiang/Jia Ting (1993), *Shehui xin qunti tanmi - Zhongguo siying qiyezhu jieceng* (On the new social stratum of Chinese private entrepreneurs), Beijing (Zhongguo fazhan chubanshe)

Qin Yan (1999), *Zhongguo zhongchan jieji. Weilai shehui jiegou de zhuliu* (China's middle class. On the main trend of a future social structure), Beijing (Zhongguo jihua chubanshe)

Qiu Baoxing (1997), "Zaojiu gao suzhi de qiyejia duiwu" (To train a contingent of high quality entrepreneurs), in: *Renmin Ribao,* 24 July

Qiushi (Truth), Beijing

Qiye Guanli (Enterprise management), Beijing

Qu Changfu (2000), "Qiyejia qunti yige jianqiang de shengyin" (A voice of entrepreneurship that becomes stronger), in: *Zhongguo Qiyejia,* 4: 38-43

Quang Truong (1987), *Agricultural Collectivization and Rural Development in Vietnam: A North/South Study, 1955-1985,* Amsterdam (Vrije Universiteit te Amsterdam)

Radford, K.J. (1988), *Strategic and Tactical Decisions,* New York, North York (Springer-Verlag)

Ramamurthy, Bhargavi (1998), *The Private Manufacturing Sector in Vietnam 1991-97: An analysis of the deceased.* Working Paper Series in Economics and Finance, No. 252, Stockholm

Redding, Gordon S. (1990), *The Spirit of Chinese Capitalism,* New York (de Gruyter)

Redding, Gordon S. (1996), "The distinct nature of Chinese capitalism", in: *The Pacific Review,* 3: 426-440

Reese, Pat Ray/Aldrich, Howard E. (1995), "Entrepreneurial Networks and Business Performance", in: Birley, Sue/MacMillan, Ian C., eds., *International Entrepreneurship,* London, New York (Routledge): 109-123

Reid, Gavin C. (1993), *Small Business Enterprise. An Economic Analysis,* London, New York (Routledge)

Renmin Ribao (People's Daily), Beijing

Reuter 8 September 1997: "Vietnam Breaks Media Silence over Rural Unrest"

Reuter 24 July 1997: "Vietnam Says Taking Action over Province Unrest"

Robison, Richard (1989), "Authoritarian States, Capitalist Owning Classes and the politics of Newly Industrialising Countries: The Case of Indonesia", in: *World Politics,* 41: 52-74

Röglin, Hans-Christian (1991), "Eigentum in einer gerechten Welt", in: *Frankfurter Allgemeine Zeitung,* 8 June

Róna-Tas, Akos (1994), "The First Shall be the Last? Entrepreneurship and Communist Cadres in the Transition from Socialism", in: *American Journal of Sociology,* July: 40-69

Rona-Tas, Akos (1995), "The Second Economy as a Subversive Force: The Erosion of Party Power in Hungary", in: Walder, Andrew G., ed., *The Waning of the Communist State. Economic Origin of Political Decline in China and Hungary,* Berkeley, Los Angeles, London (Univ. of California Press): 61 - 84

Rondinelli, Dennis A./Kasarda, John D. (1992), "Foreign Trade Potential, Small Enterprise Development and Job Creation in Developing Countries", in: *Small Busines Economics,* 4: 253-265

Rondinelli, Dennis A./Litvack, Jennie I. (1999), "Economic Reform, Social Progress, and Institutional Development: A Framework for Assessing Vietnam's Transition", in: Litvack, J.I./Rondinelli, D.A., eds., *Market Reform in Vietnam. Building Institutions for Development,* Westport, London (Quorum)

Ronnas, Per (1992), *Employment Generation through Private Entrepreneurship in Vietnam,* Genf (ILO)

Ronnas, Per (1996), "Private Entrepreneurship in the Nascent Market Economy of Vietnam. Markets and Linkages," in: McMillan, J./Naughton, B: 135-166

Ronnas, Per (1998), *The Transformation of the Private Manufacturing Sector in Vietnam in the 1990s.* Stockholm School of Economics Working Paper Series in Economics and Finance No. 241

Ronnas, Per/Ramamurthy, Bhargavi (2001), eds., *Entrepreneurship in Vietnam. Transformation and Dynamics,* Copenhagen, Singapore (Nordic Institute of Asian Studies/Institute of Southeast Asian Studies)

Rose, Richard (1994), "Postcommunism and the Problem of Trust", in: *Journal of Democracy,* 3: 18-30

Roth, Andrei (1997), "Staatliche Bürokratie und neue Eliten im posttoalitären Rumänien", in: Sterbling, Anton/Zipprian, Heinz, eds., *Max Weber und Osteuropa,* Hamburg (Krämer Verlag): 181-204

Ru Xin/Lu Xueyi/Dan Tianlun (1999), eds., *1999 nian Zhongguo shehui xingshi fenxi yu yuce* (Analysis and prospects of China's societal situation in 1999), Beijing (Shehui kexue wenxian chubanshe)

Rüegg-Sturm, Johannes (1998), "Neuere Systemtheorie und unternehmerischer Wandel", in: *Die Unternehmung*, 1: 2-17

Rueschemeyer, Dietrich/Stephens, Evelyne H./Stephens, John D. (1992), *Capitalist Development & Democracy,* Cambridge, Oxford (Polity Press)

Rüland, Jürgen (1997), "Wirtschaftswachstum und Demokratisierung in Asien: Haben die Modernisierungstheorien doch recht?", in: Schulz, Manfred, Hrsg., *Die Perspektive der Entwicklungssoziologie,* Opladen (Westdt. Verlag): 83-110

Rüland, Jürgen (1999), "Janusköpfige Mittelschichten in Südostasien", in: Becker, Bert/Rüland, Jürgen/Werz, Nikolaus: 41-75

Rutten, Mario/Upadhya, Carol (1997), eds., *Small Business Entrepreneurs in Asia and Europe. Towards a Comparative Perspective,* New Delhi, Thousand Oaks, London (Sage)

Sadowski, Christine M. (1994), "Autonomous Groups as Agents of Democratic Change in Communist and Post-Communist Eastern Europe", in: Diamond, Larry, ed., *Political Culture and Democracy in Developing Countries,* Boulder (Rienner): 155-188

Sanchez, Ron/Heene, Aimé/Thomas, Howard (1996), eds., *Dynamics of Competence-Based Competition. Theory and Practice in the New Strategic Management,* Oxford, Tarrytown, Tokyo (Pergamon)

Schak, David (1994), ed., *Entrepreneurship, Economic Growth and Social Change,* Queensland (Griffith Univ. Press)

Schellhorn, Kai M. (1992), "Politischer und wirtschaftlicher Wandel in Vietnam", in: *KAS-Auslandsinformationen,* 6: 16-21

Schubert, Gunter (1999), "Taiwans Mittelschichten - Demokratisierungsagent oder Demokratisierungsphantom?", in: Becker, Bert/Rüland, Jürgen/Werz, Nikolaus: 160-185

Schubert, Gunter/Tetzlaff, Rainer/Vennewald, Werner (1994), *Demokratisierung und politischer Wandel. Theorie und Anwendung des Konzeptes der strategischen und konfliktfähigen Gruppen,* Münster (Lit-Verlag)

Schüller, Margot (1992), "Untersuchung zur Entwicklung von Privatunternehmen", in: *China aktuell,* November: 792

Schumann, Dirk (1992), *Bayerns Unternehmer in Gesellschaft und Staat 1834-1914,* Göttingen (Vandenhoek&Ruprecht)

Schumpeter, Joseph A. (1928), "Unternehmer", in: Elster, Ludwig/Weber, Adolf/Wieser, Friedrich, Hrsg., *Handwörterbuch der Staatswissenschaft,* Bd. VIII, Jena (G. Fischer): 476-487

Schumpeter, Joseph A. (1987a), *Theorie der wirtschaftlichen Entwicklung,* Berlin (Duncker&Humblot)

Schumpeter, Joseph A. (1987b), *Beiträge zur Sozialökonomik,* Hrsg. Stephan Böhm, Wien, Köln, Graz (Böhlau)

Scott, James C. (1969), "Everyday Forms of Resistance", in: Forest D. Colburne, ed., *Everyday Forms of Peasant Resistance,* Armonk, London (Sharpe): 3-33

Scott, James C. (1976), *The Moral Economy of the Peasants. Rebellion and Subsistence in Southeast Asia,* New Haven, London (Yale University Press)

Scott, James C. (1977), "Hegemony and Peasantry", in: *Politics & Society,* 3: 267-296

Scott, James C. (1985), *Weapons of the Weak: Everyday Forms of Resistance,* New Haven (Yale University Press)

Sexton, Donald L./Smilor, Raymond W. (1986), eds., *The Art and Science of Entrepreneurship,* Cambridge/Mass. (Ballinger Publishing Co.)

Shaw, Eleanor (1997), "New Start, Growth and Development. The 'Real' Networks of Small Firms", in: Deakins, David/Jennings, Peter/Mason, Colin, eds., *Small Firms. Entrepreneurship in the Nineties,* London, McGraw-Hill: 7-17

Shehuixue Yanjiu (Sociological Studies), Beijing

Shehuizhuyi chuji jieduan yanjiu ketizu (1991) (Discussion group "Initial stage of socialism"), "Zhongguo shehuizhuyi chuji jieduan de suoyouzhi tese" (Characteristics of ownership system in the initial stage of Chinese socialism), in: *Longjiang Shehui Kexue* (Longjiang Social sciences), 3: 21-27

Shi Shenglin (2000), "Siying qiye de fazhan zhanbei" (Development strategy of private enterprises), in: *Jingji Guanli* (Enterprise Management), 4: 37

Shi Tianjian (1997), *Political Participation in Beijing*, Cambridge/Mass., London (Harvard University Press)

Shi Zhongwen/Pang Yi (1996), *Paomo jingji, toushi Zhongguo de disan zhi yan* (Bubble economy, view on China with the eyes of a third person), Beijing

Shils, Edward (1962), *Political Development in the New States*, London, The Hague, Paris (Mouton)

Shue, Vivienne (1990), "Emerging State-Society Relations in Rural China", in: Delman, J./Ostergaard, C.S./Christiansen, F., eds., *Remaking Peasant China. Problems of Rural Development and Institutions at the Start of the 1990s*, Aarhus (Arhus University Press): 60-80

Sievert, Olaf (1993), "Probleme des Übergangs von einer sozialistischen zur marktwirtschaftlichen Ordnung", in: Dichmann, Werner/Fels, Gerhard, Hrsg., *Gesellschaftliche und ökonomische Funktionen des Privateigentums*, Köln (Deutscher Inst.-Verlag): 207-242

Silverman, Bertram/Yanowitch, Murray (1997), *New Rich, New Poor, New Russia. Winners and Losers on the Russian Road to Capitalism*, Armonk, London (Sharpe)

Simmel, Georg (1994), *Philosophie des Geldes*, Frankfurt/M. (Suhrkamp)

Sixth National Congress of the Communist Party of Vietnam (1987). *Documents*, Hanoi (The Gioi Publishers)

Sjöberg, Örjan (1991), "Wirtschaftsreform in Vietnam", in: *Südostasien Informationen*, 4: 13-16

Sombart, Werner (1909), "Der kapitalistische Unternehmer", in: *Archiv für Sozialwissenschaft und Sozialpolitik*, Bd. XXIX, Tübingen: 689-758

Sombart, Werner (1969a), *Die vorkapitalistische Wirtschaft*, 1. Halbband, Berlin (Duncker&Humblot)

Sombart, Werner (1969b), *Das europäische Wirtschaftsleben im Zeitalter des Frühkapitalismus*, 2. Halbband, Berlin (Duncker&Humblot)

Sombart, Werner (1987), *Der moderne Kapitalismus*, 3 Bde., München, Berlin (Duncker&Humblot)

Stern, Lewis M. (1989), "Nguyen Van Linh's Leadership. A New Operational Code", in: *Indochina Report*, No. 151: 1-15

Stewart, Ian (1997), *Peasant Rebels*, AP 27 October

Südostasien Aktuell (Hamburg)

Sullivan, John D. (1994), "Democratization and Business Interests", in: *Journal of Democracy*, 4: 146-160

Sun Liping (1996), "Guanxi, shehui guanxi yu shehui jiegou" (Connexions, social connexions and social structure), in: *Shehuixue Yanjiu*, 5: 20-30

Sun Liping et al. (1994), "Gaige yilai Zhongguo shehui jiegou de bianqian" (Change of China's social structure since reform), in: *Zhongguo Shehui Kexue* (China's Social sciences), 2: 47-62

Sun Liping/Li Qiang/Shen Yuan (1999), "Major Trends and Hidden Concerns in China's Social-Structural Transformation for the Short- and Mid-Term Future", in: *The Chinese Economy*, 3: 5-55

Sun Wu (1990), *Wahrhaft siegt wer nicht kämpft*, Freiburg (Bauer-Verlag)

Sundhausen, Ulf (1991), "Democracy and the Middle Classes: Reflections on Political Development", in: *Australian Journal of Politics and History*, 37: 100-117

Szelenyi, Ivan (1988), *Socialist Entrepreneurs. Embourgeoisement in Rural Hungary*, Cambridge, Oxford (University of Wisconsin Press)

Szelenyi, Ivan (1995), "Le Postcommunisme, ou la revolution du "capitalisme managerial", in: *Courrier International*, Nr. 264, 23-28 November

Tanner, Murray S. (1999), *The Politics of Lawmaking in Post-Mao China. Institutions, Processes and Democratic Prospects*, Oxford (Clarendon Press)

Tarrow, Sidney (1989), *Struggle, Politics and Reform: Collective Action, Social Movements and Cycles of Protest*, Ithaca, New York Cornell Studies in International Affairs

Thang Tran Phuc (1994), "Tendencies of Change in the Vietnamese Social Class Structure in the Present Transitional Period", in: *Vietnam Social Sciences*, 2: 3-9

Thaveeporn, Vasavakul (1997), "Sectoral Politics and Strategies for State and Party Building from the VII to the VIII Congress of the Vietnamese Communist Party", in: Fforde: 81-135

Thayer, Carlyle A. (1995), "Mono-Organizational Socialism and the State", in: Kerkvliet,
    B.J.T./Porter, D.J.: 39-64
The Constitution of 1992 (1993), Hanoi (Gioi Publishers)
The Constitutions of Vietnam (1995), Hanoi (Gioi Publishers)
The Saigon Times, Ho Chi Minh-City
Thompson, Grahame/Frances, Jennifer/Levacic, Rosalind/Mitchell, Jeremy (1991), eds., *Markets,*
    Hierarchies and Networks. The Coordination of Social Life, London, Newbury Park,
    New Delhi (Sage)
Thompson, Mark R. (1999), "Mittelschichten und Demokratie: Soziale Mobilität und politische
    Transformation," in: Becker, Bert/Rüland, Jürgen/Werz, Nikolaus: 14-40
Thuc trang Lao Dong - Viec Lam O Viet Nam (1998) (Labor and Employment in Vietnam), Hanoi
    (Statistical Publishing House)
Tian Qianli (2000), *Laoban lun* (On entrepreneurial strata), Beijing (Jingji kexue chubanshe)
Tian Weidong (1997), "Siying qiyezhu jieceng shuxing zhi wo jian" (My opinion on strata affilia-
    tion of private entrepreneurs), in: *Lilun Qianyan* (Theoretical Front), 12: 16
Tiem Phan Van/Thanh Nguyen Van (1996), "Problems and Prospects of State Enterprise Reform,
    1996-2000", in: Yuen/Freeman/Huynh: 3-18
Tien Tran Huu (1996), "Society - Class Relationship in the Transitional Period to Socialism in
    Vietnam", in: *Vietnam Social Sciences*, 3: 29-35
Tiep Thu Chuyen Giao Cong Nghe Va Hien Dai Hoa Cac Doanh Nghiep Vua Va Nho (1996)
    (Attraction of technology and the modernization of small and medium enterprises), Ha-
    noi (The Gioi Publishers)
Tilly, Charles (1978), *From Mobilization to Revolution,* Reading, Menlo Park, London, Don Mills,
    Sydney (Addison-Wesley)
Ton Tich Qui (1998), "Equitization of State-Owned Enterprises", in: *Vietnam's Socio-Economic*
    Development, 14: 10-16
Tong Cuc Thong Ke (General Statistical Office) (1996), *Kinh Te. Ngoai Quoc Doanh. Thoi Mo*
    Cua 1991-1995 (Non-state economy in the period of opening up 1991-1995), Hanoi
    (Statistical Publishing House)
Tonkin, Derek (1992), "Whither Vietnam?", in: *Asian Affairs*: 295-303
Tran Du Lich (1998), "Equitization of State-Owned Enterprises: Initial Results and Obstacles", in:
    Economic Review, 1: 20-21
Tran Duc Vinh (1996), *Daten zum 'unstrukturierten' (informellen) Sektor in Vietnam*, Manuskript,
    Beitrag zur DED-Regionalkonferenz Asien, Hanoi 25-28 October
Tran Duc Vinh (1997), "Überleben Jenseits der Planwirtschaft", in: *DED-Brief*, 3: 20-22
Tran Hong Thai (1998), "Equitization of State-Owned Enterprises: Initial Results and Obstacles",
    in: *Economic Review*, 1: 15-19
Tran Minh Ngoc (1996), "Quality of Labour in Small and Medium-Sized Enterprises in Rural
    Areas", in: *Vietnam's Socio-Economic Development*, 8: 35-41
Tran Minh Tich (1996), "Nhung 'khoang toi' dang luu tam!", in: *Thuong Mai*, 30 November
Tran Ngoc Khue (1997), "Positive and Negative Influences of Market Mechanism on Social Psy-
    chology in Rennovation", in: *Vietnam Social Sciences*, 3: 59-66
Tran Thi Que (1998), *Vietnam's Agriculture. The Challenges and Achievements*, Singapore (Insti-
    tute of Southeast Asian Studies)
Tran Trung Dung (1991), "Rette sich, wer kann "[Interview], in: *Südostasien Informationen*, 4: 14
Tran Van Hoa (1999), ed., *Sectoral Analysis of Trade, Investment and Business in Vietnam*,
    Houndmills, New York (St. Martins Press)
Trinh Duy Luan (1995), "Impacts of Economic Reforms on Urban Society", in: Vu Tuan Anh, ed.,
    Economic Reform and Development in Vietnam, Hanoi (The Gioi Publishers): 134-196
Trong Nguyen Phu (1996), "Socialist Orientation and the Path to Socialism in Vietnam", in: *Viet-*
    nam Social Sciences, 4: 3-11
Truong, David H.D./Gates, Carolin L. (1992), *Effects of Government Policies on the Incentive to*
    Invest, Enterprise Behaviour and Employment. The Case Study of Vietnam, Genf (World
    Employment Programme Research, Working Paper No. 57)

Tuan Nguyen Ngoc/Long Ngo Tri/Phuong Ho (1996), "Restructuring of State-Owned Enterprises towards Industrialization and Modernizing in Vietnam", in: Yuen/Freeman/Huynh: 19-37

Tuong Lai (1997), "The Issue of Social Change After 10 Years of 'Doimoi' in Vietnam", in: *Vietnam Social Sciences*, 1: 21-28

Tuong Lai (1999), *Vai tro cua doanh nghiep nho va vua trong cong cuoc Doi Moi o Viet Nam* (The Role of medium and small enterprises in Vietnamese reform process), in: *Tap chi Xa hoi hoc* (Sociological Review), 1: 3-16

Turley, William S./Womack, Brantly (1998), "Asian Socialism's Open Doors: Guangzhou and Ho Chi Minh City", in: *The China Journal*, July: 95-143

Tyson, James/Tyson, Ann (1995), *Chinese Awakenings. Life Stories from the Unofficial China*, Boulder, San Francisco, Oxford (Westview Press)

Unger, Jonathan (1994), "'Rich Man, Poor Man': The Making of New Classes in the Countryside", in: Goodman, David S.G./Hooper, Beverley, eds., *China's Quiet Revolution. New Interactions Between State and Society*, New York (Longman Cheshire): 43-63

Unger, Jonathan (1996), „Bridges": Private Business, the Chinese Government and the Rise of New Associations", in: *The China Quarterly*, September: 795-819

Union Association of Industry and Commerce (1996), ed., *Industrial and Commercial Directory '96*, Ho Chi Minh-City

Vanhanen, Tatu (1990), *The Process of Democratization: A Comparative Study of 147 States, 1980-88*, New York (Crane Russak)

Vanhanen, Tatu (1992), ed., *Strategies of Democratization*, Washington, Philadelphia, London (Crane Russak)

Vanhanen, Tatu/Kimber, Richard (1994), "Predicting and Explaining Democratization in Eastern Europe", in: Pridham, Geoffrey/Vanhanen, Tatu, eds., *Democratization in Eastern Europe. Domestic and international perspectives*, London, New York (Routledge): 63-96

Vermeer, Eduard B./Pieke, Frank N./Chong, Woei Lien (1998), eds., *Cooperative and Collective in China's Rural Development*, Armonk and London (Sharpe)

Viet Nam News, Hanoi

Vietnam (1997), *Vietnam Slams Amnesty for Meddling in Secrets Case*, Reuter 20 October

Vietnam 1997/98 (1997), Hanoi (The Gioi Publishers)

Vietnam Economic Times, Hanoi

Vietnam Investment Review, Hanoi

Vo Dai Luoc (1996a), ed., *Vietnam's Industrialization, Modernization and Resources*, Hanoi (Social Sciences Publications)

Vo Dai Luoc (1996b), "Orientations of Industrialization Policy", in: Vo/Akie: 15-46

Vo Dai Luoc/Akie Ishida (1996), eds., *Industrialization and Modernization in Vietnam Toward 2000*, Tokyo (Social Sciences Publications)

Vo Nhan Tri (1992), *Vietnam's Economic Policy Since 1975*, Singapore (ASEAN Economic Resarche Institute)

Vo Nhan Tri/Booth, Anne (1992), "Recent Economic Developments in Vietnam", in: *Asian-Pacific Economic Literature*, 1: 16-40

Vo Thi Vuong (1997), "Equitization and Reform of State-owned Enterprises", in: *Vietnam Economic Review*, December: 5-9

Vogel, Ezra F. (1971), *Japan's New Middle Class*, Berkeley, Los Angeles, London (University of California Press)

Vokes, Richard/Palmer, Ingrid (1993), "Transition in a Centrally Planned Economy. The Impact and Potential of Economic Reform in Vietnam", in: Dixon, Chris/Drakakis-Smith, David, eds., *Economic and Social Development in Pacific Asia*, London, New York (Routledge): 169-196

von Senger, Harro (1994), *Strategeme*, Bern, München, Wien (Scherz)

von Winter, Thomas (1997), " 'Schwache Interessen': Zum kollektiven Handeln randständiger Gruppen", in: *Leviathan*, 4: 539-566

Vu Dinh Anh (2001), "Capital of Private Sector in Vietnam", in: *Vietnam Economic Review*, 1: 27-31.

Vu Hien (1997), "Van de dang vien lam kinh te tu nhan", in: *Tap Chi Cong San 1997*, August : 35-37, 40

Walder, Andrew G. (1986), *Communist Neo-Traditionalism: Work and Authority in Chinese Industry*, Berkeley (Univ. of California Press)

Wall, David (2001), "China and the WTO: The Role of the Private Sector", in: *The Journal of East Asian Affairs*, 1: 97-126

Wan Guilan/Li Xingbin (1993), "Siying jingji de duoceng tezheng" (Manifold Characteristics of Private Economy), in: *Dongbei Shida Xuebao* (Journal of Dongbei Normal University), 6: 62-66

Wang Dehua/Chen Chaozhong (1985), *Dangdai nongmin qiyejia* (Current peasant entrepreneurs), Zhengzhou (Henan renmin chubanshe)

Wang Dehua/Tang Changxi/Mei Deping (1997), "Nongcun cunji dang zuzhi zai mang sha?" (What are rural Party organizations doing?), in: *Shehui*, 10: 32-33

Wang Gan (1998), *'Friends Eating Together': Banqueting and Networking for Entrepreneurs in Shenzhen*, Paper presented to the 50th Annual Meeting of the Association for Asian Studies, Washington, D.C., March 26-29

Wang Kezhong (1990), *Zhongguo xian jieduan siying jingji tansuo* (Research on China's private economy in the current period), Shanghai

Wang Qinghai (1997), "Guanyu zhiye qiyejia peiyu de jige wenti" (On some questions of training of professional entrepreneurs), in: *Liaoning Daxue Xuebao* (Journal of Liaoning University), 1: 66-69

Wang Qingxiu (1993), "Zai shehuizhuyi shichang jingji zhong jiakuai siying jingji de fazhan" (Acceleration od development of private economy in socialist market economy), in: *Jingji Shehui Tizhi Bijiao* (Economic and social comparison), 4: 59-62

Wang Xiaodong (1996), "Lun wo guo qiyejia zhiyehua de jiben silu, zhongdian yu nandian" (Principle considerations, main emphasis and difficulties in professionalization of our entrepreneurs), in: *Zhongguo Renmin Daxue Xuebao* (Journal of the Chinese People's University), 5: 15-17

Wang Xunli (1998), "Siying jingji fazhan dui Zhongguo shehui jiegou de yingxiang", in: Yuan Fang/Liu Yingjie/Zhang Qixi, ed., *Zhongguo shehui jiegou zhuanxing* (Transformation of China's social structure), Beijing: 331-352

Wang Yong (1993), "Controls on Private Sector to be Loosened", in: *China Daily*, 4 January

Wang Yu (1993), "Shichang jingji yu fei guoying jingji" (Market economy and non-state economy), in: *Jingji Lilun Yu Jingji Guanli* (Economic theory and economic management), 4: 15-19

Wang, Fei-Ling (1998), *From Family to Market. Labor Allocation in Contemporary China*, Lanham, Boulder, New York, Oxford (Roman&Littlefield)

Wank, David L. (1993), *From State Socialism to Community Capitalism. State Power, Social Structure, and Private Enterprise in a Chinese City*, Ann Arbor, Cambridge/Mass. (Dissertation) (UMI)

Wank, David L. (1995), "Bureaucratic Patronage and Private Business: Changing Networks of Power in Urban China", in: Walder, Andrew G., ed, *The Waning of the Communist State. Economic Origin of Political Decline in China and Hungary*, Berkeley et al. (California University Press): 53-183

Wank, David L. (1996), "The Institutional Process of Market Clientelism: Guanxi and Private Business in a South China City", in: *The China Quarterly*, September: 820-838

Weber, Max (1964), *Wirtschaft und Gesellschaft*, 2. Halbband, Köln/Berlin, (Kiepenheuer&Witsch)

Weggel, Oskar (1994), *Vietnam* (unpublished manuscript)

Weggel, Oskar (1997a), "Gesamtbericht Vietnam, Laos, Kambodscha", in: *Südostasien aktuell*, 2: 123-135

Weggel, Oskar (1997b), "Gesamtbericht Vietnam, Laos, Kambodscha", in: *Südostasien aktuell*, 3: 218-225

Weggel, Oskar (1999), "Gesamtbericht Vietnam, Laos, Kambodscha", in: *Südostasien aktuell*, November: 515-535

Wei Jiafu (1999), "Qiyejia xuyao shenme suzhi" (Which qualities do entrepreneurs needs?), in: *Renmin Ribao*, 27 December

Wei Jie/Xu Youke (1996), "Zaojiu zhenzhengde qiyejia jieceng" (To create a real stratum of entrepreneurs), in: *Guanli Qianyan* (Management front), 4: 34-38
Wei Yan (1999), "Shanghai shi mingong tousu siying qiyezhu zengduo" (Grievances of migrant
workers towards private entrepreneurs in Shanghai have increased), in: *Renmin Ribao*, 9
December
Wei Zhanrong/Sun Aozhou (1994), "Lun wo guo qiyejia jieceng de peiyu" (On the cultivation of an
entrepreneurial stratum in our country), in: *Jingji Wenti Tansuo* (Discussion of economic
problems), 10: 25-27
Weinshall, Theodore D. (1993), ed., *Societal Culture and Management*, Berlin, New York (de
Gruyter)
Wellman, Berry (1988), "Structural Analysis: From Method and Metaphor to Theory and Sub-
stance", in: Wellman, B./Berkowitz, S.D.: 19-62
Wellman, Berry/Berkowitz, S.D. (1988), eds., *Social Structures: A Network Approach*, Cambridge,
New York, New Rochelle (Cambridge University Press)
Weltbank (1996), ed., *Weltentwicklungsbericht 1996: Vom Plan zum Markt*, Washington, D.C.
(World Bank)
Werhahn, Peter H. (1990), *Der Unternehmer. Seine ökonomische Funktion und gesellschaftspoliti-
sche Verantwortung*, Trier (Paulinus)
White, Gordon/Howell, Jude/Shang Xiaoyuan (1996), *In Search of Civil Society. Market Reform
and Social Change in Contemporary China*, Oxford (Clarendon Press)
Wiegersma, Nancy (1991), "Peasant Patriarchy and the Subversion of the Collective in Vietnam",
in: *Review of Radical Political Economics*, 3-4: 174-197
Wischermann, Jörg (1993), *Vietnam 1992, wirtschaftlich erholt, politisch stabil? Daten, Fakten
und Meinungen zur wirtschafts- und innenpolitischen Entwicklung*, Berlin (Deutsch-
Vietnamesische Gesellschaft)
Wischermann, Jörg (1994), *Ein Land zwischen Sozialismus und Kapitalismus - wohin steuert
Vietnam?*, Berlin (Deutsch-Vietnamesische Gesellschaft)
Wolff, Peter (1997), *Vietnam - Die unvollendete Transformation*, Köln (Weltforum Verlag)
Womack, Brantly (1992), "Reform in Vietnam. Backwards towards the Future", in: *Government
and Opposition*, 27: 177-189
Wong, John/Ma, Rong/Yang, Mu (1995), *China's Rural Entrepreneurs. Ten Case Studies*, Singa-
pore (Times Academic Press)
Woodman, Sophia (1999), "Less Dressed Up as More? Promoting Non-Profit-Making Organiza-
tions by Regulating Away Freedom of Association", in: *China Perspectives*, March-
April: 17-27
Wortman, Max S. (1986), "A Unified Framework, Research Typologies, and Research Prospects
for the Interface between Entrepreneurship and Small Business", in: Sexton/Smilor: 273-
331
Wu Guangbin (1998), *Zhongguo dangdai qiyejia chengzhang yanjiu* (Studies on the growing of
current Chinese entrepreneurs), Xi'an (Shaanxi renmin chubanshe)
Wu Jinglian (1993), "Zizhu qiye zhidu: wo guo shichang jingji tizhi de jichu" (Independent enter-
prise order: foundation of a Chinese system of market economy), in: *Zhongguo Gongye
Jingji Yanjiu* (Studies on Chinese industry economy), 1: 4-10
Xiangzhen qiye qingkuang (1996) (The situation of rural enterprises), ed. by the Department for
Rural Enterprises of the Ministry of Agriculture of the PR of China, Beijing (Nongye
chubanshe)
Xiao Liang (1992), *Siying jingji lun* (On private economy), Chengdu (Sichuan renmin chubanshe)
Xiao Liang (1997), "Xian jieduan siyou jingji yu gongyou jingji de guanxi wenti" (The problem
interrelationship between private and public economy in the current period), in: *Jingying
Zhiyou* (Friend of operation), Harbin, 2: 6-8
Xiao Zhuoji (1997b), "Suoyouzhi lilun de zhongda tupo" (Major breakthrough in the theory of
ownership system), in: *Qiushi*, 20: 20-21
Xu Ruzhong,/Lei Zhenyang (1993), "Wo guo de fei gongyou jingji: xianzhuang, zuoyong ji zoushi"
(Non-public economy of China: Situation, function and trends), in: *Shehuizhuyi Yanjiu*
(Studies on socialism), 6: 52-55

Xu Xinxin (2000), "Cong zhiye pingjia yu zeye quxiang kan Zhongguo shehui jiegou bianqian" (From the assessment of occupational prestige and choice of occupation look at China's process of social change), in: *Shehuixue Yanjiu*, 3: 67-85

Xu Zhijian (1997), "Chuangxin lirun yu qiyejia wuxing zichan" (Innovation profits and invisible asset of entrepreneurs), in: *Jingji Yanjiu*, 8: 47-50

Yan Ming/Cheng Ji (1994), *Xinbian ru dang zuzhi* (New informations on Party accession), Beijing (Zhongguo wuzi chubanshe)

Yan, Yunxiang (1996), *The Flow of Gifts: Reciprocity and Social Networks in a Chinese* Village, Stanford (Stanford University Press)

Yang Long (1998), "80 niandai Zhongguo minzhong zhengzhi canyu de jieji fenxi" (Class analysis of political participation among Chinese population in the 80s), in: *Dangdai Zhonguo Shi Yanjiu* (Studies on China's contemporary history), 4: 70-81

Yang Meibo (1996), *Dangdai Zhongguo siying qiye de guyong guanxi* (Employment relations in Chinese private enterprises), Kunming (Yunnan renmin chubanshe)

Yang, Mayfair Mei-hui (1994), *Gifts, Banquets and the Art of Social Relationships in China*, Ithaca (Cornell University Press)

Yi Cheng (1996), "Siying jingji wenti ruogan ziliao" (Material on crucial issues of private economy), in: *Dangdai Sichao* (Modern trends), 2: 11-21

Yin Zhengkun (1996), "Shilun fubai chengyin ji jienue tujing" (Discussion on the reasons of corruption and ways of solution) in: *Huazhong Ligong Daxue Xuebao* (Journal of Central China Technical University), 2: 11-15

You Ji (1995), "Corporatization, Privatization, and the New Trend in Mainland China's Economic Reform," in: *Issues & Studies*, 4: 28-61

Young, Susan (1991), "Wealth but not Security. Attitudes towards Private Business in China in the 1980s", in: *Australian Journal of Chinese Affairs*, January: 115-137

Yu Heping (1993), *Shanghui yu Zhongguo zaoqi xiandaihua* (Chambers of Commerce and China's early modernization), Shanghai (Shanghai renmin chubanshe)

Yu Qiao/Yang Zi (1993), eds., *Kuangfeng xia de Zhongguo* (Crazy China), Chongqing (Sichuan daxue chubanshe)

Yu Shaowen (1997), "Qiyejia yu quanli zhihuihua" (Entrepreneurs and the wisdom of power), in: *Zhongguo Gongshang Bao*, 6 November.

Yuan Baohua (1997), "Ying zao shehuizhuyi qiyejia chengzhang de lianghao huanjing" (Create good conditions for the arising of socialist entrepreneurs), in: *Qiye Guanli*, 192: 5-8

Zapf, Wolfgang (1970), ed., *Theorien des Sozialen Wandels*, Köln, Berlin (Kiepenheuer&Witsch)

Zapf, Wolfgang (1992), "Wandel, sozialer", in: Schäfers, Bernhard, ed., *Grundbegriffe der Soziologie*, Opladen (Leske&Budrich): 365-370

Zentralinstitut für Wirtschaftsführung (1997), ed., *Merkmale des informellen Sektors und der Schattenwirtschaft in Vietnam. Eine Fallstudie in Hanoi*, Hanoi (policy paper)

Zhang Cuo (2000), "Diaocha laoban" (Investigating bosses), in: Zhongguo Gongshang Bao, 28 April

Zhang Fuchi/Guo Yuqin (1997), eds., *Qiyejia jingshen. Xiandai qiyejia chengzhang lun* (Entrepreneurial spirit. On the arising of modern enterprises), Beijing (Qiye guanli chubanshe)

Zhang Honglin/Liu Xinhua (1996), eds., *Zenyang dang ge qiyejia* (How to become an entrepreneur), Beijing (Qiye guanli chubanshe)

Zhang Houyi (1999a), "1998-1999 nian: Zhongguo siying qiyezhu jieceng zhuangkuang" (The current situation of China's private entrepreneurs stratum in the years 1998/99), in: Ru/Lu/Dan: 482-491

Zhang Houyi (1999b), "You yizhi yijun zai tuqi. Gaige kaifang yilai siying jingji de zaisheng yu fazhan" (Rush of a new force. Revitalization and development of private economy since reform and opening), in: Zhang/Ming: 3-59

Zhang Houyi (2001), "*Siying qiyezhu de shehui shuxing*" (Social affiliation of private entrepreneurs), in: Zhonggong Fujian Shengwei Dangxiao Xuebao (Journal of the Party school of Fujian's Party committee), 10: 8-12

Zhang Houyi/Ming Lizhi (1999), eds., *Zhongguo siying qiye fazhan baogao* (Development report on China's private entrepreneurs) 1999, Beijing (Shehui kexue wenxian chubanshe)

Zhang Houyi/Ming Lizhi (2000), eds., *Zhongguo siying qiye fazhan baogao* (Development report on China's private entrepreneurs) 1978-1998, Beijing (Shehui kexue wenxian chubanshe)

Zhang Houyi/Ming Lizhi/Liang Chuanyun (2002), eds., *Zhongguo siying qiye fazhan baogao* (Development report on China's private entrepreneurs), 2001, Beijing (Shehui kexue wenxian chubanshe)

Zhang Houyi/Ming Lizhi/He an (2002), ed., *Siying qiye yu shichang jingji* (Private enterprises and market economy), Beijing (Shehui kexue wenxian chubanshe)

Zhang Jiangming/Hong Dayong/Cheng Lu/Wu Shanhui (1998), "Zhongguo chengshi zhongjian jieceng de xianzhuang ji qi weilai fazhan" (Contemporary situation and future development of China's urban middle stratum), in: *Zhongguo Renmin Daxue Xuebao* (Journal of the Chinese Peoples University), 5: 62-67

Zhang Jing (2001), "Pojie 'gugong 8 ren' jieji huaxian zhi mi" (Overcome the enigma of 'employing 8 people' as a class marker), in: *Jiangnan Luntan* (Jiangnan Forum), 12: 18/19

Zhang La'e/Hu Qinfang (1998), "Xiangzhen qiyejia chengzhang de tiaojian fenxi" (Analysis of the conditions for the growing of rural entrepreneurs), in: *Nongye Jingji Wenti*, 11: 27-30

Zhang Wanding/Li Dan (1998), "Qiyejia zhineng, juese yi tiaojian de tantao" (Discussion of the function, role and conditions of private entrepreneurs)), in: *Jingji Yanjiu* 8: 29-33

Zhang Wanli (1990), "Jinqi wo guo shehui jieji, jieceng yanjiu zongshu" (General overview on recent studies on social classes and stratification in China), in: *Zhongguo Shehui Kexue* (Social Sciences in China), 5: 173-181

Zhang Xuwu/Li Ding/Xie Minggan (1996), *Zhongguo siying jingji nianjian* (Yearbook of China's private economy), Beijing (Zhonghua gongshang lianhe chubanshe)

Zhang Xuwu/Xie Minggan/Li Ding (1994), eds., *Zhongguo siying jingji nianjian* (Yearbook of the Chinese private economy), Hongkong (Xianggang jingji daobaoshe)

Zhang Youyu (1993), "Zhongguo shehui xintai fasheng shida bianhua" (10 major changes in China's social psychology), in: *Zhongguo Shehui Bao* (China's Society Daily), 12 March

Zhang, Sufang (1998), "Weishenme shuo feigongyouzhi jingji shi shehuizhuyi shichang jingji de zhongyao zucheng bufen?" (Why does one say that the non-public economy is an important element of socialist market economy?), in: *Qiushi*, 5: 47

Zhao Desheng (1988), *Zhongguo xiandai jingji shi* (Modern economic history of the PR of China), Lanzhou (Gansu renmin chubanshe)

Zhao Pozhang (1998), "Zhongguo xuyao shijieji qiyejia" (China needs world standard entrepreneurs), in: *Zhongguo qiyejia diaocha xitong* (1998a): 524-536

Zhao Runtian/Yu Jingxu (1995), "Jingjixuejia tan ruhe miandui ershiyi shiji de Zhongguo siying jingji" (Economists discuss the face of China's private economy in the 21st century), in: *Beijing Gongren Bao* (Beijing Workers Daily), 27 October

Zhejiang tongji nianjian (Statistical Yearbook of Zhejiang) (1995), Beijing (Zhongguo tongji chubanshe)

Zhengque yindao fei gongyouzhi jingji fazhan (1996) (Correctly guide the development of non-state economy), compiled by the Association of Industry and Commerce, Gansu province, Lanzhou

Zhong Jianming/Hong Dayong/Cheng Lu/Wu Shanhui (1998), "Zhongguo chengshi: Zhongjian jieceng de xianzhuang ji qi weilai fazhan" (Situation and future development of China's urban middle stratum), in: *Zhongguo Renmin Daxue Xuebao* (Journal of Chinese People's University), 5: 62-67

Zhongguo Gongchandang di shiwu ci quanguo daibiao dahui wenjian huibian (1997) (Documents of the 15th Party Congress of the CCP), Beijing (Renmin chubanshe)

Zhongguo Gongshang Bao (China's Industry and Commerce Daily), Beijing

Zhongguo Qiyejia (China's Entrepreneurs), Beijing

Zhongguo qiyejia diaocha xitong (Research net Chinese entrepreneurs) (1997), ed., *1997 nian qiye jingyingzhe wenjuan diaocha baogao* (Research report on a questionnaire survey among enterprise managers in the year 1997), Beijing (policy paper)

Zhongguo qiyejia diaocha xitong (1998a) (Research net Chinese entrepreneurs), ed., *Zhongguo qiyejia duiwu chengzhang yu fazhan baogao* (Report on growth and development of China's entrepreneurial contingent), Beijing (Jingji kexue chubanshe)

Zhongguo qiyejia diaocha xitong (1998b) (Research net Chinese entrepreneurs), ed., *1998 Zhongguo qiye jingying guanlizhe chengzhang yu fazhan zhuanti diaocha baogao* (Special report on the growing and development of China's enterprise managers), Beijing (policy paper)

Zhongguo renkou tongji nianjian 1996 (1997) (Statistical Yearbook on China's Population), Beijing

'"Zhongguo siying qiye yanjiu' ketizu" (Authors' group "Studies on Chinese private enterprises") (1999), "1997 nian quan guo siying qiye chouxiang diaocha shuju ji fenxi" (Data and analysis of the survey among private entrepreneurs in 1997), in: Zhang/Ming: 131-166

"Zhongguo siyou qiyezhu jieceng yanjiu ketizu" (1994) (Projekt group for investigating China's private entrepreneur stratum), "Wo guo siyou qiye de jingying zhuangkuang yu siyou qiyezhu de quanti tezheng" (Private enterprises' operations and group characteristics of private entrepreneurs), in: *Zhongguo Shehui Kexue* (Social sciences in China), 4: 60-76

Zhongguo tongji nianjian (1995-2002) (China's Statistical Yearbook), Beijing (Zhonguo tongji chubanshe, various volumes)

Zhonghua Renmin Gongheguo xianfa (Constitution of the PR of China) (1999), Beijing (Falü chubanshe)

Zhou Shulian (1996), "1995 nian Zhongguo qiyejia duiwu fazhan pingshu" (Development of China's entrepreneurial contingent in 1995), in: *Jingji Guanli* (Economic Management), 2: 37-39

Zhou Xueguang (1993), "Unorganized Interests and Collective Action in Communist China", in: *American Sociological Review*, vol. 58: 54-73

Zhu Guanglei (1998), *Dangdai Zhongguo shehui ge jieceng fenxi* (Analysis of all strata in current Chinese society), Tianjin (Tianjin renmin chubanshe)

Zhuanxing shiqi Shanghai shimin shehui xintai diaocha he duice yanjiu" (1994) (Investigation of the social psychology of Shanghai's population during the period of transformation and the respective policy), in: *Shehuixue Yanjiu*, 3: 19-25

Zschoch, Barbara (1998), *Entwicklung von Kleinunternehmen in Rußland*, Frankfurt/M. (Lang-Verlag)

Zunkel, Friedrich (1962), *Der Rheinisch-Westfälische Unternehmer 1834-1879. Ein Beitrag zur Geschichte des deutschen Bürgertums im 19. Jahrhundert*, Köln, Opladen (Westdeutscher Verlag)

INDEX